T0405913

new brutalism
the invention of a style

Treatise on Concrete
Directed by Roberto Gargiani

silvia groaz
new brutalism
the invention
of a style

EPFL PRESS

A Swiss academic publisher

The graphical layout of the book and the cover design are by Paola Ranzini Pallavicini of Studio Pagina Milan, Italy. The photolithographic services were provided by Walter Bassani, Milan Italy.

EPFL PRESS

The EPFL Press is the English languageimprint of the Foundation of the Presses polytechniques et universitaires romandes (PPUR). The PPUR publishes mainly works of teaching and research of the Ecole polytechnique fédérale de Lausanne (EPFL), of universities and other institutions of higher education.

Presses polytechniques et universitaires romandes EPFL – Rolex Learning Center CM Station 10 CH-1015 Lausanne, Switzerland E-mail: info@epflpress.org Phone: +41 (0)21 693 21 30

www.epflpress.org

© 2023, first edition, EPFL Press ISBN 978-2-88915-510-1 (EPFL Press) Printed in Czech Republic

EPFL

The publisher and author express their thanks to the École polytechnique fédérale de Lausanne (EPFL) and the Faculté de l'environnement naturel, architectural et construit (ENAC) for their generous support towards the publication of this book.

Treatise on Concrete

Directed by Roberto Gargiani

The volumes of the *Treatise on Concrete* intend to offer a new
and documented vision of the evolution of construction techniques
and of the creative potential and formal expressions of concrete,
from antiquity to the present time. Each book in the series is based
on specific archival research; the analysis of scientific, technical
and iconographic original sources; and the investigation into documents
made available by companies, engineers, architects and artists.
The full spectrum of the use of concrete is covered, including
the building of foundations, ports, moles, bridges, vaults, domes,
fortresses, bunkers, houses and monuments, as well as the manufacture
of artificial stones and sculptures. In addition, the volumes will address
the theoretical issues of *béton brut*, Brutalism and the true nature of matter.
All volumes focus on the techniques and materials for the manufacture
of formwork, from wood to fabric; on the meaning of the imprint;
on the surface processing of concrete by hand or with machine;
and on the composition of the mixture.
The series of books aims to provide the scientific community with
an unique and updated reference on the historical and contemporary
uses of concrete, which will open a new chapter in the knowledge
of this crucial material for architectural construction, as well
as for masterpieces of engineering and art.

Volumes published:
Concrete, From Archeology to Invention, 1700-1769
Louis I. Kahn, Exposed Concrete and Hollow Stones, 1949-1959
Louis I. Kahn, Towards the Zero Degree of Concrete, 1960-1974
The Rhetoric of Pier Luigi Nervi, Concrete and Ferrocement Forms
German Concrete, The Science of Cement from Trass to Portland, 1819-1877
A New Era of American Architectural Concrete: From Wright to SOM

Aux 'messieurs de la plume'

Acknowledgement

This book would not have been possible without the support of Prof. Roberto Gargiani, his decisive and insightful guidance, and his time and thinking.

For the financial support of my research at various stages, I am grateful to EPFL and its excellent research framework, the Swiss National Science Foundation and the Getty Research Institute.

This research required the exploration of archival holdings and architectural journals. I would like to thank the staff of the various archives: Gudrun Krämer, Krämer Verlag; Shelley Hayreh, Avery Archives, Columbia University; Sarah Sherman, Getty Research Institute; Mari Nakahara, Library of Congress; Martin Klingbacher, Atelier 5 Archive; Ines Zalduendo, Frances Loeb Library, Harvard University; and Jennifer Garland, McGill University Archive.

My heartfelt thanks for their support and help go to the librarians of EPFL Library, especially Chantal Blanc, Catherine Sénéchaud, Jérôme Yerly, Anil Goolaub, Julien Tanari and Thomas von Allmen.

I would also like to express my gratitude to Kenneth Frampton, Denise Scott Brown and Robin Middleton for their precious insights and memories.

As well as Stanislaus von Moos, Mary McLeod, Paolo Scrivano, Laurent Stalder and Nicola Braghieri for their valuable guidance and critical feedback.

I am grateful to EPFL Press for their support in guiding me through the publication process and to Jo Nicoud-Garden for re-reading my manuscript.

Table of Contents

Roberto Gargiani
A Game of Patience for a New Art History

Despite the vast body of literature devoted to the so-called 'brutalism', *New Brutalism: The Invention of a Style* for the first time offers the reader a historical reconstruction based on all the most significant published or archival documents on the subject. In fact, the book results from the consultation of international journals and contributions published from the 1930s to 1970s, as well as recent literature. This, in addition to databases for digitalized publications, enabled the author to collect all possible critical fragments concerning New Brutalism. The historical methodology was thus confronted with the difficulty of conducting archival research in collections stored in various parts of the world, from Europe to America and Canada. The retrieval of documents relating to the genesis of a concept entailed a careful search for clues, which were often no more than a few scattered phrases hidden among others in a letter of circumstance. In the case of historical research or contemporary design, for both Warburg and Mies, God was hidden in the details. From these efforts made on this front of historical research, *New Brutalism: Invention of a Style* offers a range of documents that have never before been brought together in other, albeit authoritative, theoretical essays. The picture was then completed by a series of interviews conducted with several figures who played decisive roles in the debate on New Brutalism. Thanks to a game of patience, *New Brutalism: The Invention of a Style* has thus become the first comprehensive history of one of the most important definitions in twentieth-century architecture criticism and theory.

In organising the fragments and conducting research, the author followed a chronological and thematic sequence. These two planes intertwine in a way that anchors the historian's work to the question of chronology. Layer by layer, just like an archaeologist, the author has reassembled the fragments into a frame that is held together by a critical and philological analysis. In this way, the reader is lead into the complex maze of the definition of New Brutalism.

Decisive is the starting point of the issue of New Brutalism identified in the book: the Anglo-Saxon's anxious desire to follow Pevsner's attempt to assign contemporary events with categories able to capture their essential characteristics. The English New Art History, as presented by the author in the framework of the historical reasoning on New Burtalism, thus constitutes the substantial prelude that justifies the recourse to the complicated category of 'style'. Without the framework of New Art History and without taking into account the ambitions of one of its most brilliant disciples, Reyner Banham, the overall vision of New Brutalism and its various meanings would be blurred. Without considering the New Art History framework, even the origin itself of New Brutalism would remain harnessed solely to the events of the early 1950s and the echoes of international debates. Conversely, in order for international cultural influences to take root and find expression in England, a particular sense of New Brutalism was necessary, which was made possible by the fertile ground created by a theoretical intention that animated English criticism and the history of architecture, as evidenced in *New Brutalism: The Invention of a Style*. That starting point makes it possible to ascertain, with documents in hand, the continuities and discontinuities between the English theoretical tradition going back to Ruskin and Morris, and some of the fundamental principles of New Brutalism, enunciated since the early 1950s.

The phenomena of the 1950s, which contributed to the 'birth' of the definition, are reconsidered in an overview that goes beyond the academic questions about the inventor of the definition of New Brutalism. The book delves into the chronological phases of the events that occurred before, during and after the famous appearance of that expression in the Smithsons' article on the House in Soho. The origin and changing meanings of that definition are reconstructed against the backdrop of the vicissitudes of the various protagonists, thanks to a challenging reconstruction of significant events, through a close comparison of the various testimonies and traces found in the debate. The book's great tableau reveals the collisions and the very theoretical reasons for those collisions, between the Unité in Marseilles and Le Corbusier's béton brut, between the truth to materials of ancient English origin and the enigma – for it remains an enigma – of the role attributed to the School at Hunstanton in the definition of New Brutalism. Using the historian's scalpel, the author has dissected every stance of New Brutalism's leading protagonists, including the Smithsons and Banham.

The pages of *New Brutalism: The Invention of a Style* show and demonstrate the evolutions, uncertainties and clarifications that the two leading protagonists made around the definition of New Brutalism, also following the inputs offered by the contributions of other personalities in the phase of the 'origins' of that definition. Various and diverse actors have thus appeared on the scene, who, albeit in different ways, were all decisive in providing conceptual and historical depth to a definition precipitated in the debate without any critical and theoretical argumentation: starting with Segal and Johnson and continuing through to Summerson and Pevsner with their stances supported by the presumed authority of their role as historians.

The investigation of the literal dimension of the texts sheds light on the complexity hidden in the formula and its reception. The book offers an analysis which unravels the meaning attributed to New Brutalism by its various actors: it illustrates the attempts to make it an expressive definition of a new system of design for architecture and the city; it explains its principles by pointing out the concrete examples called upon by critics to explain the specifics of a project that could be radically New Brutalist. In the course of her demonstration, the author highlights the conflict that runs through New Brutalism, between it being reduced to a certain use of exposed materials as an alternative to that of the Modern Movement and aspiring to become the definition of a new and more general 'movement' capable of going beyond the one celebrated by Pevsner.

Starting from the English epicenter of New Brutalism, the author examines it in all its components and explores all its possible implications within the framework of New Art History, as well as its political and urbanistic concerns in the context of reconstruction. The author also takes into account the Swedish origin of the term and the significant modifications made to its prefix. From there, the book moves on to explore other countries, including the United States, Italy, and Brazil, continuing to follow the twists and turns of the debate and reconstructing assumptions about the definition and interpretation of New Brutalism. Throughout the exploration, the presence or absence of the 'New' is a theme that is constantly revisited and examined.

Thanks to the framework offered by *New Brutalism: The Invention of a Style*, it is now possible to navigate among the various and diverse New Brutalisms and Brutalisms that spread between the 1950s and 1960s in the international arena. Simultaneously, there is a latent emergence of two opposing figures. On one hand, there is the architect who constantly experiments and refuses to be held captive by a definition that suggests the emergence of a style, no matter how new or alternative it may be compared to the International Style. On the other hand, there is the critic as an artist who intends to participate as a protagonist in the debate.

The final chapter of *New Brutalism* is devoted to Banham's famous 1966 essay, which is presented for the first time through a historical reading based on the correspondence between Banham and Joedicke. This correspondence is decisive in reconstructing the publishing process of a book that decreed both the success and the end of a category that had been a point of reference in the debate for a certain span of years, first in England and then internationally. *New Brutalism: The Invention of a Style* demonstrates that the history of architecture asserts its authority as a method, which is further expanded by contemporary research software, over the increasingly fashionable but prosaic and theoretical shortcuts. Is this the New Art History for the twenty-first century?

chapter one
the british debate
in search
of a new-ism

Reactions to the International Style and the Myth
of the Pioneers of the Modern Movement

The history of the concept of New Brutalism cannot begin with the first definitions proposed by British architects and critics in the early 1950s. Failure to trace the debate that preceded those definitions risks missing the specificity of New Brutalism as formulated through the writings of its most famous protagonists: Alison and Peter Smithson, and Reyner Banham. The prefix 'New' itself takes on different values, depending on the starting point of the concept. The invention and first theorisation of New Brutalism condense the aspirations of critics and historians active in England over a period spanning from the 1930s to the late 1950s. Only by following this historical chronology is it possible to draw nearer to the secret behind New Brutalism: that of it being the latest label, one that was to become internationally famous, invented by critics who aspired to restore a specific identity to English and, more generally, Western architecture. The invention of New Brutalism emerged out of numerous attempts to find guiding lines for the debate on reconstruction. The concept would therefore long carry within itself a reflection of those attempts, perceptible in the role given to composition as an echo of aulic schemes, or in the aspiration to identify a free and even chance-driven mechanics (thanks to which the Picturesque took on unrecognisable forms), or in the value of the material roughness under the guise of which acted the value of truth rooted in nineteenth-century English theories, that did not fade over the entire course of the twentieth century.

The origins of New Brutalism are hence to be found in the debates that, from the 1940s onwards, were focused on demonstrating a possible English evolution of the Modern Movement. The need to establish guidelines for the reconstruction of bombed cities is what prompted critics to question the nation's architectural identity, with the ambition of regaining an avant-garde position in international debates. Indeed, the search for a shared 'style' is what motivated the cultural renewal underlying the proliferation of labels demonstrative of a new democratic path. In their reflections on English architectural identity, critics attributed a decisive role to the parallel intentions (albeit in different ways) of architecture and politics, in translating the political aspirations of a Labour Party that had been leading the country since 1945.[1] The search for labels was thus intertwined with economic and social factors. This is the assumption that lies behind the architectural debates, whose references aligned with, or opposed to, the social democratic political orientation.

During the 1940s, the search for guidelines for reconstruction amplified the debates that had matured in the interwar period on the question of 'style'. The use of the word 'style' needs to be considered as part of the open criticism of the International Style, which had not found a culture in England capable of adapting to or interpreting its precepts. It was around the search for the validity of a 'style' that the ideological battles pursued by the critics on the pages of magazines became increasingly bitter, taking the form of a succession of stylistic labels: 'Instead of ending the chaos of "styles" and laying the foundations of a single future new tradition, its [criticism's] actual effect has too often been to provide just one more style. [...] It became a fashion: and fashions, though exciting at first, soon grow stale.'[2] William Morris Revival, New Humanism, New Empiricism, Neo Ruskinism, Functional Tradition, or New Eclecticism are just some of the labels that were to guide reconstruction.

This new 'battle of styles' became a necessary crucible for the critical operation that accompanied the advent of new movements. Without the questioning of the principles of the International Style – perceived by English historians as a short parenthesis within the wider course of the Modern Movement – combined with the search for an English essence, the appearance of New Brutalism would not have been possible. This definition would become the receptacle of the aspirations for combining English theoretical tradition with the new search for a precise nature of materials and a new logic of composition.

The various proposals advanced by critics until the mid-1950s revolved around a concept belonging to the rhetoric of the post-war period: that of 'Englishness'.[3] 'England after the war must be England'[4] was the motto that summed up the cultural hypothesis, advocated by writers and critics, artists and architects, of principles reinforcing the national identity. Not even the most anti-conformist theses of New Brutalism would escape comparison with the cultural imperative of 'Englishness', of which the Smithsons themselves would propose a personal interpretation. The introduction of the concept of 'Englishness' only increased the interest in the cultural and symbolic aspects of architecture, with the aim of revisiting the Modern Movement by retrieving the foundations of English theoretical culture, demonstrating that 'modernism is English and that Englishness is modern'.[5] The critical operation appealed to history as a tool at the service of contemporary investigations on principles that were 'English *par excellence*'.[6]

---

[1] An example of this is the report from the symposium held in 1949 entitled 'The Kind of Architecture We Want in Britain', in which A. Boyd concluded that: 'We shall get a great architecture in England only when the working class is dominant, when the state and society are moulded by the great ideas of socialism, and when architecture is inspired by the conscious aim to celebrate and inspire the achievements of the people', Andrew Boyd, 'A Review of the Symposium – The Kind of Architecture We Want in Britain', *Keystone. Journal of the AASTA* [Associations of Architects, Surveyors and Technical Assistants] (May 1949): 96.

[2] Andrew Boyd, Colin Penn, (eds.), *Homes for the People. How Modern Building Technique Can Provide High Standard Dwellings Quickly. How They Could Be Planned and Built; What They Could Look Like and How We Can Get Them*, Association of Building Technicians [Great Britain] (London: Paul Elek Publishers, 1946).

[3] See, for example, George Orwell, 'England your England', in *The Lion and the Unicorn: Socialism and the English Genius* (London: Secker and Warburg, 1941).

[4] [n.a.], 'Rebuilding Britain', *Architectural Review*, vol. 93, no. 556 (April 1943): (85–112), 86.

[5] Nikolaus Pevsner, *The Englishness of English Art* (London: Penguin Books, 1956). This publication derives from a series of lectures about Englishness given by Pevsner between 1941 and 1942 at Birkbeck College, London, later revised for a series of episodes for BBC Radio in 1955 entitled 'The Reith Lectures: The Englishness of English Art'. Lecture 1: The Geography of Art, 16 October 1955; Lecture 2: Hogarth and Observed Life, 23 October 1955; Lecture 3: Reynolds and Detachment, 30 October 1955; Lecture 4: Perpendicular England, 6 November 1955; Lecture 5: Blake and the Planning Line, 13 November 1955; Lecture 6: Constable and the Pursuit of Nature, 20 November 1955; Lecture 7: Architecture and Planning: The Functional Approach, 27 November 1955. Pevsner's interest in national characteristics stems from his art-historical training under Wilhelm Pinder in Leipzig.

[6] Nikolaus Pevsner, 'A Short Pugin Florilegium', *Architectural Review*, vol. 94, no. 560 (August 1943): (31–34), 31.

Nikolaus Pevsner's book *Pioneers of the Modern Movement: From William Morris to Walter Gropius* created the basis for a historical vision in which England could also imagine itself a protagonist. The period from Pevsner's arrival in England in 1933 to the publication of his book in 1936 can be taken as the starting point for the aspiration to create historiographical categories and visions that, after the Modern Movement, would lead to New Brutalism. The definition of a British historiographic legacy occurred also in accordance with the consolidation of what Reyner Banham defined in 1953 as the 'New Art History'.[7] According to Banham, the New Art History can be framed as the English elaboration of German art-historical culture,[8] originated with those historians who fled to England with the advent of Nazism, such as Pevsner, Rudolf Wittkower, Ernst Gombrich, Fritz Saxl and Johannes Wilde.[9] The German historians of New Art History taught at prestigious London institutions: Pevsner at the Courtauld Institute and Wittkower at the Warburg Institute, where they guided and influenced a generation of young English critics and architects active in Liverpool (such as Colin Rowe, Robert Maxwell and James Stirling) and in the avant-garde circles in London (Reyner Banham, Alan Colquhoun, Alison and Peter Smithson and John Voelcker, to name a few).[10]

Pevsner's *Pioneers of the Modern Movement* became the authoritative reference for a vision of the Modern Movement rooted in British culture. The underlying premise was the conception of the Modern Movement as an evolutionary process, able to include antithetical positions to affirm its validity over time. Principles of continuity hence became a prerequisite for the contemporary architectural project. Yet the fruitful relationship between historiography and the project was hampered, as Pevsner noted, by a lack of specific terminological agreement attributable to a series of critics who ventured into the debate on 'style'.[11] By virtue of its ability to focus on the question of language as the foundation of a new critique, *Pioneers of Modern Movement* acted as a guideline for the English debates, framing the question of the relationship between styles and history, which also became one of the focal points of the debate on New Brutalism.

The support of architectural journals proved decisive for a new architectural, theoretical and political configuration of post-war Britain.[12] The journals oriented and recorded the debate and became a tool for outlining the principles for reconstruction,

---

[7]   Reyner Banham, 'Pelican World History of Art', *Architectural Review*, vol. 114, no. 683 (November 1953): 285–88.

[8]   In 1967 Summerson underlined the contribution of German historians to Anglo-Saxon historiography noting that: 'There was a time, within living memory, when all, or nearly all, architectural history in England was written by architects; and not only architects but by the biggest and best architects. But somewhere about 1934 the game came to an end.' John Summerson, 'Nikolaus Pevsner 1967 Gold Medallist', *RIBA Journal*, no. 74 (August 1967): 316. With the founding of the Courtauld Institute of Art in 1932 and the opening of the Warburg Library in 1933, the teaching of art-historical disciplines was established in London.

[9]   For an overview of the influence of German art-historical culture on the teaching of English art history, see David Watkin, *The Rise of Architectural History* (London: The Architectural Press, 1980), 145–60. For more recent considerations, see Mark Crinson, Richard J. Williams 'From Image to Environment: Reyner Banham's Architecture', in *The Architecture of Art History: A Historiography* (New York: Bloomsbury Visual Arts, 2018), 75–93.

[10] John Onians, 'Wilde, Pevsner, Gombrich: la "Kunstgeschichte" en Grande-Bretagne', *Perspective. Actualité en histoire de l'art*, vol. 2 (2007): 194–206.

[11] Nikolaus Pevsner, 'Canons of Criticism', *Architectural Review*, vol. 109, no. 649 (January 1951): 3–6.

[12] The *Architectural Review* represented Britain's intellectual and political elite, thanks to James Maude Richards, who was affiliated with the Modern Architectural Research Group (MARS), the British section of the Congrès internationaux d'architecture moderne (CIAM), and a founding member of the Georgian Group and the Victorian Society, associations for the preservation of architectural heritage. The weekly *Architect's Journal* dedicated several articles to the reconstruction of damaged historic buildings, as well as updating readers on the progress of the New Towns construction sites. It also included an agenda of events, exhibitions and symposia held throughout the UK. *Architect's Journal* was aligned with *Architectural Review* in its focus on national architectural identity, identified in the relationship between British building traditions and contemporary techniques of the international masters. *Architectural Design and Construction*, which became *Architectural Design* in 1946, only achieved a leading position in the debate from 1953 onwards, devoting itself until then to more technical aspects of construction and the promotion of materials and industrial products. For specific studies on the contribution of British magazines, see the theses by Steve Parnell, *Architectural Design, 1954–1972* (PhD Thesis, University of Sheffield School of Architecture, Sheffield, 2011); Erten Erdem, *Shaping 'The Second Half Century': The 'Architectural Review', 1947–1971* (PhD Thesis, Massachusetts Institute of Technology, Cambridge, 2004).

facilitating the emergence of new critical narratives. In addition to Pevsner, critics such as James Maude Richards and Hubert de Cronin Hastings, through the editorial orientation of *Architectural Review*, guided the intention to regain international prestige. There were already various initiatives during the conflict aimed at promoting reconstruction by combining the value of British heritage with the aspiration of modern architecture. This was demonstrated by examples such as Abram Games's 1942 posters, the 1943 exhibition *Towards a New Britain* at the Royal Institute of British Architects (RIBA), and the British Broadcasting Corporation (BBC) *Homes for All* broadcast in 1945.

In all these examples, the architecture of the Modern Movement was associated with Englishness, pragmatism and other values from the English tradition. 'We must go back to look forward, and tell the story of the struggle of the English people to their right way of living, the fight for an English culture which has been going on for a century and is still to be won' was the motto launched by Maxwell Fry, an influential member of the MARS Group, who was encouraging his colleagues to take a stance in international debates.[13]

The outline of an architectural orientation that would include the trilogy of 'modern', 'English' and 'new' resulted in the search for a series of precise antecedents,[14] which would demonstrate 'the continuity of tradition and show that historical precedents can be used constructively, not as an escape'.[15] The rebirth of English culture and the reconstruction of its heritage following the ravages of war seemed possible only through a national ideology, able to retrieve values and bring England 'back to the Golden Age of English design'.[16] This led to the formulation of a style that translated key historical aspects into a contemporary vocabulary, ranging from the recovery of eighteenth-century principles to the theories of those architects identified by Pevsner as being at the origin of the Modern Movement: Augustus Welby Northmore Pugin, John Ruskin and William Morris.

Principles of Truth: The Revival of Pugin, Ruskin and Morris

The origins of the ethical stance associated with the use of materials without cladding, as theorised in some of the initial definitions of New Brutalism, lay in the cult for truth professed by some of the greatest nineteenth-century English theorists. At the end of the war, the architectural debate turned towards nineteenth-century principles not only to identify 'something new but also to [...] return to the best English principles of the past'.[17] In response to the stylistic dogmas of the International Style emerged the necessity for values able to reintroduce the traditional component of craft.[18] The interest in Gothic Revival[19] was intended as a re-evocation of the factors that had contributed to the country's development of craft and urban planning principles, representing a return to the architectural concepts of 'simplicity', 'modesty', 'straightforwardness' and 'ordinariness' of nineteenth-century England.[20]

---

13 Maxwell Fry, *Fine Building* (London: Faber & Faber, 1944), 24.
14 The 1943 *Architectural Review* editorial inaugurated the operation of retrieval and cataloguing 'of authentically English antecedents', [n.a.], 'Editorial. Programme', *Architectural Review*, vol. 93, no. 556 (April 1943): 85–112.
15 James Maude Richards, 'The Second Half Century', *Architectural Review*, vol. 101, no. 601 (January 1947): 21–36.
16 John Gloag, *The English Tradition of Design* (London: Penguin Books, 1947), 15.
17 [n.a.], 'Rebuilding Britain', 107.
18 Nikolaus Pevsner, 'The Function of Craft in an Industrial Age', *Art for Everyone: Art and the State*, 16–18–19 June 1946, BBC Radio, London.
19 [n.a.], 'High Gothic', *Architects' Journal*, vol. 108, no. 2787 (July 1948): 29; [n.a.], 'The Gothic Roots of the Highly Developed Craft', *Architects' Journal*, vol. 108, no. 2790 (July 1948): 79.
20 These terms repeatedly appear in *Architectural Review* editorials from 1943 onwards, starting with William Henry Ansell, 'Foreword, Rebuilding Britain', *Architectural Review*, vol. 93, no. 556 (April 1943): (85–112), 85.

Based on *Pioneers of the Modern Movement* and under the framework of the social role of architecture, critics reiterated the origin of the Modern Movement identified in the Arts and Crafts moral imperative. In this context, notions of truth and honesty of construction were strictly linked to the use of specific materials, in close relation to the social and economic context.[21] The distinctive features of 'modern architecture' were found in the use of materials, which had to result from 'insistence upon the honest acceptance of the materials of the contemporary world'.[22] In Morris's writings, post-war critics saw an interpretation of architecture in a democratic key and a collectivist notion of the construction site.[23] This aspect of the construction site as an expression of the community was to be a characteristic of the architectural production of the 1940s, against the backdrop of the socialist policy of the welfare state.

The insistence on Ruskin's moral imperative to conceive architecture as a 'duty to the future' was motivated by a vision in which architecture could collect the traces of time on its surfaces to express a sense of 'permanence'.[24] In the first hypotheses put forward in the definition of New Brutalism, Ruskinian 'permanence' was to become a characteristic that demonstrated its deep links to the cult of 'Englishness'. But a radical difference distinguished the positions expressed in the debates on New Brutalism from those of the editors of *Architectural Review*. Indeed, the focus on the surface of materials advocated by the review was framed in the 'charm of texture' and in the exhortation to look at both the aesthetics of ruin and to anonymous industrial architecture for the richness of a local language. This would result into the new aesthetic of 'modern' architecture according to the *Architectural Review*'s editors.[25] These suggestions, evoking Ruskin's warning 'never to render the face of the wall smooth',[26] expressed the value of 'texture' through concepts such as 'familiarity', 'orderly variety' and 'art by accident'. From 1944 onwards, these themes became recurrent again through the cultural propaganda of Richards, Pevsner and Hastings. *Architectural Review* published monthly columns with collections of images that emphasised the organic functionality of nature, enlargements of unintentional marks on irregular surfaces, aerial photographs of machinery tracks on the ground, or agricultural fields that revealed a homogeneity achieved through irregular elements.[27] The formulation of a repertoire with a strong material component occurred through the communicative immediacy of images, in which the vast collection of sketches, graphics and photomontages became tools to legitimise fundamental nineteenth-century values: the cult for 'texture', 'honesty' and 'craft'.

[21] See, in this regard, Nikolaus Pevsner, *Pioneers of Modern Movement: From William Morris to Walter Gropius* (London: Faber & Faber, 1936); Nikolaus Pevsner, *An Enquiry into Industrial Art in England* (Cambridge: Cambridge University Press, 1937); Nikolaus Pevsner, *Academies of Art, Past and Present* (Cambridge: Cambridge University Press, 1940); Nikolaus Pevsner, *An Outline of European Architecture* (London: Penguin Books, 1942).

[22] Fry stressed as a distinctive feature of modern architecture the moral imperative: 'What has set architecture on a new path is no less than the return of the original moral impetus William Morris gave it at the dawn of the century, the accent upon morality being to my mind the quality which, above others, distinguishes modern architecture'. Maxwell Fry, 'The Future of Architecture', *Architects' Year Book*, vol. 1, no. 1 (1945): (7–10), 10. The honest acceptance of materials, together with 'locality, destination and character of a building' are, to quote Pugin, the characteristics hoped for in a new architecture, [n.a.], 'A Village Planned to Be Picturesque, *Architectural Review*, vol. 95, no. 566 (February 1944): 39–43. On Ruskin's echoes in modern English architecture, see also [n.a.], 'Rebuilding Britain', 110.

[23] G. D. H. Cole (ed.), *William Morris* (London: Nonesuch Press, 1934), 485; Nikolaus Pevsner, *An Outline of European Architecture*, 206.

[24] [n.a.], 'Rebuilding Britain'.

[25] [n.a.], 'Price on Picturesque Planning', *Architectural Review*, vol. 95, no. 566 (February 1944): (47–50), 48.

[26] John Rusk, *The Poetry of Architecture* (London: George Allen, 1837–38), 51–55; John Piper, 'Colour and Textures', *Architectural Review*, vol. 95, no. 566 (February 1944): (51–52), 52.

[27] Hugh Casson, 'Art by Accident', *Architectural Review*, vol. 96, no. 573 (September 1944): 63–70.

Roughness, Accident and Irregularity for a New Picturesque

Alongside the contemporary surface values considered as an expressive force in architecture, critics put forward other cultural references to English principles at a broader scale, including the layout of buildings and more generally urban questions. The articles show the aspiration to reconcile through the urban fabric the image of an essentially rural nation, attached to its landscape heritage, pursuing a rhetoric that emerged from the propaganda implemented during the war following the dramatic transformation of cities devastated by war and industrialisation. The cultural inheritance of the eighteenth-century theories of the Picturesque appeared as a point of reference for contemporary architecture, destined to continue until the second half of the 1950s. Against this 'nostalgic' and 'sentimental' vision of 'modern architecture', new generations of critics and architects were to voice their fiercest criticism and form an 'anti-Picturesque faction' that came to include all the protagonists of the 'new' identified in New Brutalism.[28]

For the editors of *Architectural Review*, the resurrection of Picturesque principles was necessary to reinforce a national genealogy for the Modern Movement, again in line with Pevsner's theories, where the legacy of William Temple, Alexander Pope, Horace Walpole and Batty Langley would be again used to deal with the emergency of reconstruction.[29] This assumption was made clear by statements affirming that the 'modern movement may be said to be nothing more than the logical development of eighteenth-century Landscape theory', and that the reconstruction of British territory must be set up under the re-enactment of the principles of the Picturesque: 'Resurrect the true theory of the picturesque [...] and apply [it] to a field [to] which it has not been consciously applied before: the city.'[30] *Architectural Review* published essays where eighteenth-century landscape theories were applied to contemporary projects, demonstrating the promise of a 'modern' capable of coexisting with its national past through the help of graphic montages published on the magazine's covers between 1944 and 1946 (see figure 1).[31]

In the Picturesque tradition Pevsner identified Britain's most decisive contribution to European 'visual culture'.[32] This critical operation is to be understood both at a rhetorical and operational level. In rhetorical terms, the Picturesque became 'a national picture-making aptitude', connected to an exaltation of the national values of Englishness.[33] The ability of the Picturesque to interpret political instances and the configuration of a national identity in the eighteenth-century needs to be considered. Indeed, Pevsner emphasised the advent of Picturesque theories concurrently with Britain's transition from an absolute monarchy to a liberal state, intimately linked with the nation's democratic genealogy. Pevsner's chosen example was that of a vital movement resulting from a theory 'conceived by philosophers, writers and *virtuosi* – not by architects'. This statement reveals Pevsner's belief that critics, and not architects, would play a crucial role in orienting the evolution of the Modern Movement.[34]

[28] Reyner Banham, 'Revenge of the Picturesque: English Architectural Polemics, 1945–1965', in John Summerson (ed.), *Concerning Architecture: Essays on Architectural Writers and Writing Presented to Nikolaus Pevsner* (London: The Penguin Press, 1968), 265–73.

[29] 'The truth of these sentences for council houses and council flats needs not to be specifically emphasised' and again, 'the application of these passages to contemporary problems of urban planning is evident', [n.a.], 'Price on Picturesque Planning'.

[30] The Editors, 'Exterior Furnishing or Sharawaggi: The Art of Making Urban Landscape', *Architectural Review*, vol. 95, no. 565 (January 1944): (3–11), 3.

[31] See, for example, the photomontages of Aalto's Paimio Sanatorium framed by the ruins of a gothic window of a church devastated by bombing during the Blitz, on the *Architectural Review* January 1944 cover, or the superimposition of Oscar Niemeyer's Dance Club plan on the Picturesque plan for the town of Chiswick, designed in 1736, on the May 1944 cover.

[32] Nikolaus Pevsner, 'The Genesis of the Picturesque', *Architectural Review*, vol. 96 (November 1944): 139–46.

[33] Ibid.

[34] Pevsner, *An Outline of European Architecture*.

1 Various covers of
Architectural Review:
• vol. 89, January 1941,
  no. 530,
  St. Paul cathedral
  on the background
  of war ruins
• vol. 95, January 1944,
  no. 565,
  Alvar Aalto's Paimio
  sanatorium framed
  by a gothic ruin
• vol. 95, May 1944,
  no. 569, Restaurant
  at Pampulha by
  Oscar Niemeyer
  and Chiswick
  Picturesque Park
• vol. 96, November
  1944, no. 575,
  Diderot's illustration
  of the human nervous
  system beside Stephen
  Switzer's plan of an
  ideal garden, 1718

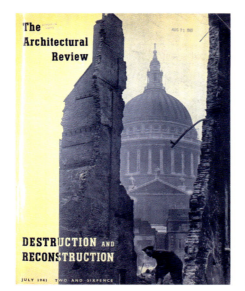

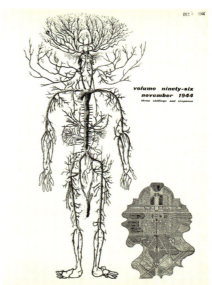

In opposition to the rationalist urban principles enunciated in the Athens Charter and in Louis Sert's essay *Can Our City Survive*, both published in 1943, and against the theories promoted by the artistic avant-garde, critics drifted away from the figurative tradition and oriented the debate towards the integration between nature and architecture. A vision was embedded in the theories of the Picturesque landscape in which 'the geometric and organic arts lie completely together', in radical opposition to the attempt 'of men by his machinery to geometrise the world'.[35] The intention was to attack the functionalism of the International Style. Pevsner's rationale followed that

[35] G. A. Jellicoe, 'A Philosophy of Landscape I', *Architects' Year Book*, vol. 1 (1945): (39–42), 42.

of Uvedale Price, who had theorised the Picturesque as a very rejection of the 'formalism' found in the Queen Anne and William III and Mary II styles.[36]

These intentions laid the foundation for the theories of 'Townscape', which appeared in 1949. Belonging to the cultural line of Richards, Pevsner, Cullen and Hastings, Townscape envisioned the application of the principles of the Picturesque to the reading of architecture both on the urban scale and the scale of the individual building. This was done through a specific terminology derived from eighteenth-century treatises, where 'modern' architecture was described according to the parameters of 'accident', 'sudden variation', 'irregularity', 'rough' and 'irritation': 'In twentieth-century terms Price's *rough* would be *abrupt*, and for *irritation* one would probably say *stimulus*'.[37] Again, in the concepts of 'roughness' and 'accident' one can read the presuppositions for some aspects that would be affirmed in the definition of New Brutalism.

Notions such as unexpected and chance became central to the critical discourse of the very early post-war period, against the background of the search for criteria for overcoming the principles of the International Style through the manipulation of material surface and spatial arrangement. 'Trust happy accidents rather than regular plans', introduce 'improprieties' against 'the present timid monotony' were the exhortations[38]. All together these intentions would determine the critical debate of the following decade, and, a few years later, lead to the birth of an orientation, New Brutalism, which ended up fulfilling the search for principles for the composition of space on the scale both of architecture and the city.

New Humanism, New Empiricism, New Monumentality

Efforts to translate nineteenth-century principles into a contemporary idiom, combined with material and spatial devices derived from eighteenth-century landscape theories, were not easily transformed into guidelines for the contemporary context, due to their nostalgic and retroactive gaze. The orientation had to be turned towards the future, pushing critics to search for other labels, which began to be accompanied by a crucial prefix: the 'New' (see figure 2).

The concept of 'modern', first identified as the expression of contemporary architecture rooted in the eighteenth- and nineteenth-century tradition, underwent a radical transformation through this prefix. The search for the definition of a 'New-ism', in which 'New' would be the key prefix for a parameter of intellectual and operative research, found its reasons for existence in the desire to reconcile an ethical and political orientation with an aesthetic character.

The term 'New Humanism' was the first 'New-ism' to re-emerge, in a fresh guise, a few months before the end of the war. It appeared on 23 November 1944 in the weekly *Architects' Journal* in the title of an anonymous review of Howard Robertson's book *Architecture Arising*.[39] The author stressed the need to define a 'national idiom' through the search for a regional architecture. The humanistic dimension, summarised with the formula 'New Humanism', identified the capacity of architecture to possess a

---

[36] [n.a.], 'Price on Picturesque Planning'.
[37] The Editors, 'Exterior Furnishing or Sharawaggi', 47: 'Although smoothness be the ground-work of beauty, yet roughness is its fringe and ornament, and that which preserves it from insipidity', in ibid.
[38] [n.a.], 'Price on Picturesque Planning', 47.
[39] [n.a.], 'The New Humanism', *Architects' Journal*, vol. 100, no. 2600 (23 November 1944): 375–76. The term New Humanism was not entirely new. In 1930, a symposium entitled *The Critique of Humanism was* organised in New York, in which Mumford and Hitchcock, among others, took part, see Paolo Scrivano, *Storia di un'idea di architettura moderna. Henry-Russell Hitchcock e l'International Style* (Milan: FrancoAngeli, 2001), 84–5). In 1934 Jerzy Waldemar-George invented the definition of neo-humanism in the art-historical field. Unlike the English New Humanism, Waldemar-George's definition was not intended to define an orientation but was described as a moral imperative to express the human presence in artworks.

2 Advertisement,
Architects' Journal,
5 August 1943, p.n.n.

'The New Humanism',
Architects' Journal,
vol. 100, 23 November
1944

Gehrard Kallmann,
'New Uncertainty',
Architectural Review,
vol. 99, March 1946

James Maude Richards,
'The New Empiricism',
Architectural Review,
vol. 102, June 1947

Robin Boyd,
'New Eclecticism',
Architectural Review,
vol. 110, September
1951

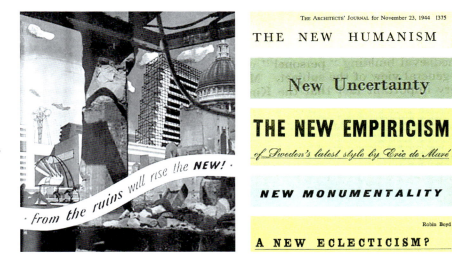

THE ARCHITECTS' JOURNAL for November 23, 1944   [375

THE NEW HUMANISM

New Uncertainty

THE NEW EMPIRICISM
of Sweden's latest style by Eric de Maré

NEW MONUMENTALITY

Robin Boyd

A NEW ECLECTICISM?

· from the ruins will rise the NEW! ·

personality 'as varied as that of an attractive human character, for it is human character which a city should reflect'.[40]

However, the author of *Architecture Arising* suggested identifying aesthetic possibilities in the past, through the observation that traditional materials were 'creeping
back into the idiom of contemporary design'. Robertson's use of the term 'back' was
rejected by *Architects' Journal*: 'It is the word "back" to which we take exception'. A
revealing contrast between 'back' and 'new' was hence made clear.

The presence of the prefix 'New', added by the magazine, demonstrated the
necessary invention of a new label able to break free from traditional precepts, one
that could literally change direction: 'The contemporary idiom should [...] show a
forward development'. However, this 'development' was suggested by *Architects'
Journal* through a truly twentieth-century vernacular, 'which recognises humanity and in which humanity can itself recognise because it is national, because it is
familiar'.[41] In this statement converged the interests resulting from the discussions
on the principles of truth, on the honest and correct use of materials, as well as on
the Picturesque, which the critics referred to as being opposed to the principles of
the machine age.[42]

The use of the term 'humanism' inserted the critical operation of *Architects' Journal* into the ongoing debate on reducing the mechanistic emphasis of the Modern
Movement. It also helped broaden the meanings of 'New' to include renewed interest in Renaissance architecture, defined as 'humanist'. However, this debate increased
the ambiguity of the term 'humanism', understood both as an aspiration to a more
human, or 'humanised' architecture, and as a reference to the classical principles of
architecture, those described by Geoffrey Scott in *The Architecture of Humanism: A
Study in the History of Taste* and that later re-emerged in Wittkower's 1949 *Architectural Principles in the Age of Humanism*.

[40] Howard P. Robertson, *Architecture Arising* (London: Faber & Faber, 1944), 46.
[41] [n.a.], 'The New Humanism', 376.
[42] About humanism in modern architecture, see Miriam Panzeri, *Architettura moderna e progetto umanistico storia,
formazione, comunità 1945–1965* (Milan: Jaca Book, 2013); Scrivano, *Storia di un'idea di architettura moderna.
Henry-Russell Hitchcock e l'International Style*.

The debate on the term 'humanism' was also influenced by Scandinavian architectural culture, which would offer powerful incentives for the invention of New Brutalism. In fact, the term 'humanism' also spread in England in the wake of Alvar Aalto's article 'The Humanizing of Architecture' published in 1940.[43] Aalto developed a coherent argument about the crisis of functionalism and the consequent need to respond to man's psychological needs, citing examples that brought English interests closer to Scandinavian architecture and to the architecture of Aalto, but also that of Asplund and Markelius. These examples had achieved, in the eyes of British critics, a regionalist interpretation of the Modern Movement corresponding with the hypotheses of New Humanism. This orientation matured in the context of the speech given by Sigfried Giedion in 1946 at the RIBA in London, where he shared his conviction of the need to overcome the mechanistic and functionalist aspects of the Modern Movement.[44] In Britain, Giedion strengthened a hitherto latent aspiration towards a unity of intents relating to psychological, artistic and technical components.

Pevsner himself appropriated the term 'humanism' in August 1945, in an article entitled 'The New Humanism'. There he compared the various editions of Anthony Bertram's book, *The House*. In contrast to the 'humanism' of Aalto and the consequent English interpretations, Pevsner demonstrated the possibility of bringing customary terms up to date by adding the prefix 'New'. His New Humanism was intended to orient post-war reconstruction favouring 'human' over the 'mechanical' traits that had characterised the architecture of the International Style.[45] Pevsner's incursions into the debate through terminological inventions must be carefully evaluated because the greatest proponent of the most in-depth theoretical positions on New Brutalism was one of his disciples.

In order to consolidate public support for the new housing policies advocated by the post-war government and, in so doing, solidify their relationship with the Labour Party, British critics (and Richards in particular) promoted a model for urban planning that was aligned with the government's reconstruction programmes. This resulted in the perpetuation of the relationship between art, politics and architecture, as advocated by Pevsner through radio broadcasts entitled 'Art for Everyone: Art and the State'.[46] The political affinity between the Labour Party and the Scandinavian welfare state made the choice of the Swedish architectural model a logical expression of architecture for a social democratic state. During the war, the photographic campaigns conducted by George Everard Kidder Smith, curator of the *Stockholm Builds* exhibition at MOMA in New York, had already helped direct the interests of British architects towards Scandinavian countries, whose architecture filled the pages of magazines.[47] It was also in the context of these interests that an artist destined to play an important role in the affirmation of New Brutalism appeared in the debate: the photographer Eric de Maré. In 1943, De Maré edited an entire issue of *Architectural Review* entitled 'Swedish Peace in War', in which the projects of Sven Markelius, Stüre Fröle and Ralph Erskine, photographed by Kidder Smith, consolidated the interest in Swedish regionalism.[48] For *Architectural Review*, these works were an example of 'progressive' architecture, capable of combining a certain degree of functionalism with local building traditions and materials.

Swedish architecture thus emerged as a model to be applied to English reconstruction. This view was supported not only by the editors of *Architectural Review*,

[43] Alvar Aalto, 'The Humanizing of Architecture', *Architectural Forum*, vol. 73 (December 1940): 505–06.
[44] [n.a.], 'Astragal: Notes & Topics: In Search of a Word', *Architects' Journal*, vol. 104, no. 2966 (17 October 1946): 274–75.
[45] Nikolaus Pevsner, 'Books. The New Humanism', *Architectural Review*, vol. 98, no. 584 (August 1945): 59–60.
[46] Nikolaus Pevsner, 'Art for Everyone: Art and the State', 16–18–19 June 1946, BBC Radio, London, 1946.
[47] George Everard Kidder Smith, *Sweden Builds: Its Modern Architecture and Land Policy Background, Development and Contribution* (New York: A. Bonnier, 1950).
[48] Sven Backström, George Everard Kidder Smith, William Holford, 'Swedish Peace in War', *Architectural Review*, vol. 94, no. 561 (September 1943).

but also by Patrick Abercrombie, author in 1943 of the Great London Plan, who identified the legislation of the Swedish welfare state as a model for social democratic Britain, 'where class or income differentials are minimalised in architectural expression'.[49]

Alongside the example of Scandinavian architecture, the definition of New Humanism included an interest in post-revolutionary Russian architecture, which from 1935 onwards was defined as 'Socialist Realism'. The issue of Socialist Realism is vital for understanding the ideological substratum that animated the definition of 'humanism' in Britain. The term's inference to Socialist Realism is in fact to be understood as a close alliance between architecture and politics, as specified the *RIBA Journal* in 1941: 'Realism demands of the artist constant active participation in the daily activities and the emotions of the people whom he serves [...] it also fundamentally implies that art is a part of the socialist dynamic'.[50]

Since the 1930s, English critics had been sensitive to Russian architectural production, and it is in this very period that we can identify the recognition of architecture as a reflection of political thought, according to an ideological vision that until then had been foreign to British culture, as Lubetkin recalled in 1932: 'To the English reader a discussion of architecture in terms of "ideology" will be somewhat startling'.[51] The interpretation of Russian architecture as an experiment in both urban reconstruction and reconstruction of a social nature fuelled the moral assumption that a consideration for social and 'human' issues should be reflected in reconstruction programmes, to recover the fracture between art, architecture and politics.[52]

The New Humanism thus outlined a synthesis on a Russian-Swedish axis, whose centre was ideological, fuelled first and foremost by a moral imperative 'providing the men in the street with something more genuine' and the desire to 'humanise' architecture by overcoming pure functionalism. Secondly, New Humanism was elaborated on a precise political affinity, which is why the term converged with debates concerning Scandinavian and Soviet architecture. Considering the positions taken by critics in the immediate post-war period, architecture therefore became a political instrument and a vehicle for civil values that an entire democratic society could share.

The formulation of a coherent language that could speak 'to the common man'[53] is to be read against the background of Britain's quest to identify a national architecture. What this language consisted of would be at the centre of the debate in the years to come, in a hesitant oscillation between the pursuit of a humanised architecture, a contemporary vernacular close to the feeling of the 'common man', attentive to human psychological needs following the example of Swedish modernism; or the proposal of a system of standardisation and prefabrication of Soviet derivation, capable of favouring a unity of scale and a coherent reading of the building; or an architecture regulated by precise geometric formulas, in search of a *modulor*. New Humanism remained suspended between a critical definition and the aspiration for a style in search of architects able to translate the theoretical horizon proposed by the magazines into an architecture that embodied the ideological values emerging from the politics of reconstruction.[54] However, without the collision between the ideological implications of Socialist Realism and the search for a theoretical horizon proposed

---

[49] Patrick Abercrombie, Bertil Hulten, *Building Modern Sweden* (London: Penguin, 1951), 3.

[50] [n.a.], 'Architecture in the USSR', *RIBA Journal*, vol. 48 (June 1941): 155–58.

[51] An entire issue of *Architectural Review* was devoted to Russian architecture, published in 1932 and edited by Robert Byron and Berthold Lubetkin: 'The Russian Scene', *Architectural Review*, vol. 71 (May 1932): 173–214.

[52] Stephen V. Ward, 'Soviet Communism and the British Planning Movement: Rational Learning or Utopian Imagining?', *Planning Perspectives*, vol. 27, no. 4 (October 2012): 499–524.

[53] [n.a.], 'Inside the Pub', *Architectural Review*, vol. 106, no. 634 (October 1949): 209–22: 'An architecture which takes full advantage of contemporary techniques and materials – but is yet fully rooted in the needs and responses of ordinary people'.

[54] James Maude Richards, 'The Wrong Turning', *Architectural Review*, vol. 105, no. 627 (March 1949): (107–112), 107.

through New Humanism, it would be impossible to understand the crucial aspect of New Brutalism's ethical stance.[55]

Another definition emerged as a consequence of the decision by British critics to drift away from the examples of Soviet Realism, following the authoritarian turn of the Stalinist regime, which represented an unacceptable model for 'democratic reconstruction'.[56] In June 1947, *Architectural Review* coined the definition New Empiricism, presented as 'a tendency to humanise the theory [of functionalism] on its aesthetic side and to get back to the earlier rationalism on the technical side'. A short unsigned article, probably written by Richards, entitled 'The New Empiricism: Sweden's Latest Style', presented the Swedish attempt to 'humanise the aesthetic expression of functionalism'.[57]

If at first the interest in Sweden converged with New Humanism through examples of large-scale projects such as hospitals, factories and social housing, under the definition of New Empiricism the focus was on the use of materials in domestic architecture and on the appeal to 'cosiness'. In the examples of Sven Backström, Sven Markelius, Sture Fröle and Ralph Erskine, Richards identified the abandonment of the functionalist cause through recourse to the 'psychological' dimension of the built environment. It is through Backström's very words, taken from a 1943 article,[58] that the term New Empiricism entered the English debate, described as 'the attempt to be more objective than the functionalists and to bring back another science, that of psychology, into the picture'.[59]

This theoretical framework was reinforced by Eric de Maré in 'The Antecedents of Sweden's Latest Style'.[60] New Empiricism was described as a liberation of local materials, such as brick and wood, from the international canons that imposed cladding and rigid formalism, in the name of a return to the 'workaday common sense' and through the resizing of architectural elements, 'in line with human aspirations'.[61] In the Swedish-only examples, New Empiricism was safe from possible authoritarian drifts. A 'new vernacular' elevated the local tradition through the technical infrastructure of the Modern Movement. In the context of Richards' aspirations for a 'new regionalism', a term derived from American criticism, the Scandinavian example became the symbol of an architecture rooted in local characteristics, as opposed to the internationalism of the 1920s.

This ambition also found strength in other definitions circulating in the international debate, such as that of the American critic Lewis Mumford, author of the definition 'Bay Region Style', which became the receptacle of a 'native and human form of modernism'.[62] It was thanks to the international echo of American regionalist concerns through the symposium organised at the MoMA in New York in 1948, entitled 'What is Happening to Modern Architecture?',[63] that Richards would reinforce the term New Empiricism, finding a commonality of intent: 'Its [Bay Region Style] recent spread in the USA is undoubtedly a symptom of the same tendency as gave rise to the New Empiricism'.[64]

[55] See also Joan Ockman, 'New Empiricism and New Humanism', *Design Book Review*, no. 41/42 (Winter/Spring 2000): 18–21.
[56] [n.a.], 'Reconstruction in the USSR', *Architectural Review*, vol. 101 (May 1947): 184. The end of the exchange between the UK and Soviet Union is marked by the May 1947 issue of *Architectural Review*, following a letter to the editors of *Architectural Review* by three Russian architects, David Ark, Andrei Bunin and Nikola Bylinkin, who refused to publish any future contributions in British magazines in response to British accusations.
[57] James Maude Richards, 'The New Empiricism: Sweden's Latest Style', *Architectural Review*, vol. 102, no. 606 (June 1947): (199–204), 199.
[58] Sven Backström, 'A Swede Looks at Sweden', *Architectural Review*, vol. 94, no. 561 (September 1943): 80.
[59] Richards, 'The New Empiricism: Sweden's Latest Style'.
[60] Eric de Maré, 'The Antecedents and Origins of Sweden's Latest Style', *Architectural Review*, vol. 103, no. 623 (January 1948): 8–22.
[61] Ibid, 18.
[62] Lewis Mumford, 'The Sky Line: Status Quo', *New Yorker*, 11 September 1947, 106–09.
[63] [n.a.], 'Architectural Symposium', *Architectural Review*, vol. 104, no. 620 (August 1948): 97–8.
[64] James Maude Richards, 'Bay Region Domestic', *Architectural Review*, vol. 104, no. 631 (October 1948): 164.

The Swedish-derived tendency immediately attracted criticism and became Giedion's target during a lecture at the Victoria and Albert Museum in London on 18 August 1948. Giedion defined New Empiricism as too general a label to succeed in establishing a credible alternative to the functionalism of the 1930s. New Empiricism appeared to Giedion as nothing more than 'a certain Nordic evasion of the real problem, which means that "cosiness is coming back into domestic work"'.[65] If placed in the general framework marked by the multiplication of definitions, Giedion's position confirms the expectations of a genre of New-ism capable of grasping and orienting contemporary trends, beyond the International Style and within the Modern Movement.

Alongside New Empiricism and New Humanism, another label entered the English debate thanks to the discussions at the sixth CIAM held in Bridgwater in 1947: New Monumentality. Formulated in 1943 in the United States by Giedion, Sert and Léger as a call for an appropriate architectural democratic language, the definition of New Monumentality acquired in England other decisive components, linked to the country's socialist and industrial traditions. The fact that Louis Kahn discussed 'Monumentality' on that occasion serves to anticipate his scepticism towards all kinds of New, including New Brutalism.[66]

Richards and the members of the MARS Group identified the egalitarian ideal as the motor for a democratisation of architecture and the consequent responsibility of the architect to realise 'the ordinary man's aspirations towards some visible expression of his collective consciousness'.[67] From these considerations emerged a visual investigation of a monumentality generated by artistic and technical practices,[68] which became the subject of debate at the symposium 'In search of a New Monumentality' organised in September 1948 by *Architectural Review*. Gregor Pulsson, Henry-Russell Hitchcock, William Holford, Sigfried Giedion, Walter Gropius, Lucio Costa and Alfred Roth were invited to discuss the adaptability of the concept of 'monumentality' to British ambitions. The report published in *Architectural Review* reveals the theoretical scaffolding of its editors, who seized the opportunity to reiterate the potential of ordinary and everyday objects to evoke a 'public feeling for perpetuation', as a synthesis of collective expression. This affirmation delimits the question of monumentality, which, while imposing itself by being 'irresistible to mind' and 'of strong emotional impact', rediscovered itself as 'slow' and 'subconscious', with an intent apparently similar to what was to be one of the principles of New Brutalism.[69]

The search for a New Monumentality occurred through the investigation of the aesthetic impact of materiality in vernacular architecture and functionality in the exalted anonymity of industrial and domestic architecture.[70] At the beginning of the 1950s, *Architectural Review*, followed by *Architect's Journal*, sought to define 'visual cases' to identify the coexistence of elements of an English vernacular tradition with contemporary technologies, expressive of a certain degree of monumentality.[71] An example of this attitude is a photograph by Charles Eames on the cover of the November 1949 issue of *Architectural Review*, where of a stack of bricks presents the 'unusual massiveness of the pilotis' and recalls other famous *pilotis* under construction. This image alluded to 'a great modern building [...] in which the functional tradition has been brought two steps closer to the realisation of a new and specifically contemporary monumentality' (see figure 3).[72]

[65] Sigfried Giedion, 'Mars & ICA', *Architects' Journal*, vol. 108, no. 2796 (September 1948): 251–52.
[66] Louis Kahn, 'Monumentality', in Paul Zucker (ed.), *New Architecture and City Planning: A Symposium* (New York: Philosophical Library, 1944), 577–88.
[67] [n.a.], 'In Search of a New Monumentality', *Architectural Review*, vol. 104, no. 621 (September 1948): 117–28.
[68] Sigfried Giedion, *A Decade of Contemporary Architecture* (Zurich: Editions Girsberger, 1954), 12.
[69] Reyner Banham, 'The New Brutalism', *Architectural Review*, vol. 118, no. 708 (December 1955): 354–61.
[70] John Summerson, 'The London Suburban Villa', *Architectural Review*, vol. 104, no. 620 (August 1948): 63–72; James Maude Richards, *The Castles on the Ground: The Anatomy of Suburbia* (London: Architectural Press, 1946).
[71] [n.a.], 'In Search of a New Monumentality', 128.
[72] Charles Eames [cover], *Architectural Review*, vol. 106, no. 635 (November 1949).

3 Cover, Photo
by Charles Eames
representing a pile of
bricks, *Architectural
Review*, vol. 106,
November 1949,
no. 635

The Cover should be looked at long ways on. It
will then be recognized as a progress photograph of
a great modern building in which, largely by means
of the poignant contrast of the expressive pattern of
the *brises-soleil* with the unusually massive form of
the *pilotis*, the functional tradition has been brought
at least two steps nearer to the realization of a new
and specifically contemporary monumentality.
For another photograph see the frontispiece.

4 James Maude
Richards, 'The Functional
Tradition', *Architectural
Review*, vol. 107,
January 1950, no. 637

The Functional Tradition for National Unification

English cultural unity was challenged by the constellation of labels in the debate. Through the polemical invective entitled 'The Next Step?', Richards warned against the dangers of stylistic confusion generated by 'phrases and catchwords [...] disguised reactions to the bad old days of style for style's sake'.[73] The search for a New-ism moved away from the initial 'battle of styles' of the immediate post-war period, towards a style that had to find 'unity, not uniformity'.[74]

This led to positions such as that of the Australian-born critic Robin Boyd, who wanted to lessen antagonism by proposing a nineteenth-century inspired label he defined as 'The New Eclecticism'.[75] Boyd unveiled to the reader the common research underlying two apparently antithetical directions, similar to two antagonists in a 'new war of the styles – the Organic versus the Functional'.[76] Boyd's incursion into this phase of the debate should not be underestimated, since he would show himself to be attentive to the evolution of New Brutalism, to the point of seeing, in the emergence of the eclectic drifts of Brutalist style, the failure of that definition.

In order to quell the battle over styles, *Architectural Review* resumed the visual re-education programme begun in 1947 under the name 'Functional Tradition'[77], a definition presented in a special issue of the magazine in January 1950.[78] Wanting to demonstrate the intermingling of the functionalism of the Modern Movement and a 'spontaneous and anonymous' architecture, the magazine engaged in a discourse of images that went beyond questions of style and focused on materials and processes dependent on local resources, through photographs of buildings and objects on whose surfaces one could read the signs of the natural or mechanical forces that had shaped them.[79] To explain the Functional Tradition, Richards emphasised 'visual perception' as a crucial tool for reading urban space and architecture, according to the emotional impact on the observer and the relationship between elements, materials and textures.[80] These reflections would be evoked in the supremacy of the image, which, in the context of the different meanings and interpretations assumed by New Brutalism, would be revealed as one of its main characteristics.

The Functional Tradition defined a repertoire that profoundly marked old and new generations of architects, who witnessed through the monthly columns the possible recovery of both the functionalism of the Modern Movement and the English building tradition.[81] Surfaces shaped by 'accidents of nature' or 'by man's lack of precision tools' acquired values 'desirable in themselves' (see figure 4).[82] 'Variety, interest

---

[73] James Maude Richards, 'The Next Step', *Architectural Review*, vol. 107 (March 1950): 165–68.

[74] Lewis Mumford, 'Monumentalism, Symbolism and Style', *Architectural Review*, vol. 105, no. 628 (April 1949): 173–80.

[75] It is unclear whether Boyd was presenting this new definition as a cultural project promoting heterogeneous research or whether it was an interrogation of the state of criticism, questioning its effectiveness. Robin Boyd, 'A New Eclecticism?', *Architectural Review*, vol. 110, no. 657 (September 1951): 151–54.

[76] By 'organic' Boyd means 'regionalistic, empirical, humanistic, romantic, irrational or merely Cottage Style'; and by 'functional', 'rational, geometric, post-cubist, mechanicist, or merely International Style', ibid., 152.

[77] For a recent account of the Functional Tradition, see Andrew Higgott, 'Eric de Maré in Search of the Functional Tradition', *AA Files*, no. 70 (Winter 2015): 140–47.

[78] [n.a.], 'The Functional Tradition', *Architectural Review*, vol. 107, no. 637 (January 1950): (3–65), 11.

[79] Ibid., 47.

[80] Ibid., 5.

[81] A prime example, also recalled by Banham, is the photograph of the Cobb breakwater at Lyme Regis, whose form exemplifies the 'strict discipline of function [...] so remarkably virile and expressive as to deserve the title of the Parthenon of the functional movement of the twentieth century', Banham, 'Revenge of the Picturesque: English Architectural Polemics, 1945–1965'. Richards and de Maré also published several books on the Functional Tradition, see James Maude Richards, *The Functional Tradition in Early Industrial Buildings* (London: Architectural Press, 1958); Eric de Maré, *The Nautical Style: An Aspect of the Functional Tradition* (London: Architectural Press, 1973).

[82] [n.a.], 'The Functional Tradition', 49.

and vitality' were the fundamental values of a series of images composing a catalogue destined to favour a change in sensibility that in the short term would lead
to the definition of a new vernacular, in which the surface value became central in
rediscovering Englishness. Within a few years, a similar visual catalogue would also
re-emerge in the artistic imagination of the avant-garde, such as the Independent
Group, although presented according to a vision that intended to override the canons of traditional beauty.

Of all attempts proposed, it was New Empiricism that took on a particular
dimension through a reunifying event. The critical commitment pursued by the magazines during the previous five years seemed to reach its goal in the autumn of 1951,
when the Festival of Britain, organised at the South Bank in memory of the Great
Exhibition of 1851, opened its doors and became the ultimate expression of the theories advocated through New Empiricism.[83] The festival was promoted by *Architectural
Review* as an attempt to put into practice the theories of Townscape,[84] demonstrating the vitality of British debates.[85] The criticism voiced against the Festival of Britain
revealed the dissatisfaction of the younger generations of critics and architects, including the Smithsons and Banham, with an architecture entrusted to 'pitched roofs, peep-
hole windows and "folky" details'.[86] The architecture staged during the Festival represented a return to a language dominated by 'cosiness', as Giedion himself put it,[87] as
the result of an attitude of disenchantment 'and a sense of guilt towards the scientific
methods and machines that have been used for destruction'.[88]

For several critics and architects, the obvious concession to tradition and the
lapse into a vernacular architecture fomented by the editors of *Architects' Journal* and
Architectural Review was a betrayal of the modernist ideal, as well as a missed opportunity to demonstrate Britain's cultural potential. This would be the main criticism
that extended the debate towards new references, thus escaping the aesthetics that
emerged from the Festival.

The Neo-Palladianism of Wittkower and Rowe

While the nostalgic ferments enunciated in New Empiricism and New Humanism
spread with fragmentary results, the 1950s saw a convergence of interest in the dis-
missal of any vernacular and regionalist references. It featured the same concern for
'humanism', not as a stylistic and psychological model but as a formal and compositional guideline, linked to England historical research and contemporary design. Publications such as Wittkower's *Architectural Principles in the Age of Humanism*, Le Corbusier's *Le Modulor* and Colin Rowe's essays on Le Corbusier had a crucial impact on
the younger generation of architects and their search for new principles. *Architectural
Principles* demonstrated the possibility of a 'humanism' beyond the Swedish or Soviet
models, devoid of any ideological framework defended by the magazines.[89] Among
the exponents of the new generation attentive to this particular meaning of 'humanism'

---

[83] On the Festival of Britain see for example: Becky Elizabeth Conekin, *The Autobiography of a Nation: The 1951
Festival of Britain, Representing Britain in the Post-war Era* (Manchester: Manchester University Press, 2003).

[84] [n.a.], 'South Bank Exhibition', *Architectural Review*, vol. 110, no. 656 (August 1951): 73–142.

[85] Monica Pidgeon, 'Editorial', *Architectural Design*, vol. 21, no. 1 (January 1951): 1.

[86] Colin St John Wilson, 'The Vertical City', *The Observer*, 17 February 1952, 8.

[87] Giedion, 'Mars & ICA'.

[88] Wilson, 'The Vertical City', 8.

[89] Rudolf Wittkower, *Architectural Principles in the Age of Humanism*, vol. 19 (London: Warburg Institute, University
of London, 1949). The book combines three articles previously published in the *Journal of the Warburg and
Courtauld Institutes*. On the reception of Wittkower's essay and its influence on post-war culture, see Alina Payne,
'Rudolf Wittkower and Architectural Principles in the Age of Modernism', *Journal of the Society of Architectural
Historians*, vol. 53, no. 3 (September 1994): 322–42.

were two of the leading figures of New Brutalism: Alison and Peter Smithson. As evidence of the influence of Wittkower's method, they commented on the publication of *Architectural Principles* as follows: 'Dr. Wittkower is regarded by the younger architects as the only art historian working in England capable of analysing buildings in spatial and plastic terms, and not in terms of derivations and dates'.[90] Wittkower was well aware of the possible influence of this essay on the new generations, as his conclusion in *Architectural Principles* demonstrates: 'The subject [theory of proportions] is again very much alive in the minds of young architects today, and they may well evolve new and unexpected solutions to this ancient problem'.[91] The book generated a fruitful input for the contemporary project, where principles of 'logic of the plan', 'precision, geometrical economy' and 'evidence of the structural skeleton' answered a contemporary concern. The series of diagrams used by Wittkower demonstrated the possibility of an a-temporal system based on essential geometric principles that found a potential contemporary application in the simplicity of geometry (see figure 5a).[92]

The operativity of Wittkower's essay consisted in its capacity to become an 'active force in the present situation', as Voelcker defined it in 1952,[93] for it promoted a critical stance that went beyond the consolidated British attitude of associating the architecture of the fifteenth and sixteenth centuries with a question of personal taste, as Geoffrey Scott had advanced.[94] *Architectural Principles* also became a reference disseminated through a series of meetings, seminars and public events centred on the theory of proportions that continued until 1955, suggesting a specific strategy of appropriation of historical examples in the compositional procedures of the Modern Movement.[95]

The success of Wittkower's theories can be measured through the early articles of Colin Rowe, his student at the Warburg Institute. Rowe's 1947 article, 'The Mathematics of the Ideal Villa', introduced a new reading of Le Corbusier's work based on the example of Wittkower's principles to contemporary architecture.[96] The Villa Stein at Garches was analysed through a comparative reading with Palladio's Villa Malcontenta, based on the analogy of the mathematical system as a means of controlling the design process. Through the scrutiny of compositional principles, Rowe inaugurated a process of architectural analysis that transcended historical periods and turned history into a tool for contemporary design. In fact, Rowe underlined the persistence of common concerns through the communicative strategy of the diagram, launching the basis for an aesthetic to be achieved through principles of symmetry and rigid systems of proportion (see figure 5b).

In *Mannerism and Modern Architecture*, published in May 1950, Rowe also read significant works of the Modern Movement in light of Mannerism, understood not as a stylistic category but as an attitude.[97] Rowe emphasised the similarity in form-finding

---

[90] Alison and Peter Smithson, 'Correspondence', *RIBA Journal*, vol. 59 (February 1952): 140.

[91] Wittkower, *Architectural Principles in the Age of Humanism*, 135.

[92] In the preface to the second edition of 1962, Wittkower acknowledged the impact of the book on the younger generation of architects: 'The book is concerned with purely historical studies of the period 1450 to 1580, but it was my most satisfying experience to have seen its impact on a young generation of architects'. Wittkower, *Architectural Principles in the Age of Humanism*, second edition (London: Warburg Institute, University of London, 1952).

[93] John Voelcker, 'Correspondence', *RIBA Journal*, vol. 59 (February 1952): 140–41.

[94] English aesthetic theories from William Hogarth, Edmund Burke, David Hume and John Ruskin repudiated classical theories of proportion and the existence of an objective, mathematical truth, in favour of a physiological and psychological sensibility and thus the essentially subjective nature of proportion.

[95] Consider also the international impact of the 1951 Milan Triennale event, i.e., the *De divina proportione* conference and exhibition, to which Le Corbusier and Wittkower were also invited.

[96] Colin Rowe, 'The Mathematics of the Ideal Villa: Palladio and Le Corbusier Compared', *Architectural Review*, vol. 101, no. 602 (February 1947): 101–04.

[97] Colin Rowe, 'Mannerism and Modern Architecture', *Architectural Review*, vol. 107, no. 641 (May 1950): 289–300.

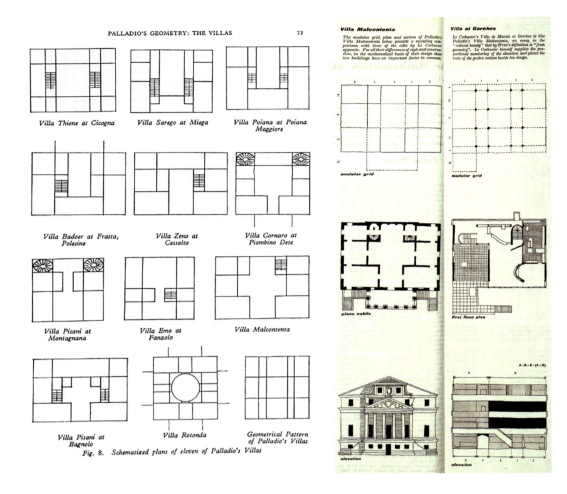

Villa Thiene at Cicogna

Villa Sarego at Miega

Villa Poiana at Poiana Maggiore

Villa Badoer at Fratta, Polesine

Villa Zeno at Cessalto

Villa Cornaro at Piombino Dese

Villa Pisani at Montagnana

Villa Emo at Fanzolo

Villa Malcontenta

Villa Pisani at Bagnolo

Villa Rotonda

Geometrical Pattern of Palladio's Villas

Fig. 8. *Schematized plans of eleven of Palladio's Villas*

Villa Malcontenta

The modular grid, plan and section of Palladio's Villa Malcontenta below provide a revealing comparison with those of the villa by Le Corbusier opposite. For all their differences of style and construction, in the mathematical basis of their design these two buildings have an important factor in common.

Villa at Garches

Le Corbusier's Villa de Moncie at Garches is like Palladio's Villa Malcontenta, an essay in the "natural beauty" that by Wren's definition is "from geometry". Le Corbusier himself supplies the proportional numbering of the elevation and places the ratio of the golden section beside his design.

modular grid

modular grid

plano nobile

first floor plan

elevation

elevation

5a Rudolf Wittkower, diagrams of Palladian villas in *Architectural Principles in the Age of Humanism*, 1949, p. 73

5b Colin Rowe, 'The Mathematics of the Ideal Villa: Palladio and Le Corbusier Compared', *Architectural Review*, vol. 101, February 1947, no. 602, pp. 102–03

strategies between architects of the sixteenth century and protagonists of the Modern Movement, such as Adolf Loos, Ferenc Molnár, Walter Gropius, Mies van der Rohe and Le Corbusier. Rowe's interest in Mannerism reactivated in the 1950s a renewed attention to transitional phases, against the background of a debate that arose after Heinrich Wölfflin's *Renaissance and Baroque*, which omitted from its analysis the very question of the interval between the two styles.

Ultimately, *Architectural Principles* was implanted into the architectural debate and became a reference for critics who, purged of nostalgic and vernacular references, were moving towards a search for absolute forms[98]. Rowe's consequent method for interpreting twentieth-century architecture through its own intrinsic historicity initiated

[98] On this subject, see the following contributions: Howard Hibbard, 'Obituary for Rudolf Wittkower', *Burlington Magazine*, vol. 114 (March 1972): 175; James Ackerman, 'Rudolf Wittkower's Influence on the History of Architecture', *Source*, vol. 8, no. 9 (1989): 87–90; Henry A. Millon, 'Rudolf Wittkower, Architectural Principles in the Age of Humanism: Its Influence on the Development and Interpretation of Modern Architecture', *Journal of the Society of Architectural Historians*, vol. 31, no. 2 (1972): 83–91; Payne, 'Rudolf Wittkower and Architectural Principles in the Age of Modernism'; Eva-Marie Neumann, 'Architectural Proportion in Britain 1945–1957', *Architectural History*, vol. 39 (1996): 197–221; Anthony Vidler, *Histories of the Immediate Present* (Cambridge, MA: MIT Press, 2008), 68–73.

a search for a renewed definition of modern architecture. The collision between different historical categories would eventually find an application in the very first definitions of New Brutalism.

This recourse to the principles of proportion contributed to new critical perspectives that searched for universal laws transcending the fifteenth century and that intersected with a real phenomenon of the 1950s: the Unité d'Habitation in Marseilles.[99] None of the stylistic labels put forward by *Architectural Review* survived in their original form after the disruptive event of the Unité, which caused the collapse of popular and vernacular myths, marking the crisis of post-war orientations that New Brutalism would have to take on.

---

[99] Peter Smithson, 'The Idea of Architecture in the '50s', *Architects' Journal*, vol. 21 (January 1960): 121–26.

chapter two
le corbusier
and béton brut

From 'Béton armé' to 'Béton brut' at the Unité in Marseille

The issues of raw material, honesty of structure and material, and humanism that accompanied the English debates were crucial in facilitating the positive reception of a building that left its mark on post-war architecture. The construction and dissemination of the Unité d'Habitation in Marseilles provoked sharp reactions in the international and especially British context, where architects were seeking solutions for reconstruction. Le Corbusier's poetics centred on the concept of *béton brut* raised debates that would amplify the Unité's cultural significance far beyond a prototype for reconstruction, laying the foundations for a new phase in architecture. The appearance of *béton brut* as demonstrated and in part theorised by Le Corbusier intersected the search for a label capable of explaining the changes occurring in the early 1950s. The construction site of the Unité confirmed the hypotheses that would be developed in the English definition of New Brutalism and, more intensely, in the style of International Brutalism.

The international phenomenon of *béton brut* resulted in continual tension in the trajectory of New Brutalism. While on the one hand, it gave authority and coherence to the English intellectual adventures, confirming a specific aspiration for the use of materials and the principle of truth, on the other hand, the success of this phenomenon would profoundly undermine the multiform ambitions of New Brutalism, causing it to sink to the point of annihilation. This triggered a dialectical challenge derived from the intellectual effort required for New Brutalism, despite its eloquent etymological roots, to put into practice the 'brutal poetry' demonstrated by Le Corbusier, without being reduced to the aesthetics of exposed material alone.

Acknowledgement of the aesthetic qualities of exposed concrete was a slow process, characterised for the most part by attempts to disguise its appearance through techniques which undermined the nature of the material and prevented its artistic potential from being explored. It was in the immediate post-war period that concrete, because of its qualities of strength, cheapness and durability, was presented as a possible material for reconstruction. In France, as early as 1946 it was heralded as the material that would give rise to a new phase in architecture.

6 Detail of the wall of a structure of the Norris Dam on the Clinch River, in Albert Caquot, 'Le béton dans la reconstruction de la France', *L'Architecture d'Aujourd'hui*, vol. 17, no. 5, December 1946, p. 41

Beton brut de coffrage. Traitement de la surface par le jeu alterné des panneaux de coffrage et de joints profonds. U.S.A.

Despite this, its superficial appearance still prevented its total acceptance: a 'mud' with a 'sad' appearance, a 'monotonous' 'grey paste', its 'excessive fidelity' still dictated work after dismantling which, as recommended in the pages of *Architecture d'Aujourd'hui*, ranged from bouchardage (bringing the concrete back to the quality of stone) to sandblasting or the insertion of cobblestones in the formworks. The range of examples also includes the method known as 'béton brut de décoffrage', described as a treatment of the surface marked by the alternating weave of the formwork panels, illustrated by an American example which appears to be the Norris Dam[1] (see figure 6).

During the construction of the Unité in Marseilles, Le Corbusier discovered that *béton armé* was not just a material, but a technical, plastic and artistic process that he would define as a concept: *béton brut*. The evolution from the technique of *béton armé* to the concept of *béton brut*, which in the 1960s became a style in its own right, can be found in Le Corbusier's gradually evolving vision, which progressively conferred on concrete a poetic character. What allows us to follow this transition is the particular attention paid by Le Corbusier to the dissemination of images, the choice of photographers, the layout of books and, ultimately, his control over the promotion of his work. Thanks to its experimental nature, the dissemination of images of the Unité did not begin once the construction site was completed but happened concurrently with the progression of daily activities, testifying to the use of photography for conveying the results of the experiments underway. Le Corbusier's ambition was also to make the Unité memorable through the exhibition of its plastic strength captured at the moment of its construction.

The artistic potential of concrete was gradually revealed through photographs and photomontages published in books or magazines, which were attentively following the experiments carried out on the Unité building site. The sculptural forms, the typological solution, the use of materials, and the particular connotation taken on by the adjective 'brut' soon began dominating the debates. This led architects from all over the word to explore the forms and artistic expressions of exposed materials, investigating concepts such as the truth of materials and structure, the vision of the

[1]   Albert Caquot, 'Le béton dans la reconstruction de la France', *L'Architecture d'Aujourd'hui*, vol. 17, no. 5 (December 1946): 37–43. The relevance of the examples of Tennessee Valley Authority's hydroelectric infrastructure for Le Corbusier has been investigated in Mardges Bacon, 'Le Corbusier and Postwar America: The TVA and Béton Brut', *Journal of the Society of Architectural Historians*, vol. 74, no. 1, (March 2015): 13–40.

building site as a process and a possible vision of architecture as art. The Unité, with its exposed concrete, revolutionised architecture to such an extent that it gave rise to a new direction, resumed in the principles of New Brutalism, freeing architecture from the dogmas of cladding and rigid geometries of the International Style.

In the first articles, special issues of magazines and in the fourth volume of the *Œuvre complète* published in 1946, Le Corbusier highlighted the Unité's urban and sociological aspects, without any specifications regarding the material finishing.[2] Concrete was initially only a corollary to the trajectory that saw the Unité as a prototype for reconstruction and the apex of Le Corbusier's urban, sociological and architectural research, as well as the concretisation of discussions within the CIAM.

In publications from 1945 to 1947, the only remarks on materials concerned the structure. 'A rigid concrete framework'[3] or 'a skeleton in *béton armé*'[4] is what would support the 350 dwellings to be built on top of an 'artificial concrete ground'.[5] The aesthetics of the *maison radieuse* were not specified even when Le Corbusier dedicated a monographic issue of the magazine *L'Homme et l'Architecture* to the Unité in 1947, in which a series of photographs of a model represented the *pilotis* in all their angles, with close-up shots that allowed their colossal scale to be perceived, or to appreciate their sculptural qualities, or even suggesting poetic associations with ancient and monumental structures.[6] However, the artistic component of the *pilotis* was linked to a plastic dimension that did not yet concern the expression of its surface.

The opening of the building site on 14 October 1947 marked the beginning of the transition from the technique of *béton armé* to the concept of *béton brut*. Against the backdrop of his research into the synthesis of the arts, Le Corbusier made explicit the expressive potential of *béton armé* in the modelling of the sculptural volumes that support and conclude the Unité, as visible in the 1948 special issue of the magazine *Architecture d'Aujourd'hui*, which was entirely dedicated to Le Corbusier.[7] The destiny of *béton armé* would be to go beyond mere technique to express an artistic intention, confirming the direct association between Le Corbusier's research into sculpture and polychrome paintings, and what was coming to light on the Marseilles site, the apex of his 'patient search' for monumental sculpture. 'They are made of reinforced concrete', he indicated about the *pilotis*, 'And this is a decidedly architectural expression of reinforced concrete: the bridge is launched between a technique and an art'.[8]

Le Corbusier's initial intention was for the surface of the cast structures to respond to the perfection of the *béton armé* technique. A pattern of lines designed by the marks of the framework would generate a 'nouvelle stéréotomie', attributing to it the quality of the polished concrete surface, not to be touched up after dismantling.[9]

[2] In 1947 a special issue dedicated to Le Corbusier was published in the magazine *L'Homme et l'Architecture*, created in 1945 by André Wogenscky; Le Corbusier, 'Unité d'Habitation à Marseille de Le Corbusier', *L'Homme et l'Architecture*, no. 11-14 (1947). The following year, *L'Architecture d'Aujourd'hui* dedicated a retrospective to Le Corbusier that ended with the presentation of the Unité, Le Corbusier, 'Unité', *L'Architecture d'Aujourd'hui*, special issue (April 1948). See also the various editions of Willy Boesiger (ed.), *Le Corbusier. Œuvre complète 1938–1946*, vol. 4 (Zurich: Éditions Girsberger, 1946).

[3] Le Corbusier, 'Marseille. Projet pour un immeuble d'état', *Techniques et architecture*, vol. 6, no. 7-8 (July 1945): 346–48.

[4] Boesiger (ed.), *Le Corbusier. Œuvre complète 1938–1946*, 186.

[5] Ibid.

[6] Le Corbusier, 'Unité d'Habitation à Marseille de Le Corbusier'.

[7] Le Corbusier, 'Unité'.

[8] The speech by Le Corbusier published in this issue was written on 20 August 1947, before the start of the Unité building site in Marseilles. Ibid., 47.

[9] On the definition of 'nouvelle stéréotomie', see Anna Rosellini's contribution, 'Oltre il "béton brut": Le Corbusier e la "nouvelle stéréotomie"', in Flaminia Bardat, Anna Rosellini, (eds.), *Arte e Architettura. Le Cornici della storia* (Milan: Bruno Mondadori, 2007), 231–58. See also Anna Rosellini, *Le Corbusier e la superficie. Dal rivestimento d'intonaco al béton brut*, (Rome: Aracne, 2013).

Collaboration with filmmakers and photographers, particularly Lucien Hervé and René Zuber, called in to immortalise each stage of the construction site, from the assembly of the formwork to the casting phase, enabled Le Corbusier to discover the results of plastic experiments and to verify the marks of the formwork impressed on the concrete surface.[10] During construction, Le Corbusier was not directly involved in the technical aspects, which were mainly supervised by André Wogenscky and Vladimir Bodiansky, who checked the results and instructed workers on the touch ups to be made to defects due to a casting and dismantling procedure that was not always carried out correctly.[11] Le Corbusier's trust in the *béton armé* technique, which in his eyes should have resulted in a surface as polished as plaster, led to the immediate filling of the honeycomb produced during the casting process.[12] The first images also began to circulate among the many architects, journalists and critics who then visited the site and helped spread the exposed concrete colossus in international magazines. From *Domus* to *Architectural Forum*, from *Bauen + Wohnen* to *L'Architecture d'Aujourd'hui* and *Architectural Review*, photographs of the Unité construction site filled the pages of magazines, confirming Le Corbusier's intention to leave the *béton armé* exposed and thus inaugurating the debate on what was already foreseen as the new post-war architecture, but in which the question of exposed concrete remained marginal.

Architecture d'Aujourd'hui and Art Brut

The idea of a synthesis of the arts, which Le Corbusier evoked on several occasions, especially from the 1940s onwards, was confirmed by a publication that laid the foundations for a crucial association in the reception of the Unité, anticipating certain discoveries that would change the very perception of *béton brut*, transforming it into an increasingly artistic concept.

The magazine *L'Architecture d'Aujourd'hui* published a special issue on the plastic arts in March 1949, which was commissioned by editor André Bloc. The purpose of the issue was to encourage architects to develop a greater sensitivity to plastic values through contemporary artists' selected examples. The issue featured Le Corbusier's images of the Unité building site, the Pavilion Suisse, and the United Nations headquarters in New York, among other works by contemporary artists.[13] The portraits of Le Corbusier in his studio, surrounded by paintings and sculptures, promoted the cause of the synthesis of the arts. But it was not only a plastic principle that was encouraged for the definition of a new aesthetic. In Bloc's introduction, the

---

[10] As early as June 1948, the photographer René Zuber, at the suggestion of the sculptor Jacques Gestalder, repeatedly visited the building site to photograph and film the progress of the works, especially during the pouring of concrete for the *pilotis* and the 'sculptures moulées'. The Unité building site also appeared in advertising and film sequences, such as *Un aperçu de la reconstruction* by André Michel (1948), *La vie commence demain* by Nicole Védrès (1950) and *La Cité radieuse* by Jean Sacha (1952), which testified to the French state's commitment to reconstruction and gave Le Corbusier an opportunity to present his work. But it was thanks to the photographs of Lucien Hervé that the Unité was featured in magazines all around the world. In December 1949, Hervé began a photographic series on the Unité building site for the magazine *France Illustration*.

[11] For a precise analysis and reconstruction of the various phases at the Unité's site in Marseilles see: Roberto Gargiani, Anna Rosellini, 'The Discovery of Béton Brut with Malfaçons: The Worksite of the Unité d'Habitation at Marseille', in *Le Corbusier; Béton Brut and Ineffable Space 1940–1965, Surface Materials and Psychophysiology of Vision* (Lausanne: PPUR, 2011), (3–61), 27; Roberto Gargiani; Anna Rosellini, 'La découverte du béton brut avec malfaçons : chronique du chantier de l'Unité d'habitation à Marseille' in Jacques Sbriglio (ed.), *Le Corbusier et la question du brutalisme* (Marseille: Parentheses, 2013), 152–79.

[12] Ibid., 29.

[13] [n.a.], '2ᵉ numéro hors-série consacré aux arts plastiques', *L'Architecture d'Aujourd'hui* (March 1949). In this issue André Bloc wanted to demonstrate the synthesis of the arts. In 1949, Bloc suggested that Le Corbusier found the Association pour une synthèse des arts plastiques, of which Henri Matisse was to be president and Charlotte Perriand one of the members. On the magazine *Architecture d'aujourd'hui*, see the thesis by Corine Girieud, *La revue Art d'aujourd'hui (1949–1954): une vision sociale de l'art* (PhD Thesis, Paris IV Sorbonne, 2011).

7 The juxtaposition of the articles 'L'art brut' and 'Marseille', *Architecture d'Aujourd'hui*, 1949, pp. 50–52

Unité's plastic shapes were framed within an artistic form of research that resonated with concepts pursued in the other arts, and in particular those of 'happy accidents' and 'praise of the irrational'. Unsurprisingly, Bloc chose these two concepts as paradigms for a new aesthetic based on an artistic vision of technique.

The layout of the issue reveals the intention to include the Unité's experiments in the panorama of contemporary art phenomena, linking them in particular to the concept of art brut that was concurrently spreading in Parisian avant-garde circles, according to the theories and practice of Jean Dubuffet.[14] The Unité was presented through close-up photographs of the platform still in construction, showing the material of the *pilotis* and the process for their manufacture, including the assembly of the formwork. The article is laid out in such a way as to be the continuation of an article on art brut by Pierre Guéguen and illustrated by a selection of photographs of objects from Prince Alfred Antonin Juritzky-Warberg's collection of polished stones resembling prehistoric statuettes and the 'objets à réaction poétique' collected by Charlotte Perriand and Fernand Léger during the 1930s. Art brut was interpreted by Guéguen according to the 'objets trouvés' selected for their organic characteristics (see figure 7). Guéguen's vision of art brut was particular. For him,

[14] See: Jean Dubuffet, *Prospectus aux amateurs de tout genre* (Paris: Gallimard, 1946).

the adjective 'brut' identified a potential form of the raw material and was placed in antithesis to the concept of 'ruiniform' and 'archaeological debris'. Guéguen's note went unnoticed by critics of the time, but the contrast between the potential form and the evocation of ruin became part of the critical reception of *béton brut* and has continued to this day.[15] The article made no reference to the Unité, but Guéguen claimed to have discussed the collection of objects he owned with Le Corbusier to 'verify the laws of nature'.[16] At first glance, the collision between art brut and what would soon be defined as the concept of *béton brut* might seem fortuitous. However, this 'happy accident', as mentioned by Bloc in the introduction, contributed to the development of poetic affinities between art brut and *béton brut* in international debates. English critics began outlining a definition – that of New Brutalism – based on those affinities, which would have the deliberate ambition of bringing together artistic and architectural research.

Le Point and the Concept of Béton Brut

From the association between artistic and technical research, *béton armé* began to be informed by a new vision that emerged once the Unité's casting work was complete. What appeared as superficial and still controllable imperfections took on the substance of 'malfaçons' that disfigured the concrete, to the point of appearing 'atrocious' and 'ferocious', prompting Le Corbusier to commission a detailed report from Candilis and Shadrach Woods to instruct the workers on how to correct the defects. 'For a long time I wondered how to hide them, how to rectify them', he would admit in the fifth volume of the *Œuvre complète* about what he defined as 'malfaçons'.[17]

The difficulty of joining together the phenomena taking place during the building site into a single concept is clear from a series of notes and publications made during 1950. That year, Le Corbusier published a second edition of the fourth volume of the *Œuvre complète*, probably in the early months of the year, adding photographs of the Unité construction site that only a few years later would prove decisive for the affirmation of the poetics of *béton brut*.[18] However, his position towards the *malfaçons* remained reserved, and his vision of the Unité was still informed by the myth of the perfect, polished *béton armé*. The photographs depicting the various stages of construction did not show the defects in the concrete and were meant to illustrate only certain parts of the building, the *pilotis*, the platform, the framework and the façade. *Béton brut* was the term used on a single occasion to characterise the concrete cast in the sector of the platform housing the *sculptures moulées* and which contributed to defining the 'aesthetics of vibrated and casted concrete'.[19]

But in 1950 a fundamental step took place in the foundation of a new vision of *béton armé*, through a slow process of accepting what at first sight seemed a failure. Despite his initial intention to obtain a smooth surface without defects, and in the impossibility of 'rectifying' all the *malfaçons*, Le Corbusier found himself fascinated by the unexpected and disconcerting result, witnessing the very process of that material in the making. It was only thanks to the expressive richness derived

[15] See, in particular, the contribution of Stanislaus von Moos, '"L'Europe après la pluie" ou, Le brutalisme face à l'histoire', in Jacques Sbriglio (ed.), *Le Corbusier et la question du brutalisme* (Marseille: Parenthèses, 2013), 64–87.

[16] Pierre Guéguen, 'Art Brut', *L'Architecture d'Aujourd'hui*, second special issue on plastic arts (March 1949), 109–12.

[17] Willy Boesiger (ed.), *Le Corbusier. Œuvre complète 1946–1952*, vol. 5 (Zurich: Éditions Girsberger, 1953).

[18] Willy Boesiger (ed.), *Le Corbusier. Œuvre complète 1938–1946*, vol. 4, 2nd ed. (Zurich: Éditions Girsberger, 1950). The preface, signed by Le Corbusier in January 1950, suggests that the volume was published early in the year.

[19] The caption reads 'Le panneaux étant demoulés. Béton brut coulé', ibid., 193.

from the faithful recording of all the site operations that concrete could become the expression of a new aesthetic. The increasingly visible and coarse defects, resulting from the inexperience of the workers and a series of adverse conditions, left an indelible imprint. This was what Le Corbusier established as the basis of a poetics that transcended the surface of concrete to encompass the entire vision of the construction process. What had appeared as a sculptural mass of concrete disfigured by defects when the first *pilotis'* formwork was dismantled in 1949 was now redeemed through a vision that elevated imperfections to artistic concepts capable of evoking those 'sensations bruts' that Le Corbusier had celebrated since the 1920s, and which amplified their aesthetic effect. 'The Unité Michelet is stuffed with eroticism, signs and scraffiti of total virulence, everywhere on the posts and walls', he noted in his notebook in the summer of 1950.[20]

This notion of the material as an artistic investigation revealed the hint of a new sensibility, elaborated on 1940s artistic concepts such as 'imprint', 'graffiti', 'automatism', and 'chance', as theorised by Dubuffet and his Compagnie de l'Art Brut founded in 1947. Dubuffet, too, embarked on a quest oriented towards primordial and rudimentary impulses evoked by the use of materials, uncontrolled expression and traces of gestures.[21] As is well known, Dubuffet and Le Corbusier made a trip to Switzerland together in 1946,[22] but Le Corbusier would never admit to an explicit connection with Dubuffet's work. Furthermore, while Dubuffet sought expressions that could be faithful to his principles for the foundation of a new art, in architecture this process was reversed and stemmed from the discovery of the impossibility of controlling the phenomena of *béton armé* and the need to accept the unconstrained expression of matter. For Le Corbusier, subjugating himself to the irrationality of a material he had tried to tame and accustoming his eye to the fascinating imperfections of *béton armé* initially seemed a defeat that only the foundation of a new poetics could redeem. Dubuffet's 'brut' and Le Corbusier's 'brut' suggest different cultural aspirations for a renewal of artistic expression in directions that end up coinciding, at least at times, with those sought by English critics and theorists. In fact, the affinity between the Unité and the contemporary artistic avant-garde sanctioned the premises for the definition of a new aesthetic that British critics would know how to assimilate and theorise.

The artistic component of the defects of *béton armé* was only made explicit in November 1950, with a monographic publication of the Unité in the special issue of the magazine *Le Point*.[23] The coincidence between Le Corbusier's notes on the effects of concrete during the same year and the publication of this special issue is evidence of a decisive step in the formulation of the concept of *béton brut* that transcended mere technical aspects. Le Corbusier carefully supervised the volume layout, he selected photographs by Hervé and seven other photographers, and suggested placing full-page images of the construction site, without borders, to amplify the magnificence of his concrete, whose details, texture and even imperfections were fully visible (see figure 8).[24]

[20] Le Corbusier, 'Carnet 50 // III Paris-Marseille b // D17', in Françoise de Franclieu (ed.), *Le Corbusier: Carnets* (Paris-Geneva: Herscher & Dessain et Tolra-Lied, 1981), p.n.n.
[21] The direct influence between Le Corbusier and Dubuffet has not yet been demonstrated, but there is a common sensibility traceable in the terms Dubuffet used to describe his art, which recall those used by Le Corbusier to describe his béton brut: 'les aberrations' considered as human faculties, 'ardour, brutality and ferocity sing', the 'mal façonné' and the 'embryonnaire' are the prerequisites for the generation of a new art. Dubuffet, *Prospectus aux amateurs de tout genre (op. cit.)*, 71; 88.
[22] The trip was undertaken in July 1946, together with the writer Jean Paulhan; *Guide d'un petit voyage en Suisse* (Paris: Gallimard, 1947).
[23] Le Corbusier, 'L'Unité d'habitation de Marseille'.
[24] Catherine de Smet, *Vers une architecture du livre. Le Corbusier: édition et mise en pages, 1912–1965* (Baden: Lars Müller Publishers, 2007), 114.

8 'Le Corbusier's Unité d'habitation de Marseille', *Le Point*, November 1950, no. 38, p. 3

Fig. 3

L'unité de Marseille. Manifestation esthétique d'un robuste, sain et loyal emploi du béton armé. Le matériau se colore avec le temps, reconstituant l'aspect des masses rocheuses des montagnes environnantes qui ont fourni l'apport essentiel de l'agglomérat.

In the final version, not all the indications were respected, but the publication responded to his desire to show a new expression of concrete on the construction site. The photograph, which in the second edition of the fourth volume of the *Œuvre complète* was a casual presence used to showcase the platform, now becomes the proclamation of the qualities of a *béton armé* that has become 'brut'. Hervé's shot occupies three quarters of the opening page of the volume and frames the junction between the *pilotis*, the platform and the exposed framework of the flat floors, taken from the bottom upwards to make the poetic and plastic value of the concrete explicit. The photograph was reworked to accentuate the contrast of *chiaroscuro*, with the intention of enhancing the *malfaçons* and irregularities of the surface, which infuse plastic effects to the in-situ concrete with respect to the prefabricated panels of the loggia parapets. In the caption, Le Corbusier summarised for the first time the qualities attributed to exposed concrete that would inform the concept of *béton brut*. As evidence, however, that this concept was still in the making, Le Corbusier again referred to the definition of *béton armé*: 'Aesthetic manifestation of a robust, healthy and faithful use of reinforced concrete. The material becomes coloured with time, reconstituting the appearance of the rocky masses of the surrounding mountains which provided the essential contribution of the agglomerate'.[25] Described in its constant change over time, as

---

[25] Le Corbusier, 'L'Unité d'habitation de Marseille', 3. The 'human' qualities attributed by Le Corbusier would be picked up by Charles Jencks and used as the basis of the 'Brutalist language', in Charles Jencks, *Le Corbusier and the Tragic View of Architecture* (London: Allen Lane, 1973), 137–157.

the bearer of a new vision not only of architecture but also of the landscape, and in particular of those rocky mountains brought back to life in the aggregates, concrete appeared personified, with a series of attributes revealing the truth of the material. The personification of concrete introduced a particular concept of humanism, which became capital for the international debate.

From the base of the *pilotis* to the top of the ventilation chimneys, what underlay the personification of *béton armé* was the total fidelity of this material in immortalising gestures, formwork imprints and even human errors. In Le Corbusier's particular sense, *béton brut* would come to encapsulate the synthesis between art and architecture, between nature and architecture, but also between human beings and architecture.

After showing the manufacturing process of the *pilotis*, with photographs of the various phases of the construction site from different angles, Le Corbusier stated, in the caption of the same photograph published in *Architecture d'Aujourd'hui* in 1949, that *béton brut* 'has entered the society of noble materials in architecture'.[26] It is perhaps no coincidence that this very image was used to announce the sublimation of *béton armé* into the concept of *béton brut*, as if that fortuitous juxtaposition of the same image with art brut might have suggested an artistic contamination of this material. Following the constellation of images presented in *Le Point*, Le Corbusier recorded the affirmation of *béton brut* through a multitude of variants, passing from the strength of the *pilotis* to the precision of the *sculptures moulées* and from the contrasts of form exalted by the unity of the material to the articulation of the imprints on the surface of the platform. He proclaimed a new 'architectural aesthetics'. However, these rare fragmentary remarks are only made in the image captions, because the concept of *béton brut* was still in the process of being developed.

The Humanism of Béton Brut

The personification of concrete announced in 1950 became, with the completion of the building site, the premise for clarification of the meaning of the concept of *béton brut*, giving it an increasingly explicit humanism. This progression was indicated by Le Corbusier both in his notebook during 1952 and in the fifth volume of the *Œuvre complète, 1946–1952*, dates that coincide with the beginning and completion of the Unité.

The announcement of the advent of the 'the new splendour of béton brut', proclaimed during the Unité's inaugural speech on 14 October 1952,[27] confirmed the aesthetic dignity and redemption of that material previously described as 'sad and grey' and now instead used 'as a raw material in the same way as stone, wood or terracotta'.[28]

The French flag hoisted on the roof of the Unité became the symbol of an international architectural achievement, the emblem of rebirth after the destruction of the war. The completion of the Unité was celebrated in the fifth volume of the *Œuvre complète, 1946–1952*, published in 1953. The sequence of projects did not follow a strict chronology but introduced the Unité as the culmination of previous concepts and

[26] Le Corbusier, 'L'Unité d'habitation de Marseille', 43.
[27] Le Corbusier, 'Cap Martin // sept 52 // INDES // NOVEMBER 1952 // une perforatrice à air comprimé // F26', in Françoise de Franclieu, *Carnets*, p.n.n.
[28] Boesiger (ed.), *Le Corbusier. Œuvre complète 1946–1952*, 190. Auguste Perret had already elevated concrete to the dignity of other materials but had supported the need for it to be processed: 'Concrete is just as beautiful and just as admirable as any other material. You just have to work it, treat it as you would treat stone', in Auguste Perret, 'L'Architecture de béton armé' [1936], republished in *Anthologie des écrits, conférences et entretiens* (Paris: Le Moniteur, 2006), 298.

research, not least 'the certainty of a possible splendour of *béton armé*'. The construction process of the Modulor's 'fantômes' introduced what Le Corbusier identified as a hymn to *béton brut*, understood as the process leading to a synthesis of art and architecture: 'When the formwork is removed, the slightest details of the moulds, the very fibre of the wood, the slightest accidents of the saw appear. Concrete, the most faithful of materials, perhaps more faithful than bronze, can take its place in architectural art and express the sculptor's intentions'.[29] In *béton brut*, Le Corbusier also saw the possibility of forging his double identity as an architect-artist who moulded the materials and gave them an artistic and not just technical nature. Tellingly, the fifth volume of the *Œuvre complète* opens with a photograph of Le Corbusier with Picasso on a visit to the Unité building site in May 1952, as if this new artistic vision of the material could have derived from the dialogue between the two masters.[30]

The discovery of the poetics of *béton brut* was explained through the process by which 'the most ferocious of malfaçons' produced on the handrail of the ramp leading to the nursery school is skilfully transformed into a 'beauty by contrast', orchestrated through a balance 'between harshness and finesse, between the dull and the intense, between precision and accident'. Through the series of images used to represent *béton brut* we can intuit a principle that he would only explain later; this definition was not used for any concrete surface left exposed (which he instead called *béton vibré* for the panels and loggias of the *brise soleil* and *béton armé* for the framework) but was exclusively used to describe the surfaces of the elements cast on site, with their plastic forms marked by unexpected signs.[31] The 'splendour of béton brut' was exemplified by the ventilation chimneys and the emergency staircase, the soffit of the platform, the surface of the *pilotis* which created 'violent contrasts' with the perfection of the glass of the entrance doors, and again by the ramp that rises to the roof, which Le Corbusier identified as the origin of the poetics, precisely where the 'malfaçon frappant' portrayed in Hervé's photograph became 'one of the constituent elements of a plastic symphony' (see figure 9).

The humanism that in November 1950 was only hinted at gradually became a pervading component, to the point of correlating the 'brutal epidermis' of concrete with human skin, in which defects must be seen as an integral aspect of human beings, therefore investing the material with an anthropomorphic charge.[32]

As the highest expression of freedom of a plastic material, *béton brut* began to be seen as the ultimate achievement of the synthesis of the arts and a model that concretised the challenges posed by reconstruction to the various CIAM. Thus, thanks to the sophisticated poetic construction that Le Corbusier imprinted on the technique of *béton brut*, the dimension of a new humanism, the concept of synthesis between art and architecture, and the principles of truth that pervaded the Unité spread internationally.

---

[29] Boesiger (ed.), *Le Corbusier. Œuvre complète 1946–1952*, 184.

[30] Le Corbusier, letter to Picasso, 23 August 1949, in Jean Jenger, *Le Corbusier: choix de lettres* (Basel: Birkhäuser Verlag, 2002), 302. On the relevance of Picasso's visit to the Unité building site and a possible influence on the artistic vision of *béton brut*, see Anna Rosellini, 'Les sculptures en béton de Picasso et Nesjar et les processus techniques de l'architecture', in *Picasso. Sculptures*, Paris, Musée national Picasso – Paris, 2017, conference proceedings, 1–7; Anna Rosellini, 'Unité d'habitation in Marseille – Experimental Artistic Device', in Ruth Baumeister (ed.), *What Moves Us? Le Corbusier and Asger Jorn in Art and Architecture* (Zurich: Scheidegger & Spiess, 2015), 38–45. The relevance of Picasso's visit would also be underlined by Stanislaus von Moos, '"L'Europe après la pluie" ou le brutalisme face à l'Histoire', in Jacques Sbriglio (ed.), *Le Corbusier et la question du brutalisme*.

[31] It was not until 1957 that Le Corbusier dedicated a paragraph to the question of *béton brut* in the sixth volume of his monograph, in which he specified the link between surface and volume and the value of imprints, in Willy Boesiger (ed.), *Le Corbusier. Œuvre complète 1952–1957*, vol. 6 (Zurich: Éditions Girsberger, 1957), 180.

[32] Boesiger (ed.), *Le Corbusier. Œuvre complète 1946–1952*, 190.

9 Le Corbusier, L'Unité d'habitation in Marseille, *L'Œuvre Complète 1946-1952*, vol. 5, 1953, p. 218

Un exemple frappant de malfaçon de béton armé considéré comme l'un des éléments constitutifs d'une symphonie plastique

The concept of 'brut', as interpreted by Le Corbusier and Dubuffet, was then free to be manipulated. It was to replace the various realisms, empiricisms and humanisms, preceded by the prefix 'New-', that had been employed in England. None of the existing labels would succeed in transforming or summarising the phenomena occurring in the reconstruction of Europe. Other critics and architects, in search of a new architecture, would have the merit of translating the simplicity of *béton brut* into unexpected trajectories, incorporating it into the definition of New Brutalism. The invention of this definition would have to wait until the end of 1953, but the cultural premises for the further development of its embryonal concepts were already in place.

chapter three
the invention of a definition: from asplund to the smithsons

The First Brutalist Building: Villa Göth

The origin of a cultural stance associated with the definition of New Brutalism is situated at the crossroads between the British search for new styles and the theoretical urban implications generated by the Unité in Marseilles. It is not surprising that British architectural culture, suffering from thirty years of exclusion from international debates, became the protagonist of an alternative to the International Style and would be receptive to the most eloquent symptom of the rebellion against its fundamental values: the Unité. In England and elsewhere, this building would orientate the debate in a totally unexpected way, setting itself as the pivot between two eras, that of cladding and that against cladding. Le Corbusier's work sanctioned a specific position in the British architectural debate, resulting in an ideological front by architects who raged against the return of the New Picturesque and New Empiricism.[1]

The search for a new humanist architecture capable of responding to the demands of reconstruction faced the question of whether foreign examples could be selected as prototypes adaptable to the British context. Diametrically opposed to the model of the English New Towns of Howardian derivation, approved by decree in 1946, the Unité imposed in the debate an ideological dichotomy between 'low-rise' and 'high-rise', and ultimately between British and international culture.

It is from this question that a sharp ideological division developed within the London County Council (LCC) architecture department,[2] marked by two opposing factions reflecting different generational visions and divergent political orientations. On one hand, there were the supporters of Unité, called the 'Hards', who were politically

---

[1] On the reception of Le Corbusier in Britain, see Adrian Forty, 'Le Corbusier's British Reputation', in Tim Benton (ed.), *Le Corbusier, Architect of the Century* (London: Hayward Gallery, 1987); Nicholas Bullock, *Building the Post-war World: Modern Architecture and Reconstruction in Britain* (London: Routledge, 2002); Kenneth Frampton, 'Notes sur la réception critique de Le Corbusier en Grande-Bretagne, 1946–1972', *Cahiers de la recherche architecturale et urbaine*, vol. 24, no. 25 (2009): 21–40; Irena Murray (ed.), *Le Corbusier and Britain: An Anthology* (London: Routledge, 2009).

[2] The London County Council (LCC) was the main local government body in the county of London, which included an architectural department in charge of the reconstruction plan.

unaligned and generally considered 'non-Marxist'. This group included architects such as Alison and Peter Smithson, Colin St John Wilson, James Stirling, Alan Colquhoun, Peter Carter, and the so-called 'AA trio' composed of Bill Howell, John Killick, and Gillian Sarsen[3] (see figure 11). On the other hand, there were the detractors of Unité, referred to as the 'Softs', who promoted a Marxist ideological framework and a nineteenth-century urban model for their idea of modernity. The Softs favored the building tradition of brick and 'low-rise' developments, following the trend of New Empiricism and the prototypes of the New Towns designed by Cleeve Barr, Rosemary Stjersted, Oliver Cox, and Philip Powell.[4]

Against the backdrop of the debate among the members of the LCC, the Lecorbuserian concept of *brut* associated with the concrete of Unité underwent an initial significant shift. Although it is not possible to establish a certain chronology of the events, we do know that the definition identified by the Softs to criticise the Hards and their vision of reconstruction was that of New Brutalism. This label was used by the Softs in a negative sense to condemn what was emerging as a new urban model, embodied in the example of the Unité. The emergence of New Brutalism was complex and unexpectedly involved a cultural trajectory that leads to Scandinavia, still seen by the English in an anti-Lecorbuserian key.[5] All the clues converge to affirm that in 1950 the term New Brutalism was already in use according to a particular connotation that found its origin in Sweden.[6]

Three members of the LCC Softs, Oliver Cox, Graeme Shankland and Michael Ventris, proponents of the Marxist wing of New Empiricism and supporters of the Sweden-England connection,[7] visited Stockholm in the summer of 1950, where they met Hans Asplund, son of Gunnar Asplund.[8] A convergence of events supports the hypothesis that Hans Asplund was the inventor of a definition that already contained the concept of 'Brutalism', but which was formed by a prefix that did not coincide with the one later used in English criticism: namely, 'Neo-Brutalism'. Asplund is said

[3] Reyner Banham, 'The New Brutalism', *Architectural Review*, vol. 118, no. 708 (December 1955): 354–61

[4] On the influence of Swedish culture and the debate within the LCC, see, in particular, Peter Carolin, 'Sense, Sensibility and Tower Blocks: The Swedish Influence on Post-war Housing in Britain', *Journal 9: Housing the Twentieth Century Nation*, no. 9 (2008): 98–112; Stephen Kite, 'Softs and Hards: Colin St John Wilson and the Contested Vision of 1950s London', in Mark Crinson, Stephen Kite, Claire Zimmerman (eds.), *Neo-Avant-Garde and Postmodern: Postwar Architecture in Britain and Beyond* (London: YC British Art, 2010), 55–77; Bullock, *Building the Postwar World: Modern Architecture and Reconstruction in Britain*. More generally on the history of the LCC, see Nicholas Merhyr Day's PhD thesis, *The Role of the Architect in Post-war Housing: A Case Study of the Housing Work of the London County Council 1939–1956* (PhD Thesis, Coventry: University of Warwick, 1988).

[5] Banham was the first to attempt a chronological reconstruction of New Brutalism, in which he specified: 'It was somewhere in this vigorous polemic that the term "The New Brutalism" was first coined'; in Banham, 'The New Brutalism', 356.

[6] The Swedish origins of the definition of New Brutalism are confirmed by a letter from Hans Asplund to Eric de Maré in 1956, published in Eric de Maré, 'Et tu, Brute?' *Architectural Review*, vol. 120 (August 1956): 72; the Smithsons then confirmed in a typescript document dated 7 March 1955 the existence of a term similar to New Brutalism in use in Scandinavia countries, E009, Alison and Peter Smithson Special Collection, Loeb Library, Harvard University, Cambridge, USA; Banham also confirms this hypothesis stating: 'There is a persistent belief that the word Brutalism (or something like it) had appeared in the English Summaries in an issue of *Byggmästaren* published late in 1950. The reference cannot now be traced, and the story must be relegated to that limbo of Modern Movement demonology where Swedes, Communists and the Town and Country Planning Association are bracketed together as different isotopes of the common Adversary', in Banham, 'The New Brutalism'; Reyner Banham, 'The Polemic before Kruschev', *The New Brutalism: Ethic or Aesthetic?* (London: Architectural Press, 1966), 11–15. Banham's supposition is not really confirmed in the journal *Byggmästaren*, in which the definition New Brutalism does not appear. Contemporary historiography also confirms this thesis, starting with Kenneth Frampton, *Modern Architecture: A Critical History* (London: Thames & Hudson, 1980).

[7] The three were known in British circles as 'Swedophiles': Ventris had lived and worked in Sweden; Cox trained at the Architectural Association where he developed a strong interest in Swedish architecture, going on an extended trip to Sweden after graduation in 1946, where he met Swedish architects and studied local housing schemes. Shankland had joined the LCC in 1946 to work on the school building development called the Hertfordshire Plan and in 1950 he was engaged by H. J. Whitfield Lewis at the Housing Department. Cox designed the Swedish-inspired Alton East residence in Roehampton, and he and Shankland later founded an architectural practice. See Otto Saumarez Smith, 'Graeme Shankland: A Sixties Architect-Planner and the Political Culture of the British Left', *Architectural History*, vol. 57 (2014): 393–422.

[8] Hans Asplund, reported in De Maré, 'Et tu, Brute?'.

10 'Villa i Uppsala',
Byggmästaren, vol. A/12,
December 1952,
pp. 256–57

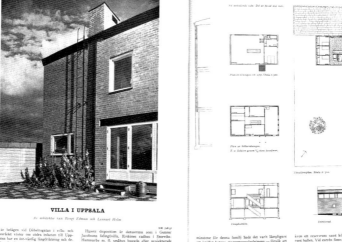

VILLA I UPPSALA

Av arkitekter s.a.r. Bengt Edman och Lennart Holm

256 Byggmästaren 1952, A 12

Byggmästaren 1952, A 12 257

to have coined this definition in January 1950 as a 'sarcastic' appellation in reference to the preparatory drawings for the Villa Göth, which was the first building realised by the Swedish architects Bengt Edman and Lennart Holm in Uppsala, with whom Asplund shared an office space.[9]

It is therefore useful to understand the architecture of the Villa Göth, not least because certain traits would re-emerge in the small house which, according to the Smithsons, marked the beginning of an aspiration to a movement identified as New Brutalism. The villa has characteristics that set it apart from the Scandinavian tradition, and it presents itself as a statement on the nature of materials, whose surface textures and structural roles are made visible.[10] The exposed bricks of the load-bearing walls are meticulously laid, studied using a 1:10 scale model to achieve a basic aesthetic, both outside and in. The absence of decorative elements drifts away from the Scandinavian vernacular tradition and reduces architecture to the expression of its materials. Concrete is modelled in the plastic but ungainly forms of the ground floor service volume, while metal is visible in the two recessed lintels of the ribbon windows on the first floor and the door on the ground floor. The wood used for the slender structure of the portico and balcony asserts a concept of architecture which, in overcoming rationalism, contains alienating aspects and disproportionate features. Even the apparently symmetrical composition of the plan betrays the academic and functionalist canons, not only in the inverted distribution of the sleeping area on the ground floor and the open-plan living room on the first floor, but also through counterpoint elements such as the services, the staircase, the fireplace and balcony, whose arrangement determines an apparently casual composition of the openings in the façade (see figure 10).

9   Ibid.
10 [n.a.], 'Villa i Uppsala,' *Byggmästaren*, vol. A/12 (December 1952): 256–58.

As Edman and Holm state in a brief description of the villa, their references belong to a precise cultural repertoire, drawing on the Swedish radicalism that found its progenitor in Sigurd Lewerentz's Villa Edstrand, recalled by the careful use of bricks and the powerful metal lintels left exposed, and enriched by Ralph Erskine's typological research for the workers' house in Storviks Hammarby and Gunnar Jacobson's villa in Lidingö.[11] Edman and Holm's theoretical view of the use of materials is explicated in a 1950 contribution to the magazine *Tegel*, where they present a brick pavilion for the Nordisk Byggnadsdags Utställning (Nordic Building Exhibition), designed at the same time as the Villa Göth.[12] The pavilion gave Edman and Holm the opportunity to question the nature of brick, studied through a panel that they defined as a 'symbol' of brick's possible configurations. Edman and Holm wanted to show the 'simple and pure' brick, put into practice in a 'direct' way, and this was then realised in Villa Göth.[13]

Villa Göth is a statement on contemporary Swedish architecture, as it is also understandable through Holm's frequent critical contributions. In 1948 he criticised the drift of Swedish architecture, to the point of ridiculing the definition of New Empiricism coined by the British. New Empiricism was the result, according to Holm, of 'hallucinations', 'funny episodes' and 'silly generalisations', contrary to the functionalist doctrine by virtue of a 'sentimental romantic' approach.[14] Holm's cultural distance from New Empiricism not only gives Villa Göth the traits of a critique against sentimentalist and vernacular canons, but also provides a further indication of the motivations that may have encouraged Cox, Ventris and Shankland to adopt the appellation New Brutalism, directed precisely against those in England who opposed the theory of New Empiricism.

The exportation of the term Neo-Brutalism from the Swedish context saw the birth of a fully British meaning of New Brutalism, which was then not specifically concerned with the honesty of the materials but was charged with the Softs' critique of the new generation, which was considered less politically committed[15]. The evolution of New Brutalism would then be coloured by passionate discussions concerning visions for future urban developments, in an open clash between the sentimentalism of New Empiricism and the heroic dimension of the Ville Radieuse.

The Unité as a Model for English Reconstruction

The transition from Swedish Neo-Brutalism to English New Brutalism needs to be seen against the backdrop of the phenomenon of the Unité and the urban and architectural vision associated with it. Le Corbusier's visits to London, the first photographs of the Unité in international journals and in the 1950 edition of *Œuvre complète* raised expectations to test Le Corbusier's theories on British ground.[16]

In 1951 the architects and engineers in charge of London's reconstruction plan visited the Marseille building site to verify, on behalf of the LCC's Housing Division, a possible 'immediate application' of Le Corbusier's urban vision and the impact of the 'vertical housing' model. Among the architects visiting the Unité was Cox, who

[11] Ibid.
[12] Bengt Edman, Lennart Holm, 'Tegelspråk', *Tegel*, vol. 4, no. 2 (1950): 46–50. An English translation of the article is published in Agneta Eriksson, Weronica Ronnefalk, *Bengt Edman: Samlade verk / Complete Works* (Stockholm: Eriksson & Ronnefalk, 1998), 20–21.
[13] Ibid.
[14] Lennart Holm, 'Ideologi och form', *Byggmästaren*, vol. 27, no. 15 (1948): 264–72.
[15] Smith, 'Graeme Shankland'.
[16] James Maude Richards, 'Le Corbusier's Œuvre complète Shorter Notice', *Architectural Review*, vol. 110, no. 657 (September 1951): 204.

was to import the term New Brutalism to London. On their return, a symposium was organised with Kenneth Easton, Moholi and King, Max Gooch, Thurston Williams, William Howell and Philip Powell, Cleeve Barr, Oliver Cox and Robin Rockel (see figure 12).[17] The terms of the debate conducted by the architects of the LCC, as published in *Architectural Review*, demonstrate the interpretation of the Unité in urban terms, measuring its potential as a new form of living. The controversy surrounding its construction and its sociological and economic impact testify to the international resonance of the criticism levelled against the Unité. 'This building and the ideas behind it have probably engendered more heat for and against than any other building since the war', says Easton in the opening of the discussion, summarising the bitter debates already dividing LCC architects into factions.[18]

The effectiveness of the Unité model in responding to the English reconstruction programme under the County of London Plan was measured through its possible configuration as a neighbourhood development, similar to Le Corbusier's concept for the town of St. Dié, and through a series of density diagrams of English precedents, such as Dolphin Square in Westminster and the Lansbury Estate. These comparisons were intended to verify the dictates that emerged from the MARS Group, the models of which would be discussed two months later at the eighth CIAM in Hoddesdon. Powell, one of the youngest members of the symposium, was the only one who immediately saw in the Unité a potential application to British culture. Starting from the Unité model, Powell would later demonstrate the adaption of that typological principle to the Victorian terrace-house, when he would build, together with John Hidalgo Moya, the Churchill Gardens residential complex in Westminster.

The remarks concerning the materiality of the Unité, despite being recognised as truly 'magnificent' and 'a great contribution to the architectural handling of concrete', were seen by the architects of the LCC as being of secondary importance. However, some of the terms used during the symposium would remain indissolubly linked to the discussions on *béton brut* and would then become part of the characteristics of the Brutalist style.[19] 'Heroic', 'crude', 'violent', 'rough effect', 'roughness of finishes' are expressions used to describe material aspects and surface patterns that cannot but be in tune with the English tradition of the 'roughness' of surfaces that emerged in the proposals of the Functional Tradition and in the 'visual re-education' programme of *Architectural Review*. The English quest for a New Humanism was also confirmed by the geometric pattern derived from the Modulor that marks the Unité, on which everyone unanimously commented: 'It looks human'.[20]

The ideological connotations associated by the Softs with the urban model of the Unité, coinciding with the sarcastic appellation of New Brutalism, are evident in Barr and Cox's accusations against Le Corbusier's 'arbitrary' choices, evident in the 'oppressive' monumentality of the building. Barr and Cox went so far as to recall that 'in Moscow Corbusier is accused of Fascist tendencies'. Underlying the accusations of fascism levelled at Le Corbusier is the cultural line of Socialist Realism. To understand the reasons for the ideological use of that Swedish Neo-Brutalism, it should not be forgotten that Cox was one of the architects who had visited Asplund in the summer of 1950.

Socialist Realism, New Empiricism, Marxist ideology and the model of the Unité became the poles of divergence that set the whole course of the debates of the 1950s.

---

[17] London County Council Division, 'Le Corbusier's Unité d'Habitation', *Architectural Review*, vol. 109 (May 1951): (292–300), 293.

[18] Ibid.

[19] 'It will be seen that however much speakers differed about the social and structural aspects of the Unité d'Habitation, about its aesthetic qualities – and in particular, curiously enough, the humanity of its staircase – there was no disagreement at all', ibid., 294.

[20] The image of the gymnasium on the roof of the Unité is introduced as follows: 'The photograph brings out with particular clarity the close relationship between Le Corbusier's paintings and buildings', ibid., 293.

11 Alison and Peter Smithson, *LCC The Smithsons were there;* collage, Alison and Peter Smithson Archive, Folder G062. Courtesy of the Frances Loeb Library. Harvard University Graduate School of Design

12 London County Council Division, 'Le Corbusier's Unité d'Habitation', *Architectural Review*, vol. 109, May 1950, pp. 292–93

The LCC Architect's Department

The Smithsons were

there;

13 Newspaper cut, 'Radiant City Lawsuit. Complaint of Brutal Realism', *The Times*, 4 December 1952, Alison and Peter Smithson Archive, Folder G059. Courtesy of the Frances Loeb Library. Harvard University Graduate School of Design

R 4 1952

"RADIANT CITY" LAWSUIT

PLAINT OF BRUTAL REALISM

OUR OWN CORRESPONDENT

PARIS, DEC. 3

Corbusier, the architect of the
ersial "Radiant City" at Mar-
(described in *The Times* of October
as being sued for 20m. francs
ges to-day, before the Tribunal
Correctionnel of Marseilles, by the
"Society for the General Aestheticism of
France." The case against him is that he
erected the 17-storey block of flats without the necessary permits, and that his
building "has drawbacks of a moral order
and is contrary to French style and
aestheticism."

They were to take shape in the achievements of the LCC between 1951 and 1955: in the projects for Ackroydon and Alton East, influenced by New Empiricism, and in the examples of Bentham Road, Alton West and Loughborough Road, commonly referred to as 'pro-Corbu' and which even Pevsner would admit had characteristics of New Brutalism.[21]

The ideological clash between the Lecorbuserian 'vertical city' and the 'low-rise' New Empiricist reconstruction is confirmed by Colin St John Wilson in the *Observer* in February 1952, at a time when the Housing Division of the LCC was defining new housing typologies. The theories of the garden-city were targeted by Wilson who accused the Town and Country Planning Committee and the pro-Swedish wing of the LCC of 'effeminacy' and ridiculed the stylistic features of New Empiricism and the vision of reconstruction dictated by 'cosiness': 'blocks of flats with pitched roofs, peep-hole windows and folky' details in the current Swedish revival'.[22] Wilson's harsh criticism led to a clash between the two factions, with Cox and Barr confronting Wilson over the ideological implications of the Unité model. The clash ended with Wilson being accused of 'throwing mud at Stalin' in front of a crowd of LCC architects who witnessed a clear polarisation: 'Communists versus the rest', as critics described it.[23] The Unité model, ideologically charged, took on the connotations of a symbol of LCC dispute, as Robert Fourneaux Jordan recalled in April 1952: 'The symbol of a controversy that is splitting the housing and planning division of the London County Council to the point of bloodshed'.[24] What hindered the acceptance of the Unité model was the identification of Le Corbusier's theories with the precepts of the International Style, which since the 1930s had distanced British critics from Le Corbusier.

The criticism of Unité made in July-August 1952 by Frederic J. Osborn, promoter of the Garden City Movement and president of the Town and Country Planning Association, should be understood along these lines.[25] Osborn represented an intellectual point of reference for the conservative generation, who were of the opinion that the Unité prototype was a sociological as well as an aesthetic failure. The monumentality of Le Corbusier's proposal, translated into a 'high flat building on stilts', was in Osborn's eyes disproportionate and dictated by a mechanistic enthusiasm that found its origins in the rhetoric of the International Style. Osborn's criticism undermined Le Corbusier's vision of urbanism, starting with the *pilotis*, described through a particular adjective that ridicules them: 'The stilts struck me as needlessly swollen, rather brutal, more anxious to demonstrate the colossal quantity of material they are carrying than to free the ground'.[26] The fact that in his list of adjectives Osborn included 'brutal', which was becoming the expressive code for the concrete of the Unité, should not be overlooked in order to understand a terminology that from time to time, albeit in different meanings, revolves around 'brut'. Osborn's criticism reveals the extent to which the anti-mechanistic components of a fringe of nineteenth-century Marxist culture were still relevant in the paradigm of the 'low-rise' model of Howardian derivation. Osborn's

[21] Nikolaus Pevsner, 'Roehampton, LCC Housing and the Picturesque Tradition, *Architectural Review*, vol. 125, no. 750 (July 1959): 21–35.

[22] 'Fear of city-scale, fear of the machine, fear of everything that the architectural innovators of the past twenty-five years have promised us. It is symptomatic of that post-war loss of nerve which, from a sense of guilt towards the scientific methods and machines that have been used for destruction, reacts with a split-minded desire to retreat into a world of cosiness', in Colin St John Wilson, 'The Vertical City', *The Observer*, 17 February 1952, 8.

[23] Banham, 'The New Brutalism', 356; see also Sarah Menin, Stephen Kite (ed.), *An Architecture of Invitation* (London: Ashgate Publishing Limited, 2005), 47; Stephen Kite, 'Softs and Hards: Colin St John Wilson and the Contested Vision of 1950s London', in Crinson, Kite, Zimmerman (eds.), *Neo-Avant-Garde and Postmodern: Postwar Architecture in Britain and Beyond (op. cit.)*: 55–77.

[24] [n.a.], 'Marseille Building Experiment: Symbol of L.C.C. Dispute', *Manchester Guardian*, 9 April 1952, 8.

[25] Frederic J. Osborn, 'Concerning Le Corbusier. Part I, *Town & Country Planning*, vol. 20, no. 99 (July 1952): 311–16; Frederic J. Osborn, 'Concerning Le Corbusier. Part II', *Town & Country Planning*, vol. 20, no. 100 (August 1952): 359–63.

[26] Osborn, 'Concerning Le Corbusier. Part I'.

sentence strikes down one of the principles of the Ville Radieuse to shake its urban vision. However, he seems to confirm, through the adjective 'brutal', the advent of the sarcastic appellation of New Brutalism in London architectural circles.

The association between the 'brutal' characteristics and the moral demands of the Unité is also reiterated in the title of a small article in the newspaper *The Times* of 4 December 1952, which appears decisive in this context: 'Radiant-City Lawsuit. Complaint of Brutal Realism'.[27] The article briefly discusses the international controversy surrounding the Unité and reports Le Corbusier's victory in the lawsuit brought against him by the Société pour l'Esthétique Générale de la France, which had declared the Unité contrary to French morality. The phrase 'brutal realism' confirms the line of associations that emerged within the context of the intellectualist vision of the reconstruction debates, which involved a clash between the Garden City promoters, Scandinavian New Empiricism, and supporters of Le Corbusier. These associations, which undermined traditional aesthetic canons, would lead to a clarification of the role of Unité within a year through the definition of New Brutalism.[28] The Smithsons would be the protagonists of this clarification, and the short article published in *The Times* would in this sense play a decisive role: they kept the newspaper clipping in their archive (see figure 13).[29]

New Movement-Classical-Complex-Human

The definition of New Brutalism that has become famous is not the one with the sarcastic meaning born in the circle of the LCC, but the one based on the brief publication by the Smithsons in December 1953.[30] In order to understand the cultural dimension that converged in that definition, it is appropriate to pin down a series of concepts belonging to the Smithsons' theoretical vision. Both their projects and artistic experiences are at the core of their theoretical reflections, which combined a continuous pondering on the work of the masters of the Modern Movement, with the aspiration for a new architectural vision for a post-war society.

Competitions such as the School at Hunstanton (1949–1954), Golden Lane (1951–52) and Sheffield University (1953), or exhibitions such as *Parallel of Life and Art* (1953) allowed the Smithsons to develop a series of concepts, such as 'new order', 'connection', 'layering', 'quality of real materials', 'juxtaposition', 'accident' and 'new attitude'. These concepts were at the core of their demonstration of the existence of a new course in architecture and would set the foundation for their definition of New Brutalism.

What the Smithsons identified on several occasions with the concept of 'new order' was first translated into the search for a compositional organisation based on geometric principles derived from Wittkower's theories, through symmetrical forms and pure geometry, experimented in the projects for the Coventry cathedral and the School at Hunstanton. 'Finite' or 'inherent order' is the principle identified by the Smithsons for a contemporary transcription of Wittkowerian theories through relationships of symmetry, harmony and modularity, in reaction to the style of the Festival of Britain and the sentimentalism of New Empiricism.[31]

27 [n.a.], 'Radiant City Lawsuit: Complaint of Brutal Realism', *The Times*, 4 December 1952.
28 Banham confirmed the origin of the definition of New Brutalism in the internal disputes of the LCC in Banham, 'The New Brutalism'.
29 The article is preserved in the Smithson archive, folder G059, Alison and Peter Smithson Special Collection, Loeb Library, Harvard University, Cambridge, USA. In 1966 Alison pointed out that the origin of the definition of New Brutalism came from reading an article published in *The Times*. Alison and Peter Smithson, 'Banham's Bumper Book on Brutalism, Discussed by Alison and Peter Smithson', *Architects' Journal*, vol. 144, no. 26 (December 1966): 1590–91.
30 P.D.S. [Alison Smithson], 'House in Soho', *Architectural Design*, vol. 23, no. 12 (December 1953): 342.
31 Peter Smithson, 'The Idea of Architecture in the 50s', *Architects' Journal*, vol. 21 (January 1960): 121–26.

From Wittkower's principles, which find confirmation in the Miesian criteria of symmetry and balance, the Smithsons reformulated the concept of 'new order' toward an increasingly accentuated articulation of forms, which extended to a reflection on the urban scale elaborated for the reconstruction of the Golden Lane block in London and for the University of Sheffield. The 'new order' was achieved in these two projects through the conception of architecture as a 'connective urban form'. The principle of connection does not only confirm the social dimension of keywords such as 'association' and 'identity' in opposition to the rationalist urban vision consolidated in the Athens Charter,[32] but becomes the pretext for a free compositional organisation. Through 'patterns' of units connected by raised 'street decks' and a differentiation between pedestrian and road traffic, the Golden Lane project defined an urban structure with different densities and routes based on the principle of 'mobility'.[33] The 'new order' thus began to take shape as the formal and social research into components and spaces that act as a link between the parts.

In order to understand the assumptions at the origin of the definition of New Brutalism, it is necessary to understand Golden Lane as a variant of the Unité d'Habitation revised in light of the English context,[34] thus offering a concrete demonstration of the reconstruction hypotheses advocated by the Hards.[35] That project also testifies to the profound impact of the Smithsons' visit to Le Corbusier's Unité.[36] It could even be argued that the graphic montage of the transposition of the Unité in the form proposed by the Smithsons, which stands on the ruins of the bombed-out block in Golden Lane, may be representative of the Hards' vision of urbanism and, by extension, of the principle of reconstruction that the Softs called 'New-Brutalist'.[37]

The compositional research on the various 'connections', experimented on in the Golden Lane residential complex, became the generating principle for the University of Sheffield project.[38] The building's flexibility is expressed not only through the design of a concrete grid in which a light metal frame is inserted to adapt it to

---

[32] Alison and Peter Smithson, 'An Urban Project: Golden Lane Housing', *Architects' Year Book*, vol. 5 (October 1953): 48–55. The month is specified in a document compiled by the Smithsons entitled 'Bibliography Built Works, Including Projects and Diagrams, from August 1948 to May 1978', E0001: 1, Alison and Peter Smithson Special Collection, Loeb Library, Harvard University, Cambridge, USA.

[33] Ibid.

[34] All the criteria adopted by the Smithsons for the Golden Lane project are a transcription of the Unité revised in the English context: from the metaphor of the 'bouteilles-bouteiller' translated into the 'structural rack', to prefabrication, the concrete cast on site, the formwork imprints to define a 'pattern', the distribution system of the 'street deck' or 'street in the air' which opens onto the 'yard gardens' as a variant of the 'rue intérieure', the plastic chimneys which crown the building. Regarding the influence of Le Corbusier, the Smithsons would state: 'As we were in practice in Bloomsbury by the spring of 1950, we could walk over to Alec Tiranti, Charlotte Street, to buy the first copy of a new *Oeuvre* as soon as he had delivery', in Alison and Peter Smithson, *The Shift Alison + Peter Smithson*, vol. 7 (London: Academy Editions, 1982), 9; Alison and Peter Smithson, *The Charged Void: Architecture* (New York: Monacelli Press, 2002), 88.

[35] The influence of Le Corbusier's works published in the *Œuvre complète* is also testified to by the following statement: 'When you open a new volume of the *Œuvre complète* you find that he has had all your best ideas already, has done what you were about to do next', quoted in Reyner Banham, 'The Last Formgiver', *Architectural Review*, vol. 139, no. 834 (August 1966): (97–98), 98; and in the monographic essay on New Brutalism, Banham, *The New Brutalism: Ethic or Aesthetic?*, 86. Adrian Forty, however, believes that the phrase was uttered during the 1950s, in Forty, 'Le Corbusier's British Reputation', in Benton (ed.), *Le Corbusier, Architect of the Century*, 35.

[36] '[L'Unité] seen by us during construction from the outside only; seen completed at the CIAM opening party during the Aix-en-Provence Congress (CIAM 9), September 1953', in Alison and Peter Smithson, *Without Rhetoric: An Architectural Aesthetic 1955–1972* (Cambridge, MA: MIT Press, 1974), 4.

[37] The similarity between Golden Lane and the Unité did not escape the critics, who promptly commented on the Smithsons' proposal as 'extremists – in the sense that Corbusier is an extremist in his design for the well-known flats at Marseilles', in [n.a.], 'Golden Lane Competition: A Selection of the Unsuccessful Entries', *Architects' Journal*, vol. 115, no. 2977 (March 1952): (358–62), 358.

[38] Alison and Peter Smithson, 'University of Sheffield, extracts from the description', 1953, folder E064, Alison and Peter Smithson Special Collection, Loeb Library, Harvard University, Cambridge, USA.

the programme,[39] but also through the differentiation of the parts, in order to favour the relationship between the different buildings: 'Highly specialised functions have been given highly identified forms'.[40] Paul Klee's studies on the relationships between forms, which he had summarised as 'indicative graphics' in his *Pedagogical Sketchbook* were in this sense fundamental for the Smithsons.[41] The recognition of different 'patterns' of use would find its theorisation in the Smithson's concept of 'space in between',[42] which in the case of Sheffield University became the starting point for experimentation on different relations between the parts. The principle of 'connection' presupposed a progressive liberation of form from pure geometry, towards what critics would identify as an 'a-formalism', recalling the contemporary artistic experiences of Informal and Action Painting.[43]

Through the emphasis given to 'connections' and 'relations', the Smithsons began an investigation into the concept of 'assemblage'. Not only did it bring tension to the modernist doctrine of the building as a single entity, but it also enriched the architectural project with contemporary artistic methods. 'Assemblage', if taken in its most radical form as the juxtaposition of different parts of the programme or the incursion of *objets trouvés*, was the prerequisite for another concept that would become key in the definition of New Brutalism: that of 'as found'. Relevant references can be found in collages by Eduardo Paolozzi, member of the Independent Group, or in the aesthetic theories by Charles and Ray Eames. Through the assembly of disparate elements and the intrusion of the ordinary, the Smithsons were looking for an aesthetic of the immediate present, as the Eames had demonstrated in their Case Study House in Santa Monica in 1949.[44]

The concept of 'assemblage' takes the form of juxtapositions of metal profiles and of *objets trouvés* staged at the School at Hunstanton, from the water tank to the exposed ducts and the sinks selected from the Hertfordshire school building programme catalogue. But it is not limited to an object-like dimension, and it became the basis for urban diagrams in the Golden Lane City extension presented at CIAM, and finally the matrix for a compositional system of parts in Sheffield.

During the drafting of the projects for Golden Lane and Sheffield, and while the building site for the School at Hunstanton was still in progress (it was not completed until 1954), the Smithsons started dwelling on other concepts deriving from matter and its configuration. The imprints of the formwork on cast-on-site concrete, a finish specified in the project for Golden Lane,[45] should be understood as a desire to

---

[39] 'The continuum containing the Administration, Arts, Physics, Chemistry, Medical School, and terminating in the Library/Architecture School is made up of structural sandwiches – a floor of flexible accommodation between reinforced concrete main floors 20 feet apart. The flexible accommodation is in lightweight construction of steel mullions, fascias, and beams, with steel decking for the intermediate floors, when required, and panel wall and window system. By this means the accommodation can be large, or small, single or double, or any combination', ibid.

[40] Smithson, 'University of Sheffield, extracts from the description', 1953.

[41] In the autumn of 1953, an exhibition of Klee's drawings and a symposium on the *Pedagogical Sketchbook* was organised at the Institute of Contemporary Art in London, in Smithson, *The Charged Void: Architecture*, 84. In 1953 the English version of Klee's *Pedagogical Sketches* was published, translated by Moholy Nagy.

[42] Banham was among the first to recognise the compositional principle of New Brutalism; Banham, 'The New Brutalism'; later critics would be Jürgen Joedicke, 'New Brutalism: Brutalismus in der Architektur', *Bauen+Wohnen*, vol. 18, no. 11 (November 1964): 421–25. The concept of the 'space in between' would be theorised by the Smithsons only in the 1970s, in Alison and Peter Smithson, 'The Space in Between', *Oppositions*, vol. 4 (October 1974): 75–78; on this subject, see Max Risselada, 'Tussenruimte / The Space Between', *OASE: Architectural Journal*, no. 51 (June 1999): 46–53.

[43] Banham, 'The New Brutalism'.

[44] The Smithsons would recognise on various occasions the influence of the Eames on their architectural practice, Alison and Peter Smithson, *Changing the Art of Inhabitation: Mies' Pieces, Eames' Dreams, the Smithsons* (London, Zurich: Artemis, 1994), 93. On this subject, see also the contribution of Beatriz Colomina, 'Koppels / Couplings', *OASE: Architectural Journal*, no. 51 (June 1999): 20–33.

[45] 'Concrete unfaced, with a designed shuttering pattern' reads the description of the project for Golden Lane, reprinted in Smithson, *The Charged Void: Architecture*, 88.

14 'Secondary
School at Hunstanton',
Architects' Journal,
vol. 118, 10 September
1953, no. 3054,
pp. 323–24

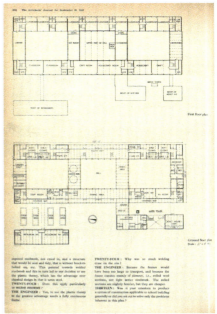

experiment with a materiality that met the Smithsons' poetics. Through the operations of 'assemblage' and 'juxtaposition', the Smithsons confirmed the use of materials according to their nature, as they arrived on the building site. Echoing Ruskin, they aimed for the 'quality of *real materials*', as they stated in an interview of September 1953 about the School at Hunstanton (see figure 14).[46] The central role of materials is declared by the desire to use them 'architecturally', that is, according to an arrangement that contributes to structural support, ornament and spatial definition. The fact that materials imply a cultural meaning depending on their substance is testified by the particular quality attributed to the brick used for the school's curtain walls, that of 'permanence'. In their reasoning, 'permanence' belongs to the English tradition and was exemplified for the Smithsons by John Vanbrugh's Seaton Delavand Hall. However, it is not only to be understood as 'solidity', in opposition to prefabricated, lightweight structures such as the ones promoted by the Hertfordshire Plan school building. For the Smithsons, 'permanence' is also the quality that gives architecture a recognisable image: 'A feeling of permanence should be a very important factor in the environment of a child'.[47]

It is worth noting that the Smithsons stressed a historical perspective in continuity with the English building tradition, from the organisation of the site to the use of materials: 'We use steel in the same way as mediaeval builders used wood'.[48] In referring to the medieval building tradition, the Smithson revealed their desire for perfect juxtaposition of the elements, to allow maximum economy and static efficiency of the metal sections, carefully welded to ensure a 'neat and tidy' structure.[49] This genuine 'reverence' for materials, whether brick, steel, glass, wood or concrete,

---

[46] [n.a.], 'Secondary School at Hunstanton', *Architects' Journal*, vol. 118, no. 3054 (10 September 1953): 323–28.
[47] Ibid., 326.
[48] Ibid.
[49] Plastic theory, developed by the engineer Baker, was admitted into the British Standards from 1948.

was to undergo, over the course of the evolution of the definition of New Brutalism, a diversion towards roughness and brutality. Paradoxically, it was the discussion of the School at Hunstanton that would offer critics the occasion for this misunderstanding.

The early debates on post-war styles, from New Picturesque to New Humanism and New Empiricism, had taken place under the banner of a reflection on architecture and urban planning. If up until the early 1950s the Smithsons' experiences had primarily been limited to competition projects, in September 1953 they had the opportunity to experiment with a figurative sensitivity that had developed out of contemporary artistic connections. Together with an engineer, a photographer and an artist from the Independent Group, Ronald Jenkins, Nigel Henderson and Eduardo Paolozzi, the Smithsons organised the exhibition *Parallel of Life and Art: An Exhibition of Landscape, Science and Art,* held from 10 September to 18 October 1953 at the Institute of Contemporary Art in London (see figure 15).[50]

New Brutalism's rise to the role of a category for a new phase of the Modern Movement was also thanks to the references that emerged through the exhibition, which catalysed a series of artistic inputs that would also enliven the Smithsons' architectural concepts. The definition of New Brutalism, which had appeared linked, by contrast and conflict, to the work of Le Corbusier, could also, thanks to the concepts deriving from *Parallel of Life and Art,* acquire its own autonomy, confronting the problems intrinsic to British culture with new artistic values that could not have been included in New Brutalism had it remained solely rooted in the adjective *brut.*

A series of concepts emerged from the alchemy of *Parallel of Life and Art* that would only later be assimilated to architecture, but for then remained tangential. The artistic references would translate into design tools, going from a composition based on the relationship between the parts to a radical material dimension. The exhibition was the bearer of a conceptual dimension in which disciplinary boundaries were broken down, bringing together art, architecture, photography and popular culture into a fundamental mixture, nourishing the complexity of New Brutalism. The more urban and theoretical dimension of that definition was not undermined but made more complex because it was articulated through creative processes occurring in the art world.

It is significant that some concepts already adopted by the Smithsons for their projects, such as 'assemblage', 'juxtaposition' and 'cross-reference'[51] are found in the text presenting the exhibition. Critics would make the parallels with contemporary artistic experiences from art informel to art brut more explicit, by occasionally associating them with the definition of New Brutalism, along the lines of the juxtaposition between art brut and the Unité in the pages of *Architecture d'Aujourd'hui* in 1949.

[50] From 1951 onwards, a group of architects, artists, sociologists and engineers organised informal meetings at the French Pub in Soho, at Banham's house or at the Institute of Contemporary Art (ICA) opened in 1948 under the direction of Dorothy Moarland. Around twenty architects attended the Independent Group, including Peter Carter, Alan Colquhoun, Geoffrey Holroyd, John Voelcker, Colin St John Wilson, Bill Howell, engineer Frank Newby and critic Reyner Banham. What the architects of the Independent Group have in common is their admiration for the figures of Mies and Le Corbusier, whose lectures they had heard at the Architectural Association and the RIBA. The most frequent members of the meetings were Richard Hamilton, Nigel Henderson, John McHale, Eduardo Paolozzi, William Turnbull, Colin St John Wilson, James Stirling, Magda Cordell, Alan Colquhoun and Alison and Peter Smithson, led by Reyner Banham, Lawrence Alloway, and Toni del Renzio. For questions related to the foundation and activities of the Independent Group, see David Robbins, *The Independent Group: Post-war Britain and the Aesthetics of Plenty* (Cambridge: MIT Press, 1990); Anne Massey, *The Independent Group: Modernism and Mass Culture in Britain, 1945–59* (Manchester: Manchester University Press, 1995); Irénée Scalbert, 'Parallel of Life and Art', *Daidalos*, vol. 75 (May 2000): 52–65; Victoria Walsh, *Nigel Henderson: Parallel of Life and Art* (London: Thames & Hudson, 2001); Claude Lichtenstein, Thomas Schregenberger, *As Found: The Discovery of the Ordinary* (London: Lars Müller Publishers, 2001); Claude Lichtenstein, 'As Found: The Discovery of the Ordinary', in Claude Lichtenstein (ed.), *British Architecture and Art of the 1950s* (London: Lars Müller Publishers, 2006); Ben Highmore, 'Walls without Museums: Anonymous History, Collective Authorship and the Document', *Visual Culture in Britain*, vol. 8, no. 2 (2007): 1–20; Anne Massey, Gregor Muir, *Institute of Contemporary Arts: 1946–1968* (Amsterdam: Roma Publications, 2014).

[51] Theo Crosby, 'Parallel of Life and Art', *Architectural Design*, vol. 23, no. 10 (October 1953): 297–98.

PARALLEL OF LIFE AND ART

Exhibition at the Institute of Contemporary Art

Report by Theo Crosby

The significance of the Pavilion d'Esprit

Below: a section of the I.C.A. Exhibition

and dome.

To be made aware of the wonder and the miracle of science and Nature, and our own poignant position between them, is surely an achievement.

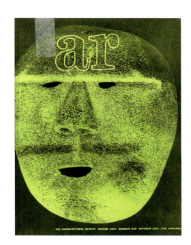

15 Theo Crosby, 'Parallel of Life and Art', *Architectural Design*, vo. 23, October 1953, no. 10, p. 297

16 Cover of *Architectural Review* with one of the images of *Parallel of Life and Art*, October 1953, no. 682

The images that came together in *Parallel of Life and Art*, debated and selected during the meetings of the Independent Group, were called 'raw material' because they bore witness to a mutable cultural magma that became a prototype for including what society commonly rejects:[52] the ugly, the grotesque, the useless.[53] This approach generated a succession of associations that critics would develop in the various definitions of New Brutalism, as well as in the wake of the emergence of pop culture. In light of the exhibition, the desire to crystallise the present was also conceptualised through an 'image' capable of acting as a 'Rosetta stone' for contemporary society, following an expression used in the catalogue of the exhibition.[54] The 'images' were suspended in the gallery space in such a way as to generate a complex form of 'order', in which disciplinary categories were disrupted through the three-dimensional assembly of inclined panels, allowing the visitor a free association of images.[55]

[52] Robbins, *The Independent Group: Post-war Britain and the Aesthetics of Plenty*. The exhibition catalogue is also held in the Smithson archives in the Harvard University Library.

[53] In the avant-garde experimentation of *Parallel of Life and Art*, the most radical culture of the Modern Movement resonated, handed down by essays such as Ozenfant's 'La peinture moderne', Giedion's 'Mechanization Takes Command', Moholy Nagy's 'Vision in Motion' or Duchamp's 'Boîte Verte'. These references, widely debated throughout 1953 in a series of presentations at the ICA entitled *Aesthetic Problems of Contemporary Art*, allowed the members of the Independent Group to grasp the connections between art, technology and industrial production within a consumer society, and some critics would see in this cultural melting pot the premises that would lead within a few months to the definition of New Brutalism.

[54] 'The exhibition will provide a key – a kind of Rosetta Stone – by which the discoveries of the sciences and the arts can be seen as aspects of the same whole, related phenomenon, parts of that New Landscape which experimental science has revealed and artists and theorists created', exhibition catalogue *Parallel of Life and Art*, in Robbins, *The Independent Group: Post-war Britain and the Aesthetics of plenty*, 129.

[55] Crosby, 'Parallel of Life and Art'.

In the exhibition catalogue, specific categories provide a key to interpreting the images, which evoke the multiform and kaleidoscopic interests necessary to overcome the Aristotelian vision and the hierarchy between the various disciplines: 'Anatomy, architecture, art, calligraphy, date 1901, landscape, movement, nature, primitive, scale of man, stress, stress structure, football, science fiction, medicine, geology, metal, ceramic'. 'Architecture' ranges from images of classic buildings of the Modern Movement, (Le Corbusier's Armé du Salut, the UN Building, Ove Arup & Partners' Dublin Bus Garage) to sacred and vernacular ancient settlements (Inuit dwellings, the cities of Erbil and Pompeii, Neptune's Temple at Paestum and Machu Picchu) to also include objects of anthropological culture such as an Aztec mask and different types of plant tissue. 'Art' is also expanded into an inclusive category, evoked by the paintings of Dubuffet, Burri and Pollock, but also by a tribal tattoo, an archaeological find from Pompeii, and other images taken from the news, such as the funeral of King George VI, an accident during a bicycle race, or the x-ray of a cat (see figure 16).

The exhibition was motivated by the desire to redefine the very concepts of 'architecture' and 'art' as acts of choice and selection, not invention. 'Accident' is another concept of surrealist derivation that the group used to justify the creative process of the exhibition:

> Accident [...] The VISUAL ENGINEER. What we call SELECTIVE ACCI-
> DENT to be good must function like the objet trouvé – a chance set of 'found'
> phenomena bringing about an order which you might ideally [have] wished/
> invented to create from scratch. It is a question of RECOGNITION.[56]

Thanks to the exhibition, the Smithsons tested artistic concepts that they could then apply to the architectural project, starting from the Dadaist 'objet trouvé', passing through the Surrealist concept of 'accident', and on to their definition of 'as found', which would later open to multiple configurations.

The works of Pollock and Burri, presented among the hundreds of images in *Parallel of Life and Art*, provided the necessary reference to challenge conventional composition through an informal, gestural and material configuration. The reference to Pollock entailed a progressive move away from the question of finite form, which would also guide architectural design towards a 'new order' and what would be theorised as 'a-formalism'. Pollock's experiments with the technique of 'dripping' were the premise for a vision of architectural design in which the notion of process became crucial. Process was seen as the antithesis of *a priori* form, to the point that, starting from considerations on New Brutalism, conceptual parallels were woven between 'action painting' and 'action architecture'.[57] Through Pollock's works, seen for the first time in Venice in 1949,[58] the Smithsons also theorised the concept of 'layering', in which the combination of fragments acquires a unitary dimension through their superimposition, which would lead to the affirmation of the concept of 'image'. 'Image system' is the expression used by the members of the Independent Group to define the principles of relationships and internal tensions within the collection of images discussed during the meetings, and which would become one of the founding criteria of New Brutalism, as defined by Banham in 1955.[59]

---

[56] Manuscript from Henderson's collection, Tate Archive, see Walsh, *Nigel Henderson*, 92.

[57] Gerhard M. Kallmann, 'The "Action" Architecture of a New Generation', *Architectural Forum*, vol. 111, no. 4 (October 1959): 132–37.

[58] During the Hunstanton construction site, the Smithsons also began to think about the concept of 'layering', visible in the overlapping of the metal frames and in the reflections of the large windows, immortalised by photographer Nigel Henderson. Richard Hamilton had already experimented with the concept of layering in the exhibition *Growth and Form*, held in the ICA Gallery from July to August 1951.

[59] 'It was necessary in the early 50s to look to the works of painter Pollock and sculptor Paolozzi for a complete image system, for an order with a structure and a certain tension, where every piece was correspondingly new in a new system of relationship', in Alison and Peter Smithson, Nigel Henderson, Theo Crosby, *Uppercase, No. 3* (London: Whitefriars, 1960); also confirmed in Alison and Peter Smithson, *Ordinariness and Light* (Cambridge: M.I.T. Press, 1970), 86.

For the Smithsons, *Parallel of Life and Art* was the necessary period of gestation that allowed them to recognise a 'new movement-classical-complex-human', as they noted in a preparatory text for the exhibition.[60] In September 1953, it might still seem premature to make a direct connection between the definition of New Brutalism, the experiments taking place in the exhibition, and the main concepts that emerged in the design projects, from 'accident' to 'juxtaposition' and the concept of 'layering'. However, that very note, 'new movement-classical-complex-human', contains a primordial attempt to line up a series of definitions, some belonging to the debate that had been going on since the 1940s, linked by hyphens to indicate the incompleteness of each word chosen for the series, and introduced by Pevsner's 'New-'. It is no coincidence that the Smithsons jotted down a quotation from James Joyce that confirms the premonition: 'This is a movement I call epiphany. (Epiphany: a reality behind the appearance)'. This note proved decisive in the historical development that led, thanks to the Smithsons, to the invention, or reuse, of an expressive word that contains within itself the synthesis of 'movement-classical-complex-human': New Brutalism. That note constitutes the indispensable and precious *trait d'union* between the cultural intentions of *Parallel of Life and Art*, the decades-long aspiration of English critics and New Art History to define a new style, the theoretical impulses and conflicts around the Unité, its *béton brut*, its *Brutal Realism*.

It is even possible to claim that the very invention of New Brutalism appears at the end to be nothing more than a philological and academic question. In fact, even if the Smithsons had used Asplund's Neo-Brutalism, or had embraced the satirical label used by the Softs of the LCC, what is essential is that *their* New Brutalism would be the synthetic transcription, in a single word and without the hyphens of the list, of an attitude that includes a variety of aspirations: first of all a vital and processual *movement*, indicated as the first word of the list; secondly, an aulic and even Platonic attitude resumed in the word *classical* – intended not academically but as a pondered attitude to be adapted to each specific case; thirdly, to a synthesis that reveals a *complex* constellation of reference which resumes at the same time the lessons of the masters of the Modern Movement and the realities of the present time; and finally, a dimension of the project that must express *human* contingencies.

The Smithsons' New Brutalism

The insight pinned down in September 1952 into that 'new movement-classical-complex-human' found a synthesis in the invention of New Brutalism in December 1953, in the pages of *Architectural Design*.[61] The Smithsons' first use of New Brutalism was in a comment accompanying a brief description of their unbuilt project for the House in Soho, their home and office in Colvill Place, a block of Georgian terrace houses demolished during the war (see figure 17). The announcement was made through an article entitled 'Small House Projects', which documented residential projects by various architects, including that of the Smithsons. The contribution was written by Alison, although

[60] 'By presenting phenomena from our various fields we can demonstrate the existence of a new movement-classical-complex-human-a fundamental outlook from common sources to future synthesis'. Alison and Peter Smithson, 'Addendum: Texts Documenting the Development of Parallel of Life and Art. 1. Sources, 1952', in Robbins, *The Independent Group: Post-war Britain and the Aesthetics of Plenty*.

[61] P.D.S. [Alison Smithson], 'House in Soho'. The Smithsons would henceforth frequently publish in *Architectural Design*, thanks to their connection with Theo Crosby, who joined the magazine's editorial team as technical editor in 1953. The definition of New Brutalism was published in the first volume of the magazine edited by Crosby. Parnell claims that the article on the House in Soho was commissioned by Monica Pidgeon in July 1953, when she met the Smithsons at CIAM in Aix-en-Provence. See Steve Parnell, *Architectural Design, 1954–1972* (Sheffield: University of Sheffield School of Architecture, 2011), 254.

17 Clipping of the article 'House in Soho', *Architectural Design*, December 1953, with handwritten substitution of the author's initials P.S.D [Peter Denham Smithson] with A.M.S [Alison Margaret Smithson], Alison and Peter Smithson Archive, Folder E003. Courtesy of the Frances Loeb Library. Harvard University Graduate School of Design

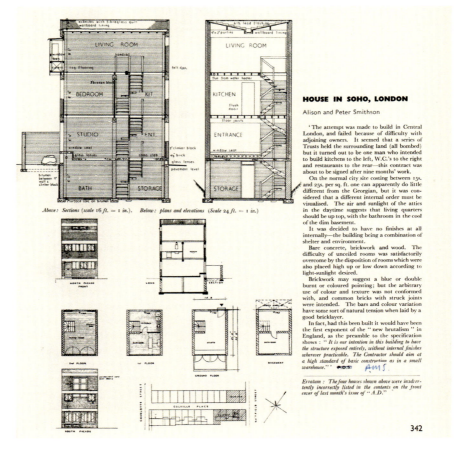

Above: Sections (scale 16 ft. = 1 in.). Below: plans and elevations (Scale 24 ft. = 1 in.)

HOUSE IN SOHO, LONDON

Alison and Peter Smithson

'The attempt was made to build in Central London, and failed because of difficulty with adjoining owners. It seemed that a series of Trusts held the surrounding land (all bombed) but it turned out to be one man who intended to build kitchens to the left, W.C.'s to the right and restaurants to the rear—this contract was about to be signed after nine months' work.

On the normal city site costing between 15s. and 25s. per sq. ft. one can apparently do little different from the Georgian, but it was considered that a different internal order must be visualised. The air and sunlight of the attics in the daytime suggests that living quarters should be up top, with the bathroom in the cool of the dim basement.

It was decided to have no finishes at all internally—the building being a combination of shelter and environment.

Bare concrete, brickwork and wood. The difficulty of unceiled rooms was satisfactorily overcome by the disposition of rooms which were also placed high up or low down according to light-sunlight desired.

Brickwork may suggest a blue or double burnt or coloured pointing; but the arbitrary use of colour and texture was not conformed with, and common bricks with struck joints were intended. The bars and colour variation have some sort of natural tension when laid by a good bricklayer.

In fact, had this been built it would have been the first exponent of the " new brutalism " in England, as the preamble to the specification shows : " *It is our intention in this building to have the structure exposed entirely, without internal finishes wherever practicable. The Contractor should aim at a high standard of basic construction as in a small warehouse.*" ' P.S.D A.M.S.

Erratum : The four houses shown above were inadvertently incorrectly listed in the contents on the front cover of last month's issue of " A.D."

342

the magazine attributed the text to Peter, signing it with the initials P.D.S. The reasons for this change would be attributed by Alison to an 'anti-feminist editorial gesture' apparently implemented by the magazine's editorial staff.[62] As to why the Smithsons did not present themselves as co-authors of the article, several hypotheses can be put forward, among which the most plausible is that of Robin Middleton: 'Alison was dictating all the time, she was the one always deciding what they were going to do. Alison was the one formulating what their image was going to be, what they were going to read, etc'.[63]

Several narratives would be perpetuated about the origin of the label New Brutalism, including an autobiographical hypothesis taken from the combination of Peter's nickname, Brutus, and Alison Smithson's first name.

In the year in which they first used the label New Brutalism, the Smithsons had the opportunity to publish two further contributions: an interview about the School

[62] 'P.S. is described as the "founder" presumably on the evidence quoted on page 10: "When Peter Smithson finally committed the phrase to print in December 1953". The quote following is part of the description of Soho House published in *Architectural Design* in December 1953, which was in fact written by Alison Smithson. "The piece was initialled A.M.S. in typescript, but this was mistranscribed, in error or as an anti-feminist editorial gesture, as P.D.S. This is how one comes to found a movement"', in Smithson, 'Banham's Bumper Book on Brutalism, Discussed by Alison and Peter Smithson'.

[63] Interview with Robin Middleton, 21 April 2018, New York.

at Hunstanton in September, while still under construction,[64] and an article on their urban theories.[65] Their willingness to associate the definition of New Brutalism with the House in Soho, rather than with the Golden Lane or Sheffield projects, or the School at Hunstanton, should be considered in light of the Smithsons' experiences and the evolution of British and international debates, and the hypothesis of a fortuitous coincidence as the article might suggest can be discarded.

Compared to the other projects, the House in Soho presents significant characteristics that confirm the intention to root New Brutalism in the principles of English culture, in the tradition of brick and craft, revised in light of a synthesis of different contemporary cultural and artistic impulses. It is also understandable that the intention was to define New Brutalism through a project that demonstrates an evolution with respect to the model of Mies in the School at Hunstanton and the Unité in Golden Lane.[66] In this sense, the scale of the project is crucial, reflecting the Smithsons' interest in the ordinary and in 'everyday life', and in which there was no trace of that heroic and colossal dimension that would instead be associated with the definition of New Brutalism by other critics. It is within the parameters of noble simplicity, domesticity, the experience of war and the consequent construction of identity through the concept of Englishness, that the Smithsons structured their first definition of New Brutalism.

Only a few previously discussed themes, such as the 'new order' and the question of the visibility of materials, were brought together in the brief description, taking on an almost manifesto-like dimension in the interpretation of the project. The concept of New Brutalism in the explanation of the House in Soho revolves around the design of a 'basic unit', reduced to a simple 'shelter and environment', to be realised with the simplicity of a 'small warehouse'. Despite the clear influence of the series of photographs of vernacular industrial architecture gathered together during the early 1950s in *Architectural Review*, the Smithsons nevertheless omitted the sentimentalism in vogue in English debates. In essence, architecture is reduced to a simple 'structure exposed entirely', the radicalism of which consists of a domesticity conceived 'without internal finishes' and with exposed ducts. In its simplicity, the design for the House in Soho refers to a roughness aesthetics capable, in the abolition of differences between interior and exterior, of compensating for the conventions of the domestic environment.

Two terms are crucial in framing the value the Smithsons placed on their New Brutalism: 'shelter' and 'environment'. The interests in primitive settlements that the Smithsons presented in the diagrams shown at the IX CIAM in 1953 converge in the 'shelter' characteristic of the House of Soho. That feature evokes a primordial need for architecture, like the contemporary primitive hut that the Smithsons would stage in the symbolic habitat of the *Patio & Pavilion* art installation at the 1956 *This Is Tomorrow* exhibition. Even the definition of their project as 'environment' can only be a critical response to the obsessions with 'comfort' brought to the fore by New Empiricism and New Humanism, here declined by the Smithsons according to the social and ordinary vision of post-war London life, as portrayed by Henderson in the streets of Bethnal Green in London and that would influence the Smithsons' 'doorstep philosophy' and 'street-thinking'.[67]

---

[64] [n.a.], 'Secondary School at Hunstanton'.

[65] Smithson, 'An Urban Project: Golden Lane Housing'.

[66] 'The House in Soho is unique even in the body of their own work. Because it is so embedded in brick culture. In the House in Soho the Smithsons are trying to ground their Brutalism in something to do with the British situation. There is something "nativistic" in trying to go into the ground and the roots of the British sensibility. They give value to craft and cottages in Scotland, to a relative archaic vernacular in the British situation. They allude to that'. According to Frampton, a 'proto-Brutalist' example that might have inspired the Smithsons for their House in Soho is Le Corbusier's Maison du Weekend of 1935. Interview with Kenneth Frampton, 2 February 2018, Columbia University, New York.

[67] Alison and Peter Smithson, 'The Built World: Urban Reidentification', *Architectural Design*, vol. 25, no. 6 (June 1955): 185–87; Smithson, 'Banham's Bumper Book on Brutalism, Discussed by Alison and Peter Smithson'.

In the description accompanying the project, it is possible to identify a number of themes that the Smithsons brought together in the development of the concept of New Brutalism, namely that of 'new order', 'basic construction', structural honesty, a vitalistic vision of materials, and finally an industrial aesthetic:[68]

> In fact, had this been built it would have been the first exponent of the 'new brutalism' in England, as the preamble to the specification shows: It is our intention in this building to have the structure exposed entirely, without internal finishes wherever practicable. The Contractor should aim at a high standard of basic construction as in a small warehouse.[69]

The 'new order' now takes on a different form from the aulic composition of Coventry, or that based on 'patterns' of Sheffield, and is associated with the search for ideal natural lighting that dictates the inversion of the living room, located on the top floor, where a large bow-window seems to reaffirm the deep link with Victorian English tradition and the exercise of re-appropriation of traditional domestic elements that would become the design theme of the 1956 Sugden House.[70]

The elaboration of concepts that emerged in *Parallel of Life and Art* was not revealed in the formulation of the Smithsons, who instead reiterated a notion of architecture as a distant confrontation with Ruskin's 'quality of real materials' and Le Corbusier's visibility of structure: 'It was decided to have no finishes at all internally', they said in their description. The Smithsons did not admit any decorative meaning for 'common bricks', 'ordinary concrete' and 'wood', other than the expression of intrinsic vitalism entrusted to their laying: 'The bars and colour variation have some sort of natural tension when laid by a good bricklayer'.

The House in Soho, despite its apparent symmetry, has an intrinsic disproportion that the Smithsons would later theorise with the concept of 'un-arty', derived from the juxtaposition of large and small openings, which appears to evoke the same disproportion found in Edman and Holm's Villa Göth. If we compare Villa Göth and the House in Soho, as the genealogy of the definition of New Brutalism would seem to suggest, then those two visions no longer appear to be so distant but show themselves as aspects of the same generational questioning of the evolution of the Modern Movement, investigated in the dimension of materials and domesticity. Unmistakable affinities weave links that suggest that the House in Soho was chosen by the Smithsons precisely in response to the work that had given rise to the definition of New Brutalism – from the exposed materials to the internal arrangement of functions, the accentuated lintels and the composition of the openings, and finally the choice of brick, the common denominator of two architectural cultures that intertwined and rejected each other, English and Swedish.

Moreover, the Smithsons' awareness of the existence of the previous definition of Neo-Brutalism is implicitly confirmed by the geographical clarification that they felt obliged to specify, perhaps in order to vindicate their personal appropriation of that definition: the Soho House would have been 'the first exponent of New Brutalism in England'. One can therefore hypothesise that the Smithsons decided to announce New Brutalism through the House in Soho as a critical response to the Villa Göth, in order to purge that definition of the negative urban vision circulating in the LCC.

---

[68] 'Ordinary concrete' is specified in the monograph and not in the 1953 article, in Smithson, *The Charged Void: Architecture*, 96.

[69] P.D.S. [Alison Smithson], 'House in Soho'.

[70] The interior layout recalls that of Le Corbusier's Maison Cook, Interview with Kenneth Frampton, 2 February 2018, Columbia University, New York.

However, the dominant feature of the House in Soho is undoubtedly the accentuated roughness underlying the definition of 'shelter', which distances the project from the reference to the Villa Göth, bringing it back into the sphere of Le Corbusier's research into the *brut* aesthetics, in the form that would be realised in the Maisons Jaoul. The Smithsons' operation does not imply the foundation of new principles with respect to those of the Modern Movement and is to be understood as the intention to reframe the definition of New Brutalism in close connection with the founding principles of visibility of materials and structure. In this sense the Smithsons wanted to link New Brutalism to their domestic project for the House in Soho, while that label was still anchored to the urban vision following the model of the Unité in Marseilles. In light of these observations, the enigma of the origin of the definition of New Brutalism can perhaps be solved.[71]

One could hypothesise that this tension towards the 'New-', which in hindsight clashes with other contemporary 'new-isms', had not yet reached full conceptualisation in the first definition of New Brutalism. The Smithsons would constantly alternate with other synonymous expressions, starting from 'new movement-classic-complex-human', or 'new attitude', 'new order' and, as will be seen later, with that of 'architecture of reality'. This hesitation is indicative of the ambivalence of a concept of New Brutalism still in the making, which the Smithsons associated with the House in Soho, perhaps only through a momentary intuition. The Smithsons' return to the definition of New Brutalism, as opposed to the other formulas, may even be fortuitous, perhaps because of that suffix '-ism' which seems to herald the possibility of a style to come.

Indeed, New Brutalism is still an uncertain concept, woven from fragments and cryptic, lapidary statements delivered to the pages of magazines, and evolving as the Smithsons' interventions unfold. For the time being, urban concerns remained detached from New Brutalism. The urban preoccupations of the Smithson were moving on a parallel line, through a series of articles published between 1953 and early 1954 such as 'An Urban Project: Golden Lane Housing' and 'What the Smithsons Think',[72] in which they reiterated the need to move beyond the New Towns model, in favour of an urban project responding to the drastic changes in post-war society, including new mass consumer goods, on the background of the discussions conducted in the Independent Group.

When the Smithsons returned to reflect on the ongoing change in architecture, concerns about the expressiveness of materials were preponderant, as evidenced by some annotations published in the summer of 1954 in the student journal *244: Journal of the University of Manchester Architecture and Planning Society* (see figure 18).[73] The contribution, entitled 'Some Notes on Architecture', is presented as a series of scattered thoughts, which denote the irresolution of some concepts suspended in enigmatic aphorisms. Their reasoning is carried out by means of contrasts, between the succession of different phases of the Modern Movement and art history, between the 'academic' modernism of the Pavilion Suisse and the new humanism of Unite's *béton brut*, between the confirmation of the reference to Pollock and the need to overcome De Stijl and Cezanne, seen as the origin of a purism that later became academic.

[71] The Smithsons did not recognise the Swedish origin of the definition, a position perhaps justified by their desire for total appropriation of the definition, presenting themselves as the sole authors. This hypothesis is also confirmed by Frampton, Interview with Kenneth Frampton, 2 February 2018, Columbia University, New York. Several scholars have attempted to frame the origin of New Brutalism, for example, see Anthony Vidler, 'Troubles with Theories V: The Brutalist Moment', *Architectural Review*, vol. 234, no. 1404 (February 2014): 96–101; Dirk van den Heuvel, 'Between Brutalists. The Banham Hypothesis and the Smithson Way of Life', *The Journal of Architecture*, vol. 20, no. 2 (April 2015): 293–308; Steve Parnell, 'The Brutal Myth', *Thresholds*, vol. 45 (August 2017): 151–58.

[72] Smithson, 'An Urban Project: Golden Lane Housing'; Five Architects, 'What the Smithsons Think', *Architects' Journal*, vol. 119, no. 3078 (February 1954): 240.

[73] Alison and Peter Smithson, 'Some Notes on Architecture', *244: Journal of the University of Manchester Architecture and Planning Society*, vol. 1 (Spring 1954): 4.

18 Alison and Peter Smithson, typescript entitled 'Some notes on architecture', January 1954, Alison and Peter Smithson Archive, Folder E004. Courtesy of the Frances Loeb Library. Harvard University Graduate School of Design

ome notes on architecture . Jan.54

With the completion of the Pavillon Suisse,Modern Arhitecture became academic.

With the completion of the Uité, _life_ has returned.

In the béton brut of the Unité a new human architecture has been born.

Technique is seen once more as a tool: the machine as a means.

A new humanism has been born.

The dead hand of de Stidl can be lifted from our backs.

Cezanne can be seen as aboring painter of little importance.

Perhaps even Pollock is more important ? Who can say.

All we know is what moves us now.

This day .

January the 23rd 1954.

We of the 50's have no one to look up to in our own country, and there is no climate of enthusiasm in which architecture can flower.

Your magazine should aim to create such a climate of enthusiasm.

Discuss real architecture, Paestum, Sunion,the Villa Adriana,Prenestina,Seaton Delaval, Vezelay, and that by real architects today, the yonger ones such asMoretti or Rudlph as well asCorbu and Mies.

Establish real standards.

Donét worry about architectural education.

Don't be taken in by the Wiemar Fallacy.

Architecture and urbanism are problems of signifant organisation.

Utter complexity made lucid.

It is more important to fail magnicently than to achieve mediocrity.

Although they do not explicitly mention New Brutalism, it is clear from the notes that the Smithsons identified in the Unité a new direction in architecture. The sensitivity for 'real materials' that had led them to trace the a-temporal quality of 'permanence' in bricks now seems able to evolve in *béton brut*, reported in French. This evolution aligns with the English debates as it becomes the genesis of a 'new humanism' for the Smithsons, which is radically different from that theorized by the *Architectural Review*, as it is precisely founded on material expression. The recurrence of 'new human' and 'new humanism' in the Smithsons' 1954 note confirms the decisive role of this term, which also appears in their list of words mentioned for the exhibition *Parallel of Life and Art*. To have jotted down this term again, preceded by the prefix 'New' to give it the status of a theoretical attitude, shortly after using New Brutalism in the article on the House in Soho, on the one hand confirms their intention to find a definition for contemporary architecture, and on the other demonstrates the uncertainties of their choice. The 1954 note also suggests that the Smithsons, in using New Brutalism, had appropriated a definition that was not their own and that they simply made it public in England. That act was, however, destined to spark a debate in England. Following the discussions on the various New-isms, the conditions for the future success of New Brutalism in catalysing certain theoretical trajectories did exist in that historical context, and that is, in fact, what happened.

Early Definitions of New Brutalism: Segal and the English Magazines

The first contribution to ensuring that the New Brutalism used by the Smithsons for the House in Soho did not remain a dead letter was made by the German-born architect Walter Segal, professor at the Architectural Association in London, who sent his observations to the magazine *Architectural Design* in February 1954.[74] Segal's letter is entitled 'The New Brutalism' and should be considered as the first complete attempt to define some of its characteristics. Segal, starting from the Smithsons' article, expanded New Brutalism in a more articulate manner through a historical perspective. The central point of his argument concerned the issue of cladding and coincided with his own education, his experimental projects on self-building, and his radical building approach marked by the Swiss modern tradition.

Segal went so far as to argue that New Brutalism consisted solely of a turn in architecture towards materials left exposed, as in the design of the House in Soho. He framed it as a critical offshoot of the Modern Movement, characterised by extreme 'nakedness'. In accordance with this principle, Segal recognised the pre-existence of a category that he defined as Brutalism, linked to the phenomena of the 1920s, and subsequently he distinguished the contemporary as Neo-Brutalism, following Asplund's original definition.

In the British debate, for the moment confined within the examples of Le Corbusier and his Unité, the brick model of the Villa Göth, and finally the exposed materials of the House in Soho, Segal included a line that took up typically Central European matrices, to which he associated three fundamental figures, called into question because of their use of uncovered materials: Hannes Meyer, Klaus Koppen and Frank Lloyd Wright.

According to Segal, Brutalism found its origin in the experiments of Meyer, recognised as 'the begetter' because he had pursued with intensity and determination an architecture devoid of cladding, as in the example of the Bundesschule des Allgemeinen Deutschen Gewerkschaftsbundes complex in Bernau, with exposed floors and brick infill walls which, according to Segal, attracted the attention of the 'brutalist pilgrims'.

More enigmatic was Segal's choice to point to Klaus Koppen's design for the 1930 competition for the Kharkov State Theatre in the Ukraine,[75] characterised by glass volumes (according to Segal's own description), as a model for a 'nakedness' which, according to him, found its greatest expression in the works of Mies. What Segal was keen to point out is that beyond the absence of cladding lies an absolute transparency that he saw as perhaps even an ethical attribute of New Brutalism. That primordial 'nakedness', in his view, indicated 'the path of the true Western Brutalist'. It goes without saying that in drawing a line of continuity between Koppen's project and the works of Mies, the latter ended up being involved in the definition of New Brutalism. Segal thus created the conditions for a literally Miesian work by Smithson to become emblematic of New Brutalism: the School at Hunstanton.

[74]   Walter Segal, 'The New Brutalism', *Architectural Design*, vol. 24, no. 2 (February 1954): 7 ad.
[75]   The first prize was won by Alfred Kastner, Eric Engerder and Carl Meyer; the second by Norman Bel Geddes and the third, presumably, by Klaus Koppen, [n.a.], '3 Americans Share Soviet Design Prize', *The New York Times*, 8 May 1931, 8.

Still driven by the construction of a genealogy for New Brutalism, Segal also referred to Frank Lloyd Wright, whom he called 'the venerable protagonist of brutalism'. In Wright's case, Segal was interested in pointing to the Usonian Houses as precedents for New Brutalism, not only because they were built with prefabricated concrete blocks and without cladding, thus in line with the House in Soho, but also because they are an expression of self-building that adds further connotations to Segal's New Brutalism, not contemplated by the Smithsons. The inclusion of Wright is significant from the point of view of a Modern Movement that went beyond the stylistic elements of the International Style, where Wright had not found a place. However, Wright's legacy would not have a decisive outcome in the conceptual evolution of New Brutalism, to the point that he would soon be replaced by a figure more in line with what was to become the phenomenon of Brutalism, namely Kahn.

In focusing on the lack of cladding as a privileged message of New Brutalism, Segal recognised the Smithsons' intervention as but a continuation. Brutalism was depicted as an orientation already underway in various geographical epicentres, declined according to regionalist traits: a 'Western Brutalism' centred on the Central European culture of Meyer and Mies, an 'English Brutalism' obsessed with 'concrete, brick and wood', and the American 'Brutalism' of Wright.[76]

Segal's 'The New Brutalism' was the first key, albeit brief, contribution to a critical reflection on whether the label appropriated by the Smithsons could become that New-ism sought after for years by British critics and New Art History. It is significant that the Smithsons read Segal's letter and kept it in their archives. They would pick up his 'The New Brutalism' again when they began to write a more articulated article on New Brutalism in 1955.[77] Segal's contribution also revealed a critical interest in the definition of New Brutalism and thus confirmed its potential for becoming the receptacle for a new theory.

Following the publication of Segal's letter, the definition of New Brutalism also became the title of an anonymous article in the 'Future' column of *Architectural Review*.[78] The initiative to publish this article, also entitled 'The New Brutalism', was of the utmost importance because it demonstrated that after the use of New Brutalism by the Smithsons and Segal, British critics felt the need to investigate the potential of this label to act as a repository for the aspiration to renew the tradition of the Modern Movement without betraying its foundations.

Architectural Review's 'The New Brutalism' was conceived in a peculiar way. It is not, in fact, a real article but a collection of small contributions, chosen and introduced by one of the magazine's editors with the explicit intention of giving authority to the definition that had just appeared in the English press. The person behind the collection and the anonymous introductory note was, most likely, Reyner Banham, who had been collaborating with the magazine as literary editor since 1952, and who, at the time of the publication of 'The New Brutalism', had begun his doctoral research at the Courtauld Institute under the guidance of Pevsner.

The editor of this collection started, as Segal did, with the Smithsons' first definition on the House in Soho. He then contacted the Smithsons requesting an explanation of what they had meant in their definition, which was published at the end of the column. The other document included confirms Banham's hand in orchestrating this contribution. It is in fact a 'forgery' based on an earlier article in the *Review*, designed to respond to Segal's criticism of English culture. The supposition that the author of 'The New Brutalism' was stung and perhaps even irritated by Segal's initiative is

[76] Segal, 'The New Brutalism'.
[77] Alison and Peter Smithson, Theo Crosby, 'The New Brutalism', *Architectural Design*, vol. 25, no. 1 (January 1955): 1.
[78] [Reyner Banham], 'The New Brutalism', *Architectural Review*, vol. 115, no. 688 (April 1954): 274–75.

proven by the fact that he did not mention Segal's article as being the first fundamental contribution to the label.

The presentation of New Brutalism to the audience of *Architectural Review* demonstrated that this label was assuming authority as well as autonomy over the description of the House in Soho, and that other values were starting to be associated with it, beyond the visibility of the structure and the use of exposed materials. New Brutalism was here introduced as a decisive phenomenon in the world of the arts and architecture, and as a necessity for contemporary criticism.

Following Pevsner's lesson in framing contemporary phenomena through a historical perspective, Banham read the embryonic definition of New Brutalism through the development of the Modern Movement and as a response to the degeneration of the International Style, placing the nascent label in the mainstream of the most experimentalist architectural culture of the twentieth century. This critical operation should also be considered against the background of English New Art History, of which it probably represents one of the most significant chapters. In Banham's historiographical construction, where the Modern Movement as defined by Pevsner possessed distinctly British, traditional traits, New Brutalism could be borrowed to find national alternatives to the International Style. It is not by coincidence that in the introduction to 'The New Brutalism' in *Architectural Review*, the most significant fragments of what had been the English debate on style reappeared. In the introduction Banham defines New Brutalism as an 'attitude' in continuity with the Modern Movement, and in contrast with the 'dry academic-abstract geometric forms' of the International Style, using an adjective, 'academic', which had also been used by the Smithsons in opposition to the plastic, expressive and figurative richness of the *béton brut* of the Unité d'Habitation.

On the delicate point of the invention and origins of the definition of New Brutalism, Banham's intervention, although brief, left many clues. He was well aware that the appearance of New Brutalism in Smithson's text on the House in Soho did not decree the moment of birth of the definition. Banham did not mention the debates going on in the LCC, nor certain possible Swedish origins, but neither did he attribute the invention of that definition to the Smithsons. One expression was significant in this regard: they, it is written about the Smithsons, had the merit of 'first using it in public'. It should not be overlooked that alongside the 'young English architects' (of whom he only named the Smithsons, or rather, to be precise, Peter alone), Banham also mentions 'artists', probably alluding to the role of *Parallel of Life and Art* in creating the cultural premises to identify New Brutalism as the definition that best reflected contemporary phenomena. Another consideration deserves to be made regarding the 'half satirically' that was placed next to New Brutalism, as if to make it clear that the author of the note knew all the nuances of the discussions between clans of friends and antagonists active in London. The positioning of New Brutalism within the Modern Movement, 'vital and British', and against the International Style, 'academic and dry', removed any sarcastic, ironic or critical connotation that some were attributing to that definition. The author of the note, under whose guise, it is worth repeating, Banham hid, was therefore convinced that New Brutalism was ready to become a category of the great history of architecture and New Art History.[79]

Among the documents published in 'The New Brutalism' was a letter from architect Kenneth Scott of Accra, Ghana. The author of the letter, tempted to act 'half satirically' again, modified the text of an article by Joseph [Giuseppe] Samonà on Wright.[80] It cannot be ruled out that Banham's intervention was behind Scott's alleged letter

---

[79] [Banham], 'The New Brutalism', 274.
[80] Joseph [Giuseppe] Samonà, 'Man, Matter and Space, *Architects' Year Book*, vol. 5 (1953): 110–22.

since the text of the letter is included in the 'Future' section under the same title 'The New Brutalism' and in continuity with Banham's comments.[81] Only a few years later Banham would admit that his intention had been to appropriate that definition, that he was in search of a 'rolling band-wagon to jump on'.[82] The body of the letter slavishly reproduces Samonà's article, except for some precise substitutions, in which the Smithson's name takes the place of Wright's and the term 'brutality' is inserted as a qualifying noun for New Brutalism, repeatedly testifying to a brutality that becomes 'essential', 'intimate', 'possible to dominate'. Regarding 'brutality', we should not forget the small article in *The Times* on Unité's 'Brutal Realism'. The editing of the article on Wright, transformed into a far-fetched description of the House in Soho, was symptomatic of a certain satirical climate that shaped the debates on the new course of architecture and the search for a 'new theory'. In fact, it is impossible not to grasp an underlying ironic and Dadaist vein, as if it were an academic game orchestrated in a circle of friends or, as Robin Middleton would later summarise: 'A theory came out from social gatherings, that resulted in a personal movement'.[83]

Banham asked the Smithsons to write a note at the end of the column, which seems to confirm that the definition of New Brutalism was a convenient choice in order to find an appropriate synthetic word for their enigmatic 'new movement-classical-complex-human'. It is probable that after having tried to replace the sequence 'movement-classical-complex-human' with 'New Brutalism', the Smithsons immediately felt the ineffectiveness of a term that for them was perhaps too contaminated by a material intention because of the Lecorbuserian *brut* at its root. It is a fact that just after succinctly launching New Brutalism in the comment on the House in Soho, they slip in another definition of their own: 'architecture of reality'.[84] This was the first attempt by the Smithsons to break away from the expression New Brutalism, and they would do so several times in the following years, without ever achieving the organic and complete definition that Banham would.

This choice must be carefully considered since their unfathomable New Brutalism would always be positioned between the well-known 'new movement-classical-complex-human' and the 'architecture of reality'. With this definition the Smithsons intended to assert an architecture that not only upheld the values of truth linked to structure and materials, as already presented in the description of the House in Soho, but that also bore witness to contemporary and popular culture. In fact, the Smithsons confirmed Banham's vision of a New Brutalism in continuity with the Modern Movement, whose epicentre is significantly identified not in the Swiss-German radicalism proposed by Segal, but in the avant-garde movements evoked in the exhibition *Parallel of Life and Art*, such as De Stijl, Dada, and Cubism. The framing of the origin of New Brutalism in those avant-gardes indicates their intention to go beyond pure geometric form in favour of a system of decomposition and assembly of elements based on a principle of relations. In this sense, the Smithsons saw in the example of De Stijl a confirmation of the principle of the continuity of space, generated by separate but related elements.[85] Moreover, this 'reality' of architecture cannot but refer to artistic experiences that staged life itself, such as Dada, reviving the same parallel between art and life that was woven through the exhibition of September 1953.

[81] [Banham], 'The New Brutalism', 275.
[82] Reyner Banham, *Fathers of Pop*, Arts Council of Great Britain. Concord Video & Film Council, UK, 1979.
[83] Interview with Robin Middleton, 21 April 2018, New York.
[84] The expression 'architecture of reality' summarised the main theses presented in the 1953 article 'The Built World: Urban Re-identification', in which the Smithsons identified a 'new order' appropriate to contemporary society and through which they criticised the Garden City and the New Towns for their nostalgia, and the Athens Charter for reducing architecture to a mechanical concept.
[85] Alison and Peter Smithson, 'The Heroic Period of Modern Architecture', *Architectural Design*, vol. 35, no. 12 (December 1965): 9.

The fact that the Smithsons, in coining their 'architecture of reality', had in mind New Brutalism, for which they were seeking alternative formulas, is confirmed by their choice of the word 'reality', which coincidentally appeared at the root of 'Brutal Realism' attributed by *The Times* to Le Corbusier's Unité in the article that they had cut out and kept. However, the expression 'architecture of reality' is probably indicative of their intention to ensure the definition's autonomy from material that New Brutalism did not allow. The appeal to reality included Ruskin's dimension of 'real materials' but was it was focused on the combination of references from popular to avant-garde culture with a new urban vision that went against the functionalist precepts of the Athens Charter. The Smithsons attributed to the 'architecture of reality' an extension that was no longer limited to the domestic scale of the House in Soho but included the urban notions of 'town', 'environment' and 'cities' that had not yet found a precise place in their definition of New Brutalism. This desire for 'reality' became a real topic of research in the debates of the 1950s, finding surprising parallels in other countries, such as Neorealism in Italy, although in that context it took on configurations far removed from the Smithsons' interests.

The construction of 'The New Brutalism' in *Architectural Review* already contained the two main trajectories of the English debate on New Brutalism: a critic who successfully exploited a definition that had appeared early in his career and two architects who were reluctant to fully identify with a definition they had used, almost by accident, and which would imprison them.

After Segal's intervention, Banham's anonymous one, and the Smithsons' clarifications, it seems clear that the New Brutalism made public in the article on the House in Soho was destined to take the place of the various New Humanisms or New Empiricisms that even the most convinced critic in the *Architectural Review* had already abandoned. From now on, British critics would use New Brutalism to explain various phenomena in progress and apply the definition from the perspective of historical analysis. However, it was still a question of articulating its scope, its peculiarities and its possible principles. It should not be forgotten that no one had so far argued what the nature of New Brutalism was. Banham's hypothesis in his column in *Architectural Review* of a trend involving not only architecture but also art was presented as a new element of its possible aesthetic and cultural epicentres. Although it is not possible to establish a definite link between New Brutalism and the exhibition *Parallel of Life and Art*, the fact remains that more than a few of the themes of the exhibition lent themselves to New Brutalism. It can even be said that what was staged in *Parallel of Life and Art* was left waiting for a definition that would summarise the vital intentions of all the ferments that ran through the different images on display. This is the context in which other discussions about the definition of New Brutalism took place.

The exhibition *Parallel of Life and Art* was reviewed in this light during a debate in June 1954 organised by Hugh Pope at the Architectural Association, to which Peter Smithson and Basil Taylor were invited.[86] The definition of New Brutalism, which began to catalyse general interest, was not developed against the background of the search for a style in architecture, but became, for the first time, directly associated with the visual universe of *Parallel of Life and Art*, defined as 'the aesthetic source of the New Brutalism'. The association of *Parallel of Life and Art* with New Brutalism, however obvious it may seem, marks another decisive moment in its clarification. The Architectural Association event was attended by Peter Smithson, who was both co-author of the exhibition and disseminator of the definition, and thus, in his own person, a carrier of a synthesis of the images selected for the exhibition and the possible meanings attributable to New Brutalism. It is thanks to this event that the cultural intentions and *brutality*

86   Huge Pope, 'Letter on New Brutalism', *Architectural Review*, vol. 115, no. 690 (June 1954): 364.

of the works exhibited in *Parallel of Life and Art* became part of the definition of New Brutalism. Precisely because these works were intended to be 'raw material' in its original state, not masked but rather rendered expressive with all its vital characteristics, some participants at the event tried to include them in the traditional categories of British criticism, thus resorting to the nineteenth-century Picturesque. Pope reported some comments describing the exhibition as 'shallow, eclectic, an example of the New Picturesque and denying the spirituality in man'.[87] The fact that he mocked New Brutalism by referring to it as a derogatory New Picturesque only confirms the extent to which the debate of the 1930s and 1940s laid the expectations for new definitions. Indeed, it was once again the British dimension of the Arts & Craft tradition that emerged as the main characteristic of New Brutalism, as Pope stated: 'New Brutalists, as masters of craft of building'. However, the Architectural Association event makes it clear that New Brutalism risked being reabsorbed into the line of Ruskin and Morris, thus being reduced to a retroactive Pevsnerian impulse anchored to the origins of the Modern Movement, rather than becoming the watchword for creative processes beyond those of the Modern Movement. If the Smithsons were still unsure about aspects of New Brutalism, the outcome of the discussions and reactions from the Architectural Association could only have strengthened their conviction for an 'architecture of reality'.

The kind of conceptual complexity that would affect New Brutalism in its English sense was already taking shape in the discussions, in which New Brutalism was passing from hand to hand. But this climax of appropriations was also what guaranteed New Brutalism's success. Where the definition probably originated, in Asplund's Sweden, the cultural conditions for the emergence of something authoritative in criticism indicating a horizon beyond the Modern Movement evidently did not exist. We should not lose sight of the fact that New Brutalism was taking on the features of a critical category in which the various theoretical and cultural ferments of England in the 1940s and 1950s were reflected, either by contrast or by continuity. And that therefore, New Brutalism, starting with its prefix, could not have the same meaning when adopted in other national and cultural contexts.

In British culture, the meaning of New Brutalism, through this process of gestation, was constantly subject to change. The dimension of the 'ordinary' and the Ruskinian 'basic unit' that characterised the Smithsons' definition of New Brutalism was gradually replaced by a revolutionary and transgressive character.

Banham's first official entry into the syncopated debate on New Brutalism was in June 1954, when he called it into question at a lecture entitled 'Disreputable Elements in Modern Architecture' at the Bartlett School of Architecture.[88] The historiographic hypothesis mentioned in the introduction of 'The New Brutalism' in *Architectural Review* was here re-stated. In proposing a possible way to overcome the crisis of CIAM, Banham reinterpreted the creative principles of 'modern architecture' in the context of the disruptive effect of the artistic phenomena presented in *Parallel of Life and Art*. All this was summed up by Banham in one word: 'disreputability'.[89] Through that word, in Banham's meaning, the 'brutality' and 'Brutal Realism' that accompanied the rise of New Brutalism found their way back into the debates. Through the parameter of 'disreputability', Banham recontextualised the evolution of architecture not in terms of honesty of structure and materials, but in the context of the artistic experiments of the Futurists and Picasso, demonstrating that it was in the category of art that he saw the potential for a renewal of architecture. While Dada, Cubism and

[87] Ibid.
[88] [n.a.], 'Astragal. Disreputable Elements', *Architects' Journal*, vol. 119, no. 3094 (17 June 1954): 723; [n.a.], 'Astragal at the Bartlett', *Architects' Journal*, vol. 120, no. 3096 (1 July 1954): 6; Reyner Banham, 'Astragal at the Bartlett', *Architects' Journal*, vol. 120, no. 3097 (8 July 1954): 36.
[89] Banham, 'Astragal at the Bartlett' (ibid.).

De Stijl had already been defined by the Smithsons as the epicentres of New Brutalism, Banham, on the other hand, discarded, by means of the criterion of 'disreputability', the two avant-garde movements, Cubism and De Stijl, as bearers of an abstract line and, consequently, of the 'academic geometry' that he had set against the affirmation of New Brutalism in April 1954.

'Up, if I may say so, to the New Brutalists!'[90] is the comment that confirms, for the first time in a signed contribution, that Banham saw in New Brutalism a direction for renewal and the potential for overcoming the functionalist principle of 'plan-structure-function' that he would soon better articulate in his famous article.

Johnson's Anti-Design

For about a year after its official appearance in 1953, New Brutalism was only discussed in English circles. First Segal, then Banham, the Smithsons, and finally Pope each added something to the construction of a new critical category, which was nevertheless still uncertain, still struggling to establish itself. Some, including the Smithsons, were even hesitant about its efficacy when considering the alternative 'architecture of reality'. *Parallel of Life and Art* laid the premises for developing the definition of New Brutalism in terms that were increasingly complex and distant from its original roots in *béton brut*, or from the late Ruskinian and Lecorbuserian vision imparted by the Smithsons. Despite their efforts, they did not demonstrate the theoretical strength necessary to describe the revolutionary scope that the definition of New Brutalism would come to have.

But the circulation of *Architectural Review* at an international level ensured the first important transplantation of that uncertain critical shoot into the American theoretical context. The first American architect who picked up the invention of New Brutalism was the one most committed to theoretical reflection, one of the authors of the famous label International Style, one who could only be interested in verifying the validity of a new category to indicate the 'directions' of contemporary architecture: Philip Johnson. Although his position was critical, his observations made a decisive contribution to clarifying design aspects of New Brutalism.

The editors of *Architectural Review* contacted Johnson, 'as an American follower of Mies van der Rohe', for a contribution on the Smithsons' School at Hunstanton, to be published in September 1954 (see figure 19).[91] The choice seems obvious if one considers the neo-Miesian character of that school, which could only be celebrated as such by an architect who until then had claimed to be an epigone of Mies. The magazine's editorial staff composed a two-voice argument, following up Johnson's article with an unsigned commentary, probably written by Banham.[92]

The double intervention thus became an opportunity to discuss New Brutalism and to extend its meaning to questions of design criteria. Whether this was the original intention of the editors or whether it was a consequence of Johnson's comment is a question that remains unresolved for the time being. The two articles by Johnson and Banham on the School at Hunstanton are written within a theoretical framework that the magazine's editors – certainly Banham himself – defined as 'design philosophy' in Johnson's case and 'radical philosophy' in Banham's case. These two different 'philosophies' of design, underpinned by New Brutalism, introduced an operative dimension into the hitherto

[90] Ibid.
[91] Philip Johnson, 'School at Hunstanton. Comment by Philip Johnson as an American Follower of Mies van der Rohe', *Architectural Review*, vol. 116, no. 693 (September 1954): 148; 152.
[92] Although the author of the article is not mentioned, the Smithsons can be completely ruled out because of the note published by the editors of *Architectural Review* at the bottom of N. A. Cowburn's letter in the November 1954 issue: 'In fact none of the prose describing and commenting on the school was by the Smithsons', *Architectural Review*, vol. 116, no. 695 (November 1954): 282. Furthermore, the article presented reasoning that Banham would explain and articulate in his December 1955 article, 'The New Brutalism'.

19 Philip Johnson and Reyner Banham, 'School at Hunstanton, Norfolk', *Architectural Review*, vol. 116, September 1954, no. 693, pp. 152–62

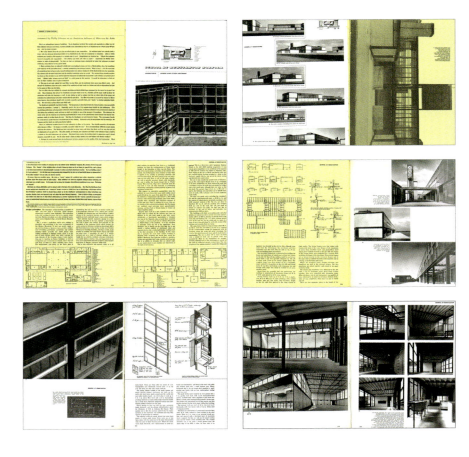

uncertain category that finally revealed New Brutalism's possible application to contemporary architecture. Banham here revealed himself to be a strategist interested in activating New Brutalism as a new and increasingly personal category of criticism.

Johnson's review of the Smithsons' school became the pretext for an intelligent critical operation, which revolved around Miesian composition and its antithesis. The qualities of the School at Hunstanton did not fail to impress Johnson: 'This is an extraordinary group of buildings', he stated without hesitation, and he particularly praised the 'formal, symmetrical' aspects that constitute a variant of Miesian principles: 'The plan is not only radical but good Mies'. The only criticisms concerned the exposed ducts, the imprecise resolution of the angles of the structure, and anything that denied the symmetry and the *a priori* form.

In his closing statements, Johnson contrasted the principles of 'composition', 'formalism' and 'elegance' found in the school with what was emerging as New Brutalism, which he defined as 'an Adolf Loos type of Anti-Design'. Johnson compared the Olympian spaces of Mies with the spatial complexity of Loos, implicitly referring to his *Raumplan* and the spatial organisation based on asymmetries and syntactic disjunctions.[93]

[93] 'Now that the Smithsons have turned against such formalistic and "composed" designs toward an Adolf Loos type of Anti-Design which they call the New Brutalism (a phrase already picked up by the Smithsons' contemporaries to defend atrocities) one wonders whether their new executed work will show the same inherent elegance', Johnson, 'School at Hunstanton. Comment by Philip Johnson as an American Follower of Mies van der Rohe', 152.

Johnson's contribution is crucial because it distinguishes the school, where specific formal criteria can be traced, from New Brutalism. Johnson thus implied that this label removes itself from the essence of design and the rules of classical composition. The opposition between 'composed design' and 'anti-design' is decisive for understanding New Brutalism from the point of view of design criteria, and, specifically, of a composition based on violent juxtapositions of shapeless and unpredictable spaces, such as those of Loos' buildings, which do not respect any Palladian axiality or any criterion of Miesian aulic spaces.

The reference to Loos, however, provides another clue to an early international interpretation of New Brutalism. The House in Soho, the project the Smithsons used to herald New Brutalism, already challenged the concept of perfection and composition. This became even clearer from the reference to Loos. On closer inspection, one could also draw a parallel between Tristan Tzara's house in Paris by Loos and the House in Soho by the Smithsons. The design of both houses expresses the archetypal form of the architrave and follows a composition of the openings dictated by the purpose of the rooms, bordering on disproportion and *ugliness*. However, Johnson seemed to imply more than mere formal coincidences between Loos' practice and the 'attitude' of New Brutalism. Imperfection as an alienating element of design also resonated in a more veiled way. After acknowledging the anti-compositional drift of New Brutalism, Johnson admonished the reader by stating that the definition of New Brutalism was used 'to defend atrocities', unequivocally recalling other 'atrocities', those Le Corbusier identified with the 'atrocious malfaçon', the origin of the concept of *béton brut*.

Johnson's portrayal of the collision between the School at Hunstanton and New Brutalism, between composition and 'anti-design' was so compelling that it would trap English critics, and Banham in particular, in a theoretical tangle difficult to resolve. When Johnson's intervention is taken into account, it becomes clearer why the Smithsons kept the School at Hunstanton away from New Brutalism, relating it instead to the small House in Soho. From this moment on, the cumbersome shadow of Mies appeared on the scene of English New Brutalism, contending with Le Corbusier's violent *brut* for the primacy of the essence hidden behind that definition.

Banham's Radical Philosophy

If Johnson contrasted the 'composed design' of the School at Hunstanton with the 'anti-design' of New Brutalism, for Banham, the school became the paradigm of his first idea of New Brutalism; it illustrated its 'philosophy', its 'principles', indeed its 'canons'. Thus, an inextricable misunderstanding began taking shape about the neo-Miesian category attributed to the school and that of New Brutalism as attributed by Banham. It should be emphasised that New Brutalism was reacting to the very specific circumstance of Johnson's interpretation, rather than becoming a concept critically articulated.

'The architects themselves would certainly disagree with Mr. Johnson's separation of Hunstanton School from the New Brutalism canon, even though the term had not been coined when the school was designed'.[94] This initial statement by Banham is surprising; it refers to 'the architects' of the school and thus suggests a certain alleged agreement between Banham and the Smithsons that the school should be considered expressive of New Brutalism. For Banham, therefore, the School at Hunstanton could not be just any old precedent of New Brutalism but had to become the model of that definition. In elevating it to the status of an emblem of New Brutalism (here Banham wanted to impersonate Oscar Wilde's 'critic as artist'), the school had to demonstrate

---

[94] [Banham], 'School at Hunstanton', 152.

its canons, given that it was the only work built by the Smithsons that could, in some way, play the role of model. Removing the chronological distance between the design of the School at Hunstanton and the year of the Smithsons' use of New Brutalism was thus in itself a sophisticated critical construction, intended to bring English architectural culture onto the international stage by trying to convince the readers of *Architectural Review* that the Smithsons' school was not neo-Miesian at all but was the first masterpiece of New Brutalism.

In taking up Johnson's challenge, Banham concentrated his reading of the school, its 'whole design', on a series of 'design principles', alluding, it would seem, to the other more famous 'principles' that had set up the English debates, those of Wittkower. The New Brutalism that Banham derived from the School at Hunstanton was not limited to a design method summarised by the principle of 'formal legibility' and of a 'new aesthetic of materials'. It also entailed a true 'radical philosophy' by virtue of an ethical principle transcending both the plan and materials, which Banham defined as an 'existential responsibility'. In 'formal legibility' Banham saw a compositional principle dictated by the criterion of 'compactness' and control of circulation, as an alternative to the 'loose disorder' of the LCC Hertfordshire school plan. It should be remembered that the notion of 'legibility' had been advanced by Wittkower as one of the fundamental criteria of Humanist architecture, and it is perhaps no coincidence that the caption of the full-page image of the School at Hunstanton mentioned the 'Palladian formality of its small-scale composition'.

Unlike Johnson, Banham was not interested in retracing the models of inspiration for the school. Banham's intention was on the contrary to demonstrate New Brutalism's charge of novelty, and therefore the Miesian characteristics of the school were neglected in favour of a 'radicalism' in the composition and use of materials. According to Banham, the inner logics of the Modern Movement could still renew themselves through New Brutalism. The tendency towards disproportion, which Johnson had associated with the 'Loos type of Anti-Design', is used by Banham to trace links to peculiar English precedents at the origin of British Modern Movement, identified not in Morris, as did his teacher Pevsner in *Pioneers*, but in Robert Smythson's Hardwick Hall, and William Butterfield's All Saints church in London.[95] Smythson and Butterfield had challenged the canons of the time to the point of becoming 'obtrusive', a characteristic that Banham also ascribes to the School at Hunstanton. What makes the Smithsons' work radical is in fact, according to Banham, 'the unorthodox principle of ruthlessness'. This term had already recently emerged in criticism, when Summerson in 1945 attributed it to Butterfield, by virtue of his inauguration of a new phase in British architecture, hybridising the Gothic Revival professed by Pugin through the polychromy of brick, grotesque and disproportionate forms and the acceptance of 'ugliness'.[96] Banham's intuition in attributing Butterfield's legacy to the definition of New Brutalism would be repeatedly confirmed by critics until the end of the 1960s.[97]

The Smithsons' compositional choice resulted for Banham in a constructive clarity that implied the principle of a 'unique material'. For Banham, this principle was useful for overcoming the abstract dimension of an *a priori* idea, in favour of a vision in which materials are left exposed and can be modelled according to their own intrinsic characteristics. Steel, and not brick, is here infused with this new vision, sharing the same care for materials as in the English tradition. 'Steel used as Queen Anne builders used brick, or Regency engineers used stone,' Banham pointed out.

[95] Elain Harwood, 'Butterfield & Brutalism', *AA Files*, no. 27 (1994): 39–46.
[96] John Summerson, 'William Butterfield, or the Glory of Ugliness, *Architectural Review*, vol. 98 (1945): 166–75.
[97] See, for example, John Summerson, *45–55 Ten Years of British Architecture* (London: Arts Council, 1956); Peter Collins, 'Neo-Butterfield. The New Brutalism: Ethic or Aesthetic (Reyner Banham)', *Progressive Architecture*, vol. 48, no. 3 (March 1967): 198–202.

The acceptance of the nature of materials was for Banham inseparable from the identification of a 'new aesthetic of materials', which imposed not only leaving them exposed, but also using them as they arrived on the building site. The total absence of the processing and finishing of materials and the impossibility of their decorative use were interpreted by Banham as artistic components, bearers of a new foundation concept for the definition of New Brutalism, that of 'as found': 'A valuation like that of the Dadaists, who accepted their materials "as found", a valuation built into the Modern Movement by Moholy-Nagy at the Bauhaus'.

The implementation of the materials according to the 'radical philosophy' of New Brutalism expressed the 'moral load' of the Modern Movement, embodied in the 'existential responsibility' that Banham identified with the conjunction between being and appearing of each component: 'Every element is truly what it appears to be'. If the trajectory of New Brutalism was to end with Banham's own question about 'ethic or aesthetic', it should be noted that in these early arguments there was nothing more than a mutual coincidence of intentions.

With Johnson's intervention and Banham's response, the definition of New Brutalism for the first time specifically concerned the architectural project, its 'formality' and 'design', in which materials were nothing more than its extreme manifestation. New Brutalism's architectural project was here articulated according to a concept of anti-design, that is, an anti-academic composition, which Banham was to discuss and more clearly conceptualise in his 1955 article. In its synthesis of architectural and artistic impulses, New Brutalism was emerging as a new direction in which every kind of cladding and controlled composition was banned, even to the point of accepting disproportion.

It is only in light of this observation that one can understand the ascription of the School at Hunstanton to the definition of New Brutalism, an operation not carried out by the Smithsons, but by Banham in response to Johnson and his concept of 'anti-design'. If one does not carefully consider the critical expedients, sophistries, ironies, reversals, inventions and calculated lies that were devised to sculpt the essence of New Brutalism, one cannot fully understand the perplexities that would arise internationally, where it would be perceived as a national issue entirely belonging to the English debate. But Banham's strength and the authority of *Architectural Review* were such that they conveyed the message of the birth of a new orientation, New Brutalism, demonstrated by a building: the School at Hunstanton. The author of all this was Banham. The Smithsons, although probably kept abreast of the various passages, were to some extent affected by the strategy pursued by the young critic who took the reins of New Brutalism.

Formalism, Roughness and Brutality

Less than a year after the Smithsons' appropriation of the definition of New Brutalism, it was no longer the House in Soho that dictated the parameters of the definition. Following Banham's critical interpretation, the School at Hunstanton catalysed the debate. For critics, the House in Soho would remain an episode, if not totally forgotten, then at least marginal in the trajectory of New Brutalism, and only a few discerning critics would recognise it as the official starting point for the New Brutalism debate. The controversial association between the school and the nascent definition of New Brutalism was commented on by readers of the *Architectural Review* during 1954 and 1955, confirming Banham's lexicon revolving around 'formalism', 'ruthlessness', and 'brutality'.

Nor did *Architects' Journal* miss the opportunity to present New Brutalism according to the composition criteria launched by Johnson and Banham.[98] The geometries dictated by a 'formal', 'extraordinary discipline' and a 'skilful mastery' of systems of proportions gave the building an intrinsic 'elegance'. Those 'unorthodoxies' of the plan and details that had pushed Johnson to distance the school from the definition of New Brutalism then formed the basis of New Brutalism, perhaps by virtue of the 'ruthlessness' that Banham had found central in the new 'attitude'. The obsession with rigorously 'exposed' materials and conduits gave the Smithson's school a markedly industrial character, to the point that the anonymous author of the article in the *Architects' Journal* went so far as to say that 'it is hard to define it as *architecture* at all'.[99]

The appearance of the definition of New Brutalism in *Architectural Review* triggered a correspondence that mostly revealed the scepticism of readers, as confirmed by T. Mellor, who defined New Brutalism as a 'funny column' suitable for entertainment 'for women architects or a page for architect's children'.[100] The School at Hunstanton provoked negative reactions, and readers did not fail to emphasise the crudeness of the building 'completely lacking grace, charm and beauty'.[101]

In light of British concerns over the dimensions of humanism and the Picturesque, the 'formalism' sanctioned as the first 'design principle' by Banham could not but be perceived as outdated, to the point that some readers summarised the proposal of New Brutalism as 'inhuman',[102] with an 'utterly un-English' character.[103] The rigidity of forms of the school contributed to suggest an architecture 'fitted into the mould of a complicated theory', nothing but a 'doctrinaire' architecture; as a reader of *Architectural Design* commented: 'In its crudity it seeks to abandon all the progress we have made towards refining and humanizing our buildings'.[104]

New Brutalism began to be perceived as a self-referential disciplinary reflection, far from the passionate sociological and ideological discussions of contemporary English debates. 'The insistence on the building and nothing but the building'[105] is just one of the considerations that led to the acceptance of a theory of New Brutalism that was far from the Smithsons' professed aspiration for an 'architecture of reality'. It is important to emphasise that in its first phase, New Brutalism was widely perceived as a subtractive process aimed at reducing architecture to structure and material expression, resulting in a 'refined architecture', as Peter Shepheard, director of the Architectural Association, attests in his 1954 opening speech for the academic year: 'Even a brutal building needs to be detailed, and I must say, whatever else I think about the New Brutalism, its exponents do seem to give the most careful thought to refining the appearance of their buildings'.[106]

In response to readers' criticisms of the School at Hunstanton, John Voelcker, a friend of the Smithsons and member of Team X, pointed out other characteristics which recalled the concepts presented in *Parallel of Life and Art*. New Brutalism meant for Voelcker an architecture derived from the articulation of parts, 'unambiguously defined as an identifiable object', summed up in the vision of a 'total idea of

[98] [n.a.], 'The New Brutalism', *Architects' Journal*, vol. 120, no. 3107 (16 September 1954): 336.

[99] Ibid.

[100] T. Mellor, 'New Brutalism', *Architectural Review*, vol. 115, no. 690 (June 1954): 364.

[101] N. A. Cowburn, 'School at Hunstanton', *Architectural Review*, vol. 116, no. 695 (November 1954): 282.

[102] A. Derek and G. de Abbott, 'The New Brutalism', *Architects' Journal*, vol. 120, no. 3108 (23 September 1954): 366.

[103] E. D. Vassiliadis, 'Hunstanton', *Architectural Review*, vol. 117, no. 698 (February 1955): 82.

[104] Alexander Aikman, 'The Hunstanton School', *Architectural Design*, vol. 25, no. 3 (March 1955): 96.

[105] Peter Bereseord, 'Correspondence: School at Hunstanton', *Architectural Review*, vol. 116, no. 695 (November 1954): 282.

[106] Peter Shepheard, 'Inaugural address by President', *Architects' Journal*, vol. 120, no. 3114 (November 1954): (569–70), 567.

the building, an image, a sign'.[107] The logic of the implementation of materials in a 'simple and direct' way strictly derived from the vision of architecture 'as an image', which would soon become a founding concept of the definition of New Brutalism. The resulting architecture, continued Voelcker, can be defined as 'brutal', but only for its rejection of any 'soft materials', alluding, it would seem, to the 'soft architecture' that generated the Softs' first appellation of New Brutalism.

Other members of the Independent Group intervened to support New Brutalism's positive input for international debates, such as the art critic Lawrence Alloway, who was eager to share British cultural vitality with the readers of the American magazine *Art News* by presenting 'a controversial subject among British architects'.[108] 'Heroic' and 'real' are the two extremes of what Alloway ascribed to the scope of New Brutalism: on the one hand the 'heroic' search for truth in structure and materials, and in particular the 'structure exposed internally' and the 'industrial fittings throughout', confirming the Smithsons' first definition based on the House in Soho; and on the other, an association of the concept of 'real' with interests in popular culture and the Independent Group's universe of images, through which architecture could find renewal and vitality. The turn to popular culture was supported by a quote from Peter Smithson reported by Alloway, where Le Corbusier's car aesthetics was interpreted in a pop key: 'The only things that are good any more are racing bicycles, jeeps (not Landrovers), racing cars'. One cannot fail to notice how Alloway's notes, and in particular the association between 'heroic' and 'real' architecture, would be taken up in the 1970s by the Smithsons in their famous motto summing up their vision of architecture: 'Things need to be ordinary and heroic at the same time'.[109] The conceptual connection between heroic and ordinary was also the Smithsons' strategy for the renewal of the Modern Movement, although in their vision the heroic dimension was included and sought after in the ordinary object, as can be deduced from the concept of 'as found'.[110] That ordinary objects can deliver a 'heroic' facet should not be surprising, if we think about the particular British declension of New Monumentality discussed at the end of the 1940s.

Alloway, as an art critic addressing the audience of *Art News*, more familiar with artistic issues than architectural ones, saw *Parallel of Life and Art* as the foundation of New Brutalism. Despite the attempt to unite on that occasion art and architecture, Alloway, apodictically affirmed that New Brutalism had 'no connection with l'*art brut*', perhaps to ward off easy conclusions dictated by assonance.

For the first time New Brutalism was presented as an international 'canon': 'Philip Johnson expressed a bold interest in it. Peter Smithson has discovered a parallel to the New Brutalism, a house by Van den Broek in Rotterdam and Kahn's Art Gallery and Design Center at Yale also appears to fit the anti-style'.[111] The first mention of the Yale Art Gallery in this list, well before Banham's famous article, cannot be overlooked.

But it is through the definition of 'anti-style' that Alloway's vision of New Brutalism needs to be framed, because it placed the Smithsons' cultural ferment in opposition to the notion of style and in line with Duchamp's and Dada's artistic research. In doing so, Alloway demonstrated the extent to which New Brutalism implied a desire for an inclusive process in architecture and a rejection of traditional concepts of beauty, order and composition.

---

[107] John Voelcker, 'Hunstanton Provides a Sense of Location', *Architects' Journal*, vol. 120, no. 3111 (October 1954): 456.

[108] Lawrence Alloway, 'Art News from London', *Art News*, vol. 53, no. 6 (October 1954): 54.

[109] Smithson, 'Without Rhetoric: An Architectural Aesthetic 1955–1972', 72.

[110] Smithson, 'The Heroic Period of Modern Architecture'.

[111] Peter Smithson discussed Van den Broek and Bakema's house in Rotterdam in 'Architect's Own House in Rotterdam', *Architectural Design*, vol. 24, no. 8 (August 1954): 227–30. However, there is no mention of the definition of New Brutalism in this article.

Smithsons' Anti-Art Architecture for a New Aesthetic

While the debate concentrated on the declination of New Brutalism in relation to the School at Hunstanton and the Miesian model, the Smithsons moved away from questions of proportions and composition to focus on the potential of architecture to absorb artistic phenomena within technical and design processes. If we follow the Smithsons' statements, we understand that for them New Brutalism consisted of a 'new theory', which subsumes artistic inputs into architecture: from the 'new attitude' entailing a vitalist vision of materials based on references to Dada to a 'new order' which, on the example of Pollock's action painting, expresses the relationships between parts to overcome traditional composition, and to an 'architecture of reality', which admits pop incursions and extends the architectural project to the urban scale.

In the winter of 1954, the Smithsons returned to New Brutalism. The second issue of *244: Journal of the University of Manchester Architecture and Planning Society* published an interview by Bill Cowburn and Michael Pearson in which the Smithsons specifically reflected on the integration of art and architecture.[112]

The concept of *béton brut* was addressed more precisely here through the pivotal example of the formwork imprints of the Unité in Marseilles. The Smithsons' interpretation of *béton brut* coincided with that of Le Corbusier, bringing New Brutalism closer to Le Corbusier's poetics of *brut* materials. Smithsons' reflections on concrete formwork implied a link between technical devices and the processes happening on the construction site, transformed into artistic phenomena. For the Smithsons, these processes were not part of the traditional synthesis of the arts but were rooted in Dada-derived phenomena assimilated in the concept of 'as found'.

The inclusion of artistic principles in the architectural project did not imply for them a simple juxtaposition of the two disciplines.[113] In their vision, artistic principles had to be absorbed within the process of architecture, from its conception to its construction. This approach was defined by the Smithsons as 'Anti-Art Architecture', which summed up, evoking Duchamp's definition of 'Anti-Art' around 1913, a cultural positioning akin to Dadaists, who had turned art into an inclusive process aimed at abolishing the difference between artistic and everyday practices in favour of a universal concept. In the Dadaist root, and in the association between art and life or, to be more explicit, between art and reality, we find a new confirmation of their research into an 'architecture of reality'.

Through the very concept of 'Anti-Art Architecture', which echoes Johnson's 'anti-design' and Alloway's 'anti-style', the Smithsons affirmed the necessity for an inclusive attitude in contemporary architecture, that is, a practice that admits the influence of popular culture, combining industrial techniques with vernacular traditions and *objets trouvés*, selected as media to express the present: 'Architecture, painting, and sculpture are manifestations of life, satisfying real need; of man and not of each other. They influence each in a poetic way, but are equally and mysteriously influenced by industrial techniques, the cinema, supersonic flight, African villages, and old tin cans'.[114]

---

[112] Bill Cowburn, Michael Pearson, 'Art in Architecture', *244: Journal of the University of Manchester Architecture and Planning Society*, vol. 2 (Winter 1954): 20. This same text, reworked, was also reprinted in June 1959 entitled *Architecture and Art*, untraced, of which the extract can be found in folder E018, Alison and Peter Smithson Special Collection, Loeb Library, Harvard University, Cambridge, USA.

[113] For a more recent analysis of the avant-garde artistic influence on New Brutalism, see, for example, Ben Highmore, *The Art of Brutalism: Rescuing Hope from Catastrophe in 1950s Britain* (New Haven: Yale University Press, 2017); Wojciech Niebrzydowski, 'The Impact of Avant-Garde Art on Brutalist Architecture', *Buildings*, vol. 11, no. 7 (2021): 290.

[114] Cowburn, Pearson, 'Art in Architecture'.

New Brutalism Will Take Many Forms

The growing interest in New Brutalism pushed the editors of *Architectural Design* to ask the Smithsons for a further text explaining their concept, published in January 1955 and considered a sort of manifesto.[115] It was once again thanks to their friendship with Theo Crosby,[116] that the Smithsons were able to publish in the magazine, and their manifesto occupied the space of the monthly editorial. The short introduction, written by Crosby, defined New Brutalism's cultural preamble: 'In 1954, a new and long overdue explosion took place in architectural theory'. In 1954, with the end of the building site of the School at Hunstanton and the definition of New Brutalism already in circulation, Crosby saw the realisation of a 'reaction' to a trend that had been present since the end of the war, represented by the 'Contemporary Style' manifested at the Festival of Britain. This opposition between the definition of New Brutalism as 'movement' and the 'style' of the Festival of Britain brought back the debates that had opposed 'movement' and 'style' during the 1940s.

Unlike Johnson, Crosby described the 'formal proportions' of the School at Hunstanton as being under Wittkower's influence, as one of the cultural extremes within which New Brutalism was defined. Crosby was the first to make the influence of Wittkower's theories on New Brutalism explicit, in a more direct way than Banham's allusions, who had discussed the 'principles' of New Brutalism and the 'Palladian' composition of the school.[117]

The Smithsons' 'manifesto' bears witness to the fact that, after various interventions, they had become aware that New Brutalism could constitute a 'new theory', radically alternative to the various labels discussed by English critics. Although an expression of the same notion of Englishness that preoccupied critics, their 'new theory' was informed by international cultural references – Dada, Pollock, art brut, the inescapable Unité and the emerging pop phenomena – that would overcome the nostalgic sentimentality of the existing proposals. In fact, the Smithsons demonstrated that they were incessantly searching for new references capable of broadening the resonance of New Brutalism, of making it complex, radically 'new' and contemporary.

The manifesto drawn up by the Smithsons again took the form of succinct aphorisms in which they not only expanded their cultural references, but also specified key dates and figures, which provide precious clues for understanding the origin of New Brutalism. Le Corbusier, framed as a pioneer of the twentieth-century architectural revolution, was evoked by the Smithsons to legitimise New Brutalism as the only possible evolution of the Modern Movement.[118] His architecture was representative of an 'image' alternative to their initial Miesian aesthetics.[119] They even went as far as to call Le Corbusier a 'practitioner' of New Brutalism, which entailed recognition by the Smithsons of the *practical* origin of New Brutalism, without the conceptual dimension that they later imprinted on that definition. The appellation therefore reveals that Le Corbusier's *béton brut* was perhaps considered by the Smithsons as a sort of zero degree of New Brutalism.

---

[115] Theo Crosby, Alison and Peter Smithson, 'The New Brutalism', *Architectural Design*, vol. 25, no. 1 (January 1955): 1. It was Banham who recognised the manifesto nature of this article, in Reyner Banham, '4.3 Manifesto', *The New Brutalism: Ethic or Aesthetic?* (London: Architectural Press, 1966), 45–47.

[116] For a recent article on the relationship between the Smithsons and Crosby, see Steve Parnell, *Architectural Design, 1954–1972*; Juliana Kei, 'New Brutalism, Again', *Architecture and Culture*, vol. 7, no. 2 (2019): 271–90.

[117] [Banham]. 'School at Hunstanton'.

[118] Crosby, 'The New Brutalism'.

[119] 'What really actually made New Brutalism a movement was the Marseille Block, that gave an image that could become brutalist architecture', from an interview with Robin Middleton, 21 April 2018, New York.

In their intention to regenerate the foundations of the Modern Movement, the Smithsons included the example of Japanese architecture, which had inspired masters from Wright to Le Corbusier, Behrens and Garnier.[120] Japanese culture was not, however, evoked as a reference for concepts of form or space, as it was for the purist aesthetic, but was considered because of the Smithsons' interest in a vitalism that also irradiates the materials. Through their reference to the film *Gate of Hell*, from 1953, which showed for the first time in colour the built and inhabited reality of traditional Japanese architecture,[121] the Smithsons transformed what was for the masters a reference to abstract forms exemplified by traditional Japanese architecture, into forms and processes related to life, materials, and the use of space. Far from deriving from geometric laws, 'FORM', written in capital letters, became for the Smithsons 'a general conception of life, a sort of reverence for the natural world, and from that for the materials of the built world'.

The reference to Japanese culture also served to distance the Smithsons' view of materials from the sentimentalist and picturesque craft dimension specific to the English context. In order to further distance New Brutalism from a possible Ruskinian revival, the Smithsons pointed to the need to frame materials within an 'intellectual appraisal' that can be traced back to the German culture of the 1920s and 30s. The Smithsons recognised Segal's genealogy outlined a year before in *Architectural Design*: 'As indeed familiars of the early German architects have prompted to remind us'. The Smithsons enriched the German genealogy of New Brutalism by including Hugo Häring's Garkau farm in Scharbeutz (1923–26). In this example the Smithsons saw a notion of 'form' no longer derived from the logic of proportions, but from the plastic expression derived from the articulation of parts. Furthermore, the reference to Häring should be read as an alternative to the Miesian model that had been the backdrop to the School at Hunstanton. In a way, Häring can be considered Mies' alter ego, and his evocation reveals the tendency, recognised from the dawn of New Brutalism, towards an expressionism as intense as that of the Unité, with material characteristics that go beyond the conventions of the International Style.

The School at Hunstanton, following the discussion on whether it belonged to the 'Brutalist canon', was also called into question for the first time by the Smithsons, as it resulted from the mixture of references that justified the affirmation of a 'new theory'. Although the Smithsons referred to the School at Hunstanton, they did not confirm its explicit affiliation to New Brutalism: 'It has been mooted that the Hunstanton School, which probably owes as much to the existence of Japanese Architecture as to Mies, is the first realisation of the New Brutalism in England'.

Ultimately, in the editorial, the Smithsons not only confirmed their position on the Unité as the origin of the 'attitude' they pursued, but for the first time they explicitly associated the definition of New Brutalism with a reflection on the urban scale until now anchored in the concept of 'architecture of reality', and which would become their predominant position during the 1960s. The notion of the 'habitat' had been the focus of their research since the 9th CIAM in 1953 where they had presented their social and urban grids.[122] However, their notion of habitat differed from the one expressed at CIAM, because it was informed by 'ecological, primeval not medieval'

[120] For an in-depth study of the influence of Japanese architecture on the theories of New Brutalism, see Juliana Yat Shun Kei, 'New Brutalism and the Myth of Japan', *Histories of Postwar Architecture*, vol. 2, no. 4 (March 2020): 242–55.

[121] In the text published in *Architectural Design* the reference to the film *Gate of Hell* is placed in a footnote, assuming a posthumous addition by the editors. In the Smithson archive, however, there is a typewritten document that testifies to the Smithsons' mention of the film, see Alison and Peter Smithson, Untitled Document, 2 October 1954, E009, Alison and Peter Smithson Special Collection, Loeb Library, Harvard University, Cambridge, USA.

[122] 'Peasant habitat' is the expression used by the Smithsons in the typescript kept in their archive. The published version is instead 'peasant dwelling forms', in Alison and Peter Smithson, Untitled document, 2 October 1954.

criteria, which were diametrically opposite to the precepts of the Athens Charter.[123] At the root of what the Smithsons saw as New Brutalism's contemporary aspects were clear 'affinities' with spontaneous forms of dwelling, such as 'peasant dwelling forms', referring to processes such as the 1936–37 master plan for Aosta in which the Italian architects BBPR reinterpreted a model of vernacular and spontaneous settlement.[124]

Despite the clarifications made by the Smithsons, often at the urging of journals, there was always a certain tension around the definition of New Brutalism, which did not adapt to a precise codification. The Smithsons also kept a certain distance from Banham who, acting from within a circle of friends, tried to channel New Brutalism towards a more historically based direction, explained through design principles. The Smithsons' definition of New Brutalism needs to be seen not as a static entity, but as an evolving concept, potentially mutable and unrecognisable. 'New Brutalism looks for roots not in a past style:life:philosophy, but in this moment of life. It will take many forms because of this finding moment', reads the preparatory typescript of the article.[125] The tendency to identify in New Brutalism a constantly changing attitude calls into question the concept of 'formal proportions', towards a disarticulation of the composition, where the various parts of the programme are allowed their own formal autonomy, even to the point of disproportion. In the concept of 'finding moment', the Miesian line of control of image and form is denied, confirming the discovery of the concept of 'as found' and the desire to respond in a 'specific way to a specific situation'. The rhetoric of the Smithsons was not bound to a single image, nor to a precise style or material, nor to a specific scale of the project, but described an 'attitude', identified with New Brutalism, at the service of society.

What was emerging was a definition of New Brutalism with vitalist and processual overtones that could not be resolved through a single form. The definition was thus destined to remain essentially ineffable within the parameters of a critique that was constantly seeking to bring together a series of categories into one style. On this occasion, when the Smithsons were called upon to take a position, all they did was to confirm the indefinability and uncertainty of the definition, carefully avoiding the setting of precepts.

This contribution resulted in the dissolution of certain references, such as the Wittkowerian theories and the Hunstanton school model. In doing so, the Smithsons questioned the certainties, through a critical operation that could appear as a desire to prevent the critics, and indirectly Banham, from giving that definition an identity derived from personal interests. One might even go so far as to read a latent conflict between the intellectual line of the Smithsons, who persisted in avoiding a clear definition, and Banham's attempts to circumscribe it. On the other hand, in the Smithsons' notes one cannot help but observe a certain distance from Banham's statements, both from his ascription of the School at Hunstanton to New Brutalism and from the 'formal legibility' put forward by Banham as his first 'design philosophy'. Deliberately sceptical of Banham's interpretation, the Smithsons created the premises for a definition intentionally excluded from the critics' game of wanting to crystallise events in progress into definitions of principles. The formulation of New Brutalism, as forged by the Smithsons, reveals its nature as an aspiration for a movement generated by architects, nourished by constant and processual design experiments, capable of bringing together antithetical models. In contrast, within a few months Banham's strategy would be diametrically opposed, when he would successfully enunciate the criteria of New Brutalism.

---

[123] Ibid.
[124] The master plan for Aosta by the BBPR is only mentioned in the typescript version, ibid.
[125] Ibid.

The Case of the School at Hunstanton

Despite the positions of the Smithsons, the School at Hunstanton ended up being a key building in the articulation of an English vision of New Brutalism. The search for a built example for the architecture of New Brutalism had been directed towards the Smithsons' school, which remained at the centre of the discussion, thus inaugurating all the consequent ambivalence linked to the Miesian model.

After the hesitations shown in the editorial of *Architectural Design*, the Smithsons were specifically called upon to clarify the ascription of the school to New Brutalism, when they were contacted by the editorial staff of the Swedish magazine *Byggmäs-taren*, which sent them a series of questions formulated by Maya Hambly.[126] It is not surprising that the magazine was interested in learning the principles of a definition that was supposed to have been invented in Sweden, by directly questioning the protagonists of its public diffusion. Although in their first definition of New Brutalism based on the House in Soho the Smithsons had underlined an implicit affinity with the Villa Göth, the fate of that definition seemed profoundly changed when framed in the perspective of the Miesian model of the school.

The series of questions posed by the magazine are identifiable through the Smithsons' answers prepared in a typewritten document dated 7 March 1955 entitled 'Answer to Questions', published in Swedish at the foot of Maya Hambly's article.[127] The Smithsons were asked to assess the relationship of the School at Hunstanton to New Brutalism, as well as the influence of the Miesian model in their work. From the repeated erasures in the document, it is evident how reluctant the Smithsons were to confirm adherence of the School at Hunstanton to the 'new theory'. At one point in their reasoning, they seem to conclude that the attribution took place by virtue of the specific vision of materials which corresponds to New Brutalism. However, they were not satisfied with this conclusion and therefore deleted it (see figure 20). The debate inaugurated by Johnson, who had distanced the building from New Brutalism, while Banham had confirmed its affiliation, entailed a complex path for the Smithsons as well, who ended up crediting Banham's indication. The uncertainties, however, demonstrate the protagonists' hesitation and the ineffability of New Brutalism, which they themselves always refused to circumscribe precisely:

1. Hunstanton School is ~~only~~ an expression of the New Brutalism ~~in its handling of materials~~.
2. We went to Mies for the vocabulary of the elements but not their formal expression ~~in its most recent buildings~~. [...] We are not rejecting the steel and glass idiom for something new: we consider all materials valid.[128]

In this short text the Smithsons confirmed 1952 as the crucial year for the origin of New Brutalism, most likely referring to the end of the Marseille construction site. Indeed, this testifies to the profound significance of a building that for the Smithsons marked the transition to a second phase of the Modern Movement, as they repeatedly stated.

The Smithsons gave further confirmation of the origin of the definition of New Brutalism within the Scandinavian debate, thus providing decisive evidence, as the question of the origins of the definition has continued to preoccupy historians to this day. In recognising the existence of an original definition used to describe other

[126] Maya Hambly, 'En ny engelsk skola', *Byggmästaren*, vol. 34, no. A6 (June 1955): 159–62.
[127] Alison Smithson, 'Answer to Questions', 7 March 1955, E009, Alison and Peter Smithson Special Collection, Loeb Library, Harvard University, Cambridge, USA.
[128] Ibid.

20 Alison and Peter
Smithson, 'Answer
to Questions', typescript
with corrections for
Byggmastaren, 7 March
1955, Alison and Peter
Smithson Archive, Folder
E009. Courtesy of
the Frances Loeb Library.
Harvard University
Graduate School of
Design

ANSWERS TO QUESTIONS

1) Hunstanton School is only an expression of the New Brutalism in the handling of materials.

2) We went to Mies for the vocabulary of the elements but not their formal expression as his most recent buildings are . It is the difference in the formal expression that is the difference between the first period of Modern Architecture and the second period which began about 1952 We are not rejecting the steel and glass idiom for something new: we consider all materials valid.

3) We naturally acknowledge our debt to Mies and all the leaders of the Modern Movement. We are in the happy position of being able to look at architecture as the expression of the Modern Movement whereas the first generation of architects had to look to ships bridges,silos and briar pipes.

*aml
7-3-55*

buildings by Scandinavian architects, they underlined the absence, in the case of Neo-Brutalism, of a statement of intent and of precise examples expressive of a theory: 'Some confusion exists in England as to the link between the New Brutalism and a similar term which has been applied to work by Scandinavian architects. Several names are mentioned in this connection but there seems to have been no clear verbal or plastic statement'.[129]

The founding 'expression' of New Brutalism was here identified in an 'anti-academic attitude', starting from a particular vision of materials, of which Le Corbusier's *béton brut* was again quoted as the first example, subsequently declined in other buildings such as the Ronchamp Chapel and the Maisons Jaoul. Due to its materiality and size, the Maisons Jaoul would mark the course of New Brutalism and serve to confirm Smithson's hypotheses advanced with the House in Soho. The principle of 'anti-academic' was subsequently extended to the composition, as Voelcker had already stressed. It is the definition of 'natural order', advanced as a possible variation of 'new order', that would become the starting point of a composition based on

[129] Alison Smithson, 'New Brutalism', typescript, 7 March 1955, E009, Alison and Peter Smithson Special Collection, Loeb Library, Harvard University, Cambridge, USA.

the articulation of forms, going beyond the limits of the individual building to the urban scale. Examples of this attitude were found by the Smithsons in the buildings of Häring, but also in those by Paul Rudolph in Florida and particularly by Aalto, who also demonstrated how the materials of New Brutalism extended beyond concrete to include brick and wood.[130]

The conclusion is provocative and confirms the Smithsons' ability to define and contradict at the same time. In a problematic and conflicting tension, the Smithsons left the definition in suspense, and moved on to give further evidence of 'a new way of thinking', established on the models of Ronchamp and the Unité in Marseilles, and Aalto's Saynätsälo urban centre: the first two for their 'rough and ready' aesthetics of *béton brut* and the second for its 'ecological' conception of the urban habitat, capable of translating the relationship between an individual and community into the 'new complexity' of the contemporary era.[131]

From the examples of Aalto and Le Corbusier came the search for a 'new aesthetic' identified with the essence of what for them corresponded to New Brutalism: 'The new aesthetic starts again with life and with a love of materials. It tries to sum up the very nature of materials and the techniques with which they are put together, and, in an altogether natural way establishes a unity between the built form and the men using it'. Again, the categories of 'shelter' and 'environment', introduced for the presentation of the House in Soho, remained central to the Smithsons' discourse.

Piranesi and Mies in Blake's New Brutalism

The Smithson's various interventions did not have the strength to shift the discussion of New Brutalism to models other than the School at Hunstanton, which continued to dictate the definition's parameters of interpretation.

The irrefutable Miesian model and Johnson's stance prompted other critics active in the United States to take an interest in the definition. American critics and journals, more interested in discussing architecture in its constructive, technological and physical sense, rarely advanced critical assessments in international theoretical debates. However, the vigorous debate on the fate of the International Style and its possible evolutions cannot be overlooked. While during the 1920s and 1930s the principles of Hitchcock and Johnson served as a theoretical input for the debate, during the 1950s those same principles crystallised into a series of rules perceived by architects as rigid and dogmatic, against which the search for new directions arose. New Brutalism happened to be assimilated into an unpredictable series of critical contexts, even though the definition was contaminated by concepts rooted in European culture, unsuitable for fully pervading the American discourse. Critics would have a varied reaction to New Brutalism, especially because they were affirming their own autonomy in outlining a path between a reaction to the International Style and the potential for renewal alluded to by the concepts of New Brutalism, such as the end of cladding and a new vision of ornament dependent on constructive processes.

However, all ethical impulses would be left aside by American culture in the process of appropriating the definition of New Brutalism, which would be reduced to concrete finishing and compositional questions concerning both the design of the plan and a process of articulation of the parts, demonstrating the intention to find, even through the definition itself, the essence of another international style.

[130] Ibid.
[131] Alison and Peter Smithson, 'The Built World: Urban Reidentification', *Architectural Design*, vol. 25, no. 6 (June 1955): 185–88.

21 Peter Blake,
'Three approaches
to architecture.
1. The New Brutalism',
Architectural Forum,
vol. 102, May 1955,
no. 5, pp. 142–45

New Brutalism was presented as one of the three possible trajectories of contemporary architecture by the American magazine *Architectural Forum*, in May 1955, in an article entitled 'Three Approaches to Architecture' (see figure 21). The autor was Peter Blake, a German architect and critic, who had fled to England to escape Nazism and then moved to the United States in the 1940s, where he graduated in architecture from the University of Pennsylvania, before working for a short period in Kahn's office.[132]

132 [Peter Blake], 'Three Approaches to Architecture', *Architectural Forum*, vol. 102, no. 5 (May 1955): 142–45. The author Peter Blake (born Peter Jost Blach) is mentioned in the bibliography archived by the Smithsons, Bibliography of New Brutalism and General Information Concerning Alison and Peter Smithson, folder E0001, Alison and Peter Smithson Special Collection, Loeb Library, Harvard University, Cambridge, USA.

Blake's was the second contribution to be published in an American magazine, after Alloway's article in *Art News*, thus demonstrating a growing interest in European debates. Starting in 1953, *Architectural Forum* inaugurated a discussion column entitled 'Architectural Trends', beginning with Eero Saarinen's famous article 'The Six Broad Currents of Modern Architecture', followed by Robert Woods Kennedy's 'After the International Style', Paul Rudolph's 'The Changing Philosophy of Architecture', and finally Walter Gropius's 'Eight Steps toward a Solid Architecture', which harshly criticised the proliferation of new stylistic labels in the current debate, guilty of crystallising ongoing processes into arid critical categories.[133]

Blake presented New Brutalism as one of the three possible facets of 'modern style'. The aim was to measure the European debates against other current American trends, such as 'Modern classicism', identified with Johnson's extension of the MoMA in New York, and international ones, such as 'romantic realism' associated with George Nakashima's timber structures. Only one work was presented to the American public as an example of New Brutalism – the School at Hunstanton. Undoubtedly, Blake carefully read the article by Johnson and Banham published in the *Architectural Review*, as well as the Smithson's commentary on the school in September 1953, as evidenced by several faithful quotations. Unlike Segal, Banham or the Smithsons, Blake's New Brutalism was not framed within a historical or conceptual vision, but was explained through its more operational precepts, limited to the visibility of structure, the use of materials and its compositional rules.

Blake was careful to present New Brutalism according to parameters that belonged to American culture, such as the concept of 'monumental', 'classic', 'elegance' and 'lightness', which he traced back to the American works of Mies. But instead of dwelling, like Johnson, on the geometric and rigorous principles that characterised the school, Blake concentrated on the elements that betrayed the apparent 'classical' image. The Miesian model was thus read in negative in the School at Hunstanton, where its architecture, from structure to composition to materials, revealed the Smithsons' intention to 'offer their meat raw'.

Blake also explained more complex concepts such as that of 'as found', purged of the Dadaist or Surrealist components advanced by Banham and the Smithsons. He dismissed it as an approach to the use of materials in their natural state and as a compositional system: 'They handle the plan as they found it, not smoothing it out. They profoundly handle their materials as they found them, too: in other words, just as they come from stock'.

Blake's contribution highlights the contradictions emerging in the English debate, the key terms of which are used to express their inadequacy: while the school seems to be driven by a principle of 'formalism' and 'Palladian' proportions, the treatment of materials delivers an effect of 'rawness' and 'romance', and although at first glance the volumes may seem 'pure' and 'classical', the acrobatic superimpositions and spatial interpenetrations reveal effects of 'weirdness' and 'drama'.

In the composition based on the juxtaposition between the parts and a rejection of 'prettiness', Blake saw not only a radical departure from the Miesian model, but also the charge of novelty contained within New Brutalism, which opens up to a dimension of 'effects of dream-fantasy': 'At first look this building is classically simple, symmetrical, stripped; it says "less is more". [...] At a second look, horns and cleft hoof poke through the innocent classical robe. This is not simple elegant modern at all, at

[133] Eero Saarinen, 'The Six Broad Currents of Modern Architecture', *Architectural Forum*, vol. 99, no. 1 (July 1953): 110–15; Robert Woods Kennedy, 'After the International Style – Then What?', *Architectural Forum*, vol. 99, no. 3 (September 1953): 130–33, 186–90; Walter Gropius, 'Eight Steps Toward a Solid Architecture', *Architectural Forum*, vol. 100, no. 2 (February 1954): 156–57; Paul Rudolph, 'The Changing Philosophy of Architecture', *Architectural Forum*, vol. 101, no. 1 (July 1954): 120–21.

all'. The dimension of the fantastic suggested to Blake an interpretation of the space of the hall with Piranesian traits, in which concrete beams, a metal structure, ducts left strictly exposed, continuous skylight windows all contribute to the definition of a 'new brutal interior': 'A Piranesian trick within Miesian space'.[134]

Futurist Connections for a 'Mechanistic Brutalism'

At this point in time, certain traits attributable to New Brutalism were starting to become more understandable and identifiable. The Smithsons still defended an open concept of New Brutalism, devoid of any dogma or principles, which proceeded and evolved as 'attitude', 'theory' and 'idea' and which could therefore extend from materials to the urban dimension. Critics, on the other hand, sought to specify New Brutalism's design principles and genealogy, going on to identify antecedents capable of conferring some authority on an emergent New Brutalism. The various interventions contributed to the elaboration of one or more possible New Brutalisms, to which, from time to time, in addition to the solid epicentre of Le Corbusier, new protagonists were ascribed, such as Meyer, Wright, Häring or Mies, confirming its malleable and expandible borders.

In its evolution, New Brutalism would become a label progressively defined by the personal interests of the critics discussing it. An example of this process of appropriation is, again, the case of Banham. At this time he was revising the 'pioneers' of the Modern Movement through his doctoral thesis, in which Futurism became a pivotal cultural epicentre to mark his distance from the historiographic reconstruction of his teacher Pevsner, as well as of authors such as Giedion and Mumford, who had reduced Futurism to a secondary episode.[135]

In the wake of the New Art History model, Banham's multiple interventions were marked by a continuous reinterpretation of historical events in close connection with current phenomena, a twofold intent that aimed on the one hand to revitalise history and on the other to legitimise the present. In this exchange between history and contemporary design, New Brutalism was for Banham an opportunity to introduce a connection that not only supported the relevance of his research, but also strongly rooted the trajectory of New Brutalism in the avant-garde. Banham's research on Futurism carried a mechanistic view of architecture and the consequent foundation of a new 'machine aesthetic'. When the Smithsons had identified Dada and Cubism as the cultural premises for New Brutalism, Banham had latched on to 'disreputability' as the characteristic intellectual attitude defended by the Smithsons. The upheaval of conventional aesthetics staged in *Parallel of Life and Art* had also confirmed for Banham the necessity of a new aesthetics carrying contemporary values for a 'second machine age'. In Banham's logic informed by his research on Futurism, the serial production of consumer goods must lead to a new aesthetic resulting from the notion of 'expendability', where the multitude of signs and symbols that belong to the popular and consumerist language, from American car design to science fiction, should find their way into architecture.[136] Hence, through affinities with Futurism, Banham intended to consolidate that anti-academic and 'anti-art' vision which represented a subversive potential towards traditional artistic values.[137]

---

[134] [Blake], 'Three Approaches to Architecture'.

[135] Lewis Mumford, *Art and Technics* (New York: Columbia Press, 1952), 54; Sigfried Giedion, *Space, Time and Architecture* (Cambridge: Harvard University Press, 1941).

[136] Reyner Banham, 'Space for Decoration', *Design*, vol. 79 (July 1955): 24–25.

[137] 'Of particular importance was Banham's interest in the Futurist painter Boccioni, who, in pursuing an artistic response unique to the new conditions of the twentieth century, he said had become the father of anti-art'. In his book *Pittura Scultura Futurista*, Boccioni wrote: 'We will put into the resulting vacuum all the germs of the power that are to be found in the example of primitives and barbarians of every race, and in the rudiments of that new sensibility emerging in all the anti-artistic manifestations of our epoch-café-chantant, gramophone, cinema, electric advertising, mechanistic architecture, skyscrapers, night-life, speed, automobiles, airplanes and so forth', in Lawrence Alloway, 'The Arts and the Mass Media', *Architectural Design*, vol. 28 (February 1958): 84–85.

In his first article dedicated to Futurism, published in the *Architectural Review* in May 1955, Banham examined the projects of Antonio Sant'Elia as an example for the integration of both aesthetic and mechanical demands of the technological era into an anti-classical and symbolic vision.[138] Banham took the opportunity to associate the question of New Brutalism with a 'mechanicist' characteristic that he attributed to the School at Hunstanton. In quoting passages from the *Manifesto of Futurist Architecture*, translated by himself, Banham dwelled on the principle of the renunciation of cladding and the affirmation of the visibility of the structure, which in Futurist architecture favoured the affirmation of a new aesthetic of the machine. It should be noted that the Futurist-informed 'machine aesthetic' radically differed from Purist and Le Corbusier's concepts, because it admitted the value of ugliness.

In his English translation of a crucial passage in the *Manifesto for Futurist Architecture*, Banham distorted the Italian term '*brutta*' and replaced it with the English adjective 'brutal' to express the congenital beauty of a house stripped of all ornament and reduced to the pure expression of its lines and its 'mechanical simplicity'. The use of the adjective 'brutal', evocative of the contemporary debate, was aimed not only at a deliberate actualisation of the Futurist aesthetic, but also conferred a particular legitimacy on New Brutalism itself: 'The reader who has been hanging on to his hat in the gale of prophecy [...] will have noted the [...] mechanicist brutalism nearly forty years before Hunstanton'.[139] By consciously translating 'ugly' as 'brutal', Banham resolved the Smithsons' intention for a truth of structure and material in a machinistic aesthetic.[140] That 'ugliness' already recognised by Banham as a possible aesthetic declination of New Brutalism through Butterfield, here found another legitimation through Sant'Elia and Marinetti. Thus, just as Segal had identified in Hannes Meyer the 'generator' of a certain Brutalism on the principle of 'nakedness', Banham traced the roots of a 'mechanistic' Brutalism back to the figure of Sant'Elia.

Banham would never abandon the idea that New Brutalism should be a wide-ranging critical reflection on contemporary culture, informed by a multitude of impulses and theories ranging from non-Aristotelian logic to American sociology and cybernetics, capable of challenging the canons of the Modern Movement through the definition of a complex and constantly changing aesthetic because it was 'expendable'. It was precisely this 1955 intuition of a 'brutalist mechanicist' that would become one of the two possible trajectories capable of reviving a New Brutalism that, in 1966, would find itself in agony.

Stirling and the Primitive Aesthetics, or the Maisons Jaoul Model

Only two years after the Smithsons' official presentation of New Brutalism, Mies and Le Corbusier were the two masters who were constantly referenced. In the plain opposition between these two figures, a British theoretical conception emerged that saw in the definition of New Brutalism the coexistence of contrasting aspects, which were at times relegated to an opposition and at others resolved in a conceptual synthesis. Miesian 'formalism' and Lecorbuserian 'roughness' seemed to define a conceptual alchemy whose traits were still unresolved, but which contained an ambivalence that would endure in

---

[138] Reyner Banham, 'Sant'Elia', *Architectural Review*, vol. 117, no. 701 (May 1955): 84–93.
[139] Ibid.
[140] The mechanistic line leading from the Futurists to the School at Hunstanton was the result of an immediate – and momentary – intuition. This is evidenced by the fact that the translation of 'ugly' with 'brutal' only occurred in the article for *Architectural Review*, and that in the writing of his doctoral thesis, all critical reference to contemporary architecture, and to Hunstanton, would be forgotten. See Reyner Banham, *The Theory of Modern Architecture 1907–1927*, PhD Thesis, University of London, Courtauld Institute of Art, 1958. Courtauld Institute THESES A680 BAN. The thesis was later published as *Theory and Design in the First Machine Age* (London: Architectural Press, 1960).

the theoretical evolution of New Brutalism. Le Corbusier's intense post-war production meant that each one of his buildings, from the Unité in Marseilles to the Maisons Jaoul and the Ronchamp Chapel, took on the role of a paradigm for evaluating the course of the Modern Movement. It is with this in mind that James Stirling measured the crisis of rationalism in order to understand the current state of architecture through the analysis of Le Corbusier's works, and in particular the Maisons Jaoul.

Stirling's view of the Modern Movement was influenced by his education under Rowe at Liverpool University School of Architecture. He adopted Rowe's binary approach in analysing architecture according to dichotomies, which in his case crystallised on the axis of technology-art, where 'technology' indicates the objectivity of engineering practice and 'art' the subjective and experimental dimension. It is through this dichotomy that Stirling revealed in contemporary architecture two opposing models: the Unité in Marseilles and the Lever House by SOM, both completed in 1952, whose apparently irreconcilable aesthetics would later surprisingly find a synthesis in the definition of New Brutalism. As for the Smithsons, the year 1952 became for Stirling the crucial date elected as a watershed in the Modern Movement: on the one hand the 'rough', 'primitive' and 'heroic' aesthetics of the Unité d'Habitation, and on the other the Miesian model of steel and curtain wall of the Lever House. This opposition, particularly felt by young architects, summed up a decisive generational stance. 'All young architects must recognise this split and take a definite attitude towards it, decide which side they are on', Stirling wrote in 1953 about the contrast between the Lever House and the Unité.[141]

In this reasoning on the masters, models and epigones of the Modern Movement, Stirling raised the question of the intrinsic value of New Brutalism, writing important reflections in his notebook of what he recognised as a 'European phenomenon'. Stirling even framed New Brutalism in opposition to technology and compositional principles and reduced it to a mere plastic search for forms not subjected to compositional rules. He illustrated his notes with diagrams highlighting the problematic relationships between art and technology, according to the classical-romantic dichotomy. New Brutalism was placed in the 'romantic' category, due to the imperfectionist traits of the surface and schizophrenic forms.

What emerged through Stirling's annotations and articles is a substantial divergence from the Smithsons' positions. It is not the mighty dimension of the Unité, nor Aalto's urban scale, nor even Mies's aulic space that Stirling included in New Brutalism, which, by virtue of the search for a plastic and finite space, ends up being exemplified by buildings of a contained and domestic size, such as Wogenscky's and Bakema's houses.[142] In this context, it is almost a coincidence that the reasoning on alternative principles within the Modern Movement, which in the case of the Smithsons led to the definition of New Brutalism, was also conducted by Stirling through a reflection on the domestic dimension of the single-family house.

The pivotal example presented by Stirling to illustrate the 'romantic' category is Bakema's house in Rotterdam, which Peter Smithson had presented in the pages of *Architectural Design* in 1954, and Alloway had consequently ascribed to New Brutalism.[143] In Bakema's example, the bricks of the load-bearing walls plastered to look like

[141] Mark Crinson (ed.), *James Stirling: Early Unpublished Writings on Architecture* (London: Routledge, 2010), 58–60. In his commentary on the Ronchamp Chapel, Stirling reiterates this opposition, in James Stirling, 'Ronchamp: Le Corbusier's Chapel and the Crisis of Rationalism', *Architectural Review*, vol. 191 (March 1956): 155–61.

[142] 'The division between constructivist (rational) and plastic (brutal) architecture is becoming more marked, the latest example being the Wogensky house. Brutalism is becoming a European phenomenon, and characteristics would appear to be no plan, material finishes, enclosed space, less interior-exterior space punctuation, not necessarily a natural structure, nor the expression of functionalism – frequently anti-technological', James Frazer Stirling, 'The Black Notebook', in Crinson (ed.), *James Stirling: Early Unpublished Writings on Architecture*, 55.

[143] Peter Smithson, 'Modern Architecture in Holland', *Architectural Design*, vol. 24, no. 8 (August 1954): 225–29; Smithson, 'Architect's Own House in Rotterdam'; Alloway, 'Art News from London' (ibid.).

concrete, suggested an idealisation of architecture in the name of an artificially produced aesthetic of the *non-finito*.

In measuring the evolution of the Modern Movement not only through the acclaimed examples of the Lever House and the Unité, but also through the domestic scale, Stirling examined the case of the Maisons Jaoul, which was to become emblematic not only for the trajectory of New Brutalism, but also for its own architectural production. While the Smithsons had recognised the essence of an 'anti-academic attitude' that confirmed the success of New Brutalism, for Stirling, the Maisons Jaoul were but a symptom of an unstoppable crisis of rationalism and a tendency towards a romantic and unattainable *non-finito*, which translated into sculptural emphasis and vernacular tendencies.[144]

The attention and interest that the Maisons Jaoul model aroused in the English context must be read against the backdrop of the debates on the search for a 'new humanism' and the visual campaign launched by *Architectural Review*. Isn't it the same material and regionalist expressiveness that Le Corbusier staged in the Maisons Jaoul – almost as if to concretise that 'neo-Ruskinism' so eagerly awaited by critics? And so, in having included the Maisons Jaoul within the trajectory of New Brutalism, weren't the Smithsons perhaps confirming, despite the foreign example, a profoundly British root? It also suggests that in their choice of domestic scale British architects were seeking the definition of a new style, which, from Villa Göth to the House in Soho, from Bakema's house to Wogenscky's, inevitably intersected with another example by Le Corbusier, the Maisons Jaoul. In this building, hopes were pinned on the demonstration of a possible contemporary version of the nineteenth-century Arts and Crafts model that English culture was still struggling to free itself from.

In the article 'Garches to Jaoul', Stirling compared the two works according to the method of his master Rowe and oriented the debate according to a binary comparison.[145] Stirling analysed the evolution from a model of abstraction, identified in the same example of the Villa at Garches used by Rowe to reaffirm the absoluteness of classical principles, to a particular material treatment visible in the Maisons Jaoul. Stirling's dissatisfaction with the Maisons Jaoul derives from Le Corbusier's abandonment of the technological and formal aspects visible in Garches, in favour of a non-technological and romantic expressiveness (see figure 22).

In 'Garches to Jaoul', Stirling aimed to shift the focus of the debate from the current outcomes of the crisis of the Modern Movement, visible in the model of the Maisons Jaoul, towards the search for foundations and origins that would allow the resurgence of technological and rationalist principles. On the contrary, the Maisons Jaoul's 'massive' and 'primitive' characteristics provided a dramatic contrast between the 'rational' features of the villa in Garches and the 'personal' ones of the Maisons Jaoul, in a tight confrontation between abstraction and materiality. It is not surprising, then, that the terms used by Stirling were purely material and at times pictorial, perhaps to accentuate the 'art-architecture' trend he defined, to the point that surfaces become 'impasto', ready to record 'variety and richness of surface' through 'unexpected' finishes that turn bricks and concrete into a 'surface depth'.

When seen in Stirling's personal trajectory, the contrast between Garches and Jaoul makes explicit his quest for a different evolution of the Modern Movement to the one hoped for by the Smithsons. The new direction of architecture, for Stirling, was only tangentially concerned with the concept of surface and material finishing, and ultimately did not coincide with the violent, 'as found' finish produced on site

[144] James Frazer Stirling, 'Garches to Jaoul', *Architectural Review*, vol. 118, no. 705 (September 1955): 145–51; Stirling, 'Ronchamp, Le Corbusier's Chapel and the Crisis of Rationalism'; James Frazer Stirling, 'Young Architects. A Personal View of the Present Situation', *Architectural Design*, vol. 28, no. 6 (June 1958): 232–40.
[145] Stirling, 'Garches to Jaoul'.

22 James Stirling, 'From Garches to Jaoul', *Architectural Review*, vol. 118, September 1955, no. 705, p. 149

and visible in the Maisons Jaoul because he judged the brickwork 'poor' by British standards. When the model of the Maisons Jaoul, and in particular the use of exposed bricks and concrete beams, became an aesthetic reference for post-war English architecture, as demonstrated by Stirling himself in the flats at Ham Common, the very material characteristics highlighted by Stirling would be associated with the definition of New Brutalism.

However, New Brutalism was a definition Stirling carefully avoided, despite identifying its roots in the trajectory of the Modern Movement. Stirling's silence on the issues of New Brutalism in regard to the Maisons Jaoul confirms a line of critics and actors who chose not to go into the merits of ongoing debates, as indeed his own master Rowe was demonstrating, despite being one of the most important post-war British critics. As the Smithsons had already identified in the Maisons Jaoul a new form of the Modern Movement,[146] Stirling's silence was therefore significant, even controversial, and heralded the refusal he would express in a few years regarding the definition. As an architect protagonist of the debate, Stirling demonstrated that he was not concerned with the definition of new labels and did not want to discuss issues that, as his notes imply, concerned intellectual rather than constructive or design aspects.

[146] Hambly, 'En ny engelsk skola'.

chapter four
banham's memorable article

A Category of the New Art History

Up until the autumn of 1955, New Brutalism was being defined and gaining significance in close relation to the projects and contributions of the Smithsons, but the intervention of Banham drastically changed the fate of this concept. Despite his initial timid intrusion in the discussions on New Brutalism, his ambition to frame the cultural phenomena of the 1950s drove him to remain inextricably linked to the historiography of New Brutalism.

Probably due to the Smithsons' inability to turn New Brutalism into the long-awaited 'new theory', Banham took advantage of a critical gap in the debate to define principles, indicate trajectories, confirm models and launch scathing invectives through a rhetoric that prevented any conciliation. Banham's intervention would have the merit of seeking initial redemption for a New Brutalism that already appeared partially nostalgic, or 'romantic', to use Stirling's words, and that had a deep connection to the principles of the early Modern Movement which destabilised the value of the prefix 'New'. But no nostalgia survived in Banham's theoretical framework, in which New Brutalism would instead be transfigured through contemporary artistic and avant-garde ferments.

Despite his previous forays into the New Brutalist debate, through two unsigned articles (the commentary on the School at Hunstanton and *Architectural Review*'s 'Future' column), the review of *Parallel of Life and Art*, and a series of letters sent to magazines, Banham had at that point not emerged as a protagonist of the debates. His personal interests in revising the Modern Movement through avant-garde trends excluded from canonical historiography would push him to appropriate the ongoing debates on New Brutalism. As he had already demonstrated in some, albeit brief, contributions, Banham was looking for alternative principles to the aesthetic compromises of New Humanism or New Empiricism, and to the theories of Townscape and Picturesque advocated, among others, by his mentor Pevsner. His articles during the years 1953–55 focused on the Futurists, Erich Mendelsohn, the aesthetics of the machine and mass culture, without forgetting his active involvement in the organisation of events that marked the London debates, such as the exhibition *Man, Machine and Motion*, as well as the various lectures held at the ICA.[1]

In the historical perspective, Banham aspired to identify a formula that, although in continuity with the principles of the Modern Movement, could condense and act in the contemporary cultural context. He was not far, in this intention, from the aspirations that in 1955 pushed various other critics to measure the evolution of the Modern Movement through the parameters of a single architect, such as Stirling through the work of Le Corbusier, Furneaux Jordan through Berthold Lubetkin, Grant Manson with regard to Sullivan and Wright, and finally Pevsner declining the theories on the Picturesque of Price and Knight in the logic of a renewal of contemporary architecture.[2]

But what differentiated Banham's approach was his desire to trace the foundation for a new vision of contemporary architecture, informed by the aesthetic and conceptual research of European or American artists, such as Dubuffet and Pollock, or those in London who gravitated around the ICA, such as Paolozzi, Hamilton, Cordell and McHale.

Thus, through his commitment to clarify the definition of New Brutalism, Banham outlined a critical framework in which contemporary debates and his own interests collided, thanks to which the fragmentary statements of the Smithsons could become a real alternative to all the stylistic definitions previously proposed. While his commentary on the School at Hunstanton, written in response to Johnson, had already provided the occasion for outlining a first 'radical philosophy', Banham then devoted an entire article to the question of New Brutalism, in which even the acclaimed example of the School at Hunstanton would be surpassed.

With the article entitled 'The New Brutalism', published in *Architectural Review* in December 1955, Banham wrote what would be remembered in historiography as the undisputed landmark contribution to that definition (see figures 23 and 24). The impact of Banham's critique not only amplified New Brutalism on an international level, but also triggered a subsequent process of appropriation by other critics.[3] Nonetheless, 'The New Brutalism' is to be read 'cum grano salis', as Banham himself warned in 1966, when he confessed the ambition that drove him to appropriate the definition.[4] Through this article, the definition of New Brutalism was to be so transfigured that a progressive divergence emerged between two interpretations of New Brutalism:[5] one that until 1955 could be identified as a concept, or, to use the Smithsons' definition, a 'spirit' and an 'attitude', and one that resulted from Banham's critical appropriation, which came to decline New Brutalism into a 'label' and a 'slogan'.

---

[1] Banham's interests are illustrated by the following articles written from 1954 to 1955: Reyner Banham, 'Object Lesson', *Architectural Review*, vol. 115, no. 690 (June 1954): 403–406; Reyner Banham, 'Mendelsohn', *Architectural Review*, vol. 116, no. 692 (August 1954): 84–93; Reyner Banham, 'The Machine Aesthetic', *Architectural Review*, vol. 117, no. 700 (April 1955): 225–28; Reyner Banham, 'Sant'Elia', *Architectural Review*, vol. 117, no. 701 (May 1955): 84–93; Reyner Banham, 'Vision in Motion', *Art*, vol. 5 (January 1955): 4; Reyner Banham, 'Vehicles of Desire', *Art*: 3; Reyner Banham, 'Art in British Advertising', *Art News & Review*, vol. 7, no. 22 (November 1955): 3; Reyner Banham, 'A Rejoinder', *Design*, vol. 19 (July 1955): 24–25; Reyner Banham, 'Where Man Meets Machine', *The Listener*, vol. 54 (September 1955): 332–33.

[2] Nikolaus Pevsner, 'C20 Picturesque: An Answer to Basil Taylor's Broadcast', *Architectural Review*, vol. 115, no. 688 (April 1954): 227–29; John Robert Furneaux Jordan, 'Lubetkin', *Architectural Review*, vol. 118, no. 703 (July 1955): 36–44; James Frazer Stirling, 'Garches to Jaoul', *Architectural Review*, vol. 118, no. 705 (September 1955): 145–51; Grant Mansons, 'Sullivan and Wright', *Architectural Review*, vol. 118, no. 707 (November 1955): 297–300.

[3] Reyner Banham, 'The New Brutalism', *Architectural Review*, vol. 118, no. 708 (December 1955): 354–61.

[4] Reyner Banham, *The New Brutalism: Ethic or Aesthetic?* (London: Architectural Press, 1966).

[5] This difference will also be revealed in New Brutalism's international reception following Banham's article. On the divergences between the Smithsons and Banham, see, in particular, the essay by Dirk van den Heuvel, 'Between Brutalists: The Banham Hypothesis and the Smithson Way of Life', *Journal of Architecture*, vol. 20, no. 2 (2015): 293–308.

23-24 Reyner Banham,
'The New Brutalism',
Architectural Review,
vol. 118, December
1955, no. 708,
pp. 354–56

In Banham's contribution, however, the controversial component is what complicates the enunciation of the concept. A sophisticated and scathing dialogue seems to run throughout the article, in which he chooses his interlocutor from a list of critics and historians from different generations who had marked the contemporary debates: from Pevsner to Johnson, from Wittkower to Rowe, and from Fourneaux Jordan to De Maré.

For Banham, the definition of New Brutalism fitted into a historiographic vision of what he defined as the New Art History.[6] His involvement at that time in doctoral research under the guidance of Pevsner is therefore decisive in that it affirms the extent to which the article on New Brutalism can be considered an appendix to his thesis. Indeed, one could even see the cause of New Brutalism as a parallel thesis to his doctoral one, to the point of being a sort of homage to the Courtauld Institute founded by a figure belonging to the New Art History: Aby Warburg. The considerations expressed from the very first lines of the article confirm that 'The New Brutalism' was an academic exercise, demonstrating Banham's role as an epigone of the New Art History. It is therefore no coincidence that the influence of the New Art historians on the British tradition was introduced by Banham as a premise for understanding the phenomenon of New Brutalism:

> One cannot begin to study the New Brutalism without realising how deeply the New Art-History has bitten into progressive English architectural thought, into teaching methods, into the common language of communication between architects and between architectural critics.[7]

Banham placed the definition of New Brutalism within the 'history of history' of the Modern Movement, whose genealogy can be traced back to Pevsner's search for the origins of that movement. In fact, by starting from the problematic destiny of the Modern Movement, the operative hypotheses of the New Art History once again became contemporary. The New Art History meant for Banham a synthesis between criticism, historiography, art and architecture, which had characterised the teachings informed by the German historiographic culture through Pevsner and Wittkower, who included architecture within a constellation of cultural phenomena. In the article Banham recognised the influence of the German art-historical tradition which significantly 'created the idea of a Modern Movement' and brought a new vision of history, capable of intervening in contemporary dynamics.[8] In 1953 Banham had already acknowledged the contribution of the New Art History to the process of emancipation from a criticism exclusively entangled in historical styles, as in the British tradition of Banister Fletcher.[9] Pevsner's historical analysis over a centuries-long time span, published in the 'Pelican World Art History' series, represented for Banham a crucial critical renewal[10]. It demonstrated a new vision of history that originated precisely 'with the arrival in the

---

6 In reference to the New Art History as defined by Banham, see also Mark Crinson, Richard J. Williams, 'From Image to Environment. Reyner Banham's Architecture', in *The Architecture of Art History. A Historiography* (London: Bloomsbury Visual Arts, 2019): 75–94.

7 Banham, 'The New Brutalism', 356.

8 'Between them [the members of the New Art History] they have also changed our ways of looking at the art of the past and the architecture of the present that is now possible for young English architects to speak calmly of a project to build a Palladian power station, and to imply thereby nothing about its detailing or its elevations, but everything about the symmetry and proportions of its plan', in Reyner Banham, 'Pelican World History of Art', *Architectural Review*, vol. 114, no. 683 (November 1953): 285–88.

9 Banister Fletcher was mentioned by Banham in 1953: 'The liberation of architecture from what Banister Fletcher would have called the "Historical Styles" was paralleled by the discovery that these styles were nothing to do with history as we now understand it and were based upon considerations of style that were no longer acceptable', in Banham, 'Pelican World History of Art'.

10 Banham had also stated that Pevsner implied accepting 'a new view of the past, for it treated (probably for the first time in English) an historical period as a whole, and dealt with architecture as one of many interrelated arts, not as a separate and specialist study', in Banham, ibid.: 286.

middle thirties of distinguished refugees from the sources of the New Architecture and the New Art-Criticism: Lubetkin, Gropius and Mendelsohn paralleled by Saxl, Wilde, Wittkower, Pevsner'.[11] It is precisely through the epigones of this school, Banham on the one hand and Rowe on the other, that one can read the extremes of a debate without which New Brutalism would have died out in a series of aporias confined to the polemics linked to the British world and more specifically to the Smithson circle. This new school of thought, in fact, should be acknowledged as having had the potential to gather all the tensions towards the search for a 'New-' still evoked in New Brutalism, creating the premises for its international theorisation.

In 'The New Brutalism', Banham framed the cursory definitions of the Smithsons within the same historical dimension activated by the New Art History, measuring it against the contemporary debates discussed at the ICA on several occasions during 1954.[12] Banham's intention was twofold: on the one hand, to historicise the phenomenon of New Brutalism, recognising several chronological phases linked to precise references and debates; and on the other, to find New Brutalism's operativity. This twofold intention was initially expressed as a liberation from the discipline of stylistic categories. New Brutalism became for Banham the expression of a new vision informed, by virtue of its origins in the New Art History, by multidisciplinary research, ranging from art to architecture but also including disparate references from music, mathematics and literature,[13] on the example of Futurism, to which he devoted his doctoral research.[14]

The Origins in Le Corbusier's Béton Brut

In reflecting on the origins of New Brutalism, Banham did not fail to consider its birth in the internal ideological factions of the LCC. In fact, from the very beginning of the article, what seems to have shaped the origin of the definition is precisely the 'battle of styles' of the 1940s, which saw the association of political ideologies with architectural values. Banham took a clear stand against the Softs, or those who, in his opinion, had reduced New Brutalism to an ironic category, by mocking a certain tendency of the Modern Movement and promoting the Picturesque and New Empiricism, following the British Marxist vision. Marxist ideology was particularly targeted, of which 'People's Architecture', the influence of Socialist Realism and the enthusiasm for Swedish architecture had become synonymous. In fact, Banham retraced the salient moments of this affair with biting phrases against the communist wing of the LCC, calling their operation a 'communist abuse'. While acknowledging the disparaging origin of New Brutalism, Banham intended to free it from any political component and redeem it from any negative connotation deriving from its ideologically 'disengaged' nature. Despite being influenced by the aesthetics of 'expendability' of American consumer goods, in which he

[11] In his review of the 'Pelican World of History of Art' series, Banham defined Pevsner as 'the precise bridge between the New Architecture and the New Art-criticism', in Banham, ibid.

[12] Banham's presentations at the ICA are illuminating in this regard, including the following lectures: 'Aesthetic Problems of Contemporary Art', 25 February 1954, ICA; 'Vision and Design by Roger Fry', for the series of lectures entitled 'Books and the Modern Movement', 16 December 1954, ICA; 'Borax, or the Thousand Horse-Power Milk', 4 March 1955; 'Man, Machine and Motion', introductory address to the Hamilton exhibition, 6 July 1955 and 21 July 1955; 'Metal in Motion – The Iconography of the Automobile', 7 July 1955.

[13] On Banham's ambiguous positioning between criticism and history, see Adrian Forty, 'Reyner Banham, "One Partially Americanized European"', in Louise Campbell (ed.), *Twentieth-Century Architecture and its Histories* (London: Society of Architectural Historians of Great Britain, 2000), 195–205.

[14] 'As a descriptive label it [New Brutalism] has two overlapping, but not identical, senses. Non-architecturally it describes the art of Dubuffet, some aspects of Jackson Pollock and of Appel, and the burlap paintings of Alberto Burri – among foreign artists – and, say, Magda Cordell or Eduardo Paolozzi and Nigel Henderson among English artists', in Banham, 'The New Brutalism', 356. Pevsner had previously made a similar point when he extended the definition of Mannerism to architecture, in Nikolaus Pevsner, *The Architecture of Mannerism* (London: The Mint, 1946, vol. 1).

saw a democratisation of design, Banham's political positioning did not clearly emerge from his articles prior to 1955, and it was only during the 1960s that he would reveal a 'left-oriented' political tendency, even though he was openly opposed to faithful adherence to dogmatic positions.[15]

What is important to note, however, is the declared coincidence between the 'non-Marxist' position, the origins of the New Brutalism and the interest in not only Le Corbusier, but more specifically his *béton brut* and the artistic constellations rooted in art brut.[16]

In particular, the Unité in Marseille was confirmed as an essential reference for any discourse on New Brutalism. Framed by the Smithsons as the progenitor of their 'new theory' by virtue of its demonstration of a 'new humanism' and of the inclusion of artistic processes in architecture, for Banham also the Unité was used to measure the validity of New Brutalism. What the Unité represented for this concept cannot be summed up solely as a prototype for reconstruction, nor as an idealistic vision for a *ville radieuse*. The use of materials and their psychological implication, which did not stop at *béton brut* but expanded to the other plastic experiments of the *toit jardin*, became the basis of the concept of New Brutalism that Banham was about to deploy. And the opening of the article almost seems to be a homage to Le Corbusier, evoking the association between 'les matières bruts' and the 'rapports emouvants' that Le Corbusier theorised in *Vers une architecture*.

The definition of New Brutalism, starting from Asplund's invention of Neo-Brutalism, altered by the internal ideological battle within the LCC, and finally fuelled by the Smithsons' aphorisms, had until that time remained suspended in a mixture of nebulous references, exemplified by the most disparate examples, in which the Miesian imprint seemed to have marked a precise direction. If the definition of New Brutalism had been made public through a project with a Lecorbuserian appearance, the example that had mainly oriented that definition was undoubtedly the School at Hunstanton, with its undeniable Miesian derivation. What, however, was clarified in Banham's article is the etymological root of the definition, identified precisely in *béton brut*, confirming the declarations of the Smithsons, who, during 1954 and 1955, had adopted the definition 'as their own, by their own desire' and who had repeatedly stated that, in the manipulation of material, they found a vital impulse for a new architecture.[17]

15 See Adrian Forty's comment: 'If Banham described himself as "Left-oriented", it emerges in his writings primarily as a demotic attack upon the values of the cultural establishment: he leaves you in no doubt whom or what he was against, but exactly who or what he was for can sometimes be a little hazy'; Banham's position is in fact against political dogmas and in particular against cultural control by the establishment, Forty, 'Reyner Banham, "One Partially Americanized European"', 203. Banham's political positions are made explicit in an article from 1964, in which he explains: 'Now if this is where we came from, it left us in a very peculiar position, vis-à-vis the normal divisions of English culture, because we had this American leaning and yet most of us are in some way Left-oriented, even protest-oriented. [...] People whose lightweight culture was American in derivation, and yet, in spite of that, were and are, of the Left, of the protesting sections of the public. It gives us a curious set of divided loyalties. We dig Pop which is acceptance-culture, capitalistic, and yet in our formal politics, if I may use the phrase, most of us belong very firmly on the other side', in Reyner Banham, 'The Atavism of the Short-distance Mini-cyclist', *Living Arts*, vol. 3, 1964, reprinted in Reyner Banham, Penny Sparkle (ed.), *Design by Choice* (London: Academy Editions, 1981), 84–85. Banham's political orientation is also confirmed by his wife Mary Banham, who recalls: 'He was a supporter of the Labour party all his life. There was a long family tradition of left-wing politics', in Mary Banham, interviewed by Corinne Julius, *National Life Story Collection: Architects' Lives*, British Library Oral History, 2001, part 10/19.
16 'Among the non-Marxist grouping there was no particular unity of programme or intention, but there was a certain community of interests, a tendency to look toward Le Corbusier, and to be aware of something called le *béton brut*, to know the quotation which appears at the head of this article, and, in the case of the more sophisticated and aesthetically literate, to know of the Art Brut of Jean Dubuffet and his connection in Paris', in Banham, 'The New Brutalism', 356.
17 See Alison and Peter Smithson, 'Some Notes on Architecture', *244: Journal of the University of Manchester Architecture and Planning Society*, vol. 1 (Spring 1954): 4; Theo Crosby, 'The New Brutalism', *Architectural Design*, vol. 25, no. 1 (January 1955): 1; Alison and Peter Smithson, Maya Hambly, 'En ny engelsk skola', *Byggmästaren*, vol. 34, no. A6 (June 1955): 159–62.

New Brutalism thus became, through Banham's operation, a concept that was both theoretical and operational, rooted in the new British criticism and art history, and forged from the combination of the poetics of Le Corbusier's *béton brut*, the theoretical impulses of the Smithsons and contemporary aesthetic concepts.

Early Brutalism

Inherent in the New Art History as described by Banham was the desire not to circumscribe the phenomenon of New Brutalism to a historiographical category crystallised in a new style. On the contrary, Banham's aim was to identify characteristics, which he called 'qualities', that could guide the recognition of New Brutalism in other contemporary buildings. The intention was to turn this blurry definition into an operational tool, making explicit the design guidelines the Smithsons hid in their formulations of their first 'manifesto'.[18] The novelty of Banham's position, what made him an active critic and the very protagonist of New Brutalism,[19] was his commitment to demonstrating its principles and validity beyond a simple synonym for the Modern Movement, as the Softs of the LCC had tried to do.[20] If we briefly retrace the gestation phases of the definition of New Brutalism, salient features noted by critics between 1954 and 1955 emerge as decisive: the 'warehouse aesthetics', the 'exhibition of structure', the 'reverence for materials', 'formal proportion', the 'Palladian' plan, and a series of concepts ranging from Johnson's 'anti-design' to Banham's 'disreputability' and 'ruthlessness'.[21]

In order to reiterate the evolutionary potential of his principles, Banham firstly framed the phenomenon within a historiographic articulation of two phases, both calibrated around the Smithsons' projects – an 'Early Brutalism', identifiable chronologically between 1949 and 1952, exemplified by the designs for the School at Hunstanton (1949), the competition for Coventry Cathedral (1951), and the House in Soho (1952); and a second phase defined as the 'furthest development of New Brutalist architecture', which included the competition designs for Golden Lane (1952) and Sheffield University (1953).

For Banham, the 'Early Brutalism' did not originate with Asplund's invention, nor with the internal discussions and polemics of the LCC but was anchored in the projects and theories of the Smithsons. Banham, as he had already specified in April 1954, confirmed the Smithsons – and specifically Alison – not as inventors, but as protagonists who used that definition for the first time 'in public'.[22]

For Banham the conceptualisation of different phases of New Brutalism corresponded to a desire to demonstrate the evolutionary process of that definition, which tended to move away from an initial phase with Miesian and neo-Palladian formal traits, and indicate a further trajectory characterised by an 'a-formalism'. The transition between the various phases of New Brutalism is in fact the decisive core of Banham's intervention. Subsequently, through a rhetorical stratagem, Banham

---

[18] Theo Crosby, 'The New Brutalism'.
[19] Banham would admit his direct involvement in the evolution of the definition of New Brutalism, particularly in the chapter 'Memoirs of a Survivor', Banham, *The New Brutalism: Ethic or Aesthetic*.
[20] On Banham's critical interest in contemporary events, see also Robert Maxwell, 'Reyner Banham: The Plenitude of Present', *Architectural Design*, vol. 51 (June 1981): 52–57. Banham's lecture given at the RIBA in London in 1961, entitled 'History of the Immediate Future' is useful to understand his notion of history.
[21] See P.D.S [Alison Smithson], 'House in Soho', *Architectural Design*, vol. 23, no. 12 (December 1953): 342; Philip Johnson, 'School at Hunstanton', *Architectural Review*, vol. 116, no. 693 (September 1954): 148–62; Crosby, 'The New Brutalism'; Alison and Peter Smithson, 'En ny engelsk skola'; [n.a.], 'Three Approaches to Architecture', *Architectural Forum*, vol. 102, no. 5 (May 1955): 142–45; [Banham], 'School at Hunstanton'.
[22] 'Alison Smithson first claimed the words in public as her own in a description of a project for a small house in Soho', Banham, 'The New Brutalism', 354.

articulated two different triads of 'quality', with similar but variable and only apparently associable parameters, concerning the plan, the structure and the materials. In the transition between the first and second phase, Banham used a constellation of different impulses, among which multidisciplinary concepts such as 'image', 'topology' and 'anti-art', which would radically alter the meaning of plan, structure and materials.

The evolution of the plan was analysed by Banham through the salient features of the examples of 'Early Brutalism', meaning the House in Soho, the School at Hunstanton and the project for Coventry Cathedral. Banham recognized among these projects a common principle of axiality and symmetry, and a regular geometric form, summed up by the first quality – the 'formal legibility of plan'.[23] In order to understand what Banham meant by 'formal' it is necessary to refer to the graphic schemes of Wittkower and Rowe.[24] To stigmatise this kind of 'Early Brutalism' plan, Banham employed the Wittkowerian definition of the 'logic of the plan'. Banham's criticism also concerned the post-war phenomena of the 'Neo-Palladian' and 'New Formalism' which identified in contemporary architecture the principles of proportions summarised by the 'Palladian approach'.[25] This definition had already been used in the image captions accompanying the September 1954 article on the School at Hunstanton and was later taken up by Blake in *Architectural Forum*. Banham was then to call the Coventry Cathedral plan 'Neo-palladian', as indicated in the caption.[26]

The notion of structure took on a different value for Banham than what had been internationally understood since the 1930s, because it was conceived to be clearly exhibited. This specification, summed up in the second quality of the 'clear exhibition of structure', was decisive in determining a very precise cultural sphere within the 1940s and 1950s, which aligned with Smithson's first definition of New Brutalism in December 1953.[27] Confirming the validity of the principle of visibility that must rule the expression of the structure, Banham asserted that materials must also be used according to their intrinsic characteristics, as summarised by the third quality: 'Valuation of material for their inherent qualities "as found"'.

The three characteristics enunciated here had already been discussed by Banham in September 1954 and had been elaborated on the basis of the School at Hunstanton: – '1, Formal legibility of plan; 2, clear exhibition of structure; and 3, valuation of materials for their inherent qualities "as found"'.[28] The evolution of these three 'qualities' was then implemented by Banham through an admittedly ambiguous and misleading list of examples, intended to confirm the strategy necessary for replacing Early Brutalism's neoplatonic and abstract characters. The list includes buildings ascribable to Hunstanton's Miesian line, including Mies's Promontory and Lakeshore Apartments, Saarinen's General Motors Technical Center, buildings by Van den Broek,

---

[23] The definition of 'formal legibility' had already been used by Banham for the plan of the School at Hunstanton; [Banham], 'School at Hunstanton', 152.

[24] Reference should be made to the diagrammatic schemes of Palladian villas made by Wittkower and published by Rudolf Wittkower, *Architectural Principles in the Age of Humanism*, vol. 19 (London: Warburg Institute, University of London, 1949) (Studies of the Warburg Institute); Colin Rowe, 'The Mathematics of the Ideal Villa: Palladio and Le Corbusier Compared', *Architectural Review*, vol. 101, no. 602 (February 1947): 101–104. For a more recent discussion of Wittkower's 'formality' and Banham's 'image', see Claire Zimmerman, 'From Legible Form to Memorable Image: Architectural Knowledge from Rudolph Wittkower to Reyner Banham', in *Candide*, vol. 5, no. 2 (February 2012): 93–108.

[25] In the brief introduction to 'New Formalism', the anonymous author specifies that 'since the publication in 1950 of Professor Wittkower's *Architectural Principles in the Age of Humanism* there has been a considerable interest among young architects in the theories of proportion of Alberti and Palladio. [...] The use of simple whole number proportions produces, as the early Renaissance shows, buildings of clarity and directness', in [n.a.], 'The New Formalism', *Architectural Design*, vol. 24, no. 4 (April 1954): 94.

[26] Banham, 'The New Brutalism', 360.

[27] P.D.S [Alison Smithson], 'House in Soho'.

[28] [Banham], 'School at Hunstanton'.

Bakema and Van Eyck, projects by 'young Englishmen affiliated with CIAM', and, in particular, the Unité in Marseille.[29]

Only the Unité, as Banham asserted, seemed capable of redeeming the 'Early Brutalism' of the formalist drift generated by the Miesian references. For in Banham's eyes, *béton brut*, contaminated as it was by the poetics of *brutal* materials and the anti-artistic principles that generated it, was the utmost expression of the fidelity to the principle of 'as found', elected as the sole quality capable of innervating the entire concept of New Brutalism, to the point of generating a 'furthest development of New Brutalist architecture'.

Anti-art and As Found: For 'une Architecture Autre'

For Banham, a new definition of New Brutalism in architecture was possible only through an expressive intensity and an attitude that admitted the unexpected, such as that practised by the artists seen as representatives of New Brutalism in art: 'In the last what characterises the New Brutalism in architecture as in painting is precisely its brutality, its *je-m'en-foutisme*, its bloody-mindedness'.[30] The images Banham selected to illustrate the definition of New Brutalism were half artworks indicative of the trend called *anti-art*, a direction Banham intended to impart to the orientation in architecture as well:[31] a painting by Pollock distinguished by 'a-formal composition in action', a photograph by Henderson depicting graffiti on a window selected for its 'formal value', a sculpture by Magda Cordell as an example of 'anti-aesthetic', a sculpture by Paolozzi indicating 'sophisticated primitivism', a work by Alberto Burri defined as 'typical Brutalist in its attitude to material', and finally a photograph from the exhibition *Parallel of Life and Art*, which, with its '100 Brutalist images', was elected by Banham as the 'locus classicus' of New Brutalism. In comparison, the two Smithsons' designs in the illustrations on the same page, the School at Hunstanton and the House in Soho, seem to declare the gap between the geometric compositions of 'Early Brutalism' and the expressiveness generated by anti-artistic research.

Banham discarded the formalism of the neo-Palladian composition and replaced it with the 'violent' immediacy of the 'image', capable of emerging as a paradigm for the architecture of the second phase of New Brutalism (and beyond). As we will see later, the concept of 'image' strictly derives from that of 'as found'. But in this context, the definition of 'as found' radically differs from the Dada-derived concept of 'as found' discussed in September 1954, according to which materials must be used as they arrive on the building site.[32] Although both concepts of 'as found' were related to the use of materials, it was the artistic avant-garde of the 1950s that resonated in Banham's 1955 article. Exemplified by the avant-garde images accompanying the article, here the concept of 'as found' demonstrated uncontrolled, violent and brutal components linked to a vision of the design project in which the process, and not the final result, was of primary importance. If the 1954 concept of 'as found' still allowed materials to be subjugated to rigid geometries, as long as their intrinsic nature was

---

[29] 'It is interesting to note,' says Banham ironically, 'that such a summary of qualities could be made to describe Marseilles, Promontory and Lakeshore apartments, General Motors Technical Centre, much recent Dutch work and several projects by younger English architects affiliated to CIAM. But, with the possible exception of Marseilles, the Brutalists would probably reject most of these buildings from the canon, and so must we, for all of these structures exhibit an excess of *suaviter in modo*, even if there is plenty of *fortiter in re* about them', in Banham, 'The New Brutalism', 357.

[30] Ibid.

[31] Banham had already associated the 'Brutalists' with 'Anti-Academic' tendencies, in Reyner Banham, 'Vehicles of Desire', *Art*, 01 September 1955, 3.

[32] [Banham], 'School at Hunstanton'.

made explicit, this new definition of 'as found' possessed a revolutionary force, similar to those artworks that bore witness to a tendency towards 'anti-art' or 'anti-beauty', by virtue of violent transgressions of the norms of artistic expression and the abolition of concepts such as order, harmony and composition.

A new architectural process that could not be assimilated to Neo-Palladian attitudes was the prerequisite for what Banham called 'architecture autre'. This definition, which became a synonym for New Brutalism, was a paraphrase of the concept of *un art autre* coined by Michel Tapié in 1952 to describe the anti-classicist and anti-formalist tendencies of European and American art, in which 'forms in process' replaced the academic concept of 'formal beauty'.[33] The reference to the concept of *art autre* also echoed the surrealist theories based on the experimentation of semi-automation techniques; the primacy of process over form, of the non-finite over absolute completeness, of the a-hierarchical and a-focal principles of Pollock's painting; and finally the negation of the category of taste and conventional beauty in favour of the affirmation of a primordial impulse, direct and spontaneous as Dada, dictated by an inclusive and non-hierarchical attitude. Banham calibrated his concept of 'architecture autre' through other disciplines, such as music. If the principle of proportions had been compared by Wittkower to musical harmony, Banham seemed almost to be responding to him when he proposed the same analogy, but this time with *musique concrete*, produced by the assemblage of 'as found' sounds, which are then synthesised and manipulated by discarding notions of harmony and melody.[34]

In *architecture autre* Banham identified a mixture of ethical and artistic impulses through which he discredited questions of symmetry, proportions and the mere function of the building.[35] The emphasis placed on *art autre* and on the attitude of the early Modern Movement concerned not only the materials, but also the very conception of the project. The alchemy of multidisciplinary references that Banham called into question to describe *une architecture autre* thus framed New Brutalism within the experiments linked to the exhibition *Parallel of Life and Art* and, in so doing, he distanced the definition from the Palladian and Wittkowerian drifts that had obscured its reception, as Banham recalled: 'Introducing this exhibition to an AA student debate Peter Smithson declared: "We are not going to talk about proportion and symmetry" and this was his declaration of war on the inherent academicism of the neo-Palladians'.

Wittkower, Rowe and the Anti-Brutalists

The 'formal legibility of plan' which underpinned the qualities of Early New Brutalism became the conceptual fulcrum against which Banham made his fiercest criticism. In fact, it cannot be denied that Banham's article is the manifesto of a precise critical attitude, summarizing the debates and controversies that characterised London in the 1950s. Different ideologies were hence reflected in it, including those of the protagonists against whom Banham himself raged.

---

[33] Del Renzio brought Michel Tapié to the attention of the members of the Independent Group after reading about his exhibition *Véhémences Confrontées* in 1951 in the Italian magazine *Spazio*. Tapié had also contributed to the introduction of Del Renzio's catalogue on the exhibition *Opposing Forces*, held at the ICA in 1953. Paolozzi was also invited to participate in Tapié's 1952 exhibition entitled *Signifiants de l'informel*. See also Michel Tapié, *Un art autre où il s'agit de nouveaux dévidages du réel* (Paris: Gabriel-Giraud et fils, 1952).

[34] 'A closely analogous development is that of musique concrète, which uses "real sounds," manipulated in a manner which resembles the manipulation of some of the photographs in *Parallel*, and does not concern itself with harmony or melody in any recognizable way', in Banham, 'The New Brutalism', 361. *Musique concrète* was a definition of French composer Pierre Schaeffer in 1948.

[35] See also the analysis by Nigel Whiteley, 'Banham and 'Otherness': Reyner Banham (1922–1988) and His Quest for an Architecture Autre', *Architectural History*, vol. 33 (1990): 188–221.

The cultural epicentre that formed the backdrop to Banham's arguments undoubtedly gravitated around the members of the Independent Group. However, the academic environment, of which Banham was a member, also inevitably resonated in certain of his positions. The most radical critique in the article was directed against 'Professor Wittkower', as Banham called him, and against some of the stances presented in *Architectural Principles in the Age of Humanism*, reprinted in a new edition in 1952.[36] This is the book against which Banham railed, yet keeping the thesis presented by Wittkower in mind helps to understand the scope of the debate on proportion, repeatedly evoked and placed at the origins of Early Brutalism.

The New Brutalism could even be considered Banham's manifesto against overly faithful recourse to academic and historicist references. Indeed, Banham's observation placed Wittkower's book at the centre of a dispute over the proper use of history, between those who advocated a literal return to the formal principles of Renaissance humanism, and those seeking a theoretical model based on universal principles.[37]

The primary aspect against which Banham railed in the article was the consequence generated by a slavish adoption of Wittkower's principles, which brought to the forefront an entirely compositional attitude and through which the works of Alberti, Bramante, Leonardo and Palladio had contributed to the principle of immutable, static and absolute beauty. Moreover, Banham recognised the use of diagrams, proportions and geometry as the preponderant academic connotation of Early Brutalism, also confirmed by the Miesian reference to perfect and ideal shapes. Thus, with the intention of freeing the definition of New Brutalism from any academic meaning, Banham underlined the novelty of the exhibition *Parallel of Life and Art*. That event favoured the development of a 'programme' instead of an 'aesthetic', distancing New Brutalism from its reduction to a 'label', precisely because of its freedom from academic categories: 'The Brutalists, observing the inherent risk of a return to pure academicism – more pronounced at Liverpool [where Wittkower teaches] than at the AA – sheered off abruptly in the other direction and were soon involved in the organisation of *Parallel of Life and Art*.'

Banham's definition of New Brutalism went as far as to declare composition freed from symmetries and regular geometries to the point of imagining a type of fluid connection of spaces traversed by circulation, extending the project beyond the architectural scale. Several impulses for renewal derived from this evolution, resulting from the mixture of liberating devices which replaced 'geometry' with 'topology', 'academism' with 'anti-art', and which found in the quality of the 'image' a synthesis of expression for an alternative vision of plan, structure and use of materials.

The Role of the Yale Art Gallery

The transition between the qualities of 'Early Brutalism' and those of the 'furthest development of New Brutalism' was orchestrated by Banham through a comparison of two buildings: Kahn's recently completed Yale Art Gallery and the Smithsons' School at

---

[36] In the preface to the third edition *Architectural Principles*, Wittkower acknowledged Banham's article: 'In a challenging article in the *Architectural Review* of December 1955 Reyner Banham tried to assess the book's influence ("for evil as well as good") on post-war British architecture', in Rudolf Wittkower, *Architectural Principles in the Age of Humanism*, 3rd edition (London: Alec Tiranti, 1962).

[37] In this context, a note by Manfredo Tafuri is illuminating: 'The general impact of Professor Wittkower's book on a whole generation of architectural students is one of the phenomena of our time. Its exposition of a body of architectural theory in which function and form were significantly linked by the objective laws governing the Cosmos (as Alberti and Palladio understood them) suddenly offered a way out of the doldrum of routine-functionalist abdications, and neo-Palladianism became the order of the day. The effect of *Architectural Principles* [...] precipitated a disputation on the proper use of history'; Manfredo Tafuri, *Ricerca del Rinascimento: principi, città, architetti*, vol. 760 (Turin: Einaudi, 1992), 5.

Hunstanton. The elements Banham brought into play for this comparison were the structure, the plan and its axialities, and the relationships between exterior and interior. The subtle comparison staged by Banham, more on a rhetorical than analytical level, gave the Smithsons' project a new meaning, devoid of any references to Wittkower and Neo-Palladian theories.

Hunstanton's technical and structural rigour, generated by the innovation of Plastic Theory, was compared to the expressive virtuosity of Kahn's tetrahedral ceiling, in which Banham identified the 'uncompromisingly frank' and 'boldly exhibited structural method' appropriate to a 'new brutalist structure'. Banham recognised in Kahn's building a disruptive potential that came close to the concept of 'image', to the point that for him the Yale Art Gallery was 'the most truly Brutalist building in the New World'.

What differentiates the two buildings, however, is the maniacal attention to detail, which is deliberately absent in Hunstanton and becomes 'arty' in Kahn's Yale Art Gallery. Banham also criticised Kahn's solution of the relation between the interior and exterior, and the imperfect axiality of the plan, betrayed by the asymmetrical entrance doors and openings. The Yale Art Gallery missed, for Banham, the uncompromising logic that should pervade every stage of the project. Instead, the compromises of the Yale Art Gallery do not allow for a coherent reading of the building and as a result its 'image' is ambiguous. It is only through a radical process, both that of the critic making judgements and that of the architect taking the logical principles of the design project to extremes, that Banham discovered something he called the 'Brutalist image'.

Regarding the reasons for the choice of the Yale Art Gallery, it should be noted that Alloway had already listed it in 1954 as one of the architectural examples for the 'anti-style' of New Brutalism.[38] Banham also stated that Ian McCallum, editor of *Architectural Review*, had suggested Kahn's building to him in early 1955.[39]

Kahn, for his part, would not comment on New Brutalism until 1960.[40] However, Colin Rowe, who had visited Kahn's studio with the painter Robert Slutzky in December 1955, informed him of the inclusion of his Yale Art Gallery among the examples of New Brutalism in a letter sent in February 1956, to which he attached a copy of *Architectural Principles* by his teacher Wittkower:

> Did you see in the *Architectural Review* a deplorable article on 'the New Brutalism' – very chauvinistic and patronising – suggesting first of all that you were a 'new brutalist', which as far as I know you would never claim to be, and then turning around and damning you because you didn't fulfil the N.B. canon. […] But one little innuendo there was, condemning pseudo-Palladian formalism, which was meant for me.[41]

Indeed, Banham's insinuation to Rowe is revealed through the very use of the example of the Yale Art Gallery, which served as a litmus test for Banham's rhetorical stratagem, one that would lead to the radical replacement of the three principles of 'Early Brutalism' through a new quality, more complex than the composition defended by Rowe, and to which Banham attributed the task of summing up the anti-artistic destructive force of 'ruthlessness', 'disreputability' and 'brutality': the quality of 'image'.

---

[38] Lawrence Alloway, 'Art News from London', *Art News*, vol. 53, no. 6 (October 1954): 54.
[39] Banham, *The New Brutalism: Ethic or Aesthetic?*, 44.
[40] James Marston Fitch, 'A Building of Rugged Fundaments', *Architectural Forum*, vol. 113, no. 1 (July 1960): 82–87.
[41] Rowe's letter to Kahn was published in Braden R. Engel, 'The Badger of Muck and Brass', *AA Files*, vol. 62 (2011): 95–98; see also Roberto Gargiani, *Louis I. Kahn: Exposed Concrete and Hollow Stones, 1949–1959* (Lausanne: EPFL Press, 2014), 109.

Image, *'Quod Visum Perturbat'*

The theoretical nucleus of the article can be summed up in the replacement of the composition of the plan based on axial principles within geometric limits, with a composition free of academic influences, as the only premise for achieving a 'new image'. The quality of 'image' is symptomatic of the interest in visual perception in the debate of the early 1950s.[42] The concept of 'image' had in fact been discussed by members of the Independent Group regarding the popular and advertising references in American magazines, and in particular by Henderson, defined by Alison Smithson as 'the original image finder'.[43] 'Multi-evocative image' was a concept that Henderson appropriated to describe his photographic research aimed at a progressive abandonment of a single focal point, in favour of a manipulated and multiple vision allowing the free associations between different forms.[44]

The appeal to the concept of 'image' corresponded, therefore, for the members of the Independent Group, to a creative re-elaboration of intellectual and visual associations, in which the notions of process, collage and montage became a principle antithetical to formal unity and an expression of a dynamic perception. 'Imageability' was also the criterion set for selecting the references for *Parallel of Life and Art*. In addition, a series of meetings entitled 'The Aesthetics Problems of Contemporary Art' was organised at the ICA between 1953 and 1954, followed by a series curated by Banham on 'Books and Modern Movement', in which he had presented Roger Fry's essay *Vision and Design*.[45] As evidence of the concept of 'image' in relation to architecture, Voelcker used 'image' to illustrate the coherence of the School at Hunstanton.[46]

Banham called into question a series of examples to clarify the concept of 'image': 'A great many things have been called "an image" – S. M. della Consolazione at Todi, a painting by Jackson Pollock, the Lever Building, the 1954 Cadillac convertible, the roofscape of the Unité at Marseilles, any of the hundred photographs in *Parallel of Life and Art*'.[47] The list illustrated different meanings of 'image' and presupposed a progressive detachment from the canons of classical beauty linked to proportions. It is not by chance that the first example was the central-plan church of Santa Maria della Consolazione, which significantly appeared on the cover of the first edition of *Architectural Principles* to sum up Wittkower's vision of Renaissance aesthetics. Wittkower had already described that plan in terms of the 'image of the vital force behind all matter', referring to a plan generated through mathematical harmonies from an a-priori

[42] Research for a psychology of vision had been advanced by James J. Gibson 'The Perception of the Visual Surfaces', in *American Journal of Psychology*, vol. 63 (1950): 367–84. Between 1952 and 1956 Gombrich was also interested in the relationship between art and visual perception, as his 1960 essay 'Art and Illusion' shows. The members of the Independent Group also showed an interest in the notion of 'image', as Theo Crosby states in 'The Search for the Image', *Architectural Design*, vol. 25, no. 3 (March 1955): 103. The notion of 'image' is also confirmed in the text of the *Parallel of Life and Art* exhibition catalogue, and confirmed by Voelker, 'Hunstanton Provides a Sense of Location', 456. For a more recent account of the question of image, see Laurent Stalder, '"New Brutalism", "Topology" and "Image": Some Remarks on the Architectural Debates in England Around 1950', *The Journal of Architecture*, vol. 13, no. 3 (2008): 263–81; Anthony Vidler, 'Another Brick in the Wall', *October*, vol. 136 (2011): 105–22.

[43] See the transcript of the interview with Alison and Peter Smithson on the occasion of the film *Fathers of Pop*, 1979, in Victoria Walsh, *Nigel Henderson: Parallel of Life and Art* (London: Thames & Hudson, 2001), 54. Banham reports that 'Henderson, an experimental photographer, is little known outside Britain though his influence was considerable (if indeed it was he who had invented their special use of the word "image" then his influence is probably crucial)', in Banham, *The New Brutalism: Ethic or Aesthetic?*, 61.

[44] Henderson's definition was based on the critic David Sylvester's 'multi-evocative sign', coined regarding the multifocal aspect of some of Paul Klee's artworks. Henderson noted how the 'multi-evocative image stood for a punchy visual matrix that triggered a number of associational ideas', in Walsh, *Nigel Henderson*, 103. Sylvester was involved in the ICA's exhibitions such as *Recent Trends in Realist Painting* and *Young Painters* (both 1952) but also in lectures (he took part in 39 events organised at the ICA during the 1950s); Anne Massey, Gregor Muir, *Institute of Contemporary Arts: 1946–1968* (Amsterdam: Roma Publications, 2014).

[45] Roger Fry, *Vision and Design* (London: Chatto & Windus, 1920).

[46] Voelcker, 'Hunstanton Provides a Sense of Location'.

[47] The Lever House was opened the same year as the Unité and had demonstrated two divergent directions of Modern architecture, as noted by Stirling. Banham, 'The New Brutalism', 358.

idea.[48] As a departure from the a-priori form, Banham suggests, through Pollock, another meaning of image, this time discovered during the dripping process, resulting in an 'all-over', a-hierarchic and a-formal composition.[49]

Cadillac, and in particular the El Dorado model presented at the London motor show in October 1954, immediately became part of the visual references associated with the definition of New Brutalism, counted among the 'overlaid imaginary' of the 'key year' of New Brutalism by Crosby,[50] and cited in March 1955 by Alison Smithson in a note clarifying the nature of New Brutalism.[51] The celebration of automobile design was the subject of the exhibition *Man, Machine and Motion*, curated by McHale and Banham in March 1955, in which cars, boats, submarines and airplanes represented the creative potential of autonomous movement, in a process of constant perfection of craftsmanship combined with the ambition of speed, not far from the Futurists studied by Banham.[52]

In this sense, New Brutalism could proclaim itself as the conclusive moment of academic aesthetics and the overcoming of the traditional notion of 'classical' beauty formulated by Thomas Aquinas, rooted in the criterion of integrity, in which the form of an object must impose precise characteristics on the material. Banham introduced his concept of beauty as an uncanny element: as *quod visum perturbat* is the singular expression used to describe the 'Brutalist image'.[53]

Banham elaborated on the criterion of 'satisfaction for the eye', with which both Rowe and Pesvner had already engaged in their discussions on Mannerism.[54] In particular, Pevsner had associated Mannerism to an architecture 'with the aim of hurting, rather than pleasing, the eye', which comes close to Banham's predilection for the 'disturbing' aesthetic.[55] In the British tradition of art theories, we should also note the inputs given by Clive Bell's *Art* published in 1914, which subversively stated that the aim of art is not beauty but the arousal of an 'aesthetic emotion'. This emotion, according to Bell, could only be activated if the artwork possesses a 'signifying form', which finds its greatest expression in the work of the 'primitives' produced by impulses impressed in matter, and hence impossible to ascribe to academic classifications.[56] Moreover, during the war, Saxl, another historian ascribed by Banham to the New Art History, had specified a necessary 'visual education' to re-orientate post-war art towards an 'appeal to the emotions'.[57] The 'visual education' pursued by *Architectural Review* at the beginning of the 1950s hence led, through Banham's operation, to outcomes other than the recovery of the vernacular.

[48] Wittkower, *Architectural Principles in the Age of Humanism*, 25.

[49] The Smithsons first saw Pollock's work at the 1950 Biennale. During 1953, Pollock's works were shown in the *Opposing Forces* exhibition at the ICA in London. Banham would also admit that he and the other members of the Independent Group 'were grappling with the Jackson Pollock phenomenon. Action painting was important to us because of its anti-formality and its quality as a record of the artist's gesture', in Reyner Banham, 'Futurism for Keeps', *Arts* (December 1960): 39.

[50] Crosby, 'The New Brutalism'.

[51] Alison Smithson, 'Answer to Questions', 7 March 1955, E009, Alison and Peter Smithson Special Collection, Loeb Library, Harvard University, Cambridge, USA. Regarding the Cadillac, Banham stated: 'In 1951 and 1952 none of us really knew how to read the forms and the symbols of the car; that was to come later when John McHale and Lawrence Alloway took over the running of the Independent Group', in *Fathers of Pop*, documentary of the Arts Council of Great Britain, Distributed by Concord Video & Film Council, 1979.

[52] See for example Reyner Banham, 'Space for Decoration', *Design*, vol. 79 (July 1955): 24–25.

[53] 'Where Thomas Aquinas supposed beauty to be *quod visum placet* (that which seen, pleases), image may be defined as *quod visum perturbat* – that which seen, affects the emotions, a situation which could subsume the pleasure caused by beauty, but is not normally taken to do so, for the New Brutalists' interests in image are commonly regarded [...] as being anti-art, or at any rate anti-beauty in the classical aesthetic sense of the word', in Banham, 'The New Brutalism', 358.

[54] Rowe, 'Mannerism and Modern Architecture'.

[55] Nikolaus Pevsner, 'The Architecture of Mannerism' (London: Routledge, 1946), 120–32.

[56] Clive Bell, *Art* (New York: Stokes, 1914).

[57] Fritz Saxl, 'Visual Education', *The Listener* (23 September 1943): 356. For the relevance of images in Saxl's and Warburg's art-historical teaching, see Katia Mazzucco, '1941 English Art and the Mediterranean. A Photographic Exhibition by the Warburg Institute in London, *Journal of Art Historiography*, no. 5 (December 2011).

In Banham's reasoning, the contrast between Thomistic beauty and the per-turbing beauty derived from the concept of *anti-art* also implied the different role that had been attributed to matter: no longer a passive role imposed by a specific form, but an active role of 'as found' and the consequent result discovered during the process, including the acceptance of what the very concept of classical beauty had excluded – disproportions, autonomy between parts, hybrids. The concept of 'as found' hence was achieved through the acceptance of unpredictable phenomena, simi-lar to those which Le Corbusier had identified in the *malfaçons*.[58] In this sense we can also understand the adjective 'perturbing' that accompanies this new definition of image, informed by psychological components exemplified by the theories intro-duced by Ernst Jentsch in 1906 and reworked by Sigmund Freud in 1919, for whom 'perturbing' acquired a psychoanalytic interpretation, in the form of the emergence of repressed traits in an unexpected and inexplicable ways, generating 'intellectual uncertainty'.[59]

The stance against Thomistic beauty and pure form was a way for Banham to criticize the precepts of truth and beauty as professed by the president of the ICA, Her-bert Read, who in the eyes of Banham and the members of the Independent Group represented an elitist and classicist attitude.[60] But although the members of the Inde-pendent Group were looking for a new system of relations in the conception of the image, through the juxtaposition of interdisciplinary references, for Banham the qual-ity of the image was aimed at undermining the concept of classical beauty, through the collision between anti-artistic practices and the academic conventions that had led to the affirmation of the Neo-Palladian, symmetrical and regular type of plan.

Banham concentrated in the concept of 'image' his critique to Wittkower and Rowe to affirm the inevitable necessity of 'a-formalism', that is, a new way of conceiv-ing architecture that included the concept of a building as a 'visual entity', which is a notion once again linked to the German art-historical tradition.

To this end, Banham proposed the use of 'topology', identified as a tool capable of revolutionising the concept of academic plan and freeing the definition of New Bru-talism from the accusation of formalism, which had been one of the most widespread criticisms since the first publications of the School at Hunstanton.[61] It was no longer a question, in fact, of sticking to the tools of the square and the compass, but, in con-trast, the plan had to be set free, through recourse to other 'mathematics' than that of Rowe and Wittkower.[62] In this way the composition is no longer restricted to a rigid and elementary geometry, but can aspire to express relations and connections, both inside and outside buildings.[63] Banham had already expressed his interest in topology a few months earlier, when he compared it to the a-hierarchy of Pollock's paintings.[64]

As a logical consequence, the recourse to topology had a decisive impact on the concept of structure, which was no longer understood as the building's skeleton, but was extended to include the relationship between the parts, thus resulting in a notion

[58] Banham had also placed the concept of 'as found' alongside the Dadaist research into the *objet trouvé*, in Banham, 'School at Hunstanton'.
[59] Ernst Jentsch, 'Zur Psychologie des Unheimlichen', *Psychiatrisch-Neurologische Wochenschrift*, vol. 8, no. 22 (25 August 1906): 195–98.
[60] 'We were against direct carving, pure form, truth, beauty, and all that [...] what we favoured was motion studies. We also favoured rough surfaces, human images, space, machinery, ignoble materials and what we termed non-art (there was a project to bury Sir Herbert Read under a book entitled *Non-Art Not Now*' (Read had published the book entitled *Art Now* in 1933)', in Banham, 'Futurism for Keeps', 33–39.
[61] [n.a.], 'The New Brutalism', *Architects' Journal*, vol. 120, no. 3107 (September 1954): 336; A. Derek, 'The New Brutalism', *Architects' Journal*, vol. 120, no. 3108 (September 1954): 366; Peter Berensford, 'School at Hunstanton', *Architectural Review*, vol. 116, no. 695 (November 1954): 282.
[62] Rowe, 'The Mathematics of the Ideal Villa: Palladio and Le Corbusier Compared'.
[63] Giedion had already discussed non-Euclidean geometry and its possible effects on the perception of space, in Sigfried Giedion, *Space, Time and Architecture* (Cambridge: Harvard University Press, 1941), 356.
[64] Reyner Banham, 'A Throw-away Aesthetic', *Industrial Design* (March 1960) [1955]: 61–65.

overcoming the limits of the single building, expanding out to the dimension of the city, as the Smithsons' own concepts such as 'cluster', 'pattern' and 'mat-building' would demonstrate.[65] Understood in this way, the concept of structure ended up summarising Banham's stance in relation to the concepts of Townscape, which had revived the theories of the Picturesque through contemporary urban conformations.

In order to trace the genealogy of the notion of form subordinated to topological relations it is necessary to go back to the scientific research of the biologist D'Arcy Thomson in his essay *On Growth and Form*, to which Hamilton had dedicated the eponymous exhibition in 1951.[66] The use of topology as an instrument for a new image had also been debated by contemporary English theorists and had been the object of investigation by Moholy-Nagy, who in *Vision in Motion* questioned the possible use of scientific notions to revolutionise the concept of static and traditional vision.[67]

The substitution of the quality of 'formal legibility of plan' with that of 'memorability as an image' thus entailed the progressive liberation of composition through three distinct ways of conceiving the project: the first, 'formal', represented for Banham the Miesian composition of the plan in the School at Hunstanton and the 'Early New Brutalism'; the second, 'non-formal', presupposed searching for a coherent image by means of circulation, independent units and the flow users, exemplified by the Lecorbuserian-style Smithsons' design for Golden Lane; the third, 'a-formal', characterised the projects of the 'furthest development of New Brutalist architecture', it rejected elementary geometry and combined the adoption of topology with the 'perturbing' force of the artistic experiments of Dubuffet and Pollock, as demonstrated by the Smithsons' competition project for the University of Sheffield.[68]

The kind of architecture envisaged by Banham was soon demonstrated not only by the Smithsons' proposal for the *Berlin Hauptstadt* competition in 1958, but also by an increasing number of international architects, who would reveal a strong attention to buildings' circulation and fluids through projects in which even technical installations were elevated to an unprecedented degree of importance, marking the architectural research of the 1960s. As shown by Kahn's plans, studded with arrows and symbols of circulation indicating various flows which became actual design tool, the logic of relations and of the 'programme' would sound the death knell for the classical composition of design.[69]

What Banham indicated, albeit implicitly, was New Brutalism as a movement for an architecture conceived as the organisation of increasingly autonomous elements, with their own aesthetic, function and expression, to the point of becoming a 'memorable image'. What seems to be missing, in this trajectory of the project towards a new aesthetic and visual research, is the ethical dimension and the 'responsibility' that the Smithsons had placed at the centre of their new 'attitude'.

[65] Alison and Peter Smithson, 'Cluster City: A New Shape for the Community', *Architectural Review*, vol. 122, no. 730 (November 1957): 333–36; Alison and Peter Smithson, 'Aesthetic of Change', *Architects' Year Book*, no. 8 (1957): 14–22.

[66] Such parallels with scientific terminology have been highlighted by Stalder, '"New Brutalism", "Topology" and "Image": Some Remarks on the Architectural Debates in England Around 1950'.

[67] László Moholy-Nagy, *Vision in Motion* (Chicago: P. Theobald, 1947).

[68] 'Sheffield remains the most consistent and extreme point reached by any Brutalist in their search for Une Architecture Autre. [...] it is the only building-design which fully matches up to the threat and promise of *Parallel of Life and Art*', in Banham, 'The New Brutalism', 361.

[69] Summerson would assert that the notion of 'programme' as a central category of modernity, in John Summerson, 'The Case for a Theory of "Modern" Architecture', *RIBA Journal*, vol. 64 (June 1957): 307–10; Laurent Stalder, 'Circuits, conduits, etcetera. Quelques notes sur le caractère normatif des infrastructures dans l'architecture de l'après-guerre', *Matières*, vol. 12 (2015): 116–25 ; for more recent stances on the notion of 'relation' in the discussion on New Brutalism see: Sarah Deyong, 'An Architectural Theory of Relations: Sigfried Giedion and Team X', in *Journal of the Society of Architectural Historian*, vol. 73, no. 2 (June 2014): 226–47; Dirk van den Heuvel, 'Rethinking Relationality', *Adaptive Behavior*, vol. 30, no. 6 (2022): 565–67.

The entirety of Banham's critical operation was functional to the shift from the academic principles of the first New Brutalism to the invention of a new idea of modernity in which the plan becomes an 'image', the structure a matrix and principle of relations, and the materials must be innervated by the anti-artistic principle of the 'as found'. Only through these three qualities would the architecture of New Brutalism succeed in overcoming the formal compositions and historicist components, to align itself with contemporary artistic phenomena capable of establishing '*rapports émouvants*', as Banham recalled at the end of his article.[70]

---

[70] 'The definition of a New Brutalist building derived from Hunstanton and Yale Art Centre, above,' concludes Banham, 'must be modified so as to exclude formality as a basic quality if it is to cover future developments and should more properly read:
1, Memorability as an Image; 2, Clear exhibition of Structure; and 3, Valuation of Materials "as found." Remembering that an Image is what affects the emotions, that structure, in its fullest sense, is the relationship of parts, and that materials "as found" are raw materials, we have worked our way back to the quotation which headed this article "L'Architecture, c'est, avec des Matières Bruts, établir des rapports émouvants," […] Even if it were true that the Brutalists speak only to one another, the fact that they have stopped speaking to Mansart, to Palladio and to Alberti would make The New Brutalism, even in its more private sense, a major contribution to the architecture of today', in Banham, 'The New Brutalism', 361.

chapter five
critical precisions: from summerson to lasdun

The Old Rigour according to Summerson

Banham's retroactive operation, in search of the theoretical outline and operative potential of New Brutalism, was welcomed by international critics as the key contribution on the subject. Despite the ambiguity that runs through the article, Banham's would be the first contribution powerful enough to spread the definition of New Brutalism in the international scene, where a fundamental evolution took place. By virtue of the breadth of Banham's discourse, New Brutalism became a stimulating subject of investigation in the search for possible origins and new examples, to which international critics would not fail to devote themselves. It is to them that we should attribute a decisive step in the formulation of New Brutalism, which evolved from an initial aspiration to a possible 'new theory' and later towards a genre of architecture ascribable to a hypothetical 'Brutalist canon'. The unresolved nature of the definition, suspended between 'movement', 'banner', 'recognition tag' and 'slogan', had already been raised by Banham, and critics soon felt the need to attribute a series of terms to New Brutalism demonstrating the uncertainty of its very nature and indicating a desire to give that definition an identity. This identity was sought through the language and words of the critics: 'idiom', 'expression', 'phenomenon', 'language' and 'phrase' were only the first in a constellation of expressions for a new style with international ambitions.

The outcome to which the definition of New Brutalism was condemned, intuitable from the very first reactions to Banham's article, was the affirmation of a true 'Brutalist style'. Underneath all debates one concept reigns undisputed. The concept of style, disliked by critics since the beginning of the twentieth century, pervades all reasoning on the configuration of post-war architecture, and, if purged of negative meanings, allows us to understand the desire to intercept and define the dynamics underway.

The trajectory of New Brutalism thus evolved within a context of problematic tension that preserved a degree of dynamism and ineffability, consistent with Smithsons' intentions not to crystallise that definition. Yet, New Brutalism was inevitably oriented towards a new form of style, declined each time with different meanings.

The critics' manipulation of the definition makes it possible to identify an interpretative margin that would lead that definition to assume an increasingly higher degree of autonomy with respect to the Smithsons' initial definitions. In doing so, the critics were joining Banham's operation to find, among built examples, other buildings that could substantiate the meanings of New Brutalism.

British critics were among the first to see in the ambiguities of New Brutalism a fertile ground between the aspirations towards the refoundation of the Modern Movement and the cultural instances active in the national debate. As part of an argument that took stock of English architecture in the previous decade, John Summerson entered the question of New Brutalism with the intention of demonstrating the presence of a certain English avant-garde. Summerson's interest in the definition of New Brutalism confirmed the immediate outcome of Banham's idea of shaping that definition within the framework of New Art History, prompting other historians to give force to New Brutalism, validating the success of Banham's second 'thesis'.

Summerson's remarks can be found in the introduction to the exhibition catalogue for *Ten Years of British Architecture, 1945–55*, organised by Trevor Dannat at the Arts Council in January 1956.[1] Summerson's comments marked the entry into the debate of a figure who was fundamental to the culture of history in England, the author of a wide history on English architecture framed as a progressive continuity from the sixteenth century onwards.[2]

In addressing the subject of New Brutalism, Summerson deployed a historical perspective that was neither Banham's nor Smithsons'. Summerson was inclined to read contemporary events under a historical filter and across the centuries, and to emphasise the elements of continuity, and therefore of tradition, rather than the 'new'. This is why Summerson's comments contain a veiled irony, for example, when he called New Brutalism a 'sub-jocular expression' and a 'nickname'. In his eyes, the contemporary debate appeared ridiculous, because it was nothing but the expression of the broad dimension of 'Englishness'. Summerson underlined the continuity of the concepts of New Brutalism when he placed the School at Hunstanton within the tradition of 'classical proportions'. He thus re-read the work of the Smithsons from the perspective of the perpetuity of the concept of the classical, a vision that would culminate in his 1963 book *The Classical Language of Architecture*, published at the height of Brutalism as a style. Bringing the interpretation of the School at Hunstanton back to the paradigm of 'classical proportion' revealed Summerson's critical stance towards Banham who had just demonstrated the overcoming of the classical dimension in his article on New Brutalism.

In addressing the discussion on contemporary architecture, Summerson identified two decisive buildings, the Unité in Marseilles and the School at Hunstanton, placed in a succession that implied a continuity and discontinuity between the examples, to reaffirm on the one hand the role of Le Corbusier as a model, but on the other hand the centrality of the British contribution. In his brief commentary, Summerson reduced New Brutalism's charge of novelty and purged its very origins from the brutal force of material. The Unité remained central to Summerson's argument, as he recognised that it was 'the only continental building of the 'forties to attract much attention in Britain'. But it was not its materiality, nor its structure, but its new systems of proportion, those of the Modulor, that would strike Summerson, overcoming any twentieth-century genre of 'manner, idiom, and the 'isms'. In Summerson's eyes, the control of the material through the modular system, as used by Le Corbusier, achieves the very scope of contemporary architecture, that is, being comprehensible in every

1 John Summerson, *45–55 Ten Years of British Architecture* (London: Arts Council, 1956).
2 John Summerson, *Architecture in Britain 1530 to 1830* (London: Penguin Books, 1958).

aspect and thus allowing a 'command of certain verities'. The mathematical device confirmed the continuity between the Unité in Marseilles and New Brutalism, which Summerson brought back to the control of the system of proportions, in the wake of a certain critical vision already present, such as that of Crosby, who had founded the Smithsons' research on the system of proportions akin to Le Corbusier's Modulor and Wittkower's diagrams.

Summerson's view of New Brutalism was not limited to a sarcastic comment on a 'jocular expression', for he needed that definition to demonstrate England's participation in the new phase of the Modern Movement. To this end Summerson recognised the vital presence of a 'radical spirit', 'of what might be described as a new radicalism' which took many forms, including that of New Brutalism. New Brutalism had already been discussed by Banham in terms of a 'radical philosophy' oriented towards a 'disreputability'. But Summerson's ascription of New Brutalism to a 'new radicalism' implies a vision of the Modern Movement that departs from Pevsner's historical interpretation, or Banham's avant-garde view, to affirm instead a problematic continuity. For Summerson, the School at Hunstanton belonged to the founding nucleus of the Modern Movement, the British 'radicalism' exemplified by Butterfield. This reference seems to open a long-distance dialogue with Banham, who had already expressed the same association in September 1954.[3] While for Banham the reference to Butterfield meant, in the context of his article, 'ruthlessness' and the use of un-cladded materials, for Summerson that same reference was enriched with other connotations that concerned the ethical and symbolic level that guaranteed a profound continuity of the British idea of Englishness.

Through the comparison with Butterfield's architecture, the School at Hunstanton was thus purged of that mixture, already active in New Brutalism, of English and international positions, such as Miesian 'formalism' and Le Corbusier's 'roughness'. Thus, through the same parallelism between the School at Hunstanton and the architecture of Butterfield, we can see the nuances that are by no means secondary between Summerson's position, centred on systems of proportion, and that of Banham who, in Butterfield, had instead found the mechanisms for the articulation of composition, brought back to the international echo generated by the Unité: the theoretical impetus crystallised in the positions against Mies and Platonism. For Summerson, New Brutalism therefore had no ambition for novelty, to the point that he summarised and replaced it with another definition, more appropriate for reaffirming the historical continuity, named 'the Old Rigour'. At this point, Summerson's replacement of the definition of New Brutalism with 'Old Rigour' sounds like a warning to Banham and the critics who left the definition suspended in uncertainty, while questioning the British ancestry of the School at Hunstanton.

Summerson's vision of the Modern Movement as an intellectual attitude and as a trajectory alien to any stylistic declination, in opposition to the American International Style, influenced other readings on the contemporary state of British architecture, such as that of Paul Reilly, critic and professor at the Faculty of Architecture in Liverpool, who, in reviewing the exhibition *Ten Years of British Architecture*, reiterated Summerson's position in counting New Brutalism among the possible 'vigorous developments' of the Modern Movement.[4] The 'intellectual and spiritual attitudes' that Reilly identified in New Brutalism justified its belonging to what Summerson called the 'new radicalism', which revived the radical thinking of the pioneers.

[3] [Reyner Banham], 'School at Hunstanton', *Architectural Review*, vol. 116, no. 693 (September 1954): 150–62.
[4] Paul Reilly, 'British Architects' Response to the Problems of Modern Living', *The Manchester Guardian*, 2 April 1956, 5.

As a result of his January 1956 contribution, Summerson was then invited to attend a symposium organised to shed light on the ambivalent nature of New Brutalism and its multiform definitions. The symposium was held in April at the ICA in London, and was attended by Toni del Renzio, a member of the Independent Group, Architectural Association student D. F. Tomlin, and engineers Ronald Kernkins and Ove Arup, who had collaborated with the Smithsons on the structural design of several of their projects, including the School at Hunstanton. The debate is summarised in the *Architects' Journal* in a contribution entitled 'New Brutalism. Defined at Last', explaining the critical confusion that still pervaded that definition.[5] 'The four speakers produced four definitions of it' was the magazine's sarcastic comment.

In this context, Summerson's statements were more decisive than at the beginning of 1956. 'I don't believe it exists', declared Summerson denying the very existence of New Brutalism, simply recognising it as a critical exercise and pastime of Banham. If Summerson had already questioned any claim to novelty in New Brutalism, through the battle between 'Old' and 'New', the still ambiguous definition became totally innocuous: 'It can't do any harm, and it may do good'.

The only positive comments on New Brutalism came from a student, Tomlin, who recognised in New Brutalism an intellectual openness and the possibility of a 'widening of mental action' for the new generations, through the 'attempt to broaden the range of techniques now available to us'. 'It has made me and my fellow students think a lot more about architecture', Tomlin continued, evoking a return to the discipline of architecture that other astute readers of *Architectural Review* had already noticed in the debates on New Brutalism.

Tomlin's comments demonstrate the extent to which the debate on New Brutalism was creeping into the student context of the Architectural Association through the lectures of Peter Smithson, who joined the school's teaching staff in 1955. In fact, during the Architectural Association Summer School of the same year, Smithson had prepared a series of lectures entitled 'Talks to Young Architects', focused on what they identified as the 'fundamentals of architecture', centred on and deduced from the experiences of De Stijl, Constructivism and Purism.[6]

Two friends of the Smithsons were also present at the symposium: the engineer Jenkins, who had collaborated on the Hunstanton project and for whom the Smithsons had designed the interiors of his residence and office, and Del Renzio, a member of the Independent Group; however, not even their comments revealed the clarity of vision one might expect. The still uncertain contours of the definition of New Brutalism, hovering between movement and theory, were at the heart of Jenkins' observation, who summed up New Brutalism as 'a movement in search of a meaning, and a meaning may come out of it'. The persistence of the Lecorbuserian matrix, found not in the theories of the Modulor but in materiality, is the only certainty to which the definition of New Brutalism was constantly bound, as testified by Del Renzio, who summarised the complex theory of New Brutalism in a succinct motto: 'Do as Corb does, not as Corb says'.[7] Ove Arup, who chaired the symposium, also refrained from any comment, confirming that in the English context New Brutalism was perceived more as a polemical and intellectual debate than a real design direction.

5 [n. a.], 'New Brutalism. Defined at Last', *Architects' Journal*, vol. 123, no. 3189 (12 April 1956): 339.
6 'Fifth Year Orientation Course 1957, based on Talks to Young Architects for the Architectural Association Summer School', 1955, typescript dated summer 1955, Alison and Peter Smithson Special Collection, Loeb Library, Harvard University: 1–3.
7 [n. a.], 'New Brutalism. Defined at Last'.

Le Corbusier's Brutal Concrete, from Zevi to Scully

Throughout the complex events described so far and without his agreement, Le Corbusier was considered one of the protagonists of New Brutalism. The Chandigarh and Ahmedabad construction sites confirmed the assumptions of the Unité in Marseilles, and the Maisons Jaoul and the Ronchamp Chapel reinforced a certain reading of New Brutalism, further shifting its theoretical focus. Emblematic of the advent of New Humanism as understood by the Smithsons, bearer of a synthesis of artistic and architectural impulses, precursor to Banham's concept of 'image', and finally progenitor of that 'anti-academic attitude', the phenomenon of *béton brut* had the ability to intercept all the concerns summarised in the debates on the fate of New Brutalism. However, Le Corbusier was neither the promoter nor the active founder of these debates and, towards the end of the 1950s, he felt obliged to express a significant distance towards them.

Le Corbusier's *béton brut* began to emerge as the fundamental parameter for New Brutalism's critical reception. Over the course of 1956 and 1957, magazines confirmed the widespread success of materials left exposed, and in particular of reinforced concrete. Several international critics recorded the textural effects derived from the various processes, often describing formal aspects, sometimes without resorting to critical definitions of any kind, and sometimes instead underlining the 'brutal' effects of that material.

The various comments following the first publications of images of Le Corbusier's buildings in Ahmedabad and Chandigarh were in this sense demonstrative of a precise cultural stance concerning the definition of New Brutalism. Richard Lannoy, a British artist, photographer and anthropologist living in India, published several photographs in *Architectural Design*, illustrating the effects of light on the bare surfaces of concrete. However, he limited his comments to the use of terms such as 'striking effect', 'textured concrete' and 'sculptural qualities', without ever employing the definition of New Brutalism, despite its then widespread use in the British context.[8]

The assonance between *béton brut* and the adjective 'brutal' was instead the premise for a direct link, made explicit in the Italian context, between Le Corbusier's works in India and the English debates. 'Le Corbusier e la poetica di un'architettura brutale' was the eloquent title chosen by the magazine *Architettura: Cronache e Storia* to characterise Le Corbusier's work in India, brought back to the centre of contemporary debates.[9] In the brief descriptive account, the author, who can be assumed to be Bruno Zevi, repeatedly evoked the plastic character of the material, defining it with the particular adjective 'brutal', due to the 'rough and grainy marks of the wooden forms' (see figure 25). The adjective 'brutal' in this context was specifically related to the English debate, and more precisely to the definition of New Brutalism. According to *Architettura: Cronache e Storia*, New Brutalism was defined specifically in relation to the work of Le Corbusier and found its *raison d'être* in the treatment of the concrete of the Unité in Marseille. Unité's concrete was defined as 'brutal' for its violent and unexpected traits, capable of breaking the rules, both in its finishing and in its form. Le Corbusier was also associated with the charisma of Picasso, thus confirming the intrinsic link between artistic practices and the experiments that occurred on the Unité building site, which had been noted by critics at the end of the 1940s. The interpretations enunciated in the contribution of *Architettura: Cronache e Storia* confirmed several links that would prove indissoluble from the reception and critical manipulation

---

[8]   Richard Lannoy, 'Two Buildings in India. Mill Owners' Association Building, Ahmedabad', *Architectural Design*, vol. 26, no. 1 (January 1956): 18–20; Richard Lannoy, 'India. House at Ahmedabad', *Architectural Design*, vol. 26, no. 3 (March 1956): 93–95.
[9]   [n.a.], 'Le Corbusier e la poetica di un'architettura brutale', *Architettura: Cronache e Storia*, vol. 26, supplement no. 3 (March 1956): 75–77.

25 'Le Corbusier e la poetica di un'architettura brutale', *Architettura: Cronache e Storia*, vol. 26, March 1956, supplement 3, p. 75

rivista delle riviste

Le Corbusier
e la poetica di un'architettura brutale

Qui, *in alto*: particolare della scala proiettante dalla facciata d'ingresso. *A sinistra*: il prospetto sud-occidentale con la rampa d'ingresso e la scala. *In basso*: gli schermi di cemento che proteggono la facciata rivolta ad oriente.
Si tratta della sede dell'Associazione della Società dei proprietari di Cotonifici a Ahmedabad, il nuovo centro industriale e amministrativo del Gujerat, Stato di Bombay, che domina la più fertile regione del cotone indiano e ha una popolazione di mezzo milione di abitanti. L'indipendenza indiana non è stata sofferta per nulla: Ahmedabad, per lungo tempo quartiere generale del Mahatma Gandhi, è divenuta, dopo la liberazione del 1947, una grande città moderna. Le Corbusier vi ha costruito tre edifici, di cui questo e il Museo sono pressoché completati. Il prospetto d'ingresso è plasticamente il più interessante. La scansione diagonale delle schermature cementizie, l'angolo smussato, la rampa, la proiezione della scala ne fanno un altro capolavoro della creatività febbrile dell'attuale Le Corbusier. Un uomo fantasiosamente scalpitante, che rifiuta di invecchiare.

of New Brutalism. Indeed, the British debates were already intrinsically linked to Le Corbusier, and to a certain artistic ascendancy of his *béton brut*, although the latter was destined to fade into the phenomenon of international Brutalism.[10]

Starting from Le Corbusier's buildings the definition of New Brutalism reached an international dimension, and progressively gained independency from the theories and works of the Smithsons, to become a tool through which critics configured new interpretations of existing buildings, which enabled the effectiveness or otherwise of this label to be determined.

---

[10] 'New Brutalism is the latest -ism, identified by *Architectural Review* to characterise a trend in the British movement. This taste can also be traced back to Le Corbusier, to his desire to break, to violently model matter, which became unexpectedly apparent from the Unity of Housing in Marseilles onwards. Le Corbusier, as so often happened to Picasso, smashes, with a single masterly and naked stroke opens a passage through which others, even the British Puritans, are unleashed', ibid.: 77.

Le Corbusier's 'brutal' works in India became the subject of an investigation into the material effects by Gio Ponti, who published a commentary on Villa Shodan in Ahmedabad in the magazine *Domus*.[11] Based on Hervé's photographic documentation of Villa Shodan, Ponti distanced that work from the British horizon and did not associate it with any style because he intended, unlike Zevi, to demonstrate a continuity with the founding principles of early twentieth-century rationalist architecture. The concept of continuity, and implicitly the concern about the fate of the Modern Movement and the direction shown by Le Corbusier, was therefore the theoretical scaffolding upon which Ponti investigated the relationships between the English debates and the phenomenon of *béton brut*. Ponti claimed a continuity, though international, through a photographic comparison staged in the volume's summary with Rietveld's Villa Schöder and demonstrated the hypothesis of the persistence of a certain underlying abstractionism that had fuelled that same culture of rationalism.

Some young London architects of the same age as the Smithsons, such as James Stirling and Denys Lasdun, began to form a common front of fundamental denial and scepticism towards the definition of New Brutalism, which they would never come to accept, either when commenting on Le Corbusier's works already ascribed to this definition, such as the Maisons Jaoul, or when their works fell victim to the critics' ascription to the label of New Brutalism. Lasdun, who in 1956 had already experimented with exposed concrete and who was to become one of the authors of a colossal reinforced concrete building in the heart of London (the South Bank complex), in a comment on the Maisons Jaoul carefully underlined the impossibility of classifying it.[12] Lasdun associated the Maisons Jaoul to adjectives belonging to an already consolidated lexical repertoire of New Brutalism. 'Aggressively', 'primitive', 'raw', 'ruthless' are terms that Lasdun reintroduced with the intention of provoking critics, including Banham, who in December established the critical boundaries of the definition of New Brutalism. His conclusion echoes Stirling's position, advancing a vision that is devoid of any stylistic concerns: 'The Jaoul Houses, likeable or not, should be hailed or challenged, but not classified'.[13]

Zevi's intuition of associating the 'brutal' treatment of matter in Le Corbusier's works with the British phenomenon of New Brutalism, continued in the magazine *Architettura: Cronache e storia* in June 1956, this time regarding the Maisons Jaoul.[14] The English debate was still the cultural reference for the magazine, which recorded Lasdun's position and summarised his theoretical conclusion, hinging on the impossibility of classifying that building. But unlike Lasdun, for *Architettura: Cronache e Storia* the Jaoul represented a synthesis of two divergent tendencies: on the one hand, the components linked to a 'cubist language' and on the other 'the new process of matter' visible in the 'brutal wall treatments'. The concept of 'brutal' thus became a decisive reading parameter, to the point that the magazine tried disseminating it in various languages, publishing, alongside the article, a series of summaries in English, French, German and Spanish, where the adjective 'brutal' attributed to the material was transposed directly to Le Corbusier: '"brutal" tendencies'; 'dit le "brutal"'; 'der letzte "brutale" Le Corbusier'; 'el "brutal"'.[15]

In the context of Le Corbusier's influence, and surprisingly, after recording the spread of New Brutalism in Sweden,[16] Eric de Maré once again used this definition to present to the readers of the *Manchester Guardian* recent trends in Brazilian architecture, in particular the treatment of concrete, which appears 'virile' and 'adventurous',

---

[11] Gio Ponti, 'Giovinezza d'oggi o splendida età di Le Corbusier?' in *Domus*, vol. 320 (July 1956): 1–4.

[12] Denys Lasdun, 'France, Maison Jaoul, Paris', *Architectural Design*, vol. 26, no. 3 (March 1956): 75–77.

[13] Ibid.

[14] [n.a.], 'Le Corbusier a terra', *Architettura: Cronache e Storia*, vol. 1, no. 8 (June 1956): 111.

[15] Ibid.

[16] Eric de Maré, 'Eric de Maré Pays a Return Visit to Sweden', *Architects' Journal*, vol. 121, no. 3125 (January 1955): 101–10.

'often crude in the manner of the New Brutalism', thus anticipating other readings, which in the 'poor' concrete used in Brazil would see a new milestone in the international spread of New Brutalism.[17]

The success of the *béton brut* technique was not always aligned with the emerging phenomenon of New Brutalism and its international spread, although an indissoluble link was emerging in critical reception to the technique. Critics often introduced new declinations and adjectives to describe the effects of *béton brut*, such as the 'ripple texture' of the UNESCO headquarters in Paris achieved by the narrow planks of the formwork, described in *Architectural Design*.[18] The terms of truthfulness and honesty of the material applied by certain actors in the debate, including Le Corbusier and the Smithsons, were on the other hand clouded, according to other critics, by the 'eccentricities' of concrete, which opened the way to 'all arsenal of misunderstanding', even becoming, in the example of the Ronchamp Chapel, an 'accumulation of lies'.[19]

The concrete of Kahn's works, including the Medical Center, the Bath House and even what Banham had defined as 'the only Brutalist building in the new world' – the Yale Art Gallery – was discussed by Walter McQuade without any mention of the phenomenon of New Brutalism, although American magazines had already recorded its presence in the debates.[20] However, the terms used by McQuade set up a repertoire that would soon be associated with New Brutalism in America. The 'mottled' concrete surfaces that express the 'muscularity' of the Yale Art Gallery or the concrete of the Bath House, which serves to 'enlarge and re-emphasise the column', are described as essential components of a 'bulky' architecture, which reiterates the 'visual importance' of the elements. It is no surprise that Banham's third category, 'memorability as an image', resonates in the very definition of 'visual importance', here declined through Kahn's treatment of concrete.[21]

The fluctuating position of the magazines at the end of the 1950s about the definition of New Brutalism can also be seen in Carlo Monotti's annotations in *Architettura: Cronache e Storia* commenting on a building that in a couple of years was to be included among the examples of Italian Brutalism: Figini and Pollini's Chiesa della Madonna dei Poveri.[22] The comments about 'the surface as if coming out of the formwork' and the 'expressive impulse' of the material did not allow the adjective 'brutal' to permeate, an adjective that had been repeatedly evoked by the same magazine and which in the Italian context seemed to be associated exclusively with the work of Le Corbusier.

Against the backdrop of the debate and the questioning of New Brutalism as style, canon, dogma, theory or even movement, Vincent Scully, an American critic and historian of architecture, raised the question of the fate of the Modern Movement through an argument related to the American context. In his contribution to the magazine *Perspecta* entitled 'Toward a Re-definition of Style', Scully defined his own historiographical vision for the 'Architecture of Democracy', in which he identified and interrogated the founding nucleus of architecture for American society.[23] In this contribution, Scully highlighted the premises for a search for complexity that would find different outlets beyond New Brutalism. With this perspective Scully traverses the history of architecture from the nineteenth century, recognising an evolutionary process

---

[17] Eric de Maré, 'Brazil's Architecture', *The Manchester Guardian*, 22 January 1957, 4.

[18] [n.a.], 'Letter from Paris. Unesco Building under Construction', *Architectural Design* (June 1957): 216.

[19] Emile Henvaux, 'La Maison', February 1957, republished in 'Ancora contro Ronchamp', *Architettura: Cronache e Storia*, vol. 3, no. 21 (July 1957): 216.

[20] Lawrence Alloway, 'Art News from London', *Art News*, vol. 53, no. 6 (October 1954): 54; [Peter Blake], 'Three Approaches to Architecture', *Architectural Forum*, vol. 102, no. 5 (May 1955): 142–45.

[21] Walter McQuade, 'Architect Louis Kahn and His Strong-boned Structures', *Architectural Forum*, vol. 107, no. 4 (October 1957): 134–43.

[22] Carlo Monotti, 'Chiesa della madonna dei poveri', *Architettura: Cronache e Storia*, vol. 3, no. 25 (November 1957): 452–57.

[23] Vincent Scully, 'Modern Architecture: Toward a Redefinition of Style', *Perspecta*, vol. 4 (1957): 4–11.

dubbed as 'classicising'. By searching for permanent values, Scully came to define the contemporary condition of architecture, found in the aspiration for an 'Architecture of Democracy', which expresses a contemporary 'New Humanism'. This definition was not new in the discussion, and it recalled the English debates, as well as the contribution of Geoffrey Scott, who had introduced this definition in the 1940s centred on the categories of 'empathy', 'experience' and 'human-body'. Scully's New Humanism, on the other hand, had clearly different characteristics, as the presence of history sublimated in 'masculine', 'primitive' and 'muscular' traits, clearly defined against the background of the advent of a new exposed concrete architecture – that proposed by Le Corbusier. From the traits of the New Humanism based on Le Corbusier's last works, Scully devised the concept of 'action', linked to the expressive force of 'modern material, reinforced concrete'. It was precisely the concept of 'action', which would later be taken up by other critics and associated with the phenomenon of New Brutalism, that carried a radical potential for the renewal of 'modern architecture'. To demonstrate that New Humanism and the concept of 'action' are linked to the material left exposed, even if Scully never made it explicit, we must consider the two images that opened and closed that same issue of the magazine: Hervé's photographs of concrete details from Le Corbusier's works in India show how the reasoning reaches its apex in the expression of the material and demonstrate how for American culture the centre of interest remains architecture, beyond political or ethical stances (see figure 26).

26 Back cover with Lucien Hervé's photos of the Palais des Filateurs and House in Ahmedabad by Le Corbusier, *Perspecta*, vol. 4, 1957

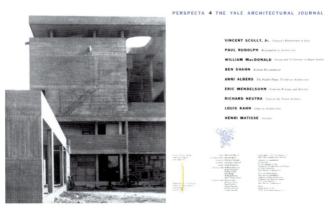

The epicentre of New Humanism, as defined by Scully, was articulated around the vitalism and historical continuity manifested in the violent action of matter, which took on those 'primitive' and 'muscular' traits, but which should not, according to Scully, be framed in a formula: 'Slogans, tags, and verbal formulas are useful, but in the end, they cannot define modern architecture or any part. At their worst, when dealing with the present, they might limit it'.[24]

The fact that Scully structured his argument on works that had become canonical for the question of New Brutalism, such as the Unité in Marseille, is a clear response to the European debate. But Scully's position is stripped of any contentious tone, demonstrating a deliberate abstention from the use of the term New Brutalism to avoid ethical and intellectual considerations unrelated to architecture.

Scully's silence coincided with the agenda of the magazine *Perspecta*, which, in turn, did not fail to propose themes that were at the origin of British New Brutalism. In the first issues of the magazine, contemporary interest in the raw treatment of materials and the ornamental and artisanal issues linked to figures such as Ruskin was paralleled with the phenomena of contemporary industrial and technological civilisation, through visual juxtaposition suggesting a critique oriented towards practical considerations, far from the British 'visual re-education' underlying the ideological and political discourse on styles. This may help us to understand the scepticism of American culture towards the definition of New Brutalism, which would be perceived as a derivative of those debates.

Even when in the pages of *Perspecta* the question of New Brutalism was more explicitly hinted at through the example of Hunstanton, within a more general discourse on 'craftsmanship' it was the 'aesthetic of materials' that was considered to trace a broader legacy, going from Viollet-le-Duc to Loos and Moholy-Nagy.[25] This is the premise for understanding the specific stylistic and surface treatments that the definition of New Brutalism, especially in its declination of international Brutalism, would assume in the North American context of the 1960s.

At this point in time, the silence of the undisputed but incidental protagonist of New Brutalism appears, to say the least, ambiguous. Le Corbusier's silence, the architect ascribed as the 'practitioner' of New Brutalism, and whose first post-war building gave rise to all the debates that divided English circles into opposing factions, challenged international critics to directly interview him on the subject.

For this reason, the Italian magazine *Zodiac* questioned Le Corbusier in 1960 about his stance on New Brutalism, in an interview about his legacy and influence on new generations.[26] *Zodiac*'s first question was about the relevance of New Brutalism, framed as an 'unpredicted consequence' of Le Corbusier's buildings. In revenge, Le Corbusier acknowledged the international diffusion of this definition but categorically rejected the appellation 'Brutalist'. His response demonstrates once again how architects were primarily concerned with the technical and constructive dimensions of architecture, while discarding its intellectual and theoretical issues. Le Corbusier's response also attempted to bring the discussion back to the intrinsic value of matter, to the truth of *béton brut* that generated everything. Sounding a clear warning against those 'messieurs de la plume' who hurriedly assign labels and categories, Le Corbusier's statement turned again to the image of a faithful material that refuses cladding:

---

[24] Ibid.
[25] Christopher Tunnard, 'The Conscious Stone', *Perspecta*, vol. 3 (1955): 22–78.
[26] [n.a.], 'Cinq questions à Le Corbusier', *Zodiac*, vol. 5 (1960): 46–51.

'Brutalist' = Anglicism. Like 'versatile' in English, it means multiplied, abundance, wealth. In French 'versatile' is a very depreciative qualitative. I used 'béton brut' (in English rough concrete). The result: total fidelity, perfect accuracy of formwork, a material that does not cheat. It replaces (it removes) cladding which is a treacherous and loose garment (which betrays). Béton brut says: I am concrete! [...] Before 'brutalism', these gentlemen of the pen had proclaimed, in order to create a sensation (and to laugh under their breath): 'This is Baroque!'[27]

This decisive statement by Le Corbusier was completely ignored by critics, who did not care to specify or investigate in more detail the limits of the complex relationships between Le Corbusier's *béton brut* and the definition of New Brutalism. Instead, they were content to have identified New Brutalism as an instrument of synthesis to describe the international phenomenon of exposed concrete, and they would continue to appeal to *béton brut* until that definition lost all its avant-garde impetus. It is easy to see this as a sign of a nascent crisis and divergence between the tools of criticism and the vision of architects, who would indeed feel distant from any attempt at categorisation.

Although the questions and answers in *Zodiac* are the only published testimony by Le Corbusier on Brutalism, he did, however, confirm his distance from that definition in two letters to Sert, in which he totally repudiated the adjective 'brutal': 'Béton brut is not the "concrete of a brute"; it is simply concrete straight from formwork'.[28] For Le Corbusier, out of the vast range of solutions he demonstrated and despite the complex relationships that this technique brings to light, *béton brut* was the manifestation of the very nature of the material and its artistic potential, a far cry from the unexpected intellectual turn that sparked the debate in England:

Béton brut was born out of the Unité d'Habitation in Marseille, where there were eighty contractors and such a massacre of concrete that it was not possible to dream of making useful connections with plaster. I decided: let's leave it all raw [brut]. I called it *béton brut*. The English immediately jumped on it and called me 'brutal'. In the end, the brute is Corbu. They called it 'the new brutality'. My friends and admirers think I'm the brute of brutal concrete.[29]

The Strict-Brutalists

Coinciding with the initial critical manipulation of New Brutalism, the official claim to the invention of that label was published. In August 1956, having noted its success, Hans Asplund intervened in the debates to affirm the paternity of the definition. The cultural connections between Sweden and England were the prerequisite for him to send his friend De Maré a letter that was published in the same magazine in which Banham had presented the theoretical framework of New Brutalism (see figure 27).[30]

The fact that the letter was published by De Maré is therefore to be seen as the Softs' response to the ongoing debate on New Brutalism. Asplund's document thus takes on the dual significance of a direct response to Banham and a written claim in reaction to his article. In transmitting Asplund's letter to the editorial staff of *Architectural Review*, De Maré used phrases that clarify the cultural climate in which the

[27] Ibid.
[28] Le Corbusier, Letter to Sert, 29 May 1961, in Anna Rosellini, 'Oltre il "béton brut": Le Corbusier e la "nouvelle stéréotomie"', in Flaminia Bardati, Anna Rosellini (eds.), *Arte e Architettura. Le Cornici della storia* (Milan: Bruno Mondadori, 2007), 231–58.
[29] Le Corbusier, Letter to Sert, 26 May 1962, quoted in Cyrille Simonnet, 'Le béton, le brut et la truelle', in Sbriglio (ed.), *Le Corbusier et la question du brutalisme*, 133.
[30] Eric de Maré, 'Et tu, Brute?' *Architectural Review*, vol. 120 (August 1956): 72.

27 Hans Asplund's
letter, 'Correspondence,
Et Tu, Brute?',
Architectural Review,
vol. 120, August 1956,
no. 715, p. 72

have been the first architect interested in street furniture; there is a sheet with six different lamp-posts, and two with a pump-cum-lamp-post.

The exhibition, which is explained in a detailed and most excellent catalogue by Dorothy Stroud, will remain open until September.

Homes of the Academy

Several proud owners of eighteenth-century houses in London have of late brought out well produced pamphlets to tell and illustrate the story of their houses (Boulton & Paul, 41, Stanhope Gate; Royal Worcester China, 30, Curzon Street; Pilkington Brothers, Selwyn House; Consolidated Zinc Corporation, Ely House, Dover Street). The Royal Academy has joined them and its librarian, Mr. S. C. Hutchison, has indeed much to say and much to show.

CORRESPONDENCE

Et Tu, Brute?

To the Editors,

Sirs,—The origin of the New Brutalism (see your article of last December) has become a subject for academic research, and you may be interested in the following letter which I have received from Hans Asplund, son of the late Gunnar Asplund: 'In January, 1950, I shared offices with my esteemed colleagues Bengt Edman and Lennart Holm. These architects were at the time designing a house in Uppsala. Judging from their drawings I called them, in a mildly sarcastic way, "Neo-Brutalists" (the Swedish word for New Brutalists). The following summer, at a jollification together with some English friends, among whom were Michael Ventris, Oliver Cox and Graeme Shankland, the term was mentioned again in a

The first New Brutalist building: see letter on this page.

definition of New Brutalism was then evolving, emphasising how it had become a subject for academic research, perhaps also referring to the symposium held in April of that year: 'The origins of the New Brutalism have become a subject for academic research'.

In a succession of contributions that sought to identify other buildings that could be ascribed to the New Brutalism movement, and following contributions by the Smithsons, Segal, Johnson, Alloway, Banham and Zevi, which called into question other works that could be ascribed to that definition, Asplund clarified his version about its invention.

In the letter, Asplund claimed to have invented the term 'Neo-brutalists' in January 1950 to connote Edman and Holm's Villa Göth in a 'mildly sarcastic way'. He then confirmed that it only entered the English debates of the 1950s after being visited by Ventris, Cox and Shankland, who belonged to the Softs' wing of the LCC. The photograph of the villa was published with the caption 'The first New Brutalist building' because it chronologically preceded the Smithsons' House in Soho.

What is surprising in this rapid evolution of events following Banham's article is the Smithsons' silence. Their reaction to the letter is still unknown and they ignored it throughout the debates. During this period, they began collecting clippings and fragments of magazines and newspapers about the ongoing debate on New Brutalism to build up an archive, which also included Asplund's letter, as well as Banham's article of December 1955, but without any annotations.

Only one of the Smithsons' contributions during 1956 attracted the attention of critics and was discussed in terms of the definition of New Brutalism. This was the installation 'Patio & Pavilion' at the exhibition *This Is Tomorrow*, curated by Crosby in August at the Whitechapel, London. The Smithsons' pavilion staged a 'habitat' reduced down to the essential and designed to accommodate a series of 'symbols'

28 Reyner Banham, 'This is Tomorrow', *Architectural Review*, vol. 120, September 1956, no. 716, p. 186

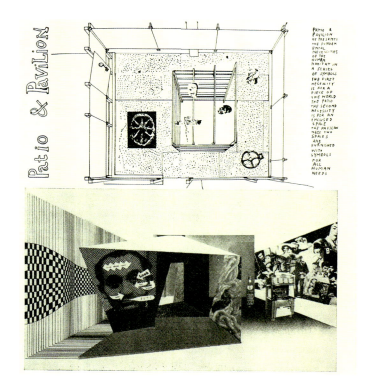

chosen and arranged by Henderson and Paolozzi and that responded to a series of primordial 'human needs' (see figure 28).[31] The allegory of a primitive and a-temporal habitat was also a theme of the Smithsons' research at the time, discussed during the IX CIAM in Dubrovnik and in various articles of the same year.[32] The pavilion was defined by the Smithsons as a 'shed', using a term that provocatively recalled Pevsner's definition of architecture, as through the word 'shed' he had distinguished the different notions of 'building' and 'architecture'.[33]

Banham reviewed the various installations presented in *This Is Tomorrow*.[34] He was deeply disappointed by 'Patio & Pavilion', as he was probably expecting a further manifestation of the 'ruthlessness', a confirmation of the anti-artistic attitude of New Brutalism. Banham did not discuss Smithson's intervention in detail; he merely dismissed it with an almost negative 'strict-Brutalist' connotation that betrays, one might almost say, the exhaustion of the theoretical force he had identified at the end of 1955. It is clear from Banham's review that it was the presence of the Smithsons alone that maintained the ascription of their pavilion to New Brutalism.

[31] Exhibition catalogue, *This Is Tomorrow*, Whitechapel Art Gallery, London, 1956. For a recent analysis of the Smithsons' pavilion, see Ben Highmore, 'Rough Poetry: "Patio and Pavilion" Revisited', *Oxford Art Journal*, vol. 29, no. 2 (2006): 269–90.

[32] Alison and Peter Smithson, 'An Alternative to the Garden City Idea', *Architectural Design*, vol. 35, no. 6 (June 1956): 229–31; Alison and Peter Smithson, 'Cluster Pattern: Images from a Sketch Book', *Architecture and Building News* (June 1956).

[33] 'A bicycle shed is a building; Lincoln Cathedral is a piece of architecture. Nearly everything that encloses space on a scale sufficient for a human being to move in is a building; the term architecture applies only to buildings designed with a view to aesthetic appeal', in Nikolaus Pevsner, *An Outline of European Architecture*, vol. 7 (London: Penguin, 1942).

[34] Reyner Banham, 'Not Quite Painting or Sculpture Either', *Architects' Journal*, vol. 124, no. 3207 (August 1956): 217–29.

Instead, it was Hamilton, McHale and Voelcker's 'Fun House' installation that succeeded in 'smashing down all the barriers' by staging the phantasmagorical universe of 1950s popular culture, with optical illusions, ultraviolet lights, collage and science fiction. These were the characteristics in which Banham could see the realisation of 'une architecture autre', the bearer of a new order subverting the classic concept of art, even though he did not use the definition of New Brutalism to describe it: 'I find it the most exciting thing I have seen in years [...] and it has, to my taste, a slight lead on the strict-Brutalist section at the back of the hall'.[35]

The reasons for this disappointment were revealed the following month in *Architectural Review*, where Banham admitted that the Smithsons pavilion was nothing more than the result of symbolic and allegorical research crossed with traditionalist rhetoric: 'The Smithson-Henderson-Paolozzi contribution showed the New Brutalists at their most submissive to traditional values'.[36] Banham also pointed out that the objects staged by Paolozzi and Henderson resulted in a disappointing 'confirmation of accepted values and symbols'.[37] Returning to his personal preference for Hamilton, McHale and Voelcker's pavilion, Banham summarised what for him were still the key concepts of New Brutalism, exemplified by 'image', 'association', 'novelty and technology', and, above all, the rejection of the discipline of geometry.[38]

For Banham, the sense of novelty and the experimental impetus of the 'Fun House' can be identified with a vital component of New Brutalism. The pavilion represented the evolving vision of New Brutalism, far from being a canon, enriched by references from the world of pop art. In contrast, the Smithsons' proposal was retrograde and anchored in an already outdated form of New Brutalism.

It was perhaps this critical interpretation by Banham that pushed the Smithsons to reposition themselves within a more contemporary discourse on pop art through what can be considered another manifesto, which appeared under the title 'But Today We Collect Ads', published in November 1956.[39]

The submerged debate about New Brutalism, which presumably continued in the meetings of the circle of friends in which it was formed, revealed itself through Banham's response to the accusations of a reader of the *Architectural Review*, Sidney H. Tasker, who mocked New Brutalism and sent a letter 'aimed at the heart of the arrant nonsense currently being written about New Brutalism'.[40] In the letter Tasker accused Banham of 'obscurity' and targeted the definition of New Brutalism, stripping it of any claim to novelty. Banham's response to the accusations reveals the process that led to the writing of the New Brutalism article: 'I was introduced to the subject much as a staff-writer on the D...ly E.p.ess [Daily Express] might have Rock 'n' Roll suddenly fall on him/her. [...] I found my subject sympathetic, though almost ineffable.'[41]

The controversy raised by the December 1955 article continued to preoccupy readers, who repeatedly discredited the definition of New Brutalism, again accusing Banham of pursuing personal interests: 'The chief asset in this struggle for power is their self-educated scribe and trumpeter, Lord Ha-Ha (played by Mr. Banham)'.[42] At

35 Ibid.
36 Reyner Banham, 'This is Tomorrow', *Architectural Review*, vol. 120, no. 716 (September 1956): 186–87.
37 Ibid.
38 'Curiously their [Hamilton, McHale and Voelcker] section seemed to have more in common with that of the New Brutalists than any other, and the clue to this kinship would appear to lie in the fact that it neither relied on abstract concepts, but on concrete images – images that carry the mass of tradition and association. Or the energy of novelty and technology, but resist classification by the geometrical disciplines by which most other exhibits were dominated', ibid.
39 Alison Smithson, 'But Today We Collect Ads', *ARK*, vol. 18 (November 1956): 49–50.
40 Sidney H. Tasker, 'Letter', *Architects' Journal*, vol. 124, no. 3213 (27 September 1956): 438–39.
41 Reyner Banham, 'Hair-cut, You!', *Architects' Journal*, vol. 124, no. 3214 (4 October 1956): 469; 471.
42 Sidney H. Tasker, 'We present for your entertainment "Under ploy-wood". Starring Reyner "teasy-weasy" Banham. This is a daring production in which everything is exposed', *Architects' Journal*, vol. 124, no. 3217 (25 October 1956): 583.

this juncture, Banham's response was eloquent: 'I am neither a founder, nor a member, of New Brutalism, but a working journalist who was asked by his editors to report back on the Brutalist Phenomenon, and I hope that my article was a reasonably responsible fulfilment of that commission'.[43]

Thoughts in Progress on the Brutalist Canon

The various controversies triggered by the correspondence on the question of New Brutalism published periodically in magazines, amplified by Summerson's sentence 'I don't believe it exists' and repeatedly evoked in various other contributions, prompted *Architectural Design*, probably at Crosby's suggestion, to undertake an investigation published in the 'Opinion' section of the April 1957 issue, entitled 'Thoughts in Progress. The New Brutalism.[44]

The section followed the traditional form of a dialogue between two characters who remained anonymous, but behind whom were hidden Denys Lasdun, who joined the magazine's editorial team in 1956, and John Davies, an architecture critic.[45] The pretext of the form of dialogue and anonymity allowed a certain freedom in the expression of opinions and no criticism was spared regarding statements by the Smithsons and Banham.

With a broader perspective on the fate of the Modern Movement, Lasdun and Davies retraced the basic principles of modern architecture and anticipated some fundamental themes of New Brutalism. Published from December 1956, the column 'Opinion' dealt with investigations that specifically concerned architecture as a system of structure and materials, their truths and fictions, through a discussion based on buildings that were decisive for the understanding of the state of the Modern Movement, such as the Seagram Building, Nervi's hangars and the Unité in Marseille.

In order to clarify the definition of New Brutalism, Lasdun and Davies delved into the diverging views between the Smithsons' first formulation and Banham's new position. In fact, while they acknowledged the clarity of Banham's position, at least in the three postulates, they challenged the Smithsons for their brevity and ambiguous statements, which had generated nothing but polemics and uncertainties.

Against the backdrop of Summerson's definition of 'Old Rigour' and Wittkower's theories of 'classical proportions', Lasdun and Davies also identified a concept linked to the British tradition, that of 'classical wholeness', which refers to Alberti's concept of interdependence between the parts and the whole. In the case of New Brutalism, the concept of 'classical wholeness' was intrinsically linked to the visibility of the architectural mechanisms, that generates an untouchable order, controlled through the choice of materials 'as found', understood as being without cladding, and with the structure left exposed.

Lasdun and Davies clarified the elements of distinction between Banham's position and that of the Smithsons. The main difference lay in Banham's introduction of the concept of topology, which affirmed a system of relations that disrupted classical symmetry, in the direction of 'a-formalism'. However, Lasdun specified how this concept undermined one of the founding essences of New Brutalism, namely, the geometric component of classical derivation. Therefore, the topology, evoked by Banham to

---

[43] Reyner Banham, reply to letter by N. Keith Scott, 'Egg-head Exposed?', *Architects' Journal*, vol. 124, no. 3216 (18 October 1956): 546.

[44] [n.a.], 'Thoughts in Progress: The New Brutalism', *Architectural Design*, vol. 27, no. 4 (April 1957): 111–13.

[45] Steve Parnell reveals the names of the authors of the 'Opinion' column and specifies that the interlocutor transcribed in italics is Lasdun. See Steve Parnell, *Architectural Design, 1954–1972* (Sheffield: University of Sheffield School of Architecture, 2011), 155–57.

free New Brutalism from the rule of proportions, altered the equilibrating nucleus first reaffirmed by Crosby and Summerson, and which Lasdun brought back to the wider concept of 'Englishness'.

The construction of New Brutalism as a critical tool was revealed in the progressive development of the reflection on the same protagonists and the same examples, which appeared from time to time in different lights. And so the School at Hunstanton demonstrated new and increasingly complex connections with New Brutalism. This was the only building that had so far been unanimously recognised by critics as the sole example of New Brutalism built architecture.

The Smithsons were also challenged for their tendency towards the vernacular and the peasant picturesque, which Lasdun and Davies found inappropriate for the contemporary characteristics of the 'atomic age'. If New Brutalism was to remain relevant, it had to be purged of any Ruskinian interpretation. It is easy to see that behind Lasdun's and Davies' criticism of the Smithsons, there was the aim at re-evaluating the debates within CIAM. Against the backdrop of a discourse of the Modern Movement that entered the debates on the heart of the cities, and a vision that admitted the influence of primitive civilisations and spontaneous settlements, the strength of the dialogue published in 'Opinion' was also evident in the desire to detach the definition of New Brutalism from that cultural and poetic universe. Instead, it was the contemporary character linked to industrial and productive civilisation that was felt to be relevant. To a certain extent, Lasdun and Davies thus restored New Brutalism to Le Corbusier's apology of '*civilisation machiniste*'.

It is clear, at this point in the English debate on New Brutalism, that this definition was rapidly becoming the victim of contradictory contaminations of impulses that went in several directions, either towards the civilisation of the contemporary machine age or towards a vernacular and nostalgic regionalism. Due to this ambivalence, it risked becoming an unusable category. In the attempts to specify it, one senses in the dialogue the fear of generating a potentially deviant category, because it was increasingly disconnected from a constructive nature, the bearer of a poetics linked to matter and structure. If ideological values were to be attributed to it, as various English critics were doing, there was a risk of transforming the definition of New Brutalism into a label with undefined limits. The debate between Lasdun and Davies thus demonstrates the difficulty of English critics and others in arriving at an inclusive, universal and, above all, comprehensible definition.

Amongst the shifting elements, the presence of Lasdun, an architect, was decisive when he discredited the Smithsons' written formulations in favour of the construction of architecture. It was at this point that the dialogue shifted focus from trying to define New Brutalism to speaking of the 'Brutalists', that is, the architects, moving into questions of detail, material and the *non-finito* as an element of novelty in relation to the International Style, understood as the decay of the heroic phase of the Modern Movement. '[Brutalists] clearly understood that a constant refinement of detail can only be devitalizing' was Lasdun's comment, which went on into a significant discussion of the new poetics of imperfection, the truth of matter and the absence of cladding. It is no coincidence that in the dialogue Le Corbusier returned to centre stage and the discussion on New Brutalism was brought back to his thought, his buildings and his writings, in particular 'roughness' or 'brutality', concepts referred to in the dialogue that are found in the pages of *Vers une architecture*. Lasdun, leaving aside more ideological or theoretical reasoning, concluded the following:

> It seems to me that any of these formulations, any of these -isms, can easily become a curse. They limit the good architects, who find themselves tied to the tails of their manifestos, they befuddle the less good, who think they

have solved their problems when all they have got is a severe attack of verbal indigestion. [...] He [the architect] should leave that to the architectural journalist.[46]

According to Lasdun, New Brutalism could have been a significant category in orienting the new architecture, if it had not been dogmatically set up by Banham in the search for absolute founding principles. Lasdun's statements on New Brutalism would find an outcome in his future poetics. If we compare his 1950s residential buildings' fine details to his 1960s concrete works, we can deduce, although he would never admit it, his true vision of New Brutalism's operative stance, beyond the conundrum of the ideological discussions.

The Smithsons' Ethics

The various definitions of New Brutalism seemed totally overwhelmed by the 'brut' root underlined as the only certainty against inconclusive theoretical wanderings. This reasoning is not valid for the case of the Smithsons, who returned to the concept of 'architecture of reality', also by virtue of their desire to advance their own concept with respect to Banham's 'architecture autre'. While Banham's preoccupation with composition was dominant at the time he invented the concept of 'architecture autre', for the Smithsons the ethical and universalistic dimension, ranging from the vision of materials to the definition of a community, was again brought back to the dimension of 'reality'. This is the very concept that they returned to in their response to the dialogue on New Brutalism published in 'Opinion'. That contribution marks an important moment in the debate on New Brutalism in England, and the two protagonists involved, the Smithsons, had the opportunity to briefly respond at the bottom of Lasdun and Davies' contribution (see figure 29).[47]

While Lasdun and Davies hinted at the possibility of an aesthetic interpretation of New Brutalism, the Smithsons brought the debate back to a much more complex and dynamic attitude that could not be reduced to exposed concrete alone. This is why they returned to the concept of 'architecture of reality', its ethical dimension and the poetics of 'as found'. This attitude prevented, precisely because of its intrinsic mechanism, the declination of architecture into a style. Thus, ethical responsibility in the use of materials and 'as found' were the Smithsons' antidotes against the possible declination of New Brutalism towards an aesthetic category in which canons could be delineated.

The Smithsons used the term 'Brutalism' for the first time without the prefix New, and this seems almost a conscious stance on the value attributed to New Brutalism, as it was taking shape through the incursions of critics who were turning the definition into a 'canon' and a series of dogmas. The Smithsons confirmed that they always understood 'Brutalism' on an ethical level, probably taking a critical stance against attempts, such as those of Banham and Lasdun, to decline that definition into a specific material and a specific finish. The ethical component of New Brutalism seems to provide a clue to the need for revision of the term, which was already being defined as a 'canon' and as a predictable dimension that emerged from Banham's comment when he implicitly criticised 'Patio & Pavilion' by calling it 'strictly Brutalist'.

[46] [n.a.], 'Thoughts in Progress; The New Brutalism', 113.
[47] Alison and Peter Smithson, 'The New Brutalism: Alison and Peter Smithson Answer the Criticism on the Opposite Page', *Architectural Design*, vol. 27, no. 4 (April 1957): 113.

29 Alison and Peter Smithson, 'Brutalism A/D', 23 February 1957, Alison and Peter Smithson Archive, Folder E009. Courtesy of the Frances Loeb Library. Harvard University Graduate School of Design

BRUTALISM   A/D   OFFICE COPY

If Academicism can be defined as yesterdays answers to todays problems, then obviously the objectives and aes- thetic technique/of a real architecture/must be in *(as a real art)* constant change.

In the immediate post-war period it seemed im- ortant to show that architecture was still possible, *and* we /determined to set against loose planning and form - abdication, a compact / disci plfined, architecture.

Simple objectives once achieved change the situat- ion, and the techniques used to achieve them become useless. So new objectives are established. From individual buildings, disci pl fin/ on the whole by *ed* classical aesthetic techniques, we moved on to an examination of/ human associations and the /form *the whole problem* / *relationship that building & community has to them.* From this study has grown a completely new attitude and a non-classical aesthetic.

Any discussion of Brutalism will miss the point if it does not take into account Brutalism's attempt *about* to be objective/"reality" - the cultural objectives of society, its urges, its techniques, and so on. Brutalism tries to face up to a mass-production socie- ty, and drag a rough poetry out of the confused and *which are at work.* powerful forces /

Up to now Brutalism has been discussed stylistica - lly , whereas its essence is ethical.

ALISON SMITHSON } FEBRUARY 23rd 1957.
PETER SMITHSON }

For N.b. see also AD - Jan 55.

As a graphic commentary on the Smithsons' note, a section of their competition project for the Sydney Opera House, designed together with Amis, W & G Howell, Killick, Jenkins and Meyrick, was published with a significant comment: 'The panel dis- cussed Brutalism on the basis of the available material; since then the Smithsons have completed several theoretical projects'.[48] This note referred to the fact that through the interventions at CIAM in 1956 and the design for the Sydney Opera House, the Smithsons were taking urban issues more and more seriously. The Smithsons in their response relativised the role that New Brutalism was assuming, tracing it back to a

[48] Ibid.

moment in their theoretical evolution when there was a need to move beyond 'classical aesthetic technics' to push architecture to consider the 'problems of human association' and the expression of the building as a symbol of a community. This was what pushed them toward a 'new attitude' and a 'non-classical aesthetic'. With this stance it becomes clear that for them New Brutalism was simply gradually becoming Brutalism, devoid of its most subversive action, and that any other declination would have risked, as they themselves noted, reducing that 'attitude' to 'style': 'Up to now Brutalism has been discussed stylistically, whereas its essence is ethical'.[49]

The unstable relationship implicit in the Smithsons' discourse was that between the notion of form and order. Elaborating on Kahn and Mies's stance on these two notions, the Smithsons included the social dimension of mass production. Their 'new order', as we have already seen, was not only a statement against the *a priori* form, but also the affirmation of a new poetics, which, through references such as Pollock and Le Corbusier, took on 'layered' and 'rough' overtones. It should also be noted that the adjective 'rough' was not in this case attributed to the material, but to a poetry that underlined the principle of the project, identified in the present condition of 'reality': 'Brutalism tries to face up to a mass-production society, and drag a rough poetry out of the confused and powerful forces which are at work'.

After attempting to free New Brutalism from its picturesque attributes and bring it back to the contemporary aesthetics for the 'atomic age', Lasdun and Davies picked up the threads that had intersected the question of New Brutalism to return to the figure of Le Corbusier. The column 'Opinion' in the following *Architectural Design* issues was dedicated to the role of technology, illustrated by photography of Le Corbusier's works in Chandigarh and Ahmedabad, all buildings in *béton brut*, assuming the role of an implicit response to the Smithsons.

One principle recovered from the debate on New Brutalism was that of the 'as found', declined by Crosby in an 'object found philosophy', no longer linked to the Smithsons' theories but extended to a broader vision, which started from the concept of a 'particular situation' against *a priori* choices.[50] Rather than placing the emphasis on materials as in the 'as found' theorised by the Smithsons, the concept of 'object found' was linked to the vision of the members of the Independent Group, as stated by Alison Smithson in her 'But Today we Collect Ads', committed to the renewal of contemporary aesthetics through the inclusion of popular culture and technology:

In the last few years a new movement has been born, brutalism, which looks for the renewal of the modern aesthetic to a number of sources – popular imagery like motor car styling, a conscious geometry, and, most important as a formal influence, the almost anonymous works of the twenties. As the early modernists loved grain elevators as symbols, so brutalists want to use our own fantastic engineering to produce an architecture of 'reality'.[51]

Style and Attitude

Ethics and aesthetics were the extremes set by the Smithsons to frame the trajectory of New Brutalism. The discussion in 'Opinion' triggered a series of responses through letters published in the June issue of *Architectural Design*, sent by protagonists of the discussion on New Brutalism, such as Voelcker and Banham, and other unknown correspondents such as W. G. Cowburn, Roderick Gradidge and Edward J. Armitage.

[49] Ibid.
[50] [n.a.], 'Thoughts in Progress, Summing up III-the "Objects found" Philosophy', *Architectural Design*, vol. 27, no. 12 (December 1957): 435–36.
[51] Theo Crosby, 'Detail, 3', *Architectural Design*, vol. 28, no. 3 (March 1958): 123–23.

Banham's identification of two moments of New Brutalism resulted in a crucial outcome. The distinction between 'Early Brutalism' and 'Furthest development of New Brutalism' became the pretext to indicate various original impulses and possible trajectories, recognising also New Brutalism's dead ends.

The School at Hunstanton established a distinction between two precise moments, confirming the existence of an initial New Brutalism, and a subsequent trajectory that ran the risk of degenerating into dogma, as Voelcker affirmed.[52] In fact, the School at Hunstanton was the outcome of the application of the principles of the Modern Movement, based on the 'rigorous articulation of predetermined parts, whether buildings, regions or towns, aided by the use of finite geometry and Cartesian analysis'.[53] The phase following Hunstanton presupposed, according to Voelcker, a definition of New Brutalism as a 're-orientation of spirit'. By virtue of a liberation from *a priori* processes, architecture assumes the function of 'resonator' to respond to multiple conditions ranging from context to use, and to the relationship between buildings, according to an approach which 'cannot be understood through stylistic analysis, although some day a comprehensible style might emerge'. His aim was to free New Brutalism from the principles that bound it to the use of a certain material and to the truth of the structure, to resituate it instead in the dynamics of the historical and technological condition of the time. Thus, the battle between style and attitude that underpinned New Brutalism was then enriched with new attributes.

Another reader, the architect William G. Cowburn, recognised in New Brutalism a vision of design that could not be reduced to style, in virtue of an 'openness' derived from a composition based on 'topology', 'as found' and 'image'.[54] For Cowburn, New Brutalism was characterised as a tension towards an 'architectural ideal', 'a general ethical response', in which materials, used 'as found', demonstrated a principle of truth. 'The surface texture and the substance look inseparable', Cowburn concluded, summarising in concrete terms the ambiguous concept of the 'as found', rooted in the 'ethical response'.[55]

Lasdun and Davies' attack on dogmas and the 'Brutalist canon' provoked a response from Banham,[56] in which he aligned himself with the Smithsons' position in a sort of retreat from the debate on New Brutalism, no longer informed by his principles: 'The Brutalist Canon is the Brutalists' affair'. In his response Banham employed the term 'Brutalists' to refer to those who sought to further define the parameters of New Brutalism to the point of making a 'Brutalist canon', clearly referring to the discussion between Davies and Lasdun. Such an assertion might also imply a distinction between the theory of New Brutalism that he advocated and the recognition of a stylistic manifestation of Brutalism.

The internal debates and polemics between Banham and other critics obscured in the British context New Brutalism's gradual internationalisation, as noted by a reader of *Architectural Design*, Edward John Armitage: 'Does the "New Brutalism" really mean anything other than the architecture of the Smithsons?'[57] Armitage also added another hypothesis on the origin of the definition of New Brutalism, namely that it derives from the nickname of Peter Smithson, then known as 'Brutus': 'Had Peter's nickname been Fido would it have been "new fidelity"?' This hypothesis would remain alive especially in the American context, and would spread especially Giedion's students, as several sources revealed in the late 1960s.

[52] John Voelcker, 'New Brutalism', *Architectural Design*, vol. 27, no. 6 (June 1957): 184.
[53] Ibid.
[54] W. G. Cowburn, 'New Brutalism', *Architectural Design*, vol. 27, no. 6 (June 1957): 184.
[55] Ibid.
[56] Reyner Banham, 'New Brutalism', *Architectural Design*, vol. 27, no. 6 (June 1957): 220.
[57] Edward John Armitage, 'Letter to the Editor', *Architectural Design*, vol. 27, no. 6 (June 1957): 184.

The assiduous comments following the publication of 'Opinion' were not limited to the pages of *Architectural Design*. Even Summerson went back to the issue of New Brutalism in his famous lecture at the RIBA in London in 1957, where Banham and Peter Smithson were also present. Summerson analysed various systems of composition in order to extract a possible contemporary 'Theory of Modern Architecture'.[58] He explicitly referred to the contemporary debate on topology, identified as a new relationship between the parts of the design project. Although he acknowledged Banham as the critic who introduced topology into contemporary discourse, Summerson did not fail to diminish Banham's theory by calling it a 'red-herring'. By virtue of the persistence of the 'classic' that underpinned the development of architecture, Summerson demonstrated the possibility of leading even the most complex and 'unfamiliar' forms back to a 'simple' generating form, based on 'geometrical absolutes'. For Banham, on the other hand, recourse to topology entailed a liberation from those very 'symbolic forms' identified in the repertoire of simple geometry. Rectangles, circles and squares belonged, for Banham, to a vision of architecture that came to an end in the 1930s, overcome by the liberating dimension of 'a-formalism' and to topology 'which does not commit you to any particular set of forms'.[59]

The discussions of compositional principles that preoccupied Summerson and Banham were ignored by Peter Smithson. The search for an 'image' was for him far from compositional concerns, and had to be understood as an 'entity' that reacted to social and urban issues: 'A social plastic entity; that is, it conceives a new way of life, a new sort of technology and a new image all in one'.[60] The concept of the process, identified in the example of Pollock's paintings, replaced from the Smithsons that of composition and geometry, and was the bearer of an ethical intention, in virtue of an approach that implied 'overtones of collaboration, co-operation between various related techniques'.[61]

[58] John Summerson, 'The Case for a Theory of "Modern" Architecture', *RIBA Journal*, vol. 64 (June 1957): 307–10.
[59] Reyner Banham, 'The Case for a Theory of "Modern" Architecture. Discussion', 312.
[60] Peter Smithson, 'The Case for a Theory of "Modern" Architecture. Discussion', 314.
[61] Ibid.

chapter six
international brutalism: from zevi to joedicke

Zevi and the First Italian Brutalist

Starting with Banham's article in December 1955, the spread of the definition of New Brutalism continued on a fragmented trajectory, marked by a proliferation of contributions through letters and brief comments. Several provided an increasing awareness of how New Brutalism was evolving and directing the course of the Modern Movement: from the debate promoted by *Architectural Design*, where the ethical stances of the Smithsons' emerged; to the international success of *béton brut* filling the pages of magazines and confirming the 'brutal' characteristics of the exposed concrete buildings; and, finally, the model of the Maisons Jaoul, which demonstrated the inclusion of 'regional' features through exposed bricks.

The appeal launched by Banham in December 1955, aimed at identifying other examples,[1] did not leave international critics indifferent. They were to be the authors of an important reformulation of the definition through the wide-ranging inclusion of new examples capable of turning a purely English question into the receptacle of national concerns and debates. The journals played a crucial role in outlining certain interpretations so that the definition could easily insert itself into various national contexts. Despite the international dessimination of the *béton brut* phenomenon from Israel to Australia and China to Brazil,[2] and the numerous architects heavily influenced by the Smithsons and the discussions of Team X, the evolution of New Brutalism as a

---

[1] After stating the set of principles, he asked, 'Are there other New Brutalist buildings beside Hunstanton?', in Reyner Banham, 'The New Brutalism', *Architectural Review*, vol. 118, no. 708 (December 1955): (354–61), 358.

[2] Recently several scholars attested the dispersion of the New Brutalist message from its origins to other countries, for example, see Philip Goad, 'Bringing It All Home: Robin Boyd and Australia's Embrace of Brutalism, 1955–1971', *Fabrications*, vol. 25, no. 2 (2015): 176–213; Andrew Murray, 'Brutal Beginnings: The New Brutalism and Western Australia in the 1950s', *The Journal of Architecture*, vol. 26, no. 8 (2021): 1219–40; Kirsten Day, Peter Raisbeck, 'The Last Laugh and Its Afterlife: Emerging Narratives in 1970s Melbourne Architecture', *Fabrications*, vol. 31, no. 3 (2021): 336–56; Jeremy Hoffmann and Hadas Nevo-Goldberst, *Aphoria – Architecture of Independence* (Tel-Aviv Yafo; Haifa: Tel-Aviv Yafo Municipality; Architectural and Landscape Heritage Research Center, Technion, 2017); Hadas Shadar (ed.), *Sunstroke: Brutalist Construction in Be'er-Sheva: Re-Examination of National Architecture* (Jerusalem: Yad Ben-Zvi, 2016); 'The Brutalist Turn' conference at the Azrieli School of Architecture, Yolanda And David Katz Faculty Of The Arts, Tel Aviv University (14–16 April 2019).

critical category was concentrated in very specific areas, particularly where critics were more receptive to theoretical discussions. This capillarity of diffusion did not proceed in the same way everywhere, and in various national contexts the debate developed autonomous concepts. It was particularly the Italian, American and German contexts that, in need of a profound reflection on the destiny of national architecture, were able to give new meanings to New Brutalism.

In the American culture, marked by a strong focus on constructive processes, a fundamental lack of interest in the theoretical questions and ethical components linked to the British debate must be noted. American critics remained refractory to the acceptance of new 'labels', except for a few who gravitated around magazines such as *Perspecta*, *Architectural Forum* and *Progressive Architecture*. In the Italian context, although there was significant debate, critical attention towards New Brutalism emerged in sporadic forms and was limited to a very precise time span, from the late 1950s to the 1960s. At the same time as the search for a new direction for post-war reconstruction, the ongoing debate on New Brutalism intercepted specific concerns regarding the use of materials and the so-called organic architecture promoted by Zevi. Another variant, different from that of the United States and Italy, characterised the German debates, which would produce a decisive stance against the Miesian model, supporting the return of certain tendencies that would be defined as expressionistic.

Other nations remained essentially uninvolved in the debates on New Brutalism. This is the case for Japan, although exposed reinforced concrete was then at the centre of the concerns of architects such as Kenzo Tange and Kunio Maekawa, who were reconfiguring the face of a new contemporary democracy. Despite a timid interest in the work of the Smithsons, they are not associated with the definition of New Brutalism. Surprisingly, the definition did not even have an effect in South America, despite the radical research into the expression of material that was particularly active in Brazil.[3] Militant debates concerning the values linked to raw material clashed in Brazil with the theory of New Brutalism, which would be identified with an attempt at Western imperialism and hegemony from which architects, in particular João Batista Vilanova Artigas, would distance themselves. Magazines of other European nations, such as Switzerland, Spain and France, seemed to avoid the question of New Brutalism; particularly surprising is the fundamental indifference of France, where one would have expected support of the definition in a Lecorbuserian key and where the pioneering experiences of Perret in exposed reinforced concrete had taken place.

It should be noted that it was in this phase of profound alteration and international expansion of New Brutalism that we see the definitive loss of the prefix New. If by speaking of 'Brutalism' the Smithsons had provided a clue as to the progressive dissolution of the ethical instances of their initial 'new theory', in the process of the internationalisation of that definition, the presence of the prefix New became a tool for critics to distinguish the original English 'attitude' from the international style of exposed concrete. Although this distinction was not rigorous, it will henceforth be the criterion adopted in the discussion and analysis of events. The critics' attribution of whether or not a building was 'brutalist', and the blurred line between New Brutalism and Brutalism has framed all discussions conducted to this day in an ambiguity undermining even the very use of the terms.[4]

---

[3] Regarding the attribution of Brutalism to the so-called Escola Paulista, refer to the following contributions: Ruth Verde Zein, *Brutalist Connections: A Refreshed Approach to Debates & Buildings* (São Paulo: Altamira, 2014); Anna Rita Emili, *Brutalismo paulista: l'architettura brasiliana tra teoria e progetto* (Castel San Pietro Romano: Manifestolibri, 2020); Margaret Becker, *Der Raum des Öffentlichen: die Escola Paulista und der Brutalismus in Brasilien* (Berlin: Reimer, 2012).

[4] Paul Walker and Antony Moulis, 'Finding Brutalism in the Architecture of John Andrews', *Fabrications*, vol. 25, no. 2 (2015): 214–33.

The Istituto di cura Marchiondi Spagliardi, built by Vittoriano Viganò in collaboration with Silvano Zorzi in Baggio, Milan, between 1956 and 1958, became an emblematic case for measuring the spread and decline of Brutalism in the international context. This work inaugurated an unprecedented meaning of that definition, which would undergo an unexpected interpretation in Italian cultural circles, which were intent on demonstrating a possible evolution of Rationalism. On 2 March 1958, in the pages of *L'Espresso*, Bruno Zevi interpreted Viganò's work according to the parameters of Brutalism in an article entitled 'I ragazzi non scappano'.[5]

Apart from the brief commentary on Le Corbusier's work in India in the January 1956 supplement of *Architettura: Cronache e Storia*, Italian publications remained silent on the events, protagonists and buildings gravitating around New Brutalism.[6] Not even Banham's article of December 1955 was mentioned in the magazines, which, from *Domus* to *Casabella*, were usually always careful to include brief accounts of international debates in special columns.

Zevi's reading of the Marchiondi Institute added a new trajectory to the discourse on Brutalism, departing drastically from Banham's theoretical presentation of the model of the School at Hunstanton. The expressiveness of the Marchiondi was used to demonstrate a new aspiration of overcoming even Lecorbuserian plasticity. In this sense, in the evolution of the definition of Brutalism, that building would be remembered as a 'surprise'.[7] It was an unexpected event that clearly defined the direction of what was becoming known as the Brutalist style. Various international critics, and in this case Zevi, highlighted in the forms of the Marchiondi Institute a 'raw' nature and a mechanical and spatial expressiveness that allowed parallels with the international phenomenon of Brutalism. Its characteristics were radically different from the architectural research carried out in the Milanese context, even though Viganò frequently reiterated cultural references belonging to the rationalist tradition, from Giuseppe Terragni to Gio Ponti.[8] According to Zevi, the use of exposed concrete was a new element on the Italian scene and this choice was celebrated and traced back to a desire to 'shun the suggestions of fashion'.

Zevi's interpretation of Viganò's building was aimed at claiming an Italian affiliation to an issue that was emerging as international, and in which the Marchiondi Institute was suited to resolving the ethical-aesthetic dilemma that the Smithsons had posed a year earlier, in 1957.[9] In the fair-faced concrete of the Marchiondi, Zevi recognised a 'psychological liberation' favoured by the use of that material, to which he attributed a 'therapeutic' function capable of educating the behaviour of children and young people. 'His reasons are not aesthetic,' Zevi observed in *L'Espresso*, 'they are dictated by a psycho-pedagogical approach worked out in close collaboration with Marchiondi's board of directors and medical advisors'. For Zevi, the structural system 'in exposed reinforced concrete, outside and inside', implied an intrinsic sense of 'security' that was not limited to the tactile and visual dimension, but radiated through the load-bearing elements. The 'certainty of a planned environment', organised according to a principle of articulation in small groups, evoked the security of a family dimension. We cannot but notice how the very programme of the Institute became a pretext for stressing the

5 Bruno Zevi, 'I ragazzi non scappano', *L'Espresso*, 2 March 1958, 16.
6 [n.a.], 'Le Corbusier e la poetica di un'architettura brutale', *Architettura: Cronache e Storia*, vol. 26, no. 3 (March 1956): 75–77.
7 Reyner Banham, *The New Brutalism: Ethic or Aesthetic?* (London: Architectural Press, 1966).
8 For an in-depth study of the Marchiondi Institute, see Franz Graf, Letizia Tedeschi (eds.), *L'Istituto Marchiondi Spagliardi di Vittorio Viganò* (Mendrisio: Mendrisio Academy Press, 2009); Roberto Gargiani, *Razionalismo emozionale per l'identità democratica nazionale 1945–1966. Eretici italiani dell'architettura razionalista* (Milan: Skira, 2021).
9 Alison and Peter Smithson, 'The New Brutalism: Alison and Peter Smithson Answer the Criticism on the Opposite Page', *Architectural Design*, vol. 27, no. 4 (April 1957): 113.

ethical and psychological components attributed to each architectural element and its materials, and we should carefully read Zevi's interpretation in light of this. Nevertheless, the psychological dimension ascribed to exposed concrete proved crucial for recognising the traits of a new humanism, of which New Brutalism sought to be the bearer from its English beginnings and to which Italian culture was particularly sensitive.

Zevi praised Viganò's 'courage' in renouncing cladding even in the interiors, in order to make the architecture 'elementary, raw, strong', all characteristics that he considered suitable for the education of the young guests of the Institute. According to Zevi, exposed concrete transmitted a sense of freedom in the expression of the material.[10] The characteristics of 'primitiveness', 'crudeness of the materials and of the forms themselves', contributed to the 'structuring of the personality'. Viganò himself had described his building with similar words a month before Zevi's comments in *L'Espresso* in an article published in Olivetti's magazine *Comunità*.[11] Where Viganò appealed to 'functionality' to justify Marchiondi's 'crudeness', Zevi on the other hand took advantage of this same feature to join the debate to the international dimension of the Brutalist trajectory. The extensive use of exposed concrete configured the Marchiondi as an 'immediately recognisable architectural organism', a definition that undoubtedly evoked the characteristic of 'memorability as an image' that Banham had placed at the head of the principles of New Brutalism. As proof of the 'memorable' dimension of Marchiondi's structures, it should be emphasised that the photographs accompanying the article in *L'Espresso* were destined to become famous throughout the world, particularly the one that shows the interior façade of the boarding school pavilion (see figure 30).

The particularly 'rough and, in some episodes, brutal imprint of architecture' led Zevi to recognise in Viganò's building traits that could be assimilated to the definition of Brutalism. 'With this work, the architect Viganò proposes himself as the first Italian "Brutalist"', Zevi stated decisively.

However, the Marchiondi made a particular definition of New Brutalism explicit, drawn along the lines of Banham's first set of principles. Zevi's definition of Brutalism transposed the theoretical and conceptual questions of English debates into a series of constructive characteristics that would contribute to the transformation of that definition into a style.[12] Zevi repositioned the plan at the head of the characteristics of Brutalism and highlighted its necessary 'readability' and intrinsic simplicity. In Zevi's definition of Brutalism, the concept of *béton brut* as described by Le Corbusier was literally reproposed, that is, concrete that has not been retouched after formwork removal. For Zevi, Brutalism also entailed that every element, from the structure to the installations, should be visible, and even the use of colour should contribute to an explicit 'violence'.

The definition of Brutalism applied to the Marchiondi Institute was motivated by Zevi's operative criticism, oriented towards a possible evolution of the Modern Movement based on Wright's organicistic line,[13] as opposed to the continuity of the

[10] For a detailed account of the correspondence between Zevi and Viganò, see Letizia Tedeschi, 'Il contributo italiano al Brutalismo: la ricezione critica dell'Istituto Marchiondi Spagliardi di Vittoriano Viganò. 1958–1968', in Graf, Tedeschi (eds.), *L'Istituto Marchiondi Spagliardi di Vittoriano Viganò*, 29–59.

[11] Vittoriano Viganò, 'L'Istituto Marchiondi a Milano-Baggio. L'internato per ragazzi difficili', *Comunità*, vol. 12, no. 57 (February 1958): 64–69.

[12] 'In England the name "the New Brutalism" has been coined for this type of architecture. It means: clear and unadorned plans, volumetries strongly accentuated in the recesses and projections but roughly prismatic, concrete structure left without finishes, as it comes from the formworks, thermal, plumbing and electrical systems all in sight, areas of violent colour, without half tones', in Zevi, 'I ragazzi non scappano'.

[13] Consider in this sense the texts published by Zevi from the 1940s onwards, including Bruno Zevi, *Verso un'architettura organica: saggio sullo sviluppo del pensiero architettonico negli ultimi 50 anni*, vol. 54 (Turin: Einaudi, 1945); Bruno Zevi, *Frank Lloyd Wright* (Milan: Il Balcone, 1947); Bruno Zevi, *Realta dell'architettura organica* (Rome: L'airone, 1950).

30 Bruno Zevi,
'I ragazzi non scappano',
L'Espresso, March 1958,
p. 16

rationalist principles professed by the Milanese cultural circles headed by Ernesto Nathan Rogers.[14] The reference to Wright did not explicitly appear in Zevi's 1958 comments, and it was only with the re-edition of his *Storia* in 1973 that he made the connection between Organicism and Brutalism clear, in particular through the category of topology interpreted not as a relationship between buildings, but as a connection to a specific context.[15]

Despite his silent presence, Wright was gradually acquiring a particular relevance in the genealogy of Brutalism, testifying to its versatility and its ability to revive the teachings of the masters, from Le Corbusier to Mies and from Aalto to Wright. Already in 1954, a few months after the Smithsons' invention, Segal had attributed to Wright the role of Brutalism's 'venerable protagonist'.[16] While Segal's reference to Wright was motivated by the need to go beyond the International Style, for Zevi it meant a stance against a Rationalism that had not admitted other cultural proposals into its principles, such as organic architecture or the New Empiricism, as he had stated in 1949 recognising the existence of a 'post-rationalist' turn.[17] He was very much aware of the 'controversy' that the Marchiondi would have raised among the 'pure rationalists'.[18] The contrast between the proposed continuity of Rationalism and Zevi's 'Post-Rationalism', which also included Brutalism, was made explicit by Zevi through BBPR's Torre Velasca and the Marchiondi Institute, two buildings that served as extremes of the debate, also on an international level. Within a few months, Banham himself

[14] Luca Molinari reported the debates against the backdrop of New Brutalism's discussion in Italy, in Luca Molinari, 'The Italian Way to New Brutalism. The Experience of Vittoriano Viganò', in *SOS Brutalism. A Global Survey. Contributions to the International Symposium in Berlin 2012*, vol. 2 (Zurich: Park Books, 2017), 85–94.

[15] Bruno Zevi, *Storia dell'architettura moderna*, vol. 136 (Turin: Einaudi, 1973).

[16] Walter Segal, 'The New Brutalism', *Architectural Design*, vol. 24, no. 2 (February 1954): 7 (ad).

[17] Bruno Zevi, 'Riconoscimento dell'architettura post-razionalista', *Comunità*, vol. 5 (September 1949): 28–29.

[18] In a letter sent to Viganò on 24 February 1958, Zevi admitted the controversial impact of the use of the definition of Brutalism: 'I have spoken to various Milanese friends about your project, and I have noticed that they have many reservations, especially about the "brutal" tone of certain details. It therefore seems to me that my article is just in time, and I think it will provoke a certain controversy with the pure rationalists', in Tedeschi, 'Il contributo italiano al Brutalismo: la ricezione critica dell'Istituto Marchiondi Spagliardi di Vittoriano Viganò. 1958–1968', 33.

would make this ongoing conflict explicit in his famous article 'Neoliberty. The Italian Retreat from Modern Architecture',[19] reworking Paolo Portoghesi's definition.[20]

The Marchiondi Institute thus became one of the references of international Brutalism and Viganò was fully recognised as one of its protagonists. 'Congratulations to the first Italian Brutalist' was the comment sent to Viganò on 3 March 1958 by an anonymous colleague.[21]

Zevi's intuition was immediately echoed in the contributions of other Italian critics. In February 1959, Renato Pedio proposed in *Architettura: Cronache e Storia* a further reading of Marchiondi in terms of Brutalism.[22] Zevi, editor-in-chief of the magazine, had in fact agreed with Viganò on the international exclusivity of Marchiondi in *Architettura: Cronache e Storia*, and entrusted Pedio with the writing of the article. Pedio was heir to the interpretation of Zevi and the definition and principles of Banham. For Pedio, 'memorability as an image' implied a visual unity, while 'as found' was simply translated into a use of materials without finishing. As Zevi had already pointed out, Brutalism was for Pedio an expression of a psychological dimension with a pedagogical and therapeutic orientation. In this sense 'Brutalism' read by Pedio 'in function of freedom' became first and foremost an 'open scheme […] aggressively inserted into the environment', a free expression of circulation and materials, put into 'action' in a way that is 'frank and real', 'stimulating, virile', in antithesis to the 'artificiality' probably identified with the cladding and rigid geometries of the International Style. Pedio's text is devoid of all controversy against the Milanese circle. His Brutalism was totally detached from theoretical or intellectual questions. He described it as being 'out of the academy', and concentrated on its 'energetic' dimension of ethics, which he saw as a real 'direction of work'. The links between exposed materials, ethics and construction staged at the Marchiondi were also highlighted by Gillo Dorfles who recognised Brutalism as being 'of importance in contemporary architecture'.[23] This vision of Brutalism anchored in the project and in the constructed substance of architecture, in its mass and plasticity, emerged precisely with the reception of the Marchiondi Institute, which indicated a possible evolution with respect to the intellectual debates that in England ran the risk of condemning the definition to a series of aporias.[24]

Viganò's reaction to his inclusion in the ranks of New Brutalism was one of silent scepticism. Disappointed by the article edited by Pedio in *L'Architettura: Cronache e Storia*, which portrayed the Marchiondi Institute as being 'in transit, entering sluggishly and leaving sluggishly', he expressed a particular vision of New Brutalism, writing to Zevi: 'And yet, Brutalism = energy!'[25] Only decades later would Viganò affirm that 'Brutalism, as an expression of violent communication and according to a stress therapy, has in itself a component which is perhaps anarchic, certainly expressionist'.[26]

[19] Reyner Banham, 'Neoliberty. The Italian Retreat from Modern Architecture', *Architectural Review*, vol. 125, no. 747 (March 1959): 231–35.

[20] Paolo Portoghesi, 'Dal Neorealismo al Neoliberty', *Comunità*, vol. 12, no. 65 (December 1958): 69–79.

[21] Tedeschi, 'Il contributo italiano al Brutalismo: la ricezione critica dell'Istituto Marchiondi Spagliardi di Vittoriano Viganò. 1958–1968', 33.

[22] Renato Pedio, 'Brutalismo in Funzione di Libertà. Il nuovo Istituto Marchiondi a Milano', *Architettura: Cronache e Storia*, vol. 3, no. 10 (February 1959): 682–88.

[23] Gillo Dorfles, 'L'Istituto Marchiondi Spagliardi a Milano', *Edilizia Moderna*, vol. 67 (August 1959): 35–46. When in 1961 Dorfles reviewed the two volumes of Benevolo's new *History of Modern Architecture*, he accused the historian of a serious omission, that of not considering 'the orientation of Brutalism', in Gillo Dorfles, 'Edizioni per architetti', *Domus*, vol. 379 (June 1961): 1–2.

[24] Tedeschi, 'Il contributo italiano al Brutalismo: la ricezione critica dell'Istituto Marchiondi Spagliardi di Vittoriano Viganò. 1958–1968', 33.

[25] Ibid.

[26] Attilio Stocchi, *Vittoriano Viganò: etica brutalista* (Turin: Testo&Immagine, 1999), 64.

Romantic, Informal, Naturalistic: Italian Variations

The entry of the 'first Italian Brutalist' into the debate did not leave the Italian magazines indifferent, as they saw in the Marchiondi a hypothesis of the development of Rationalism, as well as a critical tool to measure its validity in relation to international trends. Beyond single interpretations, Italian critics did not unanimously accept the definition of New Brutalism or its more current declination in Brutalism. The definition of Brutalism never appeared alone, but was often accompanied by other adjectives, as if to reveal an intrinsic inability to describe the complexity of contemporary phenomena. Caught up in the constellation of definitions ranging from organicism to Neo-Liberty, the fate of the definition of Brutalism in Italy was linked to a ramification of polarities, ranging from the buildings of Leonardo Ricci to those of Figini and Pollini, and to the structures of Pier Luigi Nervi. Above all, however, what is striking was the inability of critics, with a few exceptions, to develop new critical tools and categories beyond the generic and by now inadequate formula of Rationalism, to which everything basically led.

A year after Zevi's intuition, a voice supporting New Brutalism was raised by the magazine *Zodiac*, directed by Bruno Alfieri since 1957. Founded with the intention of offering a supranational contribution to contemporary architectural culture, *Zodiac* became a decisive forum for debate, publishing lengthy articles and reflections, almost in monographic form, on contemporary movements and trends. In the vast international review, the fourth issue of 1959 is almost entirely dedicated to the question of Brutalism and features contributions by Giulia Veronesi, Jules Langsner, an interview between the Smithsons, Jane Drew and Maxwell Fry and an article by Pierpaolo Santini on Viganò.[27] The various contributions were juxtaposed without a summarising critical vision that would have allowed the reader to infer a coherent position and clarify the relevance of New Brutalism, its possible declinations and its intrinsic value. However, this very issue of *Zodiac* would have an astonishing international repercussion and would become a decisive vehicle for the debate, to the point that the architectures discussed or only hinted at would become recognised examples of Brutalism.

The attempt at using the definition of Brutalism to interpret contemporary examples seemed almost forced, without a broader and more scientific review, confirming the critical observations of Sergio Bettini and Renato Bonelli, who, in the same issue of *Zodiac*, denounced a critical unpreparedness to face the crisis of the Modern Movement: 'It is no longer possible to deny that architecture criticism is in a latent crisis, in which its methods and procedures are being questioned and the very theoretical bases of artistic historiography are being denied or subverted'.[28]

To add to the ambiguity, the definition of Brutalism was introduced by an article by Veronesi about Ricci's villa in the hills near Florence.[29] For Veronesi, the villa was indicative of 'a rather extraordinary adventure for Italy, and undoubtedly dangerous: it is the adventure of the informal (call it as you like in architecture: brutalism, or wrightism, not organicism)'. The link between Wright and Brutalism is reinforced here by the use of the two terms as synonyms, but what is most striking is the introduction of the term 'informal'. The juxtaposition of Informalism and Brutalism cannot but evoke the association between artistic and architectural practices underlying the origin of English New Brutalism and the discovery of Lecorbuserian *béton brut*, which confirms the insistence on a material and a processal dimension that translates into a gestural expression. The principles linked to Tapié's concept of 'un art autre', the experiences

---

[27] *Zodiac*, vol. 4, April 1959: 73–81.
[28] Renato Bonelli, 'Estetica contemporanea e critica dell'architettura', *Zodiac*, vol. 4 (April 1959): 22–29.
[29] Giulia Veronesi, 'Du nouveau à Florence', *Zodiac*, vol. 4 (April 1959): 10–11.

of Dubuffet and the artists of art brut, intercepting Italian experiences, such as those of Burri, can be found within the Informal movement. Veronesi, sensitive to the various forms of artistic expression, thus stressed the roots of the definition of Brutalism, identified in the mixture of art and architecture.

Veronesi's interpretation of Ricci's villa was rooted in the expression of materials, in this case local stone, which takes on an 'existential' dimension. With its weight, thickness and local origin, the material becomes emblematic of an authentic, 'natural' way of making architecture. Thus, through Ricci, despite Veronesi's ambivalence, Brutalism was strongly repositioned in the rejection of a-priori form combined with a primeval and archaic choice of material. 'We hate labels', stated Veronesi, 'However, it would be difficult for us not to establish a relationship between these architectures and those that have just been named, in England, Brutalists, perhaps after the idea of Art Brut, which came from France. Brutalist architecture: the enemy of "form"'.[30]

While the influences of Wright are evident in Ricci's villa, the interpretation of his architecture in a brutalist key is an entirely Italian intuition, destined to be internationally confirmed by Creighton in an article in *Progressive Architecture*, in which he stated how Ricci 'is often characterised as "brutal"'.[31] Ricci, for his part, as well as most other architects, would only react a few years later in December 1963, confessing a distance from Brutalism, despite recognising in it a certain vital freedom to overcome pure Rationalism.[32]

The ambiguity expressed by Veronesi was also paralleled in a question posed in the article 'Ornamented Modern & Brutalism. Towards Two Movements?'[33] The subject at stake was the crisis of the Modern Movement, and the easy temptation of renewing its content without any in-depth acknowledgment of the subsequent critical implications. 'Where are architects going?' seemed to be the appeal of a group of critics caught up in confused and uncertain trajectories. Ornamented Modern and Brutalism appeared in this sense as the divergent poles of contemporary experimentation, both symptoms of an 'extremist' reaction to Rationalism: Ornamented Modern as a drastic revision of rationalist principles through ornament, symbol, symmetry and the façade conceived as a mask; and Brutalism as an extreme search for reality and truth, a desire to show 'the building for what it is', as Peter Smithson stated in the pages of *Zodiac*. We cannot ignore how these two divergent opposites would become explicit in the Postmodern discourse which, as demonstrated by Venturi and Scott Brown would be theorised on the erosion of the Brutalist discourse.

The editorial board of *Zodiac*, directed at the time by Alfieri, together with Veronesi and Angelo Tito Anselmo, also included Maxwell Fry and Jane Drew, important protagonists of the London architectural scene, who had collaborated with Le Corbusier and Pierre Jeanneret at the Chandigarh building site. The fourth issue of *Zodiac* was conceived as an opportunity to investigate the various meanings of the definition of Brutalism, questioning its main protagonists, the Smithsons, whose conversation with Drew and Fry, organised by the magazine's editorial office in London on 6 November 1958, was faithfully reported in *Zodiac*.

[30] Ibid.
[31] Thomas H. Creighton, 'European Diary', *Progressive Architecture*, vol. 41, no. 8 (August 1960): 120.
[32] 'Many years ago, I was catalogued by some critics as a "brutalist". Today I am the only "informal" Italian architect. Since I consider the currents of Brutalism and Informalism not only consequential to each other, but also the most vital of our time, I should feel satisfied after all. But I am not. It is true that Brutalism and Informalism broke the academic mould of Rationalism and geometric abstraction, bringing the artist back to the realm of mystery, of creative freedom, of fantasy, opening up new expressive and linguistic possibilities. But I feel that my human position, my intellectual commitment are different', in Leonardo Ricci, 'Nascita di un villaggio per una nuova comunità', *Domus*, vol. 409 (December 1963): (7–13), 6.
[33] [n.a.], 'Ornamented Modern & Brutalism', *Zodiac*, no. 4 (April 1959): 68–69.

The Smithsons' statements are summarised by the editors in a succinct definition of Brutalism, which radically differed from previous ones in its emphasis on its artistic and urban dimension. Indeed, this last aspect emerges in the conversation as a key point in the evolution of Brutalism:

> The concept of 'brutalist architecture' (which seems to us in a certain sense to coincide with that of art brut from France) refers to every building and (more importantly) every urban form, every plan for a city or town, which rejects the preordained idea, the beauty 'envisaged' according to theoretical directives [...]. This is one of the many ways of revolting against idealism in contemporary culture.[34]

Zodiac did not propose a catalogue of buildings to be ascribed to Brutalism but stressed the need for critics to 'recognise them in the new architecture of the whole world', according to a process first instigated by Banham. The conversation with the Smithsons was flanked by a constellation of images selected by the editors, all of which would become symbols of the Brutalist imaginary: Dubuffet's painting *Visage usagé* and Paolozzi's *St. Sebastian*, a photograph of Ricci's villa cited by Veronesi at the beginning of the volume, two images of the Marchiondi Institute and three of the extension to the Old Vic Theatre in London by Lyons, Ellis and Israel, and the inevitable School at Hunstanton. The editors of *Zodiac* added a photograph of a building that had never been included in the debate, built in 1952 and thus before the official publication of the definition of New Brutalism: Figini and Pollini's Chiesa della Madonna dei Poveri. Surprisingly, the editors did not choose the image of the main façade, with its exposed concrete framework and brick infill, but instead selected a detail of the back façade, the only point where the building seems to be entirely in exposed concrete (see figures 31–32).

In the interview, the Smithsons for the first time specified the attitude that characterised the 'brutal approach'. It consisted in the simple precept that 'the building has to reflect the way it was built'. This statement needs to be read against the background of a return to the cardinal principles of the Modern Movement in a reaction to the architecture of the 1930s and 1940s. Against a literal and stylistic 'machine building aesthetic', the Smithsons proposed the uncompromising expression of a 'machine building technology'. This expression anticipates the research of Archigram and the phenomenon of tecnomorphic architecture, which can also be interpreted as an outcome of the theories on New Brutalism. Moreover, it was precisely the 'machine building technology' that would give Banham the cue to channel the premises of New Brutalism in another direction in his 1966 monographic book. The renewed sense of the 'machine aesthetic' was anchored to the holistic concept of 'as found', which implied the use of specific materials, implemented in such a way as to overcome the restrictions of cladding: 'The whole business of materials "as found" does not imply a rejection of marble and plaster and stainless steel [...] we turned back to wood, and concrete, glass and steel, all materials which you can really get hold of'. In the Smithsons' statements, the concept of 'direct', which they had advanced in the first half of the 1950s, also returned. This time, however, it was not linked to a compositional principle, but to the use of materials, even the simplest ones: 'Let's face it, you can get a direct effect out of the most simple material'. Despite the Smithsons' intervention centred on ethics and attitudes, in the conclusion, the aesthetics of Brutalism was once again pinpointed by Maxwell Fry, stressing how New Brutalism was unfairly being reduced by critics to the use of 'London stock brick' and 'bush hammered concrete'.

---

[34] Alison and Peter Smithson, Jane Drew, Maxwell Fry, 'Conversation on Brutalism', *Zodiac*, vol. 4 (April 1959): 70–81.

31-32 'Conversation on Brutalism', *Zodiac*, vol. 4, April 1959

Mr. Peter Smithson
Mrs Alison Smithson
Miss Jane B. Drew
Mr E. Maxwell Fry

Conversation on Brutalism

The interview would have international repercussions and helped clarify some of the until then obscure aspects of the Smithsons' theory. They admitted the difficulty of trying to outline a new theory, which had often led to inconsistent statements. 'There has been an awful lot of writing by people, and construction by other people assuming what we mean', they said, almost in their own defence. 'A modern architect does not think of a theory and then build it; you assemble your buildings and your theory as you go along'.

The same volume features a critical review of the Marchiondi Institute, edited by Pier Paolo Santini.[35] While acknowledging Zevi's intuition in ascribing the Marchiondi to the ranks of international Brutalism, Santini recognised in Brutalism functionalist traits with a rationalist ancestry, visible in the 'exhibitionism' of the building programme. In virtue of this functionalist aspect, Santini attributed a particular relevance to Viganò's building, and consequently to Brutalism itself, in the Italian context. The Marchiondi Institute in fact represented a shift from strict Rationalism and in this sense successfully translated the ethical essence of English experiences into a personal language.

The question of Brutalism and its international reception continued to fascinate Alfieri, the editor of *Zodiac*, who was driven by the desire to 'recognise' other Brutalist buildings and was committed to publishing interventions by the major protagonists linked to that definition. After interrogating Le Corbusier and acknowledging his distance from it,[36] he applied Brutalism to the works of the Brazilian architect Vilanova Artigas.[37] Alfieri praised Artigas's 'courage' and 'ruthlessness' on 'brute forms' that achieved 'anti-gracious' results by negating ornaments, and expressed an ethical stance in the 'sociality' of his buildings. In Artigas's Brutalism, Alfieri even went as far as identifying Wrightian ancestry, as if this component were now inseparable from the interpretations of the editorial staff of *Zodiac*. Moreover, the Wrightian echo seemed to Alfieri to represent a controversial act, in the Brazilian context faithful to 'Lecorbuserian Rationalism'.

By comparing the various contributions on Brutalism collected in *Zodiac*, the editorial team revealed a gradual weakening of that definition and its declination into a style. Always on the lookout for new ideas and trends, it was in the introduction to issue 8 of 1961, dedicated to the United States, that the magazine recognised Brutalism as a symptom of wear and tear: 'It is from America that new ideas are now coming, and Zodiac intends to follow them closely, especially at a time of fatigue that in Italy is called "neo-liberty" and in Britain "brutalism"'. In the following issue on exposed concrete buildings, the definition of Brutalism was to all purposes avoided, even in the case of the plastic forms of Eero Saarinen's TWA terminal, defined by Dorfles as 'neo-Baroque', or in the case of Rudolph, who was unhesitatingly accused of 'eclecticism'. In that very issue, Veronesi presented Yamasaki's work. The contrast between 'Ornamented Modern' and 'Brutalism' announced in 1959 was brought back to the different use of concrete: 'The greatest care and well-finished details' characterise Yamasaki's use of this material, which can only 'abhor' Brutalism, described according to the principle of *béton brut* as 'concrete left in the raw state as it comes out of the forms'.[38]

It is not only exposed concrete that became the main feature of the definition of Brutalism, but its very 'expression', its plastic and sculptural forms. Brutalism was a definition that, despite perplexity, was used and sought after by critics to stress the expressive potential of materials and to demonstrate ongoing trends that were manifesting

[35] Pier Carlo Santini, 'The Focus is on the Young Architects', *Zodiac*, vol. 4 (April 1959): 174–79.
[36] [n.a.], 'Cinq questions à Le Corbusier', *Zodiac*, vol. 5 (1960): 46–51.
[37] Bruno Alfieri, 'João Vilanova Artigas: Ricerca Brutalista', *Zodiac*, vol. 7 (1960): 96–107.
[38] Giulia Veronesi, 'Yamasaki and Stone', *Zodiac*, vol. 8 (1961): 128–39.

themselves with increasing force on the international scene, from the buildings by Basil Spence,[39] to the structures of Ponti and Nervi, to the American works of Marcel Breuer, to John Johansen's house[40] and to Saarinen's college for Yale University.[41]

Even Gio Ponti, the architect who found in the principle of cladding his own personal poetics, when presenting his Pirelli Skyscraper in Milan, used the definition of Brutalism to describe a certain 'romanticism' of exposed concrete. In the vision of a 'romantic' Brutalism we can understand a sort of fetishisation of the material, expressed in Nervi's structure left bare on Pirelli's top floor. But the Romanticism that Ponti refers to in the definition of Brutalism also revealed a nostalgic tendency, as shown by the characterisation of 'Picturesque' given to New Brutalism: 'Some considerations could be made about the curious, let's say "romantic", aspect that reinforced concrete structures assume. (Perhaps this expression comes to mind because no exact, historical definition had yet been found for the naked aspects of reinforced concrete structures, apart from the picturesque one of New Brutalism)'.[42]

When concrete's expression resulted from an accentuated plasticity, as in the case of Breuer's Benedictine Abbey in Minnesota, for Ponti it became the pretext for overcoming a Lecorbuserian Brutalism, towards a 'dynamic romanticism', resulting in a sculptural 'new violence'.[43]

Through the magazine *Architettura: Cronache e Storia*, Zevi continued, even if only partially, to be interested in Brutalism as a way of pursuing his cause of 'Post-Rationalism', predicting 'many different futures' in order to free architecture from a 'dogmatic faith'.[44] The annexes to the Old Vic Theatre in London, presented in full-page spreads in the 1959 issue of *Zodiac*, provided Zevi with an example of British 'Post-Rationalism', aimed at a 'truthful' and intellectual architecture. The more specifically Brutalist components were identified by Zevi in the alternation between the exposed concrete structure and the brick panelling, following a trend that in Italy was becoming established with the so-called Neorealism.[45]

Zevi identified New Brutalism in a nucleus of Le Corbusier-inspired buildings, as in Affonso Reidy's museum, the Atelier 5 factory in Thun, the various works of the Japanese architects Tange and Miyagawa, and finally the Wolfon Institute by Lyon, Israel and Ellis. Through Zevi's comments, distinctive features of Brutalism emerged that were not limited solely to the exposed material. In the 'expressionistic articulations' of the parts, Zevi identified one of the fundamental traits of Brutalism, revealed in the careful composition of the plan, which entailed an 'urbanistic' conception applied to a single building. In so doing, Zevi confirmed that Brutalism had definitively overcome Palladian compositions and rigid geometries, as he stated for Spence's College House for the University of Sussex.[46]

In Brutalism as an urbanistic design strategy applied to a single building, emerges the principle of decomposition, which Zevi saw as another crucial characteristic. This particular meaning became explicit in the example of Aldo van Eyck's orphanage. As in the case of the Marchiondi Institute, the 'psychological' stances of the programme were associated with the buildings' material and design. This time, however, Brutalism

[39] Gillo Dorfles, 'Cos'è cambiato a Londra?', *Domus*, vol. 368 (July 1960): 1–2.
[40] Gio Ponti, 'A Westport, Connecticut, sulla riva del mare', *Domus*, vol. 397 (December 1962): 15–18.
[41] Gio Ponti, 'Immagini dei due "colleges" di Saarinen a Yale, con le sculture di Nivola', *Domus*, vol. 399 (February 1963): 17–26.
[42] Gio Ponti, 'Si fa con i pensieri', *Domus*, vol. 379 (June 1961): 1–34: 25.
[43] 'Nervi does not allow himself to expressions that go beyond those of a "technical poetics", in the structural justification of cement. In this construction, Breuer symbolically moves from this structural cement to the interpretation of another cement: stone cement, sculpture cement. It is no longer even Le Corbusier's concrete "new brutalism"; it is in these dynamic blocks, a "new violence"', in Gio Ponti, 'Per una abbazia benedettina nel Minnesota', *Domus*, vol. 391 (June 1962): 1–6.
[44] Giovanni Walter König, 'La seconda crisi, oggi', *Architettura: Cronache e Storia*, vol. 7, no. 73 (January 1962): 628–29.
[45] [n.a.], 'Annessi al teatro "The Old Vic" a Londra', *Architettura: Cronache e Storia*, vol. 5 (April 1960): 832–33.
[46] [n.a.], 'Brutalismo nella monumentalità', *Architettura: Cronache e Storia*, vol. 5, no. 51 (May 1960): 115.

was not limited to the 'sincere' expression of matter but was extended to the vision of an 'organism that is both urban and architectural', articulated in spatial sequences that become a 'modulated network of possibilities'. 'The existential situation had to be tackled frankly, without false sweetness,' Zevi says, 'the house is "hard"; it is brutalist'.[47] Zevi's vision of Brutalism, however, was linked to the potential of the project, or of the 'organism', to create intermediate spaces, or 'spaces in between' as the Smithsons would later theorise, through the interpenetration of functions. Only in this way, Zevi asserted, could the notion of Brutalism overcome an otherwise 'rude' architecture.

Veronesi and Ponti's intuition of juxtaposing 'informal', 'organicism', 'romanticism' and 'Brutalism', almost as if they were interchangeable definitions, was taken up by Zevi on several, albeit sporadic, occasions; in his commentary on Johansen's villa in Connecticut and Erskine's villa in Sweden, Brutalism embodied traits of an 'expressionistic, romantic, neo-organic' path.[48] But the fate of Brutalism, Zevi finally announced, could only be that of becoming a style, because of the increasing 'mannerism' of its architecture. Understood as the outcome of more and more personal research, Zevi argued that Brutalist architecture would soon lose its 'sincerity' in favour of 'self-expressive virtualisms'.[49]

If the entry of Brutalism in the Italian debates had been motivated, as Zevi confessed, by an underlying intention for controversy, mainly addressed to the editorial staff of *Casabella-Continuità*, Rogers' magazine, for its part, provided no comment on that definition until the early 1960s. Accused in 1959 by Banham of defending the most retrograde aspects of Rationalism, those that could be traced back to Neo-Liberty, the editorial staff of *Casabella* responded with an entire issue dedicated to an assessment of the English post-war experiences, published in April 1961.[50] In the editorial, Rogers complained about the lack of strong personalities in the English context, capable of provoking 'decisive ruptures'. The English contribution to contemporary architectural culture was, in Rogers' eyes, 'timid and modest, anti-monumental', capable only of reworking foreign models. Even the definition of Brutalism was by him stripped of all its violent, brutal and irreverent characteristics, to become merely an instrumental and intoxicating component of criticism.[51]

The same symptoms of 'tiredness' referred by Veronesi in *Zodiac* to tendencies such as Brutalism and Neo- Liberty, were also perceived by Aldo Rossi: 'Frankly I believe that "neo-liberty" and "brutalism" are two aspects of the same face, quite generous, all calculated, in their taste for compromise. As good as the fever for the disease is: that reveals it'.[52] Rossi's reaction was a response to the accusations of Neo-Liberty that Banham had also made against him in his 1959 article. For Rossi, Neo-Liberty and Neorealism were synonyms, and indications of the Italian tendency to combine ancient and popular references in contemporary architecture in response to the formalism of the 1950s. But in resorting to a popular taste, Rossi had critically identified the origins of another kind of style that retreated into tradition and relied on the creation of atmospheres that were more rhetorical and the result of an intellectual vision.

[47] Bruno Zevi, presentation of Jan van Goethem, 'Casa dei ragazzi ad Amsterdam', *Architettura: Cronache e Storia*, vol. 7, no. 72 (October 1961): 386–402.
[48] [n.a.], 'Erskine's Villa in Lindigö', *Architettura: Cronache e Storia*, vol. 8, no. 86 (December 1962): 538–39.
[49] Bruno Zevi, 'La registrazione veritiera di Le Corbusier', *Architettura: Cronache e Storia*, vol. 7, no. 68 (June 1961): 74–75.
[50] Ernesto Nathan Rogers, 'Appunti sull'Inghilterra e l'Italia', *Casabella-Continuità*, vol. 250 (April 1961): 1–2.
[51] 'The inability of the majority of British artists to deal with the aesthetic problem in its expressive instances, to the point of becoming a monument, is psychologically demonstrated by the favour that Brutalism (to which I do acknowledge its quality of reacting to old and new conformism) has in many young people today: it reminds me of their way of having fun, which almost never manages to become bluntly joyful without passing through drunkenness, in Rogers, 'Appunti sull'Inghilterra e l'Italia', 1.
[52] Aldo Rossi, 'Arredamento e architettura', in Guido Canella e Vittorio Gregotti (ed.), *Nuovi disegni per il mobile italiano*, (Milan: L'Osservatorio delle Arti Industriali, 1960).

Neorealism in Italy had taken a particular direction, advocated by the editorial staff of *Casabella-Continuità*, corresponding to a concrete framework and brick infill.

Rossi's critical stance towards Brutalism was also reiterated at the end of his article on Le Corbusier's La Tourette Convent, where he recognised the emergence of some 'new and very dangerous tendencies, some threatening prospects and some unresolved questions, such as to consider the very future of modern architecture precarious'.[53] In his concluding commentary, Brutalism, in its purely architectural expressions, was definitively relegated to the aporia of the copy of the master: 'Until now Le Corbusier has only served for serious, but inevitably sterile moral debates or, worse still, for the academic and foolish copies of the Brutalists'. Rossi's words resonated strongly with the arrival of Brutalism to be assimilated into a real style, exhausted in the iteration of the Le Corbusier model, while the urban dimension, dear to Rossi, was completely forgotten by him. Rossi's stance against Brutalism is not surprising if we consider that through his works he denied any aspect of truth to the very end, in order to defend an architecture of cladding, in which plaster and paint combined to confer the idea of abstraction.[54]

The Italian debate on Brutalism was also intertwined with fringes of the avant-garde culture of the 1960s, for whom Brutalism represented a revolutionary 'new art of life', founded on the total realism of construction. The controversial, intransigent and protesting components that had led to the foundation of English New Brutalism were not forgotten when, in the avant-garde magazine *Linea Sud*, a manifesto appeared by the Neapolitan artist Luigi Castellano which claimed political protest for a cultural renewal:

> We accept the 'Brutalist protest', because it clearly expresses our impatience with the inadequate and outdated terms in which the problems of the art of building today are posed; problems that today's architectural society, especially in Italy, is no longer able to understand, especially when it believes, as in the case of Brutalism, that it was a 'vain search for reality insufficiently motivated within the limits of a purely ethical problem.[55]

Premises for American Brutalism

The plastic potential of reinforced concrete and the search for new compositional principles based on the articulation of the parts were of increasing interest to American architects. In 1951 Hitchcock even suggested extending the principles of International Style to the 'articulation of structure' as a desire to go beyond pure geometry and the aesthetic purism of the curtain wall.[56] All the debates in America on the question of style and the search for a new 'ism' can be traced back to the need to go beyond the notion of 'form', through the search for elements that became increasingly plastic and sculptural, in the name of a recognition of 'individual parts', as Rudolph stated.[57] In this tension between the exhaustion of a style that had fallen victim to its own success

53 Aldo Rossi, 'Il convento de la Tourette di Le Corbusier', *Casabella-Continuità*, vol. 246 (December 1960): 4.
54 On Rossi's work, see Beatrice Lampariello, *Aldo Rossi e le forme del razionalismo esaltato. Dai progetti scolastici alla 'città analoga', 1950–1973* (Macerata: Quodlibet, 2017).
55 Luca Luigi Castellano, 'Noi insistiamo! Brutalismo. Realismo panico del costruire', *Linea sud*, vol. 0 (1963): 6.
56 'Today I should certainly add articulation of structure, probably making it the third principle', in Henry Russell Hitchcock, 'The International Style, Twenty Years After', *Architectural Record*, vol. 110, no. 2 (August 1951): (89–97), 91. See also Robin Boyd, 'Has Success Spoiled Modern Architecture?' *Architectural Forum*, vol. 111, no. 1 (July 1959): 98–103.
57 'When people attack the "box" they are really attacking the idea of form itself and the notion that the whole is more important than any individual part', in Paul Rudolph, 'Regionalism in Architecture', *Perspecta*, vol. 4 (1957): (12–19), 19; see also Peter Blake, 'Form Follows Function – Or Does It?' *Architectural Forum*, vol. 108, no. 4 (April 1958): 99–103. The supremacy of 'form' had been the subject of much debate in the US, including essays such as Susanne Langer, *Feeling and Form* (New York: Scribner 1953) and Eliel Saarinen, *Search for Form: A Fundamental Approach to Art* (New York: Reinhold Pub. Corp 1948); several MoMA exhibitions revolved around the question of 'form', such as *Form Givers at Mid-century* and *Architectural Imaginary. Four New Buildings* in 1959.

and the search for new principles, the American debate became sensitive to the issues raised by the discussions on Brutalism, which would lead to a radical revision of decisive concepts such as 'modern', 'functionalism' and 'beauty', which were translated into the concepts of 'plasticity', 'appearance' and 'imagery'.[58]

From Hitchcock and Johnson, to Scully, Boyd, Creighton and Blake, a whole host of critics, driven by different motivations and paths, launched an investigation based on a fundamental question for American culture, that is, the fate of the International Style, which was considered by some as an American declination of the Modern Movement. Therefore, by questioning its faith they were questioning their own culture and the history of American debate.[59] At this juncture it was the concept of modernity itself that was to be examined, raising reactions against the aestheticising drifts of the omnipresent 'glass box' and increasingly historicist ornamentation.[60]

Towards the end of the 1950s, decisive contributions emerged from protagonists who not surprisingly had deep ties to European culture. Some critics directly confronted the implications of Brutalism, while others assimilated its characteristics within other definitions. In this phase of renewal of the International Style, it is not surprising that critics such as Boyd and Creighton and architects such as Johnson and Kallmann were interested in concepts akin to the themes raised in the European debates on New Brutalism. Sometimes critics literally took the same concepts of New Brutalism and substituted it with another label; 'Sophisticated Functionalism', 'counter-revolution', 'New Sensualism', or 'Action Architecture' are the labels invented to describe the current phenomenon of the revolt against the 'box' through the articulation of parts, the accentuation of plastic elements and surface, up to the acceptance of processual attitudes.[61] The American tendency to discuss New Brutalism by stripping it of the prefix New is perhaps no coincidence, as if the very manipulation of that definition corresponded to an intention to purge it of the ethical principles and politicised debates that characterised its English trajectory.

On the one hand, critics were divided on the search for an exasperated and aesthetically pleasing ornamentation of the façade, as expressed in the works of Stone and Yamasaki, while on the other, at the crossroad of multiple contaminations, the free concrete forms in the 'brut' manner of Le Corbusier were becoming more and more popular.[62] A true American stance would only come during the 1960s, when Brutalism, once it had become a style in its own right, shaped the apparatus of the great democratic state machine, such as campus, hospitals, and large housing estates.[63]

[58] Peter Blake, 'Modern Architecture: Its Many Faces', *Architectural Forum*, vol. 108, no. 3 (March 1958): 76–81; Blake, 'Form Follows Function – Or Does It?'

[59] Richard Miller, 'Disenchantment and Criticism: The State of Modern Architecture', *Journal of Architectural Education*, vol. 14, no. 1 (Spring 1959): 9–12.

[60] In the early 1950s Hitchcock had already proposed a renewal of the principles of the International Style, in Hitchcock, 'The International Style, Twenty Years After'; Johnson spoke as part of a series of lectures organised by Scully at Yale University's architecture department on the question of 'modern architecture'. The transcript of the recording is now published in Philip Johnson, 'Retreat from the International Style to the Present Scene', in *Philip Johnson Writings* (New York: Oxford University Press, 1979), 84–97. On the rediscovery of ornament, see Douglas Haskell, 'Ornaments Rides Again', *Architectural Forum*, vol. 108, no. 4 (April 1958): 99–103; [n.a.], 'Architectural Coxcombry or the Desire for Ornament', *Perspecta*, vol. 5 (1959): 4–15.

[61] Blake, 'Form Follows Function – Or Does It?'; Boyd, 'The Counter-Revolution in Architecture'; Thomas Hawk Creighton, 'The New Sensualism', *Progressive Architecture*, vol. 40, no. 9 (September 1959): 141–54; Thomas Hawk Creighton, 'The New Sensualism II', *Progressive Architecture*, vol. 40, no. 10 (October 1959): 180–87; Gerhard M. Kallmann, 'The "Action" Architecture of a New Generation', *Architectural Forum*, vol. 111, no. 4 (October 1959): 132–37.

[62] Robin Boyd, 'The Counter-Revolution in Architecture', *Harper's Magazine*, vol. 219, no. 1312 (September 1959): 40–48.

[63] See in this regard the following contributions: Joan Ockman, 'How America Learned to Stop Worrying and Love Brutalism', in Maristella Casciato (ed.), *Modern Architecture: The Rise of a Heritage* (Wavre: Mardaga, 2012); Joan Ockman, 'The School of Brutalism: From Great Britain to Boston (and Beyond)', in Marc Pasnik, Michael Kubo, Chris Grimley (eds.), *Heroic. Concrete Architecture and the New Boston* (New York: The Monacelli Press, 2015), 30–47; Joan Ockman, 'The American School of Brutalism. Transformations of a Concrete Idea', in *SOS Brutalism. A Global Survey. Contributions to the International Symposium in Berlin 2012*, vol. 2 (Zurich: Park Books, 2017), 105–16.

Starting with a critique of the drifts of the Miesian model that had led architecture to hide behind the 'monotonous curtain wall' and the 'flatness' of geometric patterns,[64] Blake returned to the principles of Brutalism demonstrating to American readers the relevance of English debates for the evolution of the International Style.[65] In this context, the Smithsons' and Stirling's principle of the specific response to the specific case became for Blake the possibility for architecture to be animated by textures and three-dimensional sculptural elements, overcoming the very concept of the façade.

Towards the end of the 1950s, Robin Boyd again entered the debate on style, marginally tackling the question of Brutalism as one of several possible evolutions of the International Style and associating it to values of 'truth', 'integrity' and 'honesty'.[66] To illustrate 'the brutalist use of raw concrete', Boyd did not resort to the acclaimed examples of Le Corbusier, nor to Kahn's Yale Art Gallery, the only American example of exposed concrete building mentioned by Banham. Boyd instead chose a recent work, completed in 1958, which was unexpectedly imposing itself in the debate: the Marchiondi Institute by Viganò, presented to the American public in March 1959 in *Architectural Forum*, as an example of the versatility of reinforced concrete.[67] In its monthly review of new international architecture, the magazine praised Marchiondi's structures as 'one of the world's boldest examples of structure-conscious contemporary architecture'. For the Americans, the taste for 'rugged', 'rough' and 'stark' workmanship demonstrated the material's intrinsic versatility, which was well suited to the needs of a 'progressive education'. The article included a photograph of the façade of the boarding school pavilion, which was destined to become a pivotal image for the style of international Brutalism and which would become inextricably associated with the adjectives used to describe its concrete: 'rough', 'uncompromising' and 'rugged' entered the international vocabulary of critics announcing the new aesthetics of Brutalism.

The Marchiondi Institute also attests to the unequivocal international potential of the definition of New Brutalism, in virtue of Zevi's appropriation of Viganò as 'the first Italian "Brutalist"'.[68] If it had not been for Alfieri's editorial decision to include images of the Marchiondi Institute alongside the Smithsons' words,[69] thus giving strength to Zevi's intuition, Boyd would probably not have seen in that work the symbol of the questions posed by a new generation of architects all around the world, who could find in the monumental forms of Viganò's colossal pillars the 'brave' affirmation of structure and material. In associating Brutalism with 'raw concrete', Boyd performed two operations: the first was to omit the prefix New, and the second was to transform that definition into an adjective for a certain type of material finishing, thus repositioning an aesthetic principle at the expense of the ethical dimension recalled by Smithson just a year before.[70]

While Boyd saw Brutalism as the expression of a technique for reinforced concrete that was entirely European, Thomas Creighton, editor of *Progressive Architecture*, was concerned that the intellectualism of English debates might contaminate American discourse by distracting from constructive issues.[71] The English discussions on New Brutalism were taken up by Creighton thanks to a survey sent to him by two students from the Carnegie Mellon Institute. Creighton labelled New Brutalism as an exclusively English issue, as a 'product of the school of criticism'. Admitting the

[64] [n.a.], 'The Monotonous Curtain Wall', *Architectural Forum*, vol. 111, no. 4 (October 1959): 142–50.
[65] Blake, 'Form Follows Function – Or Does It?'
[66] Boyd, 'Has Success Spoiled Modern Architecture?'
[67] [n.a.], 'Milanese Boys' Town', *Architectural Forum*, vol. 110, no. 3 (March 1959): 223–25.
[68] Zevi, 'I ragazzi non scappano'.
[69] Fry, Drew, Smithsons, 'Ornamented Modern & Brutalism'.
[70] Smithson, 'The New Brutalism: Alison and Peter Smithson Answer the Criticism on the Opposite Page'.
[71] Thomas Hawk Creighton, 'P.S.', *Progressive Architecture*, vol. 38, no. 1 (January 1957): 216; Thomas Hawk Creighton, 'The Intellectual Fringe', *Progressive Architecture*, vol. 38, no. 6 (June 1957): 366.

difficulty in grasping its essence, Creighton denied even its effectiveness as a label, also due to the Smithsons' recent statements promoting New Brutalism's unpredictable and continuous evolution. Apart from composition issues, in which he seemed to be less interested, probably reflecting an American cultural attitude, Creighton identified in the treatment of materials and the expressive finishes a certain 'roughness' and 'crudity' which to him appeared as the real new element of New Brutalism.[72] What may come as a surprise are Creighton's perceptions of New Brutalism as a 'nostalgic' and 'reactionary' label, due to the appeal and confirmation of the first principles of the Modern Movement, which 'would only take us back in attitude'.[73] Nothing could sound more retrograde for the American culture, in which the only certainty seemed to be, as Johnson stated, that 'the battle of modern architecture has long been won'.[74]

The Carnegie Institute Student Questionnaire

The debates internationally generated on Brutalism, especially lively among the younger generation searching for new directions, can be testified by the 1958 Bachelor's thesis of two Carnegie Mellon Institute students, Marian Zdzislaw Augustyniak and Fred T. Entwistle Junior.[75] Their research was conducted in the context of a new educational orientation at the Carnegie Mellon Institute, directed since 1957 by Paul Schweikher, previously head of the faculty of architecture at Yale University and an architect with a keen interest in exposed concrete buildings. Schweikher strengthened the teaching approach introduced by his predecessor, John Knox Shear, centred on technical, structural and material knowledge in which architecture must be at the service of the formation of a 'complete man'.[76]

Augustyniak and Entwistle's thesis was the first attempt to document the debate on New Brutalism through the direct involvement of leading architects. It comprises a bibliography and a multiple-choice questionnaire entitled 'Survey of New Brutalism' that was drafted in April 1957 and sent to a total of 96 architects, critics, historians and professors, including Patrick Abercrombie, Hakon Ahlberg, Lawrence Anderson, Marcel Breuer, Gordon Bunshaft, William Dudok, George Downs, Sigfried Giedion, Walter Gropius, Le Corbusier, Wallace Harrison, Philip Johnson, Louis Kahn, William Lescaze, John Merrill, James Morehead, Richard Neutra, Nathaniel Owinga, Eero Saarinen, Paul Schweikher, John Knox Shear, Louis Skidmore, Alison and Peter Smithson, John Voelcker, Frank Lloyd Wright, and Mies van der Rohe (see figures 33–34).[77]

In the introduction New Brutalism was defined as a recent 'new architectural manifestation' that the students intended to investigate. The questionnaire was designed to collect a series of impressions in order to measure the relevance of New Brutalism in the contemporary debate.[78] The framework of the questionnaire was significantly influenced by the American cult of the evolution of technology and materials and was less concerned with conceptual aspects. The literature used by Augustyniak and

---

[72] Alison and Peter Smithson, 'Aesthetic of Change', *Architects' Year Book*, no. 8 (1957): 14–22.

[73] Creighton, 'The Intellectual Fringe', 366.

[74] Philip Johnson, preface to the book by Henry Russell Hitchcock, Arthur Drexler, *Built in USA: Post-war Architecture* (New York: Simon & Schuster, 1952), 8.

[75] Marian Z. Augustyniak, Fred T. Entwistle, *Survey of the New Brutalism*, (Pittsburgh, PA: Carnegie Institute of Technology, Department of Architecture, 1958). I thank Marian Augustyniak for sending me the Bachelor's thesis in question.

[76] John Shear Knox, 'Architecture for the Complete Man', *Architectural Record* (July 1956): 201–02.

[77] The questionnaire does not contain a complete list of the personalities contacted. However, the names can be deduced from the most significant answers given by the students, as well as from a short list at the end of the letter of invitation. A copy of the invitation letter is also kept in the archive of Louis Kahn, see Roberto Gargiani, *Louis I. Kahn: Exposed Concrete and Hollow Stones, 1949–1959* (Lausanne: EPFL Press, 2014), 108.

[78] Augustyniak, Entwistle, *Survey of the New Brutalism*, 1.

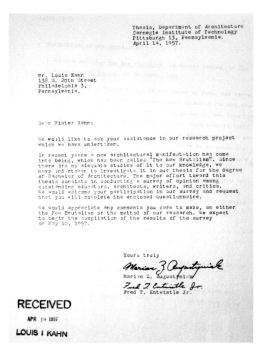

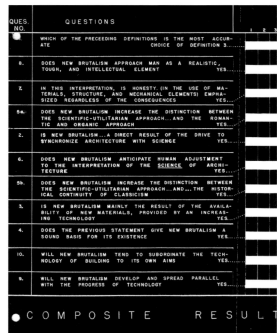

33 Marian Z. Augustyniak, Fred T. Entwistle, letter to Louis Kahn, 14 April 1957, Courtesy of Louis I. Kahn Collection, The University of Pennsylvania and the Pennsylvania Historical and Museum Commission.

34 Marian Z. Augustyniak, *Survey on New Brutalism,* Carnegie Mellon University 1957, Courtesy of Marian Z. Augustyniak

Entwistle testifies to the impact of the English discussion in America but also of the first sporadic contributions in American magazines. In fact, the questionnaire took its cue from the appearance of the two articles by Banham and Blake, published in *Architectural Review* and *Architectural Forum*, which Augustyniak and Entwistle selected as their main references. However, in their account they also recognised the Smithsons as 'the acclaimed exponent of New Brutalism'.

The questionnaire presented three possible definitions of New Brutalism, and the people contacted were asked to choose the most appropriate one. The first definition is more conceptual and based on Banham's principles of December 1955; the second suggests the more pragmatic version put forward by Blake in May 1955, focusing on the role of the elements of architecture divided into 'wall', 'skeleton', 'materials' and 'plan'; finally, a third definition was formulated by Augustyniak and Entwistle in seven points. In their definition, one senses the intention to articulate Banham's principles with a design dimension. The 'compact' plan is one of the aspects that had characterised the Neo-Palladian interpretation in the first phase of New Brutalism, traced back to Wittkower, which was here contaminated by the American principle of economy, according to which the plan must express a 'functional sequence', based on a modular and 'sub-modular' system. Some crucial aspects of New Brutalism, as theorised by Banham, undergo a translation that can be linked to the theories of vision studied by the two students, which are evident in the bibliography.[79] Banham's complex concept

[79] The texts consulted show an interest in theories of vision, such as those of Daniel Butterly, Richard Henry Guggenheimer and Herbert Read, and essays on aesthetic philosophy and art criticism, Daniel R. Butterly, *The Architecture of Vision: Or the Theory of Composition Plane-surface Design* (New York: Beechhurst Press, 1947); Richard Guggenheimer, *Sight and Insight: A Prediction of New Perceptions of Art* (London: Harper Brothers London, 1947); Herbert Read, *Art Now: An Introduction to the Theory of Modern Painting and Sculpture* (New York: Harcourt, Brace & Company, 1937).

of 'memorability' becomes for Augustyniak and Entwistle the ability of a building to convey a 'vivid total impression'. Compared to existing formulations, characteristics that had hitherto remained secondary are made explicit, such as the mechanical and technological systems and elements, which must remain 'visible and tangible'. In the logic of Carnegie Mellon Institute orientation, New Brutalism is interpreted and revised according to the criterion of economy, which also extends to the use of materials, to achieve a 'maximum effect with a minimum of materials'. The absence of a cladding emphasises the 'inherent qualities' of the materials, which are hence used 'as found'.

Following the three definitions, Augustyniak and Entwistle articulated a series of 11 multiple-choice questions with issues ranging from the collaboration of architecture, science and technology, the use of new materials, the relationship between the 'romantic and organic approach', 'classicism' and 'humanism'.

The students only received 43 answers, which were grouped together to obtain percentages. Among the received answers, it is not possible to establish whether Le Corbusier, Wright, Kahn, Johnson and Mies responded. 'The most illuminating' comments received were summarised in a four-page typewritten document, entitled 'Survey of New Brutalism'.

On the basis of the available documents, the majority of the respondents considered the students' definition of New Brutalism to be the most comprehensive, reflecting the general scepticism towards Banham's and Blake's positions. 'Many participants object to the term New Brutalism' is the summary comment. When New Brutalism was intended as a refined and almost philosophical attitude beyond simple evidence of structure or conduits, it was still perceived as an unspecified category; when, on the contrary, New Brutalism was understood as the prominence of technical and constructive aspects and as exhibited matter, the definition was clear and also indicative of a promising design process.

However, what emerged as a general critique was the absence of the necessary components for the definition of space. In this interpretation of New Brutalism, Gropius's comment was decisive. He criticised New Brutalism as 'a serious slogan invented to attract attention' and emphasised a 'lack of consideration for man's psychological needs'. In Gropius's words, one can discern the attempt of European debates to conceptualise New Brutalism and free it from the concreteness of the material. The search for the humanistic components of modern architecture explains the perplexity that even George Downs, an American architect, had towards New Brutalism, which prevented the realisation of a 'sensitive humanism'.

Shear also criticised New Brutalism as 'unnecessary and probably regrettable' because he saw it as an 'impalpable entity' over informed by theoretical debates and devoid of principles that could be translated into practical terms. This view was also shared by Saarinen, who stated: 'I am all for it [New Brutalism], if and when it is done well'.

For Hakon Ahlberg, a Swedish architect, the moral principles dictated by New Brutalism imposed a 'reaction against the multitude of materials and techniques provided by technology'. This statement implicitly suggests that the truth of materials and structure dictates a selection of precise and traditional materials. Neutra had a similar view, reducing the definition of New Brutalism to the principles of the visibility of the structure, the materials used 'as found' and the principle of 'maximum effect with a minimum of materials'.

Schweikher recognised a certain potential within New Brutalism, despite it still being an 'abstract term since the nature of the trend does not relate to the popular meaning'. For Schweikher, the survival of the definition of New Brutalism depended exclusively on its ability to gain acceptance among a wider public and on its social impact: 'The ascension or failure of New Brutalism depends mainly on its acceptance by architects, builders, users and viewers'.

The Smithsons also sent a reply, which summed up their desire to identify a new attitude. For them, the relationship between New Brutalism and new technologies revolves around the possibility for New Brutalism to remain dynamic and not crystallise in style: 'The New Brutalism professes a new spirit in a new age; it allies itself to technology and will require it to perform certain tasks, but it is not a byproduct of it. New Brutalism is primarily an idea; it puts its efforts into development of techniques in architecture based on dynamic social and technological ambitions and attitudes'. For the first time, the Smithsons clearly stated that New Brutalism consisted of an idea, and a 'new spirit', probably to distance it from a possible stylistic drift. To confirm this, they attached two images of their early projects, Sheffield University and Coventry Cathedral. Significantly, Augustyniak and Entwistle accompanied the images with the caption 'emphasis on basic structure' in the case of the Sheffield project, and 'functional areas in logical relationship to each other' for Coventry Cathedral.

The association between New Brutalism and the Smithsons was also underlined by Giedion, who specified the origin of the definition in the fusion of Peter's nickname, Brutus, and Alison, confirming Armitage's hypothesis.[80] 'About the coming about of the designation there exists the following anecdote: Mr. Smithson was called at the A.A. in London "Brutus". His wife's first name, Alison, was connected with her husband's nickname to form 'Brut-Alison', finally to Brutalism'.

The students summarise in another document the trajectory of the definition on the basis of the assumptions already presented by Banham in 1955. They recalled the Swedish origin of the term and its links with the avant-garde movements of the twentieth century, underlining its potential as an alternative to the International Style. The main characteristic identified was New Brutalism's capacity for diffusion – its definition had become 'popular' and had produced works 'in most Western countries'. In the conclusion, New Brutalism was distinguished from a movement, because it was perceived as an 'integrating force', with no claim to novelty because its principles can be traced back to the early Modern Movement into a 'coherent whole'.

Underlining relevant aspects of American culture linked to science and technology, the predominant praise in the assessment of New Brutalism was that of the economy not only of materials, but also of space. 'Economy of space' is the term coined to suggest a plan organised according to a 'simple coherence in layout' where a functionalist principle resurges, which refuses any axiality and symmetry. Palladian logics are overcome by virtue of economic reasons. Ultimately, only by aiming at a radical economy following developments in science and technology, could New Brutalism achieve humanistic aspects, affirmed Augustyniak and Entwistle. Expressive of its time, freed from ornamentation and reduced to its essential, New Brutalism was the bearer of apolitical and universal principles. A series of examples were called in to support an American genealogy; the School at Hunstanton is read against the precedents of Mies' IIT and Johnson's Glass House, and also Kahn's 'concrete space-frame' was approved for the economy of material that this system allowed. New Brutalism, as the ultimate expression of 'simplicity' and 'basic qualities', was therefore able find a certain correspondence in the 'perfectionist strain' of American industry.[81]

---

[80] Edward J. Armitage, 'Letter to the Editor', *Architectural Design*, vol. 27, no. 6 (June 1957): 184.
[81] In May 1958 Blake published an article on the theme of 'simplicity'; Peter Blake, 'The Difficult Art of Simplicity', *Architectural Forum*, vol. 108, no. 5 (May 1958): 126–31.

Kallmann's Action Architecture

While the definition of New Brutalism was being manipulated, replaced and adapted to the culture and context of the machine of the American construction industry, an architect intervened in the debate. He would become a protagonist of the American declination of Brutalism, when he built Boston City Hall in the 1960s: Gerhard Kallmann. In 1959, in *Architectural Forum*, Kallmann addressed an appeal to the new generation of American architects entitled 'The "Action" Architecture of a New Generation'.[82] In 1950, while still living in England and before moving to the United States, Kallmann had already applauded the traits of an American experimentalism in the works of Fuller, Eames, Saarinen, Mies, Wachsmann and SOM.[83]

Kallmann's was the first published American contribution to address the divergences between Banham and the Smithsons, making a clear statement about Brutalism on a conceptual level. After recontextualising the term within a 'generational' quest, Kallmann lucidly grasped how the term Brutalism was 'vivid' but at the same time 'limited' because of its etymological root that was too directly and univocally linked to Le Corbusier's *béton brut*. Labels were a limit in general, according to Kallman, because they attempted to project a dogmatic position on a 'radical new architecture' rebelling against subjugation to a single material and a set of shapes.[84]

In the wake of recent American interpretations of Brutalism, in which exposed concrete was its undisputed protagonist, Kallmann also took a critical view of Le Corbusier's *béton brut*, pointing out that the strength of the 'matières brutes' was to be understood not so much in the material itself as in the complex poetics of contrasts and tensions underlying the 'roughness'. Kallmann was not far from the vision of the Smithsons, who recognised in the 'rough poetry' of *béton brut* an ethical attitude that went beyond aesthetic questions and thus configured a definition free to evolve and change over time.[85] In order to understand the deep links between 'action architecture', Brutalism and exposed concrete it is necessary to go back over a previous Kallmann article entitled 'Vital Impulses', also from 1959. Here Kallmann presented various international trends in which 'brutalist', 'concrete' and 'action' became synonyms for an architecture capable of overcoming formal rigidity.[86]

In 'Action Architecture', Kallmann admitted he was searching for a new concept of modernity based on notions of growth of form and 'plastic' image. His quest was for a certain degree of autonomy from the masters, by virtue of an 'anti-rationalist' and 'non-directional' architecture.[87] By investigating the exhaustion of the International Style and the advent in the debates of the definition of New Brutalism, Kallmann forged his own definition and invented a formula that avoided the misunderstandings posed by an '-ism', placing a pulsating element, 'action', at the centre of the discourse.

[82] Gerhard Kallmann (1915–2012) studied at the Architectural Association in London (1936–41); he then held the position of assistant editor for the *Architectural Review* between 1945 and 1948, before moving to the United States in 1948. Kallmann, 'The "Action" Architecture of a New Generation'.

[83] Gerhard M. Kallmann, 'Towards a New Environment, the Way through Technology: America's Unrealised Potential', *Architectural Review*, vol. 108 (1950): 407–14.

[84] 'Avoiding the static position of a formed "style"', he states, 'and the play on aesthetic sensibilities exhausted in the earlier modernism, brutalists reject all pre-established conceptions imposed on materials and construction', in Kallmann, 'The "Action" Architecture of a New Generation', 135.

[85] Smithson, 'The New Brutalism: Alison and Peter Smithson Answer the Criticism on the Opposite Page'.

[86] 'They are decidedly not symptoms of disaffection of a small group. They represent impulses that are widespread, exist in many countries, overlap in their rival theories yet all converge on important issues of architectural aesthetics. Whether we identify them as a combination of "action", "brutalist", "concrete" architecture, they all have a similar shattering effect on formal eclecticism and on the rigidity, which has frozen the countenance of architecture in neo-classic formulae', in ibid.

[87] Kallmann, 'The "Action" Architecture of a New Generation', 133.

The term 'action' had already been introduced by Scully,[88] who attributed it to the expressive force of concrete and its sculptural plasticity. For Kallmann, on the other hand, 'action' became the expression of an internal vitalism of architecture. It also implied an ethical impulse that governs materials and forms, derived from construction processes rather than aesthetic objectives. Kallmann's emphasis on 'action' thus had the effect of reviving the ethical impulse of New Brutalism, which by the end of the 1950s was already declining towards a style.

It is almost certain that Kallmann's search was intrinsically linked to the cultural ferment in the United States. It is no coincidence that he defined this new course of architecture as 'radical', 'disruptive', 'violent' and 'daring', driven by a 'ruthless energy' that was in tune with the commitment of a generation entering collective protest. In this context, we should also remember Paul Rudolph's appeal when, at the beginning of the construction of Yale University Art and Architecture Building, he publicly stated: 'Theory must again overtake action'.[89] The 'theory' to which Rudolph appealed was built around a series of principles that originated through the major experiences of American architecture, from the Chicago Fair of 1893 to the International Style, but which undeniably intersected with concepts discussed in the context of New Brutalism by the Smithsons and Banham, such as the relationship between buildings and the understanding of the 'space between', the search for an 'aesthetic of change', and the need to reconsider architecture's 'visual perception'.

Kallmann Action Architecture must be read as a sequel to his 1948 idea of an 'expressive architecture' capable of infusing plastic intensity into every single part in order to defeat the formalism of a 'universal shape'.[90] The affinities between the principles of English New Brutalism and contemporary artistic practices, already stated by the Smithsons and reiterated by Banham, took on a decisive cultural dimension, inevitably paralleling the experiences of American artists on action painting and the concept of 'allover' in which 'action' entailed the liberation of artworks from aesthetic and moral dogmas.[91] Coincidentally, Peter Smithson in his 'Letter to America' recalled that 'American architecture has not yet had its Pollock'.[92] We are tempted to affirm that Kallmann's Action Architecture was hence responding to the assertion of one of the initiators of New Brutalism.

In Kallmann's view, Brutalism should be distanced from the notion of style and should not be restrained to a single material. As he proceeded to strip away all the stylistic constructs gradually superimposed onto the definition of Brutalism, Kallmann revealed the original essence of New Brutalism: the concept of the 'as found'. This concept came forth as an energetic particle, a 'vital impulse' capable of reactivating architecture through an element of 'shock' and a collision between the parts, generating a dynamic 'state of continuous discovery'.[93] The examples presented undermined the code of the International Style. In the works of Bakema, Candilis, Utzon and Le Corbusier, Kallmann identified new plastic possibilities and a richer vocabulary of forms. The vital sense of action was not limited to expected curved surfaces or shells, but mostly occurred through principles of relation and multiplication of parts, just as the Smithsons had investigated through their topological schemes.

[88] Vincent Scully, 'Modern Architecture: Toward a Redefinition of Style', *Perspecta*, vol. 4 (1957): 4–11.
[89] On this subject, see the following contributions: Paul Rudolph, 'The Changing Philosophy of Architecture', *Architectural Forum*, vol. 101, no. 1 (July 1954): 120–21; Paul Rudolph, 'Creative Use of Architectural Materials', *Progressive Architecture*, vol. 40 (April 1959): 92–94; Paul Rudolph, 'Regionalism in Architecture', *Perspecta*, vol. 4 (1957): 12–19.
[90] Gerhard M. Kallmann, in Alfred Hamilton Barr et al., 'What is Happening to Modern Architecture? A Symposium at the Museum of Modern Art', *Museum of Modern Art Bulletin*, vol. 15, no. 3 (1948): (4–21), 17.
[91] Harold Rosenberg, 'The American Action Painters', *Art News*, vol. 51, no. 8 (December 1952): 22–50.
[92] Peter Smithson, 'Letter to America', *Architectural Design*, vol. 28, no. 3 (March 1958): 93–102.
[93] Gerhard M. Kallmann, 'Vital Impulses', *Journal of Architectural Education*, vol. 14, no. 2 (Autumn 1959): 38–41.

35 Gerhard Kallmann, 'The Action Architecture of a New Generation, *Architectural Forum*, vol. 111, October 1959, no. 4, pp. 132–33; 136–37

The "action" architecture of a new generation

All other images completing Kallmann's article are to be read with the notion of action, movement and liberation in mind, such as the vivid physical power of the metal portals of the first project for the Rinascente headquarters in Rome by Franco Albini and Franca Helg and the 'brutal' materials used by Stirling and Gowan used for their 'active, actual sense of physical existence' (see figure 35). In this sense, the plasticity and strength hitherto attributed to concrete alone was extended to a wider repertoire of materials, as long as they were free from conventional geometries. The examples assembled demonstrate the existence of an architecture that projects 'pulsating images on the retina', like a stroboscopic camera capturing the process of construction and assembly of parts. The category of the 'image' theorised by Banham was here translated into the ability of architecture to immortalise the construction process, to become a 'spontaneous' and 'unpremeditated' *image* of the very act of construction, absolved of the 'censorship' of an *a priori* form.

With the concepts of topology and 'as found', the composition of the plan opens up to the insertion of elements dictated by 'chance and trouvaille' that turn architecture into an exploratory and experimental process, thus avoiding becoming a 'closed system'. Some emblematic adjectives were used by Kallmann to describe this new architectural trend, including 'vigor', 'dramatization', 'articulation', 'hyperactivity' and 'anger'. Action Architecture was framed not so much on materials as on questions of plan and composition, to the point of approaching Johnson's early intuition of the principle of 'anti-design'.

A stream of this 'action architecture' would be noticed by critics in Boston City Hall, the masterpiece designed by Kallmann, Michael McKinnell and Edward Knowles between 1962 and 1969. That building would be received not only in the wake of Le Corbusier's La Tourette, but also as the symbol of a 'tough', 'violent', 'masculine' architecture, expressive of a particular 'vigour'.[94] Kallmann confessed to recognising himself in these adjectives, which he also felt were in line with his time, giving the concrete of Boston City Hall a particular political and cultural meaning. It was remembered as 'no accident that the designers were inspired by the presidency of John F. Kennedy who, like this new City Hall, pronounced the word "vigor" with that peculiar Boston accent'.[95]

Kallmann's contribution was taken up by Collins in his comments on the construction of Boston City Hall, by Banham and Jordy and was also recorded by Italian critics, who published its translation in *Casabella*, attesting to the international scope of Kallmann's interpretative hypotheses.[96]

Action Architecture testified to the emergence in the debate of other parallel categories, as the Smithsons had already demonstrated with their alternative definitions of 'new order' and 'architecture of reality', or Banham with 'une architecture autre', Summerson with 'Old Rigour', and Lasdun with 'classical wholeness'. With the critical discourse merging into other definitions, Brutalism was rapidly emptying its scope, remaining exclusively dependent solely on the exposed concrete. Used to distinguish plastic and expressive architectures departing from the International Style it ended up affirming another international phenomenon, which we could call 'international Brutalism'.

Directions and Dilemmas beyond the International Style

During the 1960s, there was a significant reckoning in the United Stated on the design implications of Brutalism, when the panorama of exposed concrete buildings presented a wide range of expressive solutions for surface treatments, ranging from perfect control

[94] Walter McQuade, 'Toughness Before Gentility Wins in Boston', *Architectural Forum*, vol. 117 (August 1962): 96–9; [n.a.], 'La Tourette comes to Boston: Boston City Hall', *Architects' Journal*, vol. 136 (July 4, 1962): 2, 11; [n.a.], 'Boston City Hall', *Casabella-Continuità*, no. 271 (January 1963): 17–27; [n.a.], 'The New Boston City Hall', *Progressive Architecture*, vol. 44 (February 1963): 132–53; [n.a.], 'A Great Plaza for Boston's Government Center', *Architectural Record*, vol. 135 (March 1964): 190–200; [n.a.], 'Gerhard Kallmann Shows the New Boston City Hall', *Architectural Association Journal*, vol. 79 (January 1964): 313–16; M. Schmertz, 'The New Boston City Hall', *Architectural Record*, vol. 145 (February 1969): 144–50; James Marston Fitch, 'City Hall, Boston', *Architectural Review*, vol. 147 (June 1970): 398–411; Ellen Perry Berkeley, 'More Than You May Want to Know About the Boston City Hall', *Architecture plus*, vol. 1 (February 1973), no. 1: 72–77. For a more recent account of the reception of Boston City Hall, see David Monteyne, 'Boston City Hall and a History of Reception', *Journal of Architectural Education*, vol. 65, no. 1 (October 2011): 45–62; Ockman, 'The School of Brutalism: From Great Britain to Boston (and Beyond)'; Brian M. Sirman, *Concrete Changes: Architecture, Politics, and the Design of Boston City Hall* (Amherst: Bright Leaf, 2018).

[95] Wolf von Eckardt, 'Boston's New City Hall: It has Vigor, *Boston Sunday Globe*, 2 April 1967. The same allusion is also made by Paul Heyer, *Architects on Architecture; New Directions in America* (New York: Van Nostrand Reinhold, 1993), 216: 'Maybe this was influenced by the Kennedy Administration at that time, when there was more optimism about usefulness of government'.

[96] Reyner Banham, 'Stocktaking', *Architectural Review*, vol. 127, no. 756 (February 1960): 93–100; William H. Jordy, 'The Formal Image: USA, *Architectural Review*, vol. 127, no. 757 (March 1960): 156–65; Peter Collins, 'Action Architecture', *The Guardian*, 13 September 1962; Gerhard M. Kallmann, 'The "Action Architecture" of a New Generation', *Casabella-Continuità*, no. 269 (November 1962): 29–49.

through to the development of products to eliminate any possible defect, to the invention of technical expedients to include and control imperfection.[97] The definition of Brutalism, as it was being forged through Italian and British debates, posed hard challenges for American critics and architects. The quality of informal and 'violent' 'roughness', to which exposed concrete was being associated in the European context, did not find a perfect correspondence in the American architectural culture. In fact, the aesthetic and theoretical concerns that emerged with Lecorbuserian *béton brut* had already been settled in the technical system of 'Architectural Concrete', a concept that summed up the goal of technical and formal refinement combined with economy of material, in the tradition of the great American construction industry.[98]

The search for capillary control of processes, aiming for a polished surface, was linked to a particular cultural trait that Scully identified in an obsessive 'precisionism', extended to 'surface, mass, plan and structure'.[99] In his article 'The Precisionist Strain', Scully suggested that even new research coming from the European context, such as Brutalism, could not but be transfigured by American culture: 'The historical pattern now seems apparent: when closely derived from European work, American forms have always become tighter, more planar and more linear'.[100]

Scully dubbed the material expressiveness 'the humanist gesture', a definition that he traced back to Le Corbusier and that suggested the formwork imprints in *béton brut*, as he had theorised in 1955.[101] In considering the legacy of 'precisionism' in contemporary buildings, Scully confirmed, through Kahn's Richards Medical Laboratories, a certain distance between the American Architectural Concrete and *béton brut*, and could not but recognise 'the avoidance of the humanist gesture, like that of Le Corbusier, which Americans have somehow always found difficult to understand'.[102] The line of 'precisionism' enunciated by Scully did not, however, encompass the entire panorama of expressions of concrete. Some architects, precisely in reaction to the cult of perfection and influenced by the expression of Le Corbusier, would experiment with the 'unexpected', as in the first heroic *béton brut*, albeit with different cultural assumptions. If on the one hand we witness a controlled, faultless surface, on the other hand another cult of roughness was emerging, albeit through controlled textures that defied technical expedients.

In the tension between the European quest for imperfection and the American Architectural Concrete dictated by the desire to control processes, we see the possible declination of *béton brut* proposed by Scully. Through this 'precisionist strain', Scully recognised the real 'struggle' that occurred when American architects strove for a rustic surface that aimed at a 'European generosity in sculptural terms'. The roughness of the concrete experimented by American architects was, however, always the result of a precise control of the construction processes or of the surface finishing after dismantling, as the buildings of Breuer, Johansen and Rudolph demonstrate. Rudolph himself would recall the American obsession with precision, dwelling on the difference between Le Corbusier's béton brut and American concrete:

[97] At the end of the 1960s, Shilstone described three kinds of concrete, ranging from 'structural concrete', intended to be cladded, to 'concrete used architecturally' and 'architectural concrete'. By 'concrete used architecturally' Shilstone meant concrete that is not perfectly controlled: 'In most cases, small defects may even be a sought-after textural effect'. James Shilstone, 'Industry Advises', *Progressive Architecture*, vol. 48, no. 10 (October 1967): 137–38.
[98] On this subject see Roberto Gargiani, *A New Era of American Architectural Concrete. From Wright to SOM. 1940–1980*, vols. 1–3 (Lausanne: EPFL Press, 2020).
[99] Vincent Scully, 'The Precisionist Strain in American Architecture', *Art in America*, vol. 3 (1960): 46–53.
[100] Ibid.
[101] Scully, 'Modern Architecture: Toward a Redefinition of Style'.
[102] Scully, 'The Precisionist Strain in American Architecture', 53.

One of the most humanizing elements in Corbu's concrete is the oozing, dripping, and slipping of concrete between poorly placed forms. One of the reasons why American architecture has had difficulty using this medium is that our contractors take great pride with the precision of their work, which helps to give so much of it the thin, metallic-like quality.[103]

American architects would not accept all the implications of the definition of Brutalism, and in particular the total assimilation of imperfection. Although there had been a prevailing critical silence, apart from rare exceptions, there would be no lack of denials or profound distancing during the course of the 1960s. In an interview at the end of his career, Rudolph again, responding to accusation of a 'degeneration' of forms,[104] confessed in an interview that Brutalism, despite being a 'catch phrase' linked to the use of exposed concrete, for him actually had a broader purpose, including the articulation of parts, according to an interpretation that American critics often overlooked. It is no coincidence that Rudolph, in declaring his distance from the label attributed to him, referred expressly to English New Brutalism, almost as if he wished to underline, in the presence of that prefix New, that the definition belonged to English debates, and was therefore foreign to the American context.[105]

Despite a general rejection, architects accepted the definition of Brutalism if, and only if, it was to be understood beyond questions of form and surface finishing. As Kallmann had also pointed out, if Brutalism implies an 'attitude' and not a style, as the Smithsons had also repeatedly stressed, that definition is a vital tool for pursuing a reflection that transcends the individual personal idiom.

In an undated handwritten note (certainly later than 1959 and probably dating around the 1980s),[106] Rudolph wrote some thoughts on a book, the author of which was not mentioned but was only referred to as 'Mr. D'. In the notes Rudolph contested the author's reduction of New Brutalism to the mere 'intimidating' expressiveness of the material. For Rudolph, New Brutalism had instead an urbanistic scope, based on the relationship between the buildings and the scale of the city, the articulation between the parts, expressive of a concept akin to Banham's 'imageability' translated by him as 'presence from a distance'.[107]

[103] Paul Rudolph, see Richard Pommer 'The Art and Architecture Building at Yale, Once Again', *Burlington Magazine*, vol. 114, no. 837 (December 1972): (859–860), 859.

[104] Heinrich Klotz, John Wesley Cook, *Architektur im Widerspruch: Bauen in den USA von Mies van der Rohe bis Andy Warhol* (Zurich: Verlag für Architektur Artemis, 1981); Heinrich Klotz, John Wesley Cook, *Conversations with Architects: Philip Johnson, Kevin Roche, Paul Rudolph, Bertrand Goldberg, Morris Lapidus, Louis Kahn, Charles Moore, Robert Venturi & Denise Scott Brown, Lund Humphries* (Westport, CT: Praeger Publishers, 1973); Robert Venturi, Denise Scott Brown, Steven Izenour, *Learning from Las Vegas* (Cambridge, MA: MIT Press, 1972); Banham himself detected in Rudolph's work the degeneration of Brutalism towards a style of the surface, Banham, *New Brutalism. Ethic or Aesthetic?*, 1966.

[105] 'The "New Brutalism" originated in England. If I understand it correctly, they mean the very direct use of materials, the exposure of a lot of things. Well, that's about the beginning in England, so not important. The theory is about the expression of material, and so it strikes the word "new". But these terms are catch phrases. I was called a "new Brutalist" because I built in concrete sometimes. The attitude of articulating the parts is a principle in architecture, I believe, which you then use or not use. [...] In my case, I built in many different periods, so people call me all sort of names. It has nothing to do with anything as far as I am concerned', in Paul Rudolph, interview conducted by Andreas Vogler, Jan Dvorak, Yung Un Hong, Lourdes Peñeranda, Beekman Place, New York City, 23 January 1993, Paul Marvin Rudolph archive, Library of Congress Prints and Photographs Division Washington, D.C, PR 13 CN 2001:126, folder PMR-3026–3 F*.

[106] It was in fact in 1959 that the Smithsons revealed the urban dimension of Brutalism in *Zodiac*, no. 4, 1959. The notes contain reflections on the concept of 'regionalism' in the meanings put forward by Kenneth Frampton in *Modern Architecture: A Critical History* (London: Thames & Hudson, 1980).

[107] 'He [Mr. 'D'] dismisses "Brutalism" as merely a taste for the intimidating, the gratuitously hostile. This reading is not the only one for some architects found "Brutalism" is confused with their compelling need to manipulate scale in accordance with environmental demands made on a building, especially in an urban context. [...] The ability of a building to maintain appropriate sense of presence from a distance, closed range or indeed close at hand, is dependent on the architects understanding of scale', in Paul Rudolph, undated note, Paul Marvin Rudolph archive, Library of Congress Prints and Photographs Division Washington, D.C. PR 13 CN 2001:126, folder PMR-3032–1 F*.

Following the example of Kallmann's 'action architecture', other American critics started manipulating the principles of Brutalism to converge them into new definitions, less obsessed with ethics but more aimed at a formal orientation. An example of this is the 'New Sensualism' proposed by Creighton in 1959.[108] New Sensualism was nothing more than a re-elaboration of New Brutalism, as evidenced from its centre in the 'new Corbu' of the Unité in Marseilles, the Capitol in Chandigarh and the Chapel in Ronchamp, whose images accompany the article. Creighton returned to the etymological and material origins of New Brutalism, revealing, by the presence of the adjective 'new', his implicit revision of English debates. Moreover, in New Sensualism the question of the image becomes the focal point. Purged of all violent and anti-formal tendencies, the 'image' was translated by Creighton into 'emotionally moving forms and "delight" in design'.

On these assumptions, New Sensualism presented itself as a response to the 'bloody-minded' insistence of the ethics of European New Brutalism, through an all-American definition rooted in the formal possibilities of concrete.[109] All the attention paid to 'plastically sympathetic materials' only made New Sensualism the antithesis of 'Mies-type design', reiterating the conceptual clash between the two masters, Le Corbusier and Mies, and between two materials, concrete and steel.[110]

In the 1960s Johnson, the first American to enter the discussion on the definition of New Brutalism, despite his negative opinion expressed in 1954,[111] could only recognise its success and even its value as a critical tool. 'The International Style is dying [...] We are going through a foggy chaos, and the *Architectural Review* is looking for a new compelling, unifying slogan', was his comment on New Brutalism.[112] In a lecture given in November 1960 at the Architectural Association in London, he placed New Brutalism in a historiographical perspective that echoed the 1940s search for a 'New-ism': 'It is sometimes useful to have labels to hang on to or disagree with. The English are wonderfully good at it. They invented something called the New Empiricism, which came from Sweden. It did not last long, even in the *Review*. Then came Brutalism and so on'.[113]

After the 1954 exchange between Banham and Johnson on the School at Hunstanton, which generated an initial internationalisation of New Brutalism, in the 1960s the two critics met again on the prestigious stage of the MoMA in New York. The public debate, entitled 'International Style, Death or Metamorphosis?', organised on 30 March 1961, was supposed to include a discussion between Johnson, Banham and Giedion, who instead declined the invitation. For Banham, it was the first opportunity to visit the United States, where he had been invited 'to disagree with me on a platform', as Johnson stated in his invitation letter.[114] Johnson's speech was imbued with a controversial vein directed against Brutalism and Banham himself, whose book *Theory and Design in the First Machine Age* he had already criticised.[115] In the conclusion of his speech, Johnson distinguished three trends that originated from the ashes

---

[108] Creighton, 'The New Sensualism'; Creighton, 'The New Sensualism II'.

[109] Under 'New Sensualism' Creighton included the plastic forms of Le Corbusier, Wright, Niemeyer, Candela, Kahn and Saarinen as well as the more ornamental research of Stone and Yamasaki, through to the 'metallic' concrete of SOM and the 'desert-concrete' of Wright. The examples presented by Creighton demonstrate a formal repertoire based on a move away from technological functionalism towards a register of intuitive forms evoking a 'sensuous plasticity', 'sensual delight', 'sculptural concept', 'romantic expressionism', in ibid.

[110] 'The criticism of lack of relationship between form and purpose is perhaps no stronger than it would be in an evaluation of the rectilinear, Mies-type design of which the New Sensualism is the antithesis', in ibid.

[111] Johnson, 'School at Hunstanton'.

[112] Philip Johnson, 'Where Are We At?', *Architectural Review*, vol. 127, no. 763 (September 1960): 173–75.

[113] Philip Johnson, 'Informal Talk', Architectural Association, London, November 1960, in Helen M. Franc (ed.), *Philip Johnson. Writings* (New York: Oxford University Press, 1979): (104–116), 108.

[114] Mary Banham, interviewed by Corinne Julius, *National Life Story Collection: Architects' Lives*, British Library Oral History, 2001, part 10/19.

[115] 'It is a wonderful and perverse book', says Johnson about *Theory and Design of the First Machine Age*, whose mechanistic interpretation he criticised above all. Johnson, 'Where Are We At?'.

of the International Style: one that took up its principles, identifiable in the works of Mies, SOM, Pei and Creig Ellwood; a second, defined as 'what the English call Brutalism – not a good name, but a name', whose models were both European, such as the Maisons Jaoul, and American, such as the works of Rudolph and Katselas; and a final trend named 'Neo-Historicism'. If in 1954 Johnson had attributed to New Brutalism an irreverence capable of disrupting the principles of composition associating it with the concept of 'anti-design', here he noted in Brutalism an 'attitude, not a Style'. In the American context, noted Johnson, Brutalism was subverting the 'regular skeletal rhythms' of the International Style and was rapidly transforming into a constellation of formal expedients: 'The intention is strength, originality and a certain crudeness'.[116]

Banham did not respond to Johnson's controversial declaration and did not defend Brutalism, as on other occasions when he had been challenged.[117] In his speech, New Brutalism was not even mentioned, as if to indicate a progressive loss of relevance in contemporary debates.

On his side, Giedion presented his position on the course of architecture after the International Style in the introduction to the second edition and thirteenth reprint of *Space, Time and Architecture*, entitled 'Architecture in the 1960s: Hopes and Fears'.[118] On that occasion he advanced the definition of 'playboy architecture [...] an architecture treated as playboys treat life, jumping from one sensation to another and quickly bored with everything'. A profound criticism of the concept of style was highlighted by Giedion through the definition of 'playboy architecture', which demonstrated, as he had already announced in 1958, a deep uncertainty.[119]

Brutalism as one of the possible phases following the International Style was also recognised by Boyd in a speech entitled 'Directions and Dilemmas' given at the 1964 International Design Conference in Aspen.[120] In an attempt to periodise recent history, Boyd, like Johnson, recognised an evolutionary succession of post-war architecture subdivided into three phases, which passed from a literal interpretation of the principles of functionalism towards a 'Fun phase' characterised by an accentuated formalism, and culminated in a third phase, where Brutalism was included: 'The third phase is not a style, for it takes many shapes, but it has recognisable characteristics. It is formal but not stiff'. In his book *The Puzzle of Architecture*, Boyd defined the third phase as 'Counter-revolution' and specified its formal characteristics, anchored in the myth of the 'significant form', monolithism and sculpturalism.[121] 'Asymmetry, fragmentation, extroversion' and the desire to build entirely with a single material were the principles behind Brutalism according to Boyd. The examples listed demonstrated the wide spread of Brutalism in the American and international context, such as Kahn's Laboratories, Tange's Kurashiki Town Hall and Rudolph's Yale Art and Architecture Building. Most interestingly, both Boyd and other Anglo-Saxon critics, as well as the architects of the Counter-Revolution themselves, insistently used the expression 'significant

[116] Philip Johnson, typescript for the lecture 'International Style, Death or Metamorphosis?', 30 March 1961, Museum of Modern Art Archive, Philip Johnson Collection, Series I: Writings, Statements and Speeches, folder I.53a: 1–9.
[117] Reyner Banham, 'New Brutalism', *Architectural Design*, vol. 06, no. 27 (June 1957): 220.
[118] Sigfried Giedion, *Space, Time and Architecture*, 2nd edition, 13th reprint (Cambridge, MA: Harvard University Press, 1962).
[119] 'There is a word that we refrain from using to describe contemporary art. This is the word "style". [...] "Style" did not come into general use to describe specific periods until the nineteenth century, when different periods of architecture were analyzed according to a materialistic description of details of form. Today, the moment we fence architecture in within a notion of "style" we open the door to a purely formalistic approach. Purely formalist comparisons have about the same effect on the history of art as a bulldozer upon a flower garden. Everything becomes flattened into nothingness, and the underlying roots are destroyed', in Sigfried Giedion, *Architecture, You and Me: The Diary of a Development* (Cambridge, MA: Harvard University Press, 1958), 138.
[120] Robin Boyd, *Direction and Dilemmas*, 1964, The Getty Research Institute, Special Collections and Visual Resources, International Design Conference in Aspen Records, no. 2007. M.7., IDCA 1964, Box 11.
[121] Robin Boyd, *The Puzzle of Architecture* (Carlton: Melbourne University Press, 1965).

form' to designate the search for a new intensity of architectural image. 'Significant form', 'imageability' and 'figurability' are recurrent terms in the writings of Saarinen, Stone and Rudolph. *Béton brut* as interpreted through American construction culture, together with the concept of a vigorous, heroic 'significant form' superimposed on that of 'image', proved to be the canons that marked the Brutalist trajectory in America.

At the beginning of the 1960s, a wide range of examples were added to the emerging style of American Brutalism, demonstrating an impatience to define this new international style, which included almost exclusively exposed concrete buildings, such as the works of Kahn and Rudolph, the office building for Vic Maitland Associates in Pittsburgh by Tasso Katselas, the Central Fire Station in New Haven by Earl P. Carlin, Peter Millard and Paul Pozzi[122] and Johansen's house in Connecticut.[123] In all these cases, the rudimentary technique of *béton brut* from Marseilles or Chandigarh, which originated in the practical and economic constraints of the construction site, became a formal taste once it landed in America. Le Corbusier's concrete acted as the parameter for measuring a very precise style, expressive of 'virile', 'violent' and 'vigorous' effects. These are the adjectives that characterised latter manifestations of American Brutalism, which thus ended up exemplifying the gradual transition from the perfectionism of Architectural Concrete to the controlled roughness of an Americanised *béton brut*.

The reaction of critics to Le Corbusier's unusual *béton brut* for Harvard's Carpenter Center is therefore not surprising. There Le Corbusier did not reproduce the *malfaçons* that he had accepted in Marseilles or Chandigarh but sought to exploit the skills of American industry, which was capable of producing a perfectly polished concrete.[124] The well-known 'rough-finished concrete', which had become 'Le Corbusier's trademark', was commented on in *Engineering News-Record* with a significant headline: 'Le Corbusier Smooths his Style for U.S. Debut at Harvard'.[125] Similar comments appeared in the pages of major American magazines, including *Progressive Architecture*, *Architectural Record* and *Architectural Forum*, where critics bluntly noted that Le Corbusier's '*beton* is not so *brut*';[126] 'It isn't very good Corbu. Take a look at his European or Indian buildings – where the concrete is really brutal. [...] It looks like a caricature of a real Corbu building'.[127]

During the 1960s, two leading architects, Johnson and Kahn, but also minor ones, such as Carlin, became more explicit in their criticism of Brutalism. Johnson limited its relevance to the European context, delegitimising its impact on the American context. In order to highlight the distance from American culture, Johnson went as far as emphasising its historicist aspects derived from the German Expressionist of the 1920s. With regard to Carlin, Millard and Pozzi's firestation in New Haven, Johnson confirmed the presence of historicist traits tending towards expressive exaggeration.[128] This provoked

---

[122] [n.a.], 'Eight Annual Design Award', *Progressive Architecture*, vol. 42, no. 1 (January 1961): (96–199), 106.

[123] [n.a.], 'Labyrinthian Environs', *Progressive Architecture*, vol. 43, no. 5 (May 1962): 181–87.

[124] On the Carpenter Center see Eduard F. Sekler, William Curtis, Jr., *Le Corbusier at Work: The Genesis of the Carpenter Center for the Visual Arts* (London, Cambridge, MA: Harvard University Press, 1978); Roberto Gargiani, Anna Rosellini, *Le Corbusier. Béton Brut and Ineffable Space, 1940–1965. Surfaces, Materials and Psychophysiology of Vision* (Lausanne: EPFL Press, 2011), 527–44; Gargiani, *A New Era of American Architectural Concrete. From Wright to SOM. 1940–1980*.

[125] [n.a.] 'Le Corbusier Smooths His Style for U.S. Debut at Harvard', *Engineering News-Record*, vol. 170, no. 14 (4 April 1963): (80–82), 82.

[126] [n.a.], 'Le Corbusier Designs for Harvard', *Architectural Record*, vol. 133, no. 4 (April 1963): (151–58), 151; John Dixon, 'Corbu's Centre Rises at Harvard', *Progressive Architecture*, vol. 43, no. 12 (December 1962): 43.

[127] [n.a.] 'Le Corbusier at Harvard: A Disaster, or a Bold Step Forward?' *Architectural Forum*, vol. 119, no. 4 (April 1963): (104–07). 105. The commentary is taken from a fictitious dialogue organised from comments in vogue at the time of the completion of the Carpenter Center.

[128] 'Frankly I wouldn't build a building like any one of these, but I hope I can take a liberal attitude about these things. [...] That is part of the architecture of the brutalist movement – to give it the bad name used in England – to exaggerate the very thing you have. It is also more historical than you know; it is a revival of a strong movement of the '20s in Germany called Expressionism. It also undoubtedly reflects the Angry Young Men and all that, but it does represent an architectural Expressionism more than anything. It seems to me that the younger generation is going in this direction – all of Italy, most of England, and very little in the United States', in Johnson, 'Eight Annual Design Award', 156.

Carlin's reaction in July 1961, with a comment that reveals a particular affinity with the Smithsons' description of the House in Soho, where the absence of internal cladding was the predominant feature. Carlin's remarks also emphasised the value, typically American, of economy: 'Apparently we are now brutalists, so the building is of raw, hairy concrete. We intend no interior finishing, except that which is built in. [...] We think we have achieved a low-maintenance building'.[129] Carlin's surprise, similar to that of Viganò, Ricci, Rudolph and other architects who had been associated, in spite of themselves, with the definition of Brutalism, reveals the unbridgeable gap between critics and architects, the former manipulating current definitions and launching new styles, and the others inevitably distancing themselves from these intellectual operations. Carlin's comment also revealed a similar attitude to that expressed by Kahn, his former professor. The attempt to ascribe Kahn's architecture to the ranks of New Brutalism had already raised Colin Rowe's concerns when, in 1956, he informed Kahn of Banham's 'deplorable article'.[130] Kahn had not taken a public position at the time, nor was his opinion on Brutalism revealed until 1960, when, in an article on the Richards Medical Laboratories, author James Marton Fitch reported Kahn's stance.[131] Kahn's comment allows us to understand how the labels proposed by critics were perceived by architects as nothing more than a useless intellectual exercise far from the real concerns of design, as Le Corbusier had also pointed out:

> Much of his recent work, including this building, has been linked to the movement called *the new brutalism*. Such a suggestion Kahn brushes impatiently aside. For him the term connotes an attitude, an intellectual posture external to the act of designing and consciously applied to it like a coat of paint.[132]

One can only assume Kahn's reaction when Scully, a close friend of his, also applied the definition of Brutalism to his buildings in both *Modern Architecture: The Architecture of Democracy* in 1960 and in the monograph dedicated to him in 1962.[133] Although he avoided the definition of Brutalism in his 1957 essay on Le Corbusier, Scully felt compelled to mention Kahn's ascription to the Brutalist movement that had now taken on an international dimension. In the association between a 'meticulously realistic' and 'heroic' approach found in the Richards Medical Laboratories, he identified affinities with the 'English trend' of brick and exposed concrete led by the Smithsons.[134] In his monograph on Kahn, Scully returned to English New Brutalism and the legacy of the masters. Not by coincidence, Scully's understanding of Brutalism was linked to the 1950s Palladian ascendancy, when geometry and diagrammatic plans were still the bastions of a new form of architecture. This 'Wittkowerian' phase of New Brutalism is the one that allows the strongest affinities with Kahn's work, as Banham also recognised.[135] The influence of the Maisons Jaoul noted by Scully on the Chestnut Hill house ties

[129] Earl P. Carlin, 'P/A Design Award. Central Fire Station', *Progressive Architecture*, vol. 42, no. 7 (July 1961): (132–35), 132.
[130] Colin Rowe, letter to Kahn, in Braden R. Engel, 'The Badger of Muck and Brass', *AA Files*, vol. 62 (2011): 95–98.
[131] James Marston Fitch, 'A Building of Rugged Fundaments', *Architectural Forum*, vol. 113 (July 1960): 82–87.
[132] Ibid.
[133] Vincent Scully, *Modern Architecture: The Architecture of Democracy* (New York: George Brazilier, 1961); Vincent Scully, *Louis I. Kahn* (New York: George Brazilier, 1962). On the question of Brutalism in the Yale Art Gallery, see Roberto Gargiani, *Louis I. Kahn. Exposed Concrete and Hollow Stones, 1949–1959* (Lausanne: EPFL Press, 2014), 51ff. See also Denise Scott Brown, 'A Worm's Eye View of Recent Architectural History, *Architectural Record*, vol. 172, no. 2 (February 1984): (69–81), 71–73.
[134] Scully, *Modern Architecture*, 39.
[135] 'Their [Alison and Peter Smithson] Hunstanton School of 1951–53, the first moment of the English "New Brutalism", was based upon a toughening of Mies, and they ascribed its intrinsic symmetry to Renaissance and, by extension academic precedent as well, citing Wittkower's Architectural Principles in the Age of Humanism, of 1949, as their authority. Later the Brutalists, like Kahn himself, were to be more permanently influenced by the Maisons Jaoul', in Scully, *Louis I. Kahn*, 20–21.

another level of affinity between Kahn and Brutalism, establishing a new stylistic canon for American Brutalism around a particular layout of the 'spattered windows, which suggest both Le Corbusier and the English Brutalists'.[136]

The progressive diffusion of Brutalism in the American context was attributed by critics to the state of 'chaoticism' and 'confusion' that pervaded architecture, strengthened by the affirmation of individual poetics over a set of common agreements. Several magazines attempted critical assessments of the contemporary state of American architecture, through symposia among leading American critics and architects, with the intention of identifying a new common line capable of resolving the ongoing fragmentation of architectural culture, under pressure from European debates.[137] What the critics were most concerned about was the tendency for architects to respond with rapid 'action', reiterating the concept made famous by Kallmann, to the detriment of a 'long term vision', as Gilbert Herbert pointed out, lamenting the fact of being 'plagued by a plethora of coined labels. We are confused by an infinity of isms [...] with which we play the game of building today'.[138]

Creighton, the editor-in-chief of *Progressive Architecture*, organised a symposium in 1961 to overcome the antagonisms, in an attempt reminiscent of Richards' critical operation to end the 'battle of styles' of the early 1950s. The attendees were Mies, Yamasaki, Sert, Ellwood, Buckmister Fuller, Schweikher, Kahn, Creighton and Johnson. Despite the vital presence of free expression, in Creighton's words we glimpse the ultimate fate of Brutalism, entangled in the struggle between the Miesian and Lecorbuserian models, between ethics and aesthetics and, finally, between 'attitude' and 'style': 'The issues in architecture today do not seem to be plasticity vs. modularity, smooth skin vs. articulation, Mies vs. Corbu, or even steel vs. concrete. There will be lingering structuralism and increasing historicism; there will be emotional expressions that we will call sensualism, and there will be angry expressions that we will call brutalism'.[139]

Pevsner and Stirling vs. the Brutalist Aesthetics

In England, the country that witnessed the origin of New Brutalism, the investigation into the multifaceted aspects of the evolution of the Modern Movement continued with radically different challenges than in the United States. All the topics discussed since the beginning of the 1950s converged into a building that would become crucial for the international reception of New Brutalism. The Flats at Ham Common, built in 1958 by Stirling and Gowan, are to be read as a concrete response to the identity debate on 'Englishness', translated into a contemporary regionalist architecture.[140] The hypotheses of New Brutalism, from the new aesthetic for the 'atomic age', to questions on the role of technology, to the attitudes of the 'angry young men', to pop culture, are intertwined in this building with concepts advanced by Stirling and Gowan, such as 'the style for the job' and the 'multi-aesthetic'.

Considering Stirling's utter silence on New Brutalism in his article on the Maisons Jaoul, coupled with the succinct remarks in his notebook, one can understand his scepticism when Banham described, in July 1958, the housing estate at Ham Common as 'the most accessible example there is of the New Brutalism'.[141] Banham's consideration was built on the parallel with the Maisons Jaoul, which Stirling criticized for its 'poor

[136] Ibid., 35.
[137] Gilbert Herbert, 'Notes in Passing', *Arts & Architecture*, vol. 78, no. 12 (December 1961): 9.
[138] Ibid.
[139] Thomas Creighton, 'The Sixties. A P/A Symposium on the State of Architecture. Part III', *Progressive Architecture*, vol. 42, no. 5 (May 1961): 136–41.
[140] James Frazer Stirling, 'Regionalism and Modern Architecture', *Architects' Year Book*, vol. 8 (1957): 62–68.
[141] Reyner Banham, 'Plucky Jims', *New Statesman*, vol. 49 (July 1958): 83–84.

brickwork' and 'roughness'. Similarly to many other architects, Stirling rejected the appellation 'New Brutalist' with a dry 'we do not consider ourselves "new brutalist"'.[142] For Stirling, New Brutalism was nothing more than an attempt by critics to redeem English culture through the invention of a 'journalistic' definition that pretended to be internationalist but in fact concealed the limited post-war English architectural production.[143]

While New Brutalism had originally been an attempt by architects to formulate a definition capable of grasping a new architectural direction from Smithson to Asplund, at the beginning of the 1960s the definition had inexorably entered the exclusive use of critics and led to increasing distance by architects, as Stirling's emblematic comment demonstrates, in which the only valid contribution of New Brutalism was reduced to the principle of 'as found', as he would state in 1959:

> The 'new brutalism', a term which we used to regard on the one hand as
> a narrow interpretation of one aspect of architecture, specifically the use
> of materials and components 'as found' – an already established attitude;
> and on the other hand, as a well-intentioned but over patriotic attempt to
> elevate English architecture to an international status.[144]

Stirling's comments, also reported by Banham in his famous 1966 book, conceal the fear that New Brutalism could give rise to associations that would damage architects, delivering an image of 'pretentiousness, artiness, and irresponsibility'.[145] While some features of the Flats at Ham Common may in fact recall a Brutalist approach, such as the use of 'simple and everyday materials', load-bearing walls 'calculated structurally to get the maximum of window openings', and floors 'patterned by the formwork', the reasons advanced by the architects are to be found in the economic limits imposed by the client. Like Stirling and Carlin, several architects justified the use of a 'basic unit' by the economy of construction site logic:[146] 'We do not know if this specification is in accord with the "new Brutalism"', commented Stirling as he discarded the label, ironically presupposing an overlap between the critical concept of New Brutalism and the direct pragmatism of the 'specifications'.

The concept of Stirling and Gowan's 'style for the job', which recalls the Smithsons' principle of a specific response to a specific case, discards any *a priori* solutions. Banham did not miss the opportunity to pick up this concept in his article 'Machine Aesthetes' published in August 1958.[147] In returning to New Brutalism, which by then enjoyed 'international currency', Banham demonstrated the legacy of the 1920s 'machine aesthetic' and its potential contemporary adaptation for a revolutionary architectural form, especially thanks to a material such as reinforced concrete. This material, according to Banham, fell victim to the myth of a 'false aesthetic' which favoured smooth, perfect surfaces, modelled in pure geometric shapes, 'whereas structural and material truth suggests that it should be used rough-textured in complex vault-forms'. Banham re-centred Brutalism in the abandonment of cladding and the honesty of materials, according to a mechanistic approach of engineering memory:

[142] James Frazer Stirling, 'Plucky Jims' New Brutalism', *New Statesman*, vol. 50 (July 1958): 116.
[143] 'Your architectural correspondent is correct in assuming that we do not consider ourselves "new brutalist" in regard to the design of the flats at Ham Common. ("New Brutalist" is a journalistic tag applied to some designers of architectural credit, in a morale-boosting attempt to sanctify a movement as "Britain's contribution" and to cover up for the poor showing of our post-war architecture)', in ibid.
[144] James Frazer Stirling, 'Afterthoughts on the Flats at Ham Common', *Architecture and Building* (May 1959): (167–69), 167.
[145] 'Whatever the term might initially have meant it is clear from recent and repeated derisive journalistic asides, that it must now have created in the public eye an image of pretentiousness, artiness, and irresponsibility, and as such the continuation of its use can only be detrimental to modern architecture in this country', ibid.
[146] P.D.S [Alison Smithson], 'House in Soho', *Architectural Design*, vol. 23, no. 12 (December 1953): 342.
[147] Reyner Banham, 'Machine Aesthetes', *New Statesman*, vol. 52 (August 1958): 192–93.

> The Brutalists and Team Ten connections […] put surface covering behind
> them, except where functionally indicated. Furthermore they have been
> honest about materials as one might hope an engineer would be, and they
> have been sufficiently courageous in their mechanistic convictions to build
> in brick, and to let the brick appear.[148]

The label of New Brutalism, 'the much battered term', became an inescapable tool in
contemporary discourse to describe what was emerging as a new 'international unity',
despite the explicit criticisms that this definition was attracting.[149] 'To leave concrete
unfinished is the latest vogue', said *Architectural Review* about the various buildings
following the so-called 'brutalistic approach'.[150] 'It has been a period when an enter-
prising manufacturer could have put a do-it-yourself pundit-kit in which the aspiring
theorist had only to fill in the blank in the phrase The New (...) -ism and set up in business', recalled *Architectural Review*,[151] bringing together under a single definition works
as disparate as George Brera's villa in Cologny, André Wogensky's oeuvre, and Eiji
Miyagawa's No. 5 Building in Japan.[152]

Even Pevsner, in commenting on the residential complex in Roehampton, built by
the LCC between 1952 and 1958, did not fail to emphasise its traits akin to New Brutalism.[153] Pevsner, tracing Roehampton's references between the Swedish and Lecorbuserian models, made explicit the division of factions within the LCC and the debates
that had polarised the architects into Softs and Hards. Alton East and West are in fact
two buildings constituting the Roehampton Estate. Alton East was built in 1952 by
members of the Softs' wing, Robert Matthew, Cleve Barr, Michael Powell, Oliver Cox,
Mrs. Stjerrnstedt, J. N. Wall and H. P. Harrison. According to Pevsner it represents
the quintessence of the English tradition, from the informal picturesque root to the
model of the Crescent of Bath and finds in Swedish architecture the irrefutable 'foreign
source'. Alton West was instead the result of a radical change within the LCC, when,
starting from 1958, Leslie Martin entered as head of the Housing Division and was in
charge of Alton West, together with Colin Lucas, John Partridge, W. G. Howell, John
Killick, John Killick, S. F. Amis, J. R. Galley and R. Stout. For Pevsner, the details of the
side facades, the insertion into the site, and the rigidity of the slabs were the result of
the undeniable 'deliberate violence of the brutalists [...] demonstrating the fruitful influence of Le Corbusier's recent style and in particular the Marseille block'. In the caption
accompanying the image of Alton West's *béton brut*, Pevsner commented:

> Brutalism is a label which ought perhaps to be avoided. Yet the details of
> the end walls and the backs of the shopping terraces at Roehampton have
> that pride in béton brut and that delight in chunky shapes which justifies
> the term in reference to Le Corbusier at Chandigarh and to this most recent
> part of the Roehampton Estate.[154]

In Pevsner's eyes, New Brutalism responded to a desire to 'recover phantasy', visible not
only in the 'chunky concrete of the English Brutalists', but also in the sculptural forms of
the Ronchamp Chapel, in the chequered openings of the 'English non-Brutalists', and
finally in the American examples in which architecture is covered by infinite 'arbitrary

---

[148] Ibid., 193.
[149] Banham, 'Stocktaking', 98.
[150] J. Eastwick-Field, 'Out of the Form, *Architectural Review*, vol. 125, no. 749 (June 1959): 386–97.
[151] [n.a.], 'Architecture after 1960', *Architectural Review*, vol. 127, no. 755 (January 1960): 9.
[152] [n.a.] 'Epigonen' and 'No.5 Building', *Architectural Review*, vol. 127, no. 758 (April 1960): 224.
[153] Nikolaus Pevsner, 'Roehampton, LCC Housing and the Picturesque Tradition', *Architectural Review*, vol. 125,
no. 750 (July 1959): 21–35.
[154] Ibid., 34.

patterns'. Le Corbusier was targeted by Pevsner. Pevsner already defined his 'second phase' 'ambiguous', when reporting the state of abandon of Le Corbusier's buildings during the war.[155] The Ville Savoye with its ruined plasterwork could not but reveal, according to Pevsner, a flagrant affinity with his more recent works, and in particular with the treatment of the bricks of the Maisons Jaoul. The tendency to the 'non-finito', the roughness, the sympathy for the accident were symbols for Pevsner of the power of nature to endow Le Corbusier's early villas: 'Act of God, correcting act of Le Corbusier, or Act of God, improving Early Le Corbusier into Late Le Corbusier'.[156]

In the early 1960s, English historians and critics, from Summerson to Pevsner and Banham, questioned the value of history for contemporary design, both to understand its intrinsic development and to outline practical responses. We should not forget that Banham framed the events that led to the birth of New Brutalism within the influence of history, at the beginning of his 1955 article. 'What has been the influence of contemporary architectural historians on the history of contemporary architecture?' was his rhetorical question about the contribution of New Art History to the architectural debate.[157]

The question left unanswered in 1955 was then taken up in 'Stocktaking', where Banham read New Brutalism against the legacy of 'recent history', and its potential for resolving the contemporary dilemma between tradition and technology.[158] The founding concepts of New Brutalism, and in particular 'as found', are re-read by Banham as a continuation of the tradition of the 1920s and 1930s, where architecture was taking advantage of scientific discoveries. In the examples of the application of plastic theory in the School at Hunstanton and the exposed services in the Flats at Ham Common, Banham noted 'the rediscovery of science as a dynamic force' and 'an insistence that all the qualities of a material are equally relevant'.

In the 1961 lecture entitled 'Modern Architecture and the Historian – or the Return of Historicism', at the RIBA in London, Pevsner's speech challenged New Brutalism, which had already provoked a historicist interpretation (such as that of Segal and later Johnson) from the moment it first appeared in public.[159] In tracing a line of continuity between the works of the early Modern Movement and those of the postwar period, Pevsner accused the 'first Italian Brutalist' of pure historicism, to the point that the Marchiondi Institute was for him a plagiarism of the school in Harlem by the Dutch architect J. W. E. Buys of 1928, whose images are juxtaposed and accompanied by the ironic caption: 'Not another view of the same building'[160] (see figure 36). No novelty could be claimed by New Brutalism, according to Pevsner, for whom even the most well-known example of English New Brutalism at the time, Stirling and Gowan's Flats at Ham Common, was paralleled to a building by Michel de Klerk, due to the 'curious way in which odd bits, ledges and chunks of some kind stick out'.[161] The main defendant in Pevsner's discourse, however, remains Le Corbusier, guilty of spreading a new 'style', capable only of producing 'outrageous stimulation' through a consolidated repertoire of 'standard motifs'. Here he was referring to the 'heavy chunk of concrete with a segmental arch' of the Maisons Joaul, to the 'Ronchamp windows' and 'chequerboard pattern' of the Unité in Marseilles.

---

[155] Nikolaus Pevsner, 'Time and Le Corbusier', *Architectural Review*, vol. 125, no. 746 (March 1959): 159–65.

[156] Ibid., 160.

[157] Banham, 'The New Brutalism'.

[158] Banham, 'Stocktaking'.

[159] Nikolaus Pevsner, 'Modern Architecture and the Historian – Or the Return of Historicism', *RIBA Journal*, no. 68 (April 1961): 230–40.

[160] Ibid.

[161] Joedicke comments on the 'startling similarities' between Häring's view of materials and rejection of form *a priori* and the 'Brutalist connections', in an article that would bring Häring's work to attention: Jürgen Joedicke, 'Häring at Gargkau', *Architectural Review*, vol. 127, no. 759 (May 1960): 313–18. The article precedes Joedicke's monograph on Häring in the collection he edited: Jürgen Joedicke, *Hugo Häring: Schriften, Entwürfe, Bauten*, Dokumente der modernen Architektur, vol. 4 (Stuttgart: Karl Krämer, 1965).

36 Nikolaus Pevsner, 'Modern Architecture and the Historian', *RIBA Journal*, April 1961, no. 68, p. 235

So now neo-de-Stijl. Figure 16 is some of the celebrated furniture designed by Rietveld about 1917–18, and figures 17 and 18 are a recent dressing table by Howell, Killick and Partridge,14 and another exhibited recently by the Central School of Art and Crafts and commented on in the DIA Year Book. In architecture, neo-de-Stijl is, I think, just as striking. Figure 19 is a building at Harlem by the Dutch architect, J. W. E. Buys, illustrated in 1928,15 and figure 20 shows not another view of the same building, but the Marchiondi Institute in Milan by Vittoriano Viganò of 1957.16 Figure 21, again by Buys, is the Volharding, at The Hague, also of 1926, and figure 22 a café of 1958 by Marcello d'Olivo.17

Pevsner's dissatisfaction with contemporary architecture, which in his eyes coincided with the 'style' derived from Le Corbusier, is clearly expressed in a letter sent on 19 December 1961 to De Cronin, editor of *Architectural Review*, in which he confessed his intention to leave the magazine's editorial staff: 'As I am getting older, I find myself more and more out of sympathy with what is going on in architecture and what we as a "modern" paper, have to put in. I am an inveterate puritan and thirties-man'.[162] Pevsner then listed a series of works, all connected to the New Brutalism debate, with which he could not conceal a major disagreement. The works of Le Corbusier in Chandigarh and Ronchamp, but also the English examples of Chamberlin and Powell with the Barbican Estate, Basil Spence in Brighton, Robert Matthew's Imperial Institute and Leslie Martin's Caius College, were for Pevsner the symptoms of a phase that he hoped would be 'an interlude as brief as Art Nouveau or Expressionism, and that after that it will be right again'[163].

Pevsner's fears that the style originated by Le Corbusier would give rise to a series of copies are also expressed in the inaugural address of the Art and Architecture Building at Yale University, when he voiced a harsh criticism to Rudolph: 'It is all very masculine, a violent stimulus to students'. Pevsner warned the students, however, 'not to imitate what you now have around you... woe to him who imitates Paul Rudolph. The result will be a catastrophe'.[164]

Certainly, Pevsner's history is one based on styles and pioneers. His efforts to define an English genealogy to the Modern Movement could not but lead him to a direct comparison between the heroic experiences of the beginning of the century and the current outcomes of a modernity in crisis. Through the article 'Modern Architecture and the Historian – or the Return of Historicism', published a few months

[162] Nikolaus Pevsner, letter to De Cronin, 19 December 1961, Nikolaus Pevsner papers, 1903–1982, The Getty Research Institute, Special Collection, Series I General Correspondence, Box 1, Folder 840209.

[163] Ibid.

[164] Pevsner's comments are reported in [n.a.], 'Arts and Architecture Opens at Yale, *Architectural Forum*, vol. 119, no. 6 (December 1963): 7. Pevsner proudly recalled Rudolph Hall's inaugural address, to the point of mentioning his criticism in a 1973 letter to Ada Louise Huxtable, in response to her article 'The Building You Love to Hate'. Nikolaus Pevsner, letter to Ada Louise Huxtable, 21 May 1973, Nikolaus Pevsner Miscellaneous Papers, 1957–1979, The Getty Research Institute, Special Collection, Series I Correspondence 1962–1977, no. 2003.M.34, Box 5, Folder 2. Pevsner's entire speech is published in Nikolaus Pevsner, *Studies in Art, Architecture, and Design* (New York: Walker and Company, 1968), 260–65.

after Banham's famous doctoral thesis,[165] we are also able to measure the divergences between Pevsner and his disciple.[166] The relationship between Banham and Pevsner was recalled by his wife Mary Banham as one of deep mutual esteem, despite the conceptual disagreements:

> He [Banham] loved him dearly, but he disagreed with him profoundly. [...] Pevsner thought Banham's thesis would have been a continuation of his own previous studies, about Modern Architecture and design immediately before Banham's period. When the thesis came out it was extremely revisionist and not at all what Pevsner was saying.[167]

In his letter of resignation from the editorial staff of *Architectural Review*, Pevsner suggested that Banham took his place: 'This is my funeral [...] [Banham] can look after history; for inconsiderate or even impossible that he sometimes still is, he keeps his scholarship out of the fray'.[168] Pevsner was always ready to defend Banham, even when he received letters from eminent figures such as Gropius[169] or Peter Clarke, president of the Victorian Society, complaining about Banham's irreverent attitude.[170]

At the meeting at the RIBA, Banham was aware of Pevsner's accusation against him and underlined the cultural distance from his teacher, who interpreted the examples of Brutalism in a nostalgic neo-historicist way:

> It gives me curious pleasure to come up to the dock in the wake of two such eminent men. I am a 'Pevsnerian' by 15 years constant indoctrination and a 'Summersonian' by ten years admiration. I do not think, however, I am here either as a 'Pevsnerian' or a 'Summersonian': I am here because I have written about the period which produced the works imitated by the Neo Historians and possibly as a representative of my generation.[171]

In the early 1960s, Banham returned in depth to the principles of New Brutalism for the first time since 1955, through three contributions: 'History of the Immediate Future', 'The World of the Brutalists. Opinion & Intention in British Architecture' and finally 'Apropos the Smithsons'. Any concerns about clarifying its principles or adding new examples, as was the case in the 1950s, became secondary to his intention to save the definition from becoming a style.

Banham's real response to Pevsner's position took place in a lecture given at the RIBA on 7 February 1961.[172] The title of Banham's lecture summed up his criticism of Pevsner. 'History of the Immediate Future' was Banham's motto against a view of

---

[165] Reyner Banham, *Theory and Design in the First Machine Age* (London: Architectural Press, 1960).

[166] On the relationship between Banham and Pevsner, see also Nigel Whiteley, *Reyner Banham: Historian of the Immediate Future* (Cambridge, MA: MIT Press, 2002), 365 ff.

[167] Mary Banham, interviewed by Corinne Julius, *National Life Story Collection: Architects' Lives*, British Library Oral History, 2001, part 10/19.

[168] Pevsner, letter to De Cronin, 3.

[169] Peter Clarke, letter to Pevsner, 28 May 1963; Walter Gropius, letter to Pevsner, 15 January 1962, Nikolaus Pevsner papers, 1903–1982, The Getty Research Institute, Special Collection, Series I General Correspondence, Box 2, Folder 840209. In his letter, Gropius denounced Banham's harsh criticism of him in his review of Kenzo Tange's book *Katsura*, for which Gropius had written the introduction. Banham had explicitly accused Gropius of treating Japanese architecture in a 'complete absence of historical perspective'; see Reyner Banham, 'Views and Reviews: Book Reviews – Aesthetic or Technic?' *Architectural Review*, vol. 130, no. 778 (December 1961): 375.

[170] 'We have had trouble of this kind with Dr. Banham before and we are always trying to restrain him. He is of course an extremely intelligent man and a first-class journalist. But as soon as he is outside his scholarship strictly speaking, he tends to write too well and commit errors of tact for the sake of good writing', in Nikolaus Pevsner, letter to Gropius, 24 January 1962, Nikolaus Pevsner papers, 1903–1982, The Getty Research Institute, Special Collection, Series I General Correspondence, Box 2, Folder 840209.

[171] Banham, reply to Pevsner in 'Modern Architecture and the Historian – Or the Return of Historicism'.

[172] Rainer Banham, 'The History of the Immediate Future', *RIBA Journal*, vol. 68 (April 1961): 252–57.

history that stumbled over Pevsner's historicism.[173] Banham chose a pivotal but often criticised example to measure the validity of New Brutalism. Declared neo-historicist by Pevsner and ridiculed by the *Architects' Journal* as a retrograde and constrictive example,[174] the Marchiondi Institute became central in Banham's discourse.[175] Thanks to Zevi's intuition, Banham recognised the potential of the Marchiondi for becoming a decisive example: 'Zevi came nearest when he called it New Brutalist', Banham affirmed, endorsing the association between Viganò's work and New Brutalism. 'I know what Zevi meant, and I think he was right in making the Brutalist comparison'. Two buildings marked the new direction of Brutalism in the early 1960s: the Marchiondi Institute and the Flats at Ham Common, representing the aesthetic extremes of an intense debate whose protagonists, once again, were the critics and not the architects.

Banham took the opportunity of an article in the *New Statesman* to stress the alliance against the 'picturesque informalism' between New Brutalism and the Smithsons, presented as 'the architectural conscience of their generation'.[176] The intrinsic incoherence and 'discontinuity' of Smithsons' designs was due, according to Banham, to a principle that he had always placed at the head of New Brutalism: the conception of design 'without formalistic preconception'. The Smithsons' rejection of formal coherence constituted the ethical core of the New Brutalism proposal: 'The Smithsons are not offering a style, but a set of moral responsibilities to man and society'.[177] However, there is a radical difference of vision between the Smithsons and Banham regarding the ethical essence of New Brutalism. While for the Smithsons the ethical tension was resolved in the 'town building', for Banham the very concept of the building would be the spokesman for a radically future-oriented vision. 'Every building must be a prototype of the future city', was Banham's statement induced by an intention to dispel all neo-historicist doubts.

The main discussions in London circles, as evidenced by Pevsner's and Banham's interventions, focused on the operational value of history, the dreaded danger of historicism and revival, and finally the closure of architecture into a self-referential discourse. Banham's positions in this sense promoted a vital and necessary disciplinary openness. In defence of New Brutalism, Banham reiterated the inclusive nature of architectural design, which needed to be constantly fed by other disciplines in order to escape being reduced to a style: 'The standards have to come from outside architecture [...] and are apt to be different from one building to the next'.[178] The 'standards' considered by Banham derived from the mixture of artistic practices and architectural principles underlying the concept of *une architecture autre*, such as the 'anti-formal plans' of Pollock, the 'visible and tangible material qualities' as in the practice of Dubuffet and Paolozzi, and a 'mechanically advanced and expendable' consciousness found in pop experiences. 'The next move for architecture', he added, 'is to follow human sciences inside the human being'. What Banham pursued and outlined was an opening up of the architectural discourse to the biological and psychological sciences,

[173] The accusation of revival against New Brutalism would persist throughout the 1960s. Even Brett, Le Corbusier's British detractor, would point out that 'Too much bloody architecture: Peter Smithson's despairing cry echoes back via brutalism and functionalism to Adolf Loos, Lethaby and William Morris', in Lionel Brett, 'Architecture. Paris and London', *The London Magazine* (June 1963): 66–68.

[174] [n.a.], 'Astragal. Brutalism for the Backward', *Architects' Journal*, vol. 129, no. 3338 (February 1959): 287–88. In a note ironically entitled 'Brutalism for the Backward' in the 'Astragal' column, *Architects' Journal* announced the advent of New Brutalism in Italy: 'A little late in the day it seems to me the Italians have got on to Brutalism'. The interior of the Marchiondi is described as 'too pretty and crowded to satisfy English Brutalists, but the exterior has massive and rough-shuttered quality that should satisfy anybody who likes their architecture tough and uncompromising, and looks as though it's made of timber rather than concrete'.

[175] Banham, 'The History of the Immediate Future'.

[176] Banham, 'Apropos the Smithsons'.

[177] Ibid.

[178] Banham, 'The History of the Immediate Future', 253.

which would be able to respond to an architecture 'for the future', responding to the accusation of historicisms from London's academic elite.[179]

Unlike Stirling, who saw New Brutalism as a nostalgic and romantic affirmation of the status quo, for Banham New Brutalism continued to presuppose a critical and subversive reaction to the establishment. At the beginning of the 1950s, the proposal of New Brutalism was clearly set up by Banham as a provocative alternative to the Picturesque and 'sentimentalism' professed by his teacher Pevsner. It cannot be ignored that Banham's most intransigent statements during the 1960s were accusations against the editorial staff of the *Architectural Review*, and more generally against the English academic elite. 'The Brutalists, while they come almost entirely from provincial schools of architecture, are neither leftish nor insular', he stated in 1961, specifying that 'the first target of the Brutalists 'could not have been more specifically leftish and insular' – the so-called William Morris Revival.[180]

In the article 'The World of the Brutalists. Opinion & Intention in British Architecture, 1951–60', published in the American *Texas Quarterly*, Banham took stock of the trajectory of New Brutalism with greater freedom, as demonstrated by his scathing attacks on the London academic and politicised context. The political tension of the English debates was the reason for the 'reaction' that led to the origins of New Brutalism. In fact, what had allowed the radicalisation of New Brutalism, 'overriding [a] gentlemen's agreement',[181] was precisely the attack against the political control of artistic expressions instituted by the London cultural elites. New Brutalism would have never happened without the harsh critique of the 1940s 'State Department style', which Banham defined as a 'local variant of Zhdanov's Social Realism', referring to the canons drawn up by Andrej Aleksandrovič Zdanov for the control of Soviet cultural production. Only the 'moral load' of the early Modern Movement, expressed through the truth of structure and materials, could redeem an architecture otherwise dissipated in nostalgic revivals: 'If a piece of steel appeared to hold something up, then it did; if a wall was made of brick then it showed on both sides, no plaster, no paint; if water came from a tap it got there through a visible pipe'.[182]

Among the theories summarised by Banham, alongside the truth of structure and materials – namely the 'as found' – composition was confirmed as a crucial device in contrasting the 'leftish' vision crystallised in the recovery of the Picturesque and expressed through an 'informality of plan' defended by a 'soft-touch architecture'.

In fact, the 'a-formalism' characteristic of the second phase of New Brutalism derived for Banham from a cultural universe that attacked traditional canons of beauty and the moderate vision of London's cultural socialist elite, mockingly referred to as the 'Anglo-pink intelligentsia'. He seemed, indeed, to mock Pevsner's accusations when he stated: 'The New Brutalism in architecture marks the resolution of a phoney dilemma between routine modernism and period of revival; and it does so by means of the same expedient of Brutalism – going back to the principle of the pioneers'.[183] The evocation in this context of the pioneers, the founders of Modern Movement, will be instrumental in Pevsner's criticism of New Brutalism during the 1960s.

[179] Laurent Stalder, '"New Brutalism", "Topology" and "Image": Some Remarks on the Architectural Debates in England Around 1950', *The Journal of Architecture*, vol. 13, no. 3 (2008): 263–81.

[180] Reyner Banham, 'The World of the Brutalists. Opinion & Intention in British Architecture, 1951–60', *Texas Quarterly*, vol. 4, no. 3 (October 1961): 129–38.

[181] [Reyner Banham], 'School at Hunstanton', *Architectural Review*, vol. 116, no. 693 (September 1954): 150–162.

[182] Banham, 'The World of the Brutalists. Opinion & Intention in British Architecture, 1951–60'.

[183] Reyner Banham, 'Black and White Magazine Show', *New Statesman*, 2 June 1961: 889.

The Essential Ethic of Brutalism Is in Town Building

For Brutalism to survive as an 'attitude' and not a 'style', it had to entail a broader vision which, at the dawn of the 1960s, transcended fidelity to a single material and implied an ethical stance. The very architectural project, called upon to respond to increasingly complex contexts and programmes, took on a measure that invested the scale of the city, urged on by research that pushed architecture to go beyond the single object and expand into the urban fabric.

The Smithsons' interventions had so far been only marginally considered by international critics, if not for their initial remarks on materials and their use. The uncompromising ethical vision, the inflexible intention not to crystallise New Brutalism in a series of formal principles, and finally the development of the design project through principles of relationship and not of form, had passed almost unnoticed by critics who were instead focussed on discerning the formal and aesthetic similarities of a nascent, newly international style.

In 1959, for the interview in the fourth volume of *Zodiac*, the Smithsons signed one of the most decisive interventions for the trajectory of New Brutalism, which concerned its potential extension to the urban scale.[184] Discussions held during the CIAMs, from 1953 onwards, and their involvement with Team X, had only motivated the Smithsons to extend the scope of architecture beyond the single building.[185] According to the Smithsons, a contemporary urban project needed to implement its 'responsibility to the whole of town building'. Opposed to the urban plan promoted by CIAM, defined by Peter Smithson as 'sleek, anonymous, neutral and hygienic', each building was to be conceived as part of an urban whole, through a reflection that Alison Smithson extended to every scale of the project.

> [We] started working on the field of town building because it was obvious that it was no longer possible to break the situation with a few buildings of the calibre of Garches, but one had to be thinking on a much bigger scale somehow that if you only go *one* house to do it somehow had to imply the whole system of town building by expressing it in itself.[186]

Attacking the 'functionalism' defended by the Athens Charter, by virtue of a new ethical dimension implicit in the term 'responsibility', the Smithsons set urban design on the reciprocal relationship between buildings and interstitial spaces: 'The way the buildings themselves fit together and interact with each other', specified Peter Smithson. The extension of New Brutalism to the dimension of the city was understood as the ethical and unique essence that the Smithsons intended to perpetuate through that definition. Peter Smithson clearly summarised the foundation of New Brutalism with a sentence that was destined to change its boundaries: 'I think that the essential ethic of brutalism is in town building'.[187] The particular expression 'town building' cannot be understood simply as a synonym for urbanism, since it suggests an ideal extension of the building to the scale of the city. The very concept of 'topology', as evoked by Banham, carried in it an urbanistic vision and the potential of revolutionising the academic plan through

---

[184] Smithsons, 'Conversation on Brutalism'.

[185] Alison and Peter Smithson, *Ordinariness and Light* (Cambridge, MA: MIT Press, 1970); Alison and Peter Smithson, *The Charged Void: Urbanism* (New York: Monacelli Press, 2002); Alison Smithson, *The Emergence of Team 10 out of C.I.A.M.: Documents* (London: Architectural Association, 1982). For recent observations, see Laurent Stalder, 'Cluster Buildings', in Uta Hassler (ed.), *Bauten der Boomjahre* (Zurich: Infolio, 2010), 44–55; Hadas Steiner, 'Life at the Threshold', *October*, vol. 136 (2011): 133–55; Laurent Stalder, 'Circuits, conduits, et cetera. Quelques notes sur le caractère normatif des infrastructures dans l'architecture de l'après-guerre', *Matières*, vol. 12 (2015): 23–31.

[186] [Alison] Smithson, 'Conversation on Brutalism'.

[187] Ibid., 74.

the analysis of the complex relationships inside and outside the building. As critics had already shown, the examples that enrich the evolution or clarify the origins of Brutalism, such as the Marchiondi Institute, the annexes to the Old Vic Theatre, the orphanage in Amsterdam, and Aalto's dormitory at MIT, increasingly expressed a distributional mechanics developed from the interior of the building that extended outwards, taking on a significant urban dimension. The Golden Lane competition entry, based on the image of a deformed, extended and articulated Unité, was in this sense explanatory of the transition from the concept of the building as a 'machine' to urban mechanics. Zevi had already noted an urbanistic principle that could make New Brutalism evolve towards an urban dimension, and this would be one of the traits that the architects would feel most affinity with during the 1960s.

It cannot be ignored that the discussions that led to the definition of New Brutalism were primarily concerned with purely urban issues, situated in the clash of models for reconstruction where the New Town plan and the Unité were in opposition. In 1959, the Smithsons attempted to definitively close that original debate, proposing a model based on concepts such as 'mobility, connection, network' in which the hypotheses of the 'architecture of reality' and 'New Brutalism' were finally and officially brought together.[188] The Smithsons declared their pursuit of a 'functional' vision of urban space that consisted in recognising 'that the space in towns has to indicate that it is a net communication'. The functionalism evoked by the Smithsons diverged from the same notion applied to the context of CIAM: 'Our functionalism means accepting the realities of the situation, with all their contradictions and confusions, and trying to do something with them' with the aim of defining a new 'community structure', as they had pointed out in 1957.[189]

The Smithsons' urban vision centred on the concept of 'connectedness', understood not only as physical connections that include roads 'at the scale of the motor car movement', but also virtual connections, through household appliances and devices, which must be reflected in the built architecture and urban form: 'Ideas are communicated by press, television, radio and so on, advertising, which practically knots the whole world into a net of relationships where people understand each other'.[190] All the reasoning carried out by the Smithsons and the other members of Team X was functional to the inclusion of social and technological aspects in the urban project, capable of representing 'the aspirations, the artifacts, the roots, the modes of transportation and communication of present day society', for which they would try to develop an aesthetic 'appropriate to mechanized building' and an alternative terminology.[191]

This variant of New Brutalism extended to 'town building', used as synonyms, thus served for imagining urban scenarios radically different from the rationalist model and the English tradition, in which the city was conceived from principles of movement, portraying the symbol of a technological civilisation. In this sense, the project for Berlin Hauptstadt in 1958, conceived together with Peter Sigmond, is significant because geometric control was replaced by social rather than spatial organisation. 'Association, identity, growth and change' became the parameters for controlling and designing urban development.[192] A new 'pattern' of horizontal and vertical connec-

---

[188] In 1958 the Smithsons had already put forward the hypothesis that urban expansion should be pursued from the perspective of mobility, in Alison and Peter Smithson, 'Mobility Road Systems', *Architectural Design*, vol. 28, no. 10 (October 1958): 385–88.

[189] Alison and Peter Smithson, 'Cluster City: A New Shape for the Community', *Architectural Review*, vol. 122 (November 1957): 333–36. See also Smithsons, 'Aesthetic of Change'.

[190] Smithsons, 'Conversation on Brutalism'.

[191] [n.a.] 'Death of CIAM', *Architectural Design*, vol. 29 (October 1959): A/5. On alternative terminology, see, for example, Smithson, 'Cluster City: A New Shape for the Community', 333–36.

[192] Peter Smithson, 'The Idea of Architecture in the '50s', *Architects' Journal*, vol. 21 (January 1960): 121–26; Alison and Peter Smithson, 'Fix', *Architectural Review*, vol. 128, no. 766 (December 1960): 437–39.

tions was superimposed on the existing reality of the city, demonstrating the potential for overcoming the functionalist city.[193] The Smithsons' research, from their architectural to urban vision, shows affinities with the work of Kahn who, along with Le Corbusier, Mies and Aalto, was undoubtedly one of the masters who radically influenced the various trajectories of Brutalism. The Smithsons looked with interest at his 1953 plan for Philadelphia, which was also informed by a desire to 'find expression from the order of movement'.[194] The Smithsons would even repropose Kahn's terminology for their Berlin plan.[195]

The Smithsons' urban theories, published during the 1960s in several international magazines such as *Uppercase*, *Forum*, *Casabella* and then combined into a book, were to find concrete expression in the Economist Building and Robin Hood Gardens.[196] This last project, begun in 1966, needs to be read as the culmination of the search for an 'architecture of reality', resulting from a precise topography and a relation between the building and its context, in which the rationalist slab flexes and refuses isolation.[197]

Anti-Miesian Brutalism by Pehnt and Joedicke

The unresolved clash between the two masters, Le Corbusier and Mies, placed at the heart of New Brutalism since its initial hypotheses, found a possible clarification through the investigations pursued by German critics. As already pointed out, each nation looked to the phenomenon of Brutalism as a possible expression of its own cultural challenges. Dissatisfaction with the abstraction and 'monotony' of the curtain wall, understood primarily as an element of American import, reached a critical peak in Germany towards the end of the 1950s, against the backdrop of the Bauhaus debates in West Germany and the discourse on prefabrication and standardisation in the East.

The search for a monumentality expressed through concrete shapes, as in the works of Hugh Stubbins and Ulrich Müther, reactivated a conceptual line derived from the German tradition.[198] The whole debate on Brutalism, rooted in the Modern Movement, was demonstrating, through the growing number of examples, a tendency towards the expressiveness of a mechanics that concerns the building as well as the city. The consequence of all this was the conception of architecture as an eloquent device, conceived in such a way that each 'organ' was left visible to express its function. The expressiveness often ascribed to Brutalism would be seized upon by German critics to revive the critical category of expressionism, perceived as a true and distinctive German trait. The legacy of 1920s German architecture – evoked by Segal as an ancestor of New Brutalism[199] and confirmed by the Smithsons, who also included Häring among their references[200] – was crucial in constructing a genealogy of Brutalism, alternative

[193] Banham reveals in the Smithsons' proposal the demonstration of the outdated urban discourses of CIAMs. Banham refers specifically to Gropius's speech at CIAM 6 in Bridgwater, where he stated that, in essence, the city of Berlin could not be re-planned precisely because of the rigidity of the existing urban fabric; in Banham, *The New Brutalism: Ethic or Aesthetic?*, 74.

[194] Louis I. Kahn, 'Toward a Plan for Midtown Philadelphia', *Perspecta*, vol. 2 (1953): 10–27.

[195] On this subject, see also Irénée Scalbert, 'Architecture Is Not Made with the Brain', in Max Risselada (ed.), *Alison and Peter Smithson: A Critical Anthology* (Barcelona: Ediciones Poligrafa, 2011): (188–205), 192.

[196] For Frampton 'it becomes evident that the Economist development is a built part, or even the full size "mock up" of a unit within an overall proposition first made by them for the centre of Berlin', in Kenneth Frampton, 'The Economist and the Haupstadt', *Architectural Design*, vol. 137 (February 1965): 61–62.

[197] Peter Eisenmann, 'From Golden Lane to Robin Hood Gardens. Or if you follow the Yellow Brick Road, it may not lead to Golders Green', *Oppositions*, vol. 1 (September 1973): 27–56.

[198] Adrian Von Buttlar, 'Brutalism in Germany. The Pathos of Progress as Aesthetic Revolt', in *SOS Brutalism: A Global Survey*, 63–75.

[199] Segal, 'The New Brutalism'.

[200] Theo Crosby, 'The New Brutalism', *Architectural Design*, vol. 25, no. 1 (January 1955): 1.

to that of Le Corbuser's *béton brut* or to the British 'angry young men', but linked to the principles of construction and assembly of parts. It is not surprising, therefore, that the debate on Brutalism, once it became an international phenomenon, torn as it was between antagonistic and contradictory references, attracted the attention of German critics and historians. Two critics were decisive in this context, Wolfgang Pehnt and Jürgen Joedicke. They would go so far as to involve Banham for an encyclopaedia entry and for the preparation of the most famous books on Brutalism.

One of the first significant contributions demonstrating that German critics were sensitive to the issues of Brutalism was written by the art historian Udo Kultermann in 1958.[201] Significantly, the article is entitled 'Une architecture autre', following the definition invented by Banham in 1955. In it Kultermann acknowledged the intellectual debt to Banham and summarised his positions and principles. However, he extended the definition of *architecture autre* beyond that of Banham. For Kultermann, 'architecture autre' defined a visionary trajectory of plastic and sculptural structures inaugurated by Gaudi, based on the abolishment of the right angle and a liberation of form, such as in the works of Enrico Castiglioni, Michel Andrault, Eero Saarinen, Le Corbusier, Félix Candela, John Johansen and others. Kultermann associated 'architecture autre' with a mixture that was no longer, as it was for Banham, between art and architecture but, instead, between engineering and architecture.

Banham did not miss the extrapolation of the concept of 'une architecture autre' from the context of New Brutalism and criticised Kallmann for having limited the meaning of that concept to 'purely formal alternatives to "rectangular" architecture', to the point that he dedicated, in his 1966 book, a chapter to explain his 'architecture autre'.[202] What Banham meant by that concept radically transcended any formal issue, and found its origin in the artistic experiences of 'un art autre', in action painting and *musique concrète*.[203]

In his 1958 first volume dedicated to contemporary architecture Kultermann acknowledged the overuse of labels to describe contemporary architecture.[204] Ascribing the use of labels to a retroactive critical operation, Kultermann highlighted the complex relationship between critics and architects.[205] In retracing the phases of Brutalism, following Banham's trajectory, Kultermann exploited the reaction against those classical compositional principles derived from Palladio to set Brutalism in 'antithesis' to the perfectionism of the Miesian tradition. This opposition was not new, if we consider that American culture, with Blake and Johnson, had already inaugurated the distinction between the Miesian model and the principles of Brutalism. But, while for Johnson the antagonism concerned questions of composition, for Kultermann Brutalism became an expression of the search for an architecture based on 'necessary' principles of construction, space and materials. Kultermann's contribution opened the German debate on the antagonism between Brutalism and the Miesian model.

The art historian Wolfgang Pehnt, in 'Was ist Brutalismus. Zur Architekturgeschichte des letzten Jahrfünft', put forward hypotheses for a definition of the Brutalist canon.[206] The validity of the article lies not only in the historical retrospective on Brutalism, but also in the questioning of its critical and practical relevance for contem-

[201] Udo Kultermann, 'Une Architecture Autre. Ein neugeknüpfter Faden der architektonischen Entwiklung', *Baukunst und Werkform*, vol. 11, no. 8 (August 1958): 425–41.

[202] Banham, 'A Note on "une architecture autre"', *The New Brutalism: Ethic or Aesthetic?*, 68–69.

[203] Ibid., 68.

[204] Udo Kultermann, *Baukunst der Gegenwart: Dokumente des neuen Bauens in der Welt* (Tübingen: Wasmuth, 1958).

[205] 'Contemporary architecture has been given many names that have been used in retrospect to describe certain tendencies in its development. These terms can either be linked to past style designations or have a forward-looking function, namely when they seek to characterise a certain new intention', ibid., 4.

[206] Wolfgang Pehnt, 'Was ist Brutalismus? Zur Architekturgeschichte des letzten Jahrfünfts', *Das Kunstwerk*, vol. 14, no. 3 (March 1960): 14–23.

porary architecture. In a recent publication, Pehnt confessed his dissatisfaction at the absence of German examples in the debate of the 1960s and the consequent need to spread the definition of New Brutalism in Germany: 'One often perceives something first when there are terms to describe it'.[207]

After a brief introduction on the English origin and its artistic roots, Pehnt categorised examples of buildings now internationally associated with Brutalism, under specific geographical areas: in England, in addition to the works of the Smithsons, he included the annexes to the Old Vic Theatre in London; in Italy, the Marchiondi Institute by Viganò, the Torre Velasca, the house in Sperlonga by Mario De Renzi, the office tower in San Donato Milanese by Marcello Nizzoli and Mario Oliveri, the village for children in Trieste by Marcello D'Olivo and the villa near Florence by Ricci; and finally, Saarinen's college at Yale represented for Pehnt the crucial example for an American Brutalism that admits historicist tendencies. The works examined by Pehnt irrefutably demonstrate the influence of the 1959 volume of *Zodiac*, where all the buildings mentioned were presented in that issue (see figure 37).

Among the disparate examples, Pehnt identified a possible common denominator in the search for an accentuation and clarity of construction. Aware of the role of the Miesian model for the trajectory of Brutalism, Pehnt was interested in releasing that connection from the debate, so that Brutalism could establish itself as the overcoming of the post-International Style schematism identified in Mies' work. Pehnt thus framed Brutalism in the legacy of precise plastic elements, such as the projecting staircase of Aalto's MIT dormitory, the tapered and curved pillars of Nervi's Berta Stadium and, of course, in the Unité's safety staircase in Marseille, which demonstrated a neo-expressionistic functionalism. Pehnt dedicated a full-page photograph to each of these three examples, making explicit the contemporary meaning of Brutalism as the echo of a plastic, 'expressionist' and 'voluminous' architecture.

It is no coincidence that Pehnt emphasised Brutalism's aversion to a 'light' architecture, identified in the works of Mies, Johnson and SOM. Pehnt gave strength to an interpretation that had begun to emerge in the contrast between the Lecorbuserian and Miesian models. Works at the opposite of Brutalism, according to Pehnt, are identifiable in the examples ranging from Lever House to the Seagram Building and Crown Hall, including Mies' IIT. Pehnt's crucial contribution also concerned the definition itself, the ambiguous coexistence in the debates of New Brutalism and Brutalism and the problematic assonance with the term 'brutal'.[208]

Pehnt's considerations in 1960, and the importance of Brutalism in the international debate on the Modern Movement, prompted him to contact Banham for a contribution in the first encyclopaedia of modern architecture. Edited by Pehnt on behalf of the publisher Gerd Hatje for the Stuttgart-based Deutsche Bücherbund, the *Knaurs Lexicon der modernen Architektur* was conceived as a compendium for understanding significant moments in the history of architecture since 1851 and consisted of a series of entries written by leading experts on each subject.[209] The inclusion of the entry 'Brutalismus' in the *Lexikon* demonstrates, as written in Pehnt's preface, that Brutalism was considered 'one of the principal manifestations of Modern Architecture'. The appearance of the 'rugged forms' characteristic of a new course in contemporary architecture was once again built upon the antagonism towards the Miesian model found in the works of SOM and Stone, criticised for the 'excessively smooth form of this boneless type of decorative architecture'. Pehnt here recalled the opposition between Brutalism and Ornamented Modern posed by *Zodiac* but framed it as a clash with the 'classical balance found in the creations of Mies van der Rohe'. The introduction also presented the formal traits characteristic of the international phenomenon of Brutalism, still contrasted with the 'elegance of the decorator-architects':

---

[207] Wolfgang Pehnt, 'Living Traces. Churches in the Brutalist Era', *SOS Brutalism: A Global Survey*, (41–46), 46.
[208] Réjean Legault, 'The Trajectories of Brutalism. England, Germany and Beyond', *SOS Brutalism: A Global Survey*, 21–25.
[209] Wolfgang Pehnt (ed.), *Knaurs Lexikon der modernen Architektur* (Munich, Zurich: Hatje, 1963).

37 Wolfgang Pehnt,
'Was ist Brutalismus?
Zur Architekturgeschichte
des letzten Jahrfünft',
Das Kunstwerk, March
1960, no. 3, pp. 14–23

WOLFGANG PEHNT

WAS IST BRUTALISMUS?

Zur Architekturgeschichte des letzten Jahrfünfts

Rough, granular and contrasty textures such as brick and exposed concrete with the shuttering marks showing up as coarsely as possible [...] Acute or obtuse angles reign supreme, with a tendency to hard, dissonant articulation of the individual parts of a building. The visual scale is constantly jumping and small units are abruptly confronted with large ones. Detail, like overall form, is block-shaped and heavy in appearance.[210]

The flashpoint on 'Brutalismus' offered Banham the opportunity to return to its origins, principles, and contemporary manifestations, and it constitutes a decisive text as it anticipates considerations that Banham would make explicit in his famous 1966 book (see figure 38). His reconstruction ignored the role played by the House in Soho and its materials and instead started from the 'purely Miesian' and 'puritanical' School at Hunstanton, described as 'the first truly Brutalist Building'. Brutalism then incorporated a constellation of other existing tendencies, ranging from the phenomenon of *béton brut* to Pollock's a-formalism. In their juncture, Banham pointed out that 'the Brutalism of the uncompromising exhibition of materials became allied to a Brutalism of form'. One might consider this statement as the ultimate landing place of Brutalism as a style, which Banham also fully acknowledged. Resuming the conclusions expressed in 1961 in *Texas Quarterly*, Banham emphasised a substantial difference between the original New Brutalism and its international manifestation, anticipating the conclusions of his 1966 book.[211]

Since its inception, the definition of New Brutalism had been split between opposites, from the ambivalent role of the masters to the opposition between ethics and style. Banham pointed to the Smithsons' interest in both Le Corbusier and Mies for their 'uncompromising ruthlessness' which translated into 'their intellectual clarity, their honest presentation of structure and materials'. The Smithsons' further extension of that definition to the urban dimension was not considered by Banham, who limited its relevance to an argument about the internal mechanisms of the building: 'The fundamental aim of Brutalism at all times has been to find a structural, spatial, organisational and material concept that is "necessary" [...] and then express it with complete honesty in a form that will be a unique and memorable image'.[212] The buildings selected to support the phenomenon of Brutalism are significant. In addition to the ubiquitous examples of the Unité, the School at Hunstanton and the Marchiondi Institute, Banham chose two works by van der Brock and Bakema, the Town Hall complex in Marl and the Church of the Resurrection in Schiedam, the Economist Building by the Smithsons, and Park Hill Housing Estate in Sheffield by Lynn and Smith. The inclusion of buildings still being constructed or in the design phase demonstrated a contemporary value of Brutalism that Banham did not fail to emphasise. In particular, Park Hill represented for Banham the application of vital urban planning theories linked to the conception of design, which resulted in an open and continuous urban structure.

The case of the School at Hunstanton raised problematic questions for Banham as well. Although in the entry 'Brutalismus' it was explicitly anchored to that definition, of which it served as the real progenitor, the building's Miesian imprint induced Banham to include the School at Hunstanton also under the entry 'Neoklassizismus'.[213] Wittkower's rediscovery of the roots of the classical tradition was in fact recognised as the primary source of the project for Hunstanton, once again placed in parallel with the plan of the Yale Art Gallery, as theorised in 1955.

---

[210] Pehnt, 'Introduction', in ibid., 24.
[211] Banham, 'The World of the Brutalists. Opinion & Intention in British Architecture, 1951–60'.
[212] Banham, 'Brutalismus', in *Knaurs Lexikon der modernen Architektur*, 63.
[213] Banham, 'Neoklassizismus', in *Knaurs Lexikon der modernen Architektur*, 202–205.

38 Reyner Banham, 'Brutalismus', Wolfgang Pehnt (ed.), *Knaurs Lexikon der Modernen Architektur*, 1963, pp. 54–57

J. H. van den Broek und Jacob B. Bakema. Rathauskomplex. Marl, im Bau. Modell.

Unten: J. H. van den Broek und Jacob B. Bakema. Auferstehungskirche. Schiedam, 1957.

Broek, J. H. van den, *1898 in Rotterdam. Der Name des Architektenteams J. H. van den Broek und Jacob B. → Bakema ist eng mit dem neuen Bauen im Holland der Nachkriegszeit und vor allem mit dem Wiederaufbau Rotterdams verbunden. Van den Broek ist Professor an der Technischen Hochschule in Delft, wo er selber 1924 sein Examen abgelegt hat. 1927 ließ er sich als selbständiger Architekt in Rotterdam nieder; 1937 assoziierte er sich mit J. A. → Brinkman, 1948 mit J. B. Bakema.
Architektur und soziale Haltung sind im Werk von den Broeks und Bakemas untrennbar miteinander verbunden. Das Einkaufszentrum Lijnbaan in Rotterdam (1953), eine differenziert gegliederte Fußgängerstraße mit niedrigen Ladenbauten, bedeutete einen Beitrag zu

einer neuen Urbanität; der Rathauskomplex in Marl (im Bau), bei dem der alte Gedanke der Stadtkrone modern interpretiert ist, gibt einer aufstrebenden Industriestadt das zusammenfassende Zentrum. Wohnbaukomplexe und Schulen nehmen im Werk der beiden Architekten einen breiten Raum ein (Schulbauten in Brielle, 1948–57; Montessori-Lyzeum in Rotterdam, 1958).
Van den Broek und Bakema haben auch für andere Bauaufgaben Lösungen gefunden, in denen Bakemas Wort von der Architektur als dreidimensionalem Ausdruck menschlicher Verhaltensweisen verwirklicht wird. Es entstanden Ausstellungsbauten (Niederländischer Pavillon auf den Weltausstellungen Paris 1937 und Brüssel 1958), Bürobauten (Van Ommeren in Antwerpen, 1939; N. B. ten Cate in Almelo, 1954), Kaufhäuser (Ter Meulen Wassen van Vorst in Rotterdam, 1951; Galeries Modernes in Rotterdam, 1956), Industrieanlagen, Laboratorien und Forschungsinstitute für die Technische Hochschule in Delft. Die beiden Kirchen in Schiedam (1957) und in Nagele im Nordostpolder (1959) sind strenge Kuben, die aus dem Wechsel geschlossener, verglaster und durchbrochener Flächen leben.
Literatur: J. H. van den Broek, *Creative krachten in de architectonische conceptie*, Delft; 1948. Jürgen Joedicke, *Architektur und Städtebau, Das Werk der Architekten van den Broek und Bakema*, Stuttgart; in Vorbereitung.

J. J. Vriend

Brutalismus. Der Brutalismus gab einer Stimmung Ausdruck, die in den fünfziger Jahren unter den jüngeren Architekten der westlichen Welt weitverbreitet war. Sein Ursprung kann mit einiger Genauigkeit festgelegt werden. Giedions etymologische Deutung («Brute – Alison») trifft zwar nicht zu, doch stammt das Wort «Brutalismus» tatsächlich aus der Familie Smithson: Alison → Smithson oder Guy Oddie, ein Freund der Familie, der Peter Smithson «Brutus» nannte, sprachen im Frühsommer 1954 als erste vom «Neuen Brutalismus».
Was sollte nun diese Bezeichnung bedeuten? Voraussetzung war ein Gefühl der Stagnation, das teils auf die allgemeinen Schwierigkeiten auf dem Baumarkt im Nachkriegsengland zurückging, teils auf die Behendigkeit der kompromißfreudigen Älteren, die wohletabliert waren und ihre Bauaufträge hatten. Die Bauweise dieser älteren Architekten wurde von der politischen Linken als «Neuer Humanismus», von der Rechten als «Neuer Empirismus» charakterisiert. Das Schlagwort «Neuer Brutalismus» sollte diese beiden Bezeichnungen parodieren, machte aber gleichzeitig auf einige Eigenschaften des Stiles aufmerksam, den die Smith-

sons und ihre Generation schätzten und mitbegründeten.
Als Standard setzten sie sich die kompromißlose Architektur von → Mies van der Rohe und → Le Corbusier, ihre intellektuelle Klarheit, ihre ehrliche Darstellung von Konstruktion und Material. Gleichzeitig spürten sie in der Arbeit dieser Meister eine Tradition jenseits von Stilen und Moden. Unter den Werken der Vergangenheit galt ihre Bewunderung besonders der Strenge und dem Formalismus von Palladio, der heroischen Größe der englischen Barockarchitekten Vanbrugh und Hawksmore und den klargeschnittenen, massiven Formen der Ingenieurbauten aus dem frühen 19. Jahrhundert.
Die Architektur der Brutalisten war jedoch zu Beginn ganz im Stile Mies van der Rohes. Sicherlich trug ein Anflug von englischem Puritanismus zu der Entscheidung für ein schlichtes, elegantes Konstruktionssystem bei, denn gleichzeitig wurden jeder Vorwand und jede Verhüllung strikt abgelehnt. Nicht nur Konstruktion und Material, sondern auch die technischen Installationen wurden sichtbar gemacht. Bei dem ersten wirklich brutalistischen Bau, der Hunstanton School in England (1954),

Le Corbusier. Unité d'Habitation. Marseille, 1947–52. Detail der Stützen im Erdgeschoß.

Rechts oben: Jack Lynn und Ivor Smith. Wohnsiedlung Park Hill. Sheffield, 1955–61.

werden Stahl und Ziegel mit einer Ehrlichkeit verwendet, die sogar Mies van der Rohe übertrifft. Darüber hinaus sind auch Rohre, elektrische Leitungen und andere technische Einrichtungen unverkleidet. Die Strenge dieses Bauwerks erregte weltweites Aufsehen, und man suchte nach internationalen Vergleichsmöglichkeiten. Ein verwandtes Beispiel, das Art Center an der Yale University (1952–54) von Louis → Kahn, wirkte in dieser Beziehung überzeugender als das Werk Mies van der Rohes, denn auch Kahn setzte sich mit dem rohen Baumaterial auseinander und legte die Installationen frei.
In dieser Zeit verschmolz der anfängliche puritanische Extremismus der englischen Brutalisten mit einer internationalen Bewegung, die nur entfernt vergleichbare Ziele hatte. Ursprünge dieser Bewegung waren so unterschiedliche Entwicklungen wie die informelle Malerei von Jackson Pollock, der informelle Grundriß von Ronchamp, der *art brut* von Dubuffet und der *béton brut* der Unité d'Habitation in Marseille. Der Brutalismus der kompromißlosen Schaustellung von Materialien verband sich mit einem Brutalismus der Form; die deutliche Symmetrie der Hunstanton School und die verborgene Symmetrie des Yale Art Center machten einer rücksichtslosen Ehrlichkeit im Ausdruck der Funktionszonen und ihrer Beziehungen zueinander Platz. Selbst die leicht übertragbare, rechtwinklige Geometrie – von

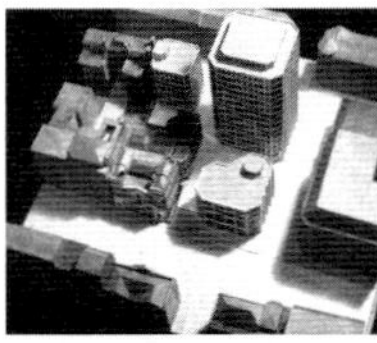

der abstrakten Malerei abgeleitet –, die die Funktionalisten zu Beginn akzeptiert hatten, wurde nun aufgegeben. Statt dessen basierte das neue Kompositionsprinzip auf der Topographie des Geländes und der Topologie der inneren Verkehrswege, was der Grundriß und die Lage von Park Hill in Sheffield (1955–61) deutlich machen (entworfen im Städtischen Baubüro von Jack Lynn und Ivor Smith).
Wenn man den Brutalismus eines Bauwerks wie Park Hill versteht, wird einem klar, daß man diese Bezeichnung nicht auf die modisch-sentimentale Architektur eines Leonardo Ricci anwenden sollte – wie man auch aus Architekten wie Juan → O'Gorman und Paolo → Soleri keine «Brutalisten» machen kann. Der Brutalismus unternimmt den Versuch, die moralischen Imperative durchzusetzen, die durch die Pioniere des 19. Jahrhunderts Eingang in die Tradition der modernen Architektur fanden. Die Verwendung von Sichtbeton oder die freigelegten Stahlkonstruktionen sind nur ein Symptom dieser Bestrebungen. Peter Smithson sagte einmal: «Wir bewundern auch die Materie der Goldfarbe, wo sie nötig ist». Das grundlegende Ziel des Brutalismus war zu jeder Zeit, eine Konzeption zu finden, die von Konstruktion, Raum, Organisation und Material her für ein bestimmtes Gebäude im Sinne von Smithson «notwendig» ist. Diese Konzeption, mit völliger Ehrlichkeit ausgedrückt, führt zum unverwechselbaren architektonischen Bild. Dabei geben die anderen bildenden Künste nicht ein ästhetisches Vorbild, sondern ein Beispiel für die Methode; die Brutalisten bewundern den Design amerikanischer Autos genauso wie den japanischen Ise-Schrein. Beide hatten keinen sichtbaren Einfluß auf die brutalistische Architektur, aber beide sind ein Beispiel für Bilder, die aus bestimmten Verhältnissen und Notwendigkeiten heraus geschaffen wurden. Der Nachdruck, den die Brutalisten bei der Konzeption eines Bauwerks auf die gegebenen und notwendigen Faktoren legten, veranlaßte Sir John Summerson zu einem Vergleich mit dem Rigorismus von Lodoli und anderen radikalen Theoretikern der italienischen Aufklärung im ausgehenden 18. Jahrhundert.
Unter diesen Voraussetzungen ist das Istituto Marchiondi von Vittorio Viganò (1957) das

Alison und Peter Smithson. Hunstanton School. Norfolk, 1954.

Alison und Peter Smithson. Economist Building. London, im Bau. Modell.

Vittoriano Viganò. Istituto Marchiondi. Mailand, 1957.

Seite 57: Erik Bryggman. Friedhofskapelle. Turku, 1938–41.

einzige brutalistische Gebäude Italiens, obwohl es sich auf den ersten Blick nicht so weit von der modernen Bewegung zu entfernen scheint wie die Werke der → Neoliberty-Anhänger. Stilistisch spiegelt das Istituto Marchiondi die Ideen, wenn nicht sogar das Werk → Terragnis und der *architettura razionalista* wider, deren Vorstellungen ähnlich streng von den Forderungen des Bauprogramms her bestimmt waren.
Das Istituto Marchiondi macht auf die Verbindung des Brutalismus mit den Architekturtraditionen aufmerksam. Bei aller Aggressivität und Kompromißlosigkeit entfernt sich der Brutalismus nicht grundsätzlich von den herkömmlichen architektonischen Auffassungen, und man kann ihn keineswegs mit dem technischen Extremismus von Buckminster → Fuller oder den radikalen Funktionsanalysen vergleichen, die der Nuffield Trust in England entwickelte. Am ehesten kann man Vergleiche mit *action-painting* und konkreter Musik anstellen: Die Aktionsmalerei gab die letzten Reste formaler Komposition auf, akzeptierte aber weiterhin so «abgenutzte» Traditionen wie Farbe, Leinwand und rechtwinkliges Bildformat, die vorher schon verschiedentlich von modernen Malern abgelehnt worden waren. Die konkrete Musik verwandte nicht mehr die gefälligen Töne, die von künstlichen Musikinstrumenten erzeugt werden, sondern «wirkliche» Geräusche, entfernte sich aber sonst kaum von dem, was frühere moderne Komponisten von der musikalischen Überlieferung unangetastet gelassen hatten. Ähnlich zogen die Brutalisten der fiktiven Oberfläche die «Realität» von Stahl und Beton vor und lehnten die formale Komposition ab. Trotzdem beruhten ihre Theorien und Werke immer auf den grundlegenden Traditionen der Baukunst. Es ist im übrigen interessant, die Arbeit der Brutalisten mit der eines Architekten zu vergleichen, den sie bewundern, ohne seine Gestaltung zu imitieren: Bei Smithsons Projekt für das Economist Building in London (im Bau) sind die drei Baukörper zwanglos um eine unregelmäßige Piazza gruppiert. Der einfache klassizistische Turm des Seagram Building in New York (1958) erhebt sich dagegen in der Mittelachse eines formal streng konzipierten Vorhofes. Die irreguläre Piazza für den Economist vermittelt einen echteren Eindruck von den organisatorischen und topologischen Erfordernissen dieses bestimmten Funktionsprogramms, als es eine Nachahmung von Mies van der Rohes Komposition vermocht hätte. Und doch haben die Smithsons bei ihrem Projekt nicht etwa eine radikale Lösung des Verhältnisses zwischen Gebäude, Fußgängerzone und Autoverkehr geliefert, sondern – wie es

auch beim Seagram Building der Fall ist – die Bauvolumen auf eine Fußgängerplattform gesetzt, von der alle Fahrzeuge verbannt sind.
Der Brutalismus ist also eine starke reformerische Bewegung innerhalb des modernen architektonischen Denkens und kein revolutionärer Umsturzversuch. Andererseits könnte der Rückgriff der Brutalisten auf grundlegende funktionalistische Prinzipien gewissermaßen nebenher zu einem Verzicht auf viele kleinere Kompromisse führen, der letzten Endes doch einer folgenreichen Revolution gleichkäme.

Reyner Banham

Bryggman, Erik, *1891 in Turku, †1955 in Turku. Bryggman, der 1916 das Architekturdiplom am Polytechnikum Helsinki erwarb, begann seine Berufstätigkeit als Mitarbeiter an einer Reihe von wichtigen Projekten: das Gefallenendenkmal in Helsinki, das er zusammen mit dem Bildhauer Ilkka entwarf, das Freiheitsdenkmal in Oulu, gemeinsam mit dem Bildhauer Saskelin, sowie die Restaurierung

It was to be a German architectural historian who would become the protagonist, albeit silent and forgotten, of the debate on Brutalism: Jürgen Joedicke. Unlike Pehnt and Kultermann, Joedicke trained as an architect at the Technische Hochschule in Stuttgart, where he completed a thesis on the relationship between construction and form in 1953. Joedicke's most decisive interventions were not carried out in Germany, but in Switzerland, where, however, the theoretical international questions on the affirmation of exposed concrete remained marginal.[214] It was only from 1958 onwards, when Franz Füeg became editor of the magazine *Bauen + Wohnen*, that critical positions began to emerge and evaluate the legacy of the masters and the essence of the concept of 'modern architecture', as well issues of form and construction.

The desire of Swiss critics not to attribute the labels circulating in the debate at the time was reflected in the glaring absence of the definition of Brutalism, which appeared only occasionally just to confirm a distance from intellectual discourse and a total rejection of critical categories. According to Füeg, Brutalism could only lead to an exclusively superficial and formal interpretation of architecture, preventing critical objectivity: 'Slogans and catch-words are insidious' is his statement.[215] 'Unfortunately, the word "brutalism", which designates a direction in architecture, is quite literary and induces emotions that complicate objective appreciation', said the editorial staff of *Bauen + Wohnen* about the monographic issue on New Brutalism in *Zodiac*, defined not without perplexity as 'an architecture magazine for which words are more important than images.'[216] When critics, all coming from a pro-Germanic epicentre, such as Benedikt Huber, used the category of New Brutalism, it was limited to describe what was already consolidated in the international debate, such as the British examples, or the works of Le Corbusier and Viganò, but it was never extended to include similar Swiss examples, also characterised by the use of 'untreated, massive, unfinished' concrete.[217] Huber's sense of the wear and tear of styles in Swiss architectural culture in the 1960s is the reason why the definition of New Brutalism was carefully avoided even when, in discussing the works of Walter Förderer, Ernst Gisel, Lorenz Moser, Werner Gantenbein and Wolfgang Behles, parallels were drawn with themes already ascribed to the definition of New Brutalism, such as *tachisme* and action painting, or the notion of chance and irregularity of form.[218]

The explicit reference to Le Corbusier in Jacques Schader's Kantonsschule in Zurich, Fritz Haller's Schulhaus Wasgenring in Basel, and Atelier 5's Siedlung Halen was recognised in *Bauen + Wohnen* by Joedicke as a Swiss stand against the domination of technique and geometrically controlled form. The desire not to merge the international experiences of New Brutalism and the Swiss examples seems justified, according to Joedicke, by a particular Swiss attitude: 'Swiss mentality is such that it welcomes the unusual only with circumspection'.[219]

Symptomatic of the rejection of the intellectual elaborations encompassed by New Brutalism was the choice of the editors of *Bauen + Wohnen* to republish Le Corbusier's stance against this definition in 1963. 'Béton brut says: I am concrete!'[220] had said Le Corbusier on that occasion, rejecting the definition of Brutalism. This statement,

[214] See Silvia Groaz, 'The Swiss Principle of Béton Brut: Betonkonstruktion', in Salvatore Aprea, Nicola Navone, Laurent Stalder (eds.), *Concrete in Switzerland. Histories from the Recent Past* (Lausanne: EPFL Press, 2021), 105–114.

[215] Franz Füeg, 'Kristalline Architektur', *Bauen + Wohnen*, vol. 14, no. 12 (December 1960): 427.

[216] [n.a.], 'Buchbesprechungen', *Bauen + Wohnen*, vol. 13, no. 10 (October 1959): 28.

[217] Benedikt Huber, 'Epigonen', *Das Werk: Architektur und Kunst*, vol. 46, no. 12 (April 1959): 224–25.

[218] Benedikt Huber, 'Architektur des Zufalls', *Das Werk: Architektur und Kunst*, vol. 50, no. 7 (July 1963): 264–71.

[219] Jürgen Joedicke, '1930–1960', *Bauen + Wohnen*, vol. 15, no. 10 (October 1961): 360–73.

[220] [n.a.], 'Am Rande: 5 Fragen an Le Corbusier', *Bauen + Wohnen*', vol. 17, no. 3 (March 1963): 95–96; original publication: 'Cinq questions à Le Corbusier', *Zodiac*, vol. 5 (1960): 46–51.

in which Swiss culture could only recognise itself, became a bulwark of the affirmation of material against the easy temptation to categorise architecture into styles.

Despite an initial lack of interest in the question of New Brutalism, in November 1964 the magazine *Bauen + Wohnen* became, thanks to Joedicke, a protagonist and vehicle for its international affirmation when it published an issue entitled *Brutalismus in der Architektur*.[221] This change was due to the presence of Joedicke, who had been on the magazine's editorial board since 1963 and who had been in contact with Banham since November 1962 for the publication of the book *New Brutalism: Ethic or Aesthetic?* The monograph issue on New Brutalism was conceived by Joedicke as an anticipation of Banham's book, and included also its international manifestations in the United States, England, Germany and Holland.

The success of Brutalism was measured by Joedicke against its ability to act as a crucible for international concerns, even though he recognised its slow decline and the loss of its original theoretical momentum. Brutalism, said Joedicke, fell victim to the 'wear and tear of all passing fashions'.[222] Joedicke demonstrated his awareness of the seminal articles published by Banham and the Smithsons over the previous decade, and recognised the malleability of the definition, capable of 'adapting to our age and our needs'.

Pehnt's declared antagonism to the Miesian model was evident in all those aspects of Brutalism defined in opposition to the 'emotional frigidity of Mies van der Rohe's architecture'. Unlike Pehnt, who emphasised the contrast between the Miesian model and Brutalism on the basis of sculptural forms and rough surfaces, Joedicke drew a comparison based on a divergent compositional process. No other critic had ever before dealt so explicitly and in such detail with the compositional approach of Brutalism. If Joedicke identified in Mies a compositional procedure that started from a basic absolute form, generally rectangular, subsequently subdivided according to functions, in the compositional approach of Brutalism the starting point was the juxtaposition, accentuation and articulation of the various parts of the programme: 'The starting point is not a great form, but the particular form'. The emblematic image identified by Joedicke to explain the particular composition of Brutalism is the 'cluster', which reflected the contemporary urban theories of the Smithsons and their considerations regarding the concept of 'town building'. To express this compositional mechanism, Joedicke used the definition of 'urbanistic principle', similar in intent to the concept recognised by Zevi. It is therefore no coincidence that Joedicke chose the same examples as Zevi to illustrate this principle, such as Van Eyck's orphanage but also works by Bakema, Candilis and Kahn. From this design process, which entails a specific form for each part of the programme, derives the whole series of formal characteristics that Joedicke identified in the overhangs and protruding volumes for different functions or in the unusual, angular or staggered openings to highlight a spatial sequence.

Joedicke was carefully following the evolution, outcome and also possible decline of Brutalism through the 'exhibitionism of form for its own sake' or through the oversizing of the load-bearing elements for a taste of 'heaviness'. Far from the original orthodox principle of 'as found', 'Brutalism of the surface' was the definition used for the tendency towards an artificial roughness, obtained by the manipulation of the compound and aggregates, or by sandblasting and bush-hammering reinforced concrete, the 'preferred material of the Brutalists'. The excessive exhibitionism of forms and the 'structured' surface started to demonstrate the weakening of New Brutalism's

---

[221] Jürgen Joedicke, 'New Brutalism: Brutalismus in der Architektur', *Bauen+Wohnen*, vol. 18, no. 11 (November 1964): 421–25.
[222] Ibid.

initial intentions, to the point that 'some reduce Brutalism to the notion of a rough surface', when originally 'Brutalism was not about the cosmetics of the facade', highlighted Joedicke.[223]

In the mid-1960s, Brutalism was in a position where it could either redeem its ethical impetus and elevate the fate of the Modern Movement in crisis or, on the contrary, become imprisoned in a catalogue of formal solutions and thus be relegated to the status of a 'passing fad'. It would be Banham's task to bring the Brutalist trajectory to completion, to deflagrate its aporias and resolve the dilemma that the Smithsons posed in 1957: 'Ethics or aesthetics?' This seemed to be the pressing question of international critics waiting for a crucial intervention, when Brutalism's pending destiny would be revealed.

[223] Ibid.

chapter seven

the new brutalism: ethic or aesthetic? by joedicke and banham

Joedicke's Proposal for a Monograph on New Brutalism

The act that sanctioned the perennity of New Brutalism, confirming its nature as a critical tool and not a movement, was the monographic book written by Banham in 1966, entitled *The New Brutalism: Ethic or Aesthetic?*[1] Had it not been for that book, New Brutalism would have been condemned to fragmentary appearances in the pages of magazines or in short paragraphs of some narratives on the Modern Movement.

The efforts made until then to make sense of the definition of New Brutalism still appeared to be disjointed impulses in need of revision: from Smithsons' clarifications to Banham's flashpoint in the *Knaurs Lexicon*, and from the investigations into the design processes and formal characteristics preluding a veritable 'canon' up to the attempts at historicisation, all had extended and drastically altered the meaning of the definition. The fate of the Modern Movement seemed sealed, and with the death of its main masters during the 1960s, the discussion on the relevance or otherwise of their principles gave way to the end of architecture's 'heroic period'. Consequently, other values going beyond the truth of materials and structure were able to enter the debate.

On closer inspection, as Banham demonstrated in 1955, there were already different phases and, it could even be argued, different New Brutalisms. This was not only because of the dual identity of Brutalism and New Brutalism, which, as we have seen, enclosed different meanings depending on the context, but also because of the various, sometimes antithetical, orientations that this definition had assumed over the

---

[1]   Reyner Banham, *The New Brutalism: Ethic or Aesthetic?* (London: Architectural Press, 1966); Reyner Banham, *Brutalismus in der Architektur.* Dokumente der modernen Architektur. Beiträge zur Interpretation und Dokumentation der Baukunst, no. 5 (Stuttgart: Krämer Verlag, 1966). The exchanges between Joedicke and Banham have already been partially discussed by Réjean Legault in a lecture entitled 'Agendas, Actors and Authorship: Reconsidering *The New Brutalism: Ethic or Aesthetic?*' on the occasion of the conference 'Actors and Vehicles of Architectural Criticism', on 4 October 2016 at the University of Bologna. Although he did not cite the source of the documents he consulted, it is likely that Legault was referring to the letters held in the Krämer Verlag archive. The correspondence that led to the publication of the book has been presented in Silvia Groaz, 'La genèse du livre *The New Brutalism: Ethic or Aesthetic?* A travers les échanges épistolaires de Banham et Joedicke de 1962 à 1966', *Matières*, no. 14 (2018): 90–101.

course of little more than a decade. After the manipulations of Italian, American and German critics, it was clear that the definition of New Brutalism had started to show cracks and gaps, which critics with sharp analytical tools were revealing.

Was it still possible, in the mid-1960s, to coherently reconstruct the events that generated the definition? What value could a definition aiming at universal coherence in a historical moment marked by a multitude of directions still have? Furthermore, how was it then possible to explain the apparent incongruity between the original definition, born in the Smithson circle, and the international phenomenon of exposed concrete? These and other questions, which Banham was called upon to answer, were at the origin of the editorial adventure which guided the book *The New Brutalism: Ethic or Aesthetic?*

The story of the commission and the publication of the book began when Joedicke contacted Banham, on 6 November 1962, to ask him to write the fifth volume of the series he was directing, 'Dokumente der modernen Architektur, Beiträge zur Interpretation und Dokumentation der Baukunst', published by Krämer Verlag.[2] The thematic succession presented through the five previous volumes of the series had engaged Joedicke as early as 1960, when he outlined his intention to deal with the historical, constructive and sociological aspects of contemporary architecture in a 'documentary' manner.[3] Joedicke recognised Banham as the authority of what he saw as a trend, Brutalism, which he intended to investigate for his own cultural purpose, entirely linked to the German debate. From the very first letter, Joedicke shared with Banham his own vision of Brutalism and the cultural strategy that was guiding his intention to dedicate a book to that subject. For him, the 'slogan' of New Brutalism, as he defined it, outlined a trend in an 'antithesis to the movement represented by Mies, the early Saarinen, and early Skidmore, Owings and Merrill who strived for the technical perfection of the aesthetic ideal'.[4] There was no doubt that Joedicke suggested that Banham revise New Brutalism in order to make it a category in contrast with the international diffusion, particularly present in Germany, of the system of the curtain wall with regular metal rods which arose from the examples of Mies, as Pehnt had already pointed out.[5]

Joedicke's intention was to publish an book that provided a historical outline, documenting the most significant examples of various contemporary artistic phenomena. With the aim of offering a new and broader interpretation of the category, useful for the foundation of a German non-Miesian orientation, Joedicke drafted the first ideas for a book that would also include a wide range of architects, demonstrating the existence of a 'widespread movement'.[6] The British case, which was at the origin of the definition of New Brutalism, would become, in the perspective outlined by Joedicke, simply the corollary of a wider reasoning. 'I don't think of dealing with the English group (Smithsons etc.) only', Joedicke pointed out to Banham, probably alluding to Stirling and Gowan, Lasdun, Colin St John Wilson and Lyons, Israel and Ellis.[7]

The letters between Joedicke, Banham and the staff involved in the publication, between November 1962 and September 1966, when the book was published, allow us to reconstruct the various critical interpretations of Brutalism, clarify certain of Banham's concepts, and understand the reasons for some of the final choices that made *New Brutalism: Ethic or Aesthetic?* an internationally successful book.

[2] Jürgen Joedicke, letter to Reyner Banham, 6 November 1962, Krämer Verlag Archive, Stuttgart, 1–2.
[3] Oscar Newman, *CIAM '59 in Otterlo: Arbeitsgruppe für die Gestaltung soziologischer und visueller Zusammenhänge*, vol. 1, Dokumente der modernen Architektur (Zurich: Girsberger, 1961).
[4] Joedicke, letter to Reyner Banham, 6 November 1962, 2.
[5] Wolfgang Pehnt, 'Was ist Brutalismus? Zur Architekturgeschichte des letzten Jahrfünfts', *Das Kunstwerk*, vol. 14, no. 3 (March 1960): 14–23.
[6] Ibid.
[7] Joedicke, letter to Reyner Banham, 6 November 1962, 2.

In accepting Joedicke's proposal, Banham replied with only a brief and conventional formula of thanks for having approached him 'as author of the proposed volume on Brutalism in your series'.[8] At that time his only concern was the exclusivity of his rights, held by the publishing house Architectural Press which, at the end was in fact involved alongside Krämer Verlag for the English edition. Banham's reaction to Joedicke's proposal, however, remained detached throughout the following months. It would be Joedicke's tenacity in wanting a book on New Brutalism, the editorial commitment of Krämer Verlag and the support of Architectural Press that made it possible to publish a book in which, at least initially, Banham did not seem to be interested, dedicated as he was to researching building services in twentieth-century architecture for the Graham Foundation and on the point of moving to the United States.

Following Banham's response, Joedicke presented his project, provisionally entitled 'New Brutalism', to Karl Krämer senior and junior, owners of Krämer Verlag, to editor Heinz Krehl and to translator Nora von Mülendahl.[9] From the outset, Joedicke revealed the cultural motivations, deeply rooted in German criticism, that led him to take an interest in Brutalism. For Joedicke, Brutalism was understood as a 'trend' that he described as 'a counter movement to the Miesian vision'. The same New Brutalism that had included Mies in the origins of the British definition with the School in Hunstanton, was then turned into a tool for deep criticism of Mies in the German context.

The structure of the Brutalist book was discussed in letters between Joedicke and Banham during the first months of 1963.[10] As a draft of the book, Banham sent Joedicke a reproduction of his 1955 article, 'The New Brutalism',[11] accompanied by 'numerous annotations clipped on to it' currently untraced[12]. In his notes, which can be guessed through Joedicke's remarks and answers, Banham must have emphasised the need to historicise New Brutalism, to examine its double aspect of 'reaction and action', almost suggesting that it belonged to the phenomena of the early 1950s rather than to those of the mid-1960s. In this new historical perspective, Banham accepted Joedicke's proposal to question the role played by Japanese culture, which he said needed 'to be evaluated'. Also in these first exchanges, Banham let Joedicke know of his intention to consider the 'general response' to Le Corbusier's Ronchamp Chapel and La Tourette Convent. These two buildings had been widely cited in international contributions as indications of a new, emerging 'plastic' style, sometimes associated with Brutalism, as can be seen in the interventions of the Smithsons, Kallmann, Pevsner, Stirling, Creighton and Rossi.[13]

Banham, in approaching the book project, intended to emphasise buildings by Le Corbusier, confirming the shift in the vision of New Brutalism from the first Smithsons' definition to a Brutalism that had tended in the direction of Le Corbusier's *béton brut*. In order to grasp the specificity of New Brutalism, Banham also proposed a

[8] Reyner Banham, letter to Jürgen Joedicke, 13 November 1962, Krämer Verlag Archive, Stuttgart, 1.
[9] Jürgen Joedicke, Gedächtnisprotokoll der Besprechung im KKV, 28 November 1962, Krämer Verlag Archive, Stuttgart, 1.
[10] Reyner Banham, letter to Jürgen Joedicke, 19 November 1962, Krämer Verlag Archive, Stuttgart, 1.
[11] Reyner Banham, 'The New Brutalism', *Architectural Review*, vol. 118, no. 708 (December 1955): 354–61.
[12] No documents relating to the New Brutalism book have yet been found among Banham's archival collections at The Getty Research Center, nor in his private archive. According to information conveyed to the author by Ben Banham (Reyner Banham's son), it has been reported that Banham used to dispose of his documents by burning them whenever the piles accumulated on his desk.
[13] Gerhard M. Kallmann, 'The "Action" Architecture of a New Generation', *Architectural Forum*, vol. 111, no. 4 (October 1959): 132–37; Nikolaus Pevsner, 'Roehampton, LCC Housing and the Picturesque Tradition', *Architectural Review*, vol. 125, no. 750 (July 1959): 21–35; Thomas Hawk Creighton, 'The New Sensualism', *Progressive Architecture*, vol. 40, no. 9 (September 1959): 141–54; James Frazer Stirling, 'Ronchamp, Le Corbusier's Chapel and the Crisis of Rationalism', *Architectural Review*, vol. 119, no. 711 (March 1956): 155–61; Aldo Rossi, 'Le Il convento de la Tourette di Le Corbusier', *Casabella-Continuità*, vol. 246 (December 1960): 4. The Smithsons had discussed Ronchamp and La Tourette several times: Theo Crosby, 'The New Brutalism', *Architectural Design*, vol. 25, no. 1 (January 1955): 1; Alison Smithson, 'Couvent de la Tourette: Le Corbusier', *Architectural Design*, vol. 28, no. 11 (November 1958): 462.

philological investigation of the term itself and an in-depth examination of the role played by what he defined as 'non-art manifestations', probably alluding to the phenomenon of anti-art, as he then explained in the book.

In the notes sent to Joedicke, Banham must also have suggested analysing in detail some 'Brutalist' buildings that had not been included in the category up to that time and examining 'visitors' reactions' to Brutalist buildings – their 'vision and emotion'. Banham expressed his intention to delve into the very meaning of architecture, or rather its 'impartiality', that is, the ability of the building to show its function in relation to the author's poetics, and the understanding, from an architectural perspective, of the urban scale. 'These annotations', Banham explains, prompting Joedicke's comments, 'do not necessarily represent my definite intentions, but I think they prove a useful basis'.[14] More than a decade after the origin of New Brutalism, the various misunderstandings and misconceptions that continued to characterise the debate convinced Banham of the need for a publication that could clarify the still ambiguous definition. To this end, as he used to do in preparation of a new book, he organised a symposium with his students from the Bartlett School of Architecture, which demonstrated that the question of New Brutalism was 'in need of historical explanation'.[15]

It is possible to deduce Banham's notes from Joedicke's response summarised in one of the most significant documents in the epistolary making of *New Brutalism: Ethic or Aesthetic?*[16] Joedicke appropriated Banham's definition of New Brutalism as a phenomenon of 'reaction and action', to reiterate his promotion of an orientation opposed to Miesian aesthetics, defined as 'technical perfection as aesthetic ideal'. From Joedicke's perspective there was an urgent need to reconsider the current phase of the debate, marked by a variety of formalistic stances that he included in the category of 'eclecticism'. This term, which Joedicke employed in his correspondence with Banham, ended up being included in the book. It should be pointed out, however, that the eclecticism Joedicke referred to is not the same as that of Banham. In fact, for Joedicke that category was used to encompass all international reactions to the spread of the rigidity of Mies's poetics:

> Compared with this tendency, at present Brutalism seems to gain special influence, especially after it turned out that various other attempts being in contrast to the view of Mies, led to eclecticism. Brutalism is one of the very few alternatives to the 'Technical Perfection' architecture.[17]

While Brutalism was proposed to counter the imperturbable reiteration of the 'Technical Perfection' of Miesian ascendancy, Joedicke was nonetheless concerned with the 'aberrations' of the phenomenon, namely 'the exhibitionist excess' and 'the haptic surface degraded to an ornament'.[18]

The notes also reveal Joedicke's attempt to historicise Brutalism well beyond British borders. In his concern to find solid models, Joedicke suggested including Le Corbusier's Maisons Jaoul, which in fact played a decisive role in the published version of the book. Joedicke also pointed to Bakema's early buildings, in particular the Rotterdam-Zuidplein civic centre and the Brielle school, already counted among the

[14] Reyner Banham, letter to Jürgen Joedicke, 9 May 1963, Krämer Verlag Archive, Stuttgart, 1.
[15] 'When I subsequently mounted an experimental seminar on the subject, my students soon made it clear that large and important aspects of Brutalism were already in need of historical explanation'. Banham, *The New Brutalism: Ethic or Aesthetic?*, preface. To date, there are no documents available that record the discussions that took place during the seminar at the Bartlett School of Architecture in London. However, Adrian Forty recalls Banham's custom of discussing with his students during a seminar focused on the theme of books in preparation, in Adrian Forty, interview with author, 19 January 2019, Zurich.
[16] Jürgen Joedicke, letter to Reyner Banham, 5 June 1963, Krämer Verlag Archive, Stuttgart, 1–3.
[17] Ibid., 1.
[18] Ibid., 2.

examples of New Brutalism by Kallmann, Stirling and Peter Smithson, and which Banham also included in the entry for the *Knaurs Lexikon*.[19] Aalto, and especially his town hall in Säynätsalo, was confirmed by Joedicke as indispensable for the understanding of New Brutalism, as Pehnt, Boyd and Scully revealed. Aalto had also been discussed several times by the Smithsons, who reiterated his influence on their reflections while coining the term New Brutalism.[20] In invoking Berlage's Amsterdam Stock Exchange, Joedicke suggested a broader historicisation based on the truth of the material and the visibility of services, which reveals how for him Brutalism was an intrinsic component of the Modern Movement.

In addition, Joedicke suggested documenting Brutalist buildings through a rich sequence of plans and photographs,[21] as if to transform a difficult-to-understand category into a more clearly illustrated orientation through a popular book. Joedicke intended to use photographic illustration to call the buildings directly into question, in order to free Brutalism from the categories he defined as ideological:

> I think this [inclusion of illustrations] would not only serve for better understanding of the subject, but also please our publishers. However, here too I feel it is important to compare the buildings with the architects' statements which often prove to be ~~pure theory~~ ideology only [strikethrough in original].[22]

With the intention of illustrating the change in meaning of the term over time, Joedicke proposed to compare the Smithsons' School at Hunstanton with 'another characteristic example of our days'. This was suggested to resolve what he called the 'problem of Non-identity', that is, a dissociation between the architects' statements and the form of the building. This issue seemed of such crucial importance in the discussion of Brutalism that Joedicke expressly asked Banham to address the way in which 'the theoretical statement can be evident in the building at all'.[23]

In the development of the book's proposal, the three qualities Banham enunciated in 1955 were still relevant. The question of composition seemed to play a more important role for Joedicke than the supremacy of the image, as evidenced by the fact that he listed the first of Banham's series of principles. Thus, as a corollary to Banham's three qualities, Joedicke proposed adding what he called 'super-concepts', in an attempt to orient Brutalism towards a trajectory other than that of style: 'vision and emotions', 'impartiality' (referred to 'Objektivität' in a German note) and 'space-forming' (or 'Raumbildung'), which described the design principle of assembling the various parts of the programme.[24]

However, the spectrum of style haunted Brutalism and its 'mannerist' and 'eclectic' tendencies against Miesian perfection. Joedicke recommended that Banham develop some arguments and critical judgements to counteract the over-design tendency:

---

[19] Kallmann, 'The "Action" Architecture of a New Generation'; James Frazer Stirling, 'The Black Notebook', in Mark Crinson (ed.), *James Stirling: Early Unpublished Writings on Architecture* (London: Routledge, 2010), 55; Peter Smithson, 'Modern Architecture in Holland', *Architectural Design*, vol. 101, no. 3 (August 1954): 68–70; Wolfgang Pehnt (ed.), *Knaurs Lexikon der modernen Architektur* (Munich, Zurich: Hatje, 1963).

[20] Robin Boyd, 'The Counter-Revolution in Architecture', *Harper's Magazine*, vol. 219, no. 1312 (September 1959): 40–48; Scully, 'Modern Architecture'; Pehnt, 'Was ist Brutalismus? Zur Architekturgeschichte des letzten Jahrfünfts'; Alison and Peter Smithson, 'Banham's Bumper Book on Brutalism, discussed by Alison and Peter Smithson', *Architects' Journal*, vol. 144, no. 26 (December 1966): 1590–91.

[21] Listed works include the Smithsons' School at Hunstanton, the Yale Art Gallery and Kahn's Medical Research Center, and residential works in Preston and Ham Common by Stirling and Gowan.

[22] Jürgen Joedicke, letter to Reyner Banham, 5 June 1963, Krämer Verlag Archive, Stuttgart, 1–3.

[23] Ibid., 2

[24] The concepts are mentioned in English with German translation on the side. Joedicke would specify these characteristics in his article, 'New Brutalism: Brutalismus in der Architektur', *Bauen+Wohnen*, vol. 18, no. 11 (November 1964): 421–25.

It may happen that on dealing with the subject Brutalism the problem of Mannerism will arise. To my surprise I noticed that in Brutalism there exists already a certain regularity of forms – an interesting phenomenon. I feel in the design for Brutalist buildings there is often the problem of over-designing (Ubergestaltung) – that means, too much is being done so that the desired effect is failing. Saying it quite simply: where there is always something happening, nobody is able to notice anything in detail. Finally the question of expression arises in this connection, an extremely interesting problem of Brutalism.[25]

The letter was accompanied by a proposal for a 'List of Buildings', many of which were in Germany and Switzerland and published in international magazines between 1960 and 1962.[26] The buildings list confirms a precise cultural project – Joedicke's not Banham's – aimed at demonstrating the contemporary value of Brutalism as a critical reaction against Miesian 'Technical Perfection'.

Towards the Final Structure of the Book

The first meeting between Banham, Joedicke, the editors and the translator took place at Krämer Verlag in Stuttgart, on 16 and 17 December 1963. On this occasion the general structure of the book, its contents, format and graphics were defined. Banham also expressed his opinion on the format of the book, which he wanted to be pocket-sized and economical, aimed at a student audience. During the course of the exchanges he also specified, in response to Joedicke's proposal to have one section dedicated only to the text, and one to the pictures, that 'a clear separation of narrative and picture section will probably not be possible'.

At the meeting, although he said that Banham was 'absolutely free in preparing and arranging the book', Joedicke summarised the development of the book in seven points, according to a historiographical sequence, opening with the 'situation in 1950' and the 'various impacts' of architects such as Le Corbusier, Bakema and Tange; 'origin of the term "New Brutalism" in Britain, definition, relations to fine arts'; 'change of the term over time'; 'significant characteristics of New Brutalism'; 'examples'; and concluded with 'the situation of today'.[27] Joedicke's premise was not designed to identify Brutalism as a historical definition, unlike his proposal to extend the definition to examples such as Berlage, but, on the contrary, he wanted to encourage discussion of a category whose meaning was still *in the making*. For Joedicke, Brutalism was highly valuable precisely because it was continuously evolving.

From the minutes of the discussions, it seems that Banham complied with the editorial decisions and agreed with the quantity of examples and illustrations suggested by Joedicke. Banham also proposed including an anthology of texts, comprising the Smithsons' articles and excerpts from the 1953 catalogue of *Parallel of Life and Art*, in which Smithson, Paolozzi and Henderson had collected a selection of images and defined a list of categories demonstrative of the variety of their interests, far beyond the discipline of architecture alone.

[25] Jürgen Joedicke, letter to Reyner Banham, 5 June 1963, 1–3, Krämer Verlag Archive, Stuttgart, 3.
[26] The first list included the following architects: Stirling and Gowan, Lasdun, Martin, Rich, Shepard Robson and Associates, Smithson, Colin St John Wilson, Alex Hardy, Kahn, Paul Rudolph, Bakema, Aldo van Eyck, Candilis/Josic/Woods, Mario Galvagni and Carlo Fallenberg, Vittano Viganò, Tigan, Tange, Maekawa, Cramer/Jaray/Paillard, Atelier 5, Ernst Gisel, Foederer/Otto/Zwimpfer, Günther Behnisch, Kalus Ernst, Fahling/Gogel/Pfankich, Roland Ostertag, Walter Schwagenscheidt, and Oswald Mathias Ungers.
[27] Karl Krämer, protocol from memory of Dr Banham's visit on 16 and 17 December 1963, 1–2, Krämer Verlag Archive, Stuttgart, 1.

The sequence of text and illustrations preoccupied Banham, who was waiting for definitive indications to adapt his manuscript. The cultural line that was to guide the choice of iconography and the final draft of the book, scheduled for June 1964, was summarised in a typewritten document prepared by Joedicke during the meeting in Stuttgart. On that occasion, after listing the thematic chapters of the book, arranged in chronological order, Joedicke suggested opening the book with cultural and political considerations concerning the immediate post-war context, from 1949 to 1952, with particular attention given to the debates that emerged during the Bergamo and Hoddesdon CIAMs. He then advised Banham to focus on the legacy of the masters, specifically the influence of Le Corbusier and Mies. This more general premise was to serve as a guide to understanding the events of 1952–1955, the Smithsons' positions in the debates over the return of Wittkower's classicism, their early projects (Coventry Cathedral, House in Soho, School at Hunstanton), the role of the Yale Art Gallery, and the comments of Johnson and 'the young Miesians', probably identified as the students trained at the Illinois Institute of Technology under Mies. The period from 1955 to 1958, which coincided with a second phase of Brutalism, was identified by Joedicke as a period of 'Anti-Classicism', which characterised the Smithsons' revolt against Palladian geometries and the beginning of the collaborations with the Independent Group that led to the exhibition *Parallel of Life and Art*. In this section Banham was also called upon to explain the relationship between New Brutalism and art brut. The role of Ronchamp, the Maisons Jaoul, the House of the Future, the project for the University of Sheffield and the Flats at Ham Common lent themselves, according to Joedicke, to an opportunity to reflect on the difference between 'Brutalism as modern Primitivism versus Brutalism as founding doctrine'. In the phenomena of the second phase of Brutalism, Joedicke recognised a contrast between a Primitivist line from Le Corbusier and a strengthening of Brutalist canon.

In Joedicke's scheme, another chapter was to be dedicated to the urbanistic principles, moving from the criticism raised to the CIAM in Aix-en-Provence in 1953 to the constitution of Team X in Dubrovnik in 1956 and the dissolution of the CIAM in Otterlo in 1959. The discussion on urbanistic principles was to be put in parallel with urban projects that demonstrated the potential of building conceived according to an 'urbanistic principle', such as Berlin Hauptstadt and the recently completed Preston Housing by Stirling and Gowan. In conclusion, Joedicke pointed to a section entitled 'Return to Architecture', covering the period between 1958 and 1963. In this phase, which was to take stock of the contemporary situation, Joedicke defined several trajectories: one characterised by a technology animated by a fantastic vision, which Joedicke identified as a new aspiration to an 'rejection of pure technicism', exemplified by Buckminster Fuller and the CLASP prefabrication system; another comprising the tendency towards 'Historicisms', which Joedicke framed in a sphere of nostalgia identified with the works of Viganò and Ungers; and finally the established forms of international Brutalism, including recent works such as Kahn's Richards Medical Institute, van Eyck's Amsterdam Orphanage, Tange's Nishinan Cultural Center and works by other Japanese architects.[28]

Banham's drafting of the book fell behind schedule due to the increasing number of contributions on the personalities listed under Brutalism, at least according to his justification.[29] As a concrete example, he cited Scully's 1962 essay on Kahn, who 'has done most of the rough work in that particular case', recognizing the ascription of Kahn's works to the international phenomenon of Brutalism.[30]

[28] Jürgen Joedicke, 'Abriss des geplanten Buches von Reyner Banham: New Brutalism', Archive Krämer Verlag, Stuttgart.
[29] Reyner Banham, letter to Joedicke, April 1964, Krämer Verlag Archive, Stuttgart, 1.
[30] Roberto Gargiani, *Louis I. Kahn: Exposed Concrete and Hollow Stones, 1949–1959* (Lausanne: EPFL Press, 2014), 108.

Contrary to Banham's expectations, who was inclined to consider Brutalism as an essentially closed chapter of the architectural debate, the international press was paying increasing attention to the issue, as confirmed by articles by Zevi, Kultermann, Kallmann, Boyd, the editors of *Zodiac* and many others. This continuous elaboration on Brutalism encouraged Banham to pursue the writing of the book: 'Although this has slowed down my rate of writing, it has proven to be a fascinating study'.[31] 'A comprehensive view only will enable us at last to decide what is to be included or not' was the prompt reaction of Joedicke who invited Banham to participate in the November 1964 issue of *Bauen + Wohnen*.[32]

In his correspondence, Joedicke showed that he was always on the lookout for 'Brutalist buildings'. While Joedicke tried to expand the cases, Banham was more selective and critical, always pursuing a vision of New Brutalism not in terms of form but in terms of principles. The cases under discussion proposed by Joedicke show that Brutalism was to be identified only with buildings in exposed reinforced concrete and that the book would give, at least in the sequence of images, an international panorama of works in *béton brut*. The suggestion of including works in brick and even more fantastic visions such as those of Buckminster Fuller remained marginal in the correspondence. Opinions between Joedicke and Banham often diverged. This was the case with Joedicke's proposal to include among Brutalist buildings, alongside Tange's Nishinan Cultural Center, Rudolph's Yale University's School of Art and Architecture and Married Student Housing, Sir Leslie Martin and Wilson's Caius College in Cambridge, as well as Rodney Gordon and Owen Luder's Eros House in London. Banham's critical reaction was against the formalist nature of certain buildings such as the Eros House. For Banham, this list demonstrated a 'superficial use of Brutalist forms', to which Joedicke commented that 'today this superficial application of Brutalist forms prevails over the intellectual concern which originally led to Brutalism'.[33] Even the acclaimed examples of Brutalism, such as the Marchiondi Institute was now seen by Joedicke not only as an example of 'Historicismus', as Pevsner had noted,[34] but even as a demonstration of a 'superficial use of Brutalist forms', due to the 'protruding lavatories as plastic means to divide the facade'.

From the end of 1964 until September 1966, the final structure of the book was developed. Winifred Constable and Muriel Fulton from the Architectural Press were entrusted with the collection of illustrations of already published buildings, while Krämer Verlag was responsible for contacting the architects.[35] One emblematic image seems to be of particular concern to Banham, who returned several times to the need to include the photograph of a drive-in cinema seen in an aerial photograph of Los Angeles. That precise image was functional in demonstrating a potential extreme outcome of Brutalism, made explicit by a structure that becomes the 'perfect example of non-architecture [where] there was nothing to see'.[36]

Le Corbusier did not bother responding personally to the request for images on 22 December 1964, and it was his secretary who sent the photographs indicated in the list, which included works that corresponded to the chronology of New Brutalism, such as the Unité d'Habitation in Marseille and the Maisons Jaoul, but also earlier projects

[31] Reyner Banham, letter to Jürgen Joedicke, 14 April 1964, Krämer Verlag Archive, Stuttgart, 1.

[32] Jürgen Joedicke, 'Brutalismus in der Architektur', *Bauen+Wohnen*, vol. 20, no. 12 (December 1964): 19–24.

[33] Jürgen Joedicke, letter to Reyner Banham, 8 June 1964, Krämer Verlag Archive, Stuttgart, 1.

[34] Nikolaus Pevsner, 'Modern Architecture and the Historian – or the Return of Historicism', *RIBA Journal*, no. 68 (April 1961): 230–40.

[35] The following architects were contacted: Bengt Edman, Aldo van Eyck, Figini and Pollini, Forderer+Otto+Zeimpfer, Pedro Freitag, Atelier 5, BBPR, Geir Grung, Louis Kahn, Mies van der Rohe, Kiyonori Kikutake, Le Corbusier, Sigurd Lewerentz, Kunio Mayekawa, Makoto Tanaka, Paul Rudolph, Oswald Mathias Ungers, Peter Smithson and Vittoriano Viganò.

[36] Reyner Banham, letter to Nora von Mühlendahl, 20 February 1966, Krämer Verlag Archive, Stuttgart.

from the 1950s, such as the Cité Permanente in La Sainte Baume, the Hotel à Cap Martin, Roq et Rob, the Maison Fueter and the St. Diè factory, as well as a work from the 1930s, the Petite Maison in Boulogne-sur-Seine. For the first time, the Petite Maison was included in the discourse as an emblematic antecedent of the Maisons Jaoul.

Confirming Kahn's distance from Brutalism,[37] he did not respond at all to the six letters sent to him over the course of eight months for images of the Yale Art Gallery. Banham had specified that he was interested in publishing photographs of the street façade, the interior, and in particular the concrete surface in the interior staircase. The Smithsons did not seem particularly interested in the publishing of the book either, as evidenced by the delays in their response. From the few lines of reply written by Peter Smithson to Karl Krämer, one can guess that the Smithsons in May 1965 had tried to discuss the publication with Banham, who was 'very elusive', perhaps to conceal the sharp conclusions Banham was formulating about them in the manuscript.

Van Eyck and Ungers, on the other hand, were interested in their works being classified as 'Brutalist buildings'. Van Eyck presented a careful selection of images for what he imagined would be a publication that was anything but 'neutral – certainly not if its subject is New Brutalism!'[38] For his part, Ungers suggested publishing images of the Haus Reimbold in Cologne believing it 'should be classified under New Brutalism'.[39]

In his successful attempt at documenting and expanding contemporary Brutalism, Joedicke continued to believe in the 'unique alternative to Mies' that had pushed him to undertake the publication, and also the possibility of going beyond the Modern Movement and the lesson of its masters. From some of his notes we understand that Brutalism for him was 'a response to the cosmetics of the façade', pushed as far as 'primitivisms'. 'A slogan? A stylistic idea? A challenge?' are the questions he prepared to advertise Banham's book. Only the last one, the 'challenge', contained the sense of his vision of the New Brutalism of the future.

The design of the book was clarified during Banham's last visit to Stuttgart on 28 March 1965, when it was decided that the reference images that did not concern the 'brutalist constructions' should flank the text printed on grey paper, while those from the list of crucial examples would be printed on glossy white paper. Joedicke was pleased with the editorial achievement and the form taken by the fifth book in his series. 'This book is a resumé of a movement which started from England and has become world-wide today,' he wrote to Banham.[40]

Banham completed the manuscript on 19 July 1965. Von Mühlendahl, who was responsible for the German translation, drew up a list of questions for the author, some of which were decisive for understanding the value of the category and concerned the relationship between 'New Brutalism' and 'béton brut' ('Is Brutalism and béton brut the same?', she asked Banham), the reduction of Brutalism to pure form ('Reduzierung Brutalismus als Form'), and even the possibility of using the typical prefix in use for stylistic categories ('Neobrutalistisch').[41] This was the decisive point of the whole theoretical framework of Banham's book, from which the differences between him and Joedicke derived. The list of Brutalist buildings that Joedicke was able to document through Banham's book was the demonstration of the existence of a new 'International Style', of a different kind from the one decreed at the beginning of the 1930s, but a style, nonetheless. Banham was well aware of this academic declination of New Brutalism, which constituted a real 'disappointment': 'As Brutalism

[37] James Marston Fitch, 'A Building of Rugged Fundaments', *Architectural Forum*, vol. 113 (July 1960): 82–87.
[38] Aldo van Eyck, letter to Krehl, 30 December 1964, Krämer Verlag Archive, Stuttgart, 1–2.
[39] Oswald Mathias Ungers, letter to Krehl, 7 January 1965, Krämer Verlag Archive, Stuttgart, 1.
[40] Jürgen Joedicke, letter to Banham, 6 April 1965, Krämer Verlag Archive, Stuttgart.
[41] Nora von Mühlendahl, 'Fragen an Dr. Banham', undated document, Krämer Verlag Archive, Stuttgart, 1–3.

became a world style it ceased to be what it had been when it was an English movement, and that it was Le Corbusier who put his imprint on the word', he wrote to Joedicke in December 1966.[42]

Banham's New Brutalism: From Materials to Ethics

The publication of *The New Brutalism: Ethic or Aesthetic?* established New Brutalism as an exhausted phenomenon of the Modern Movement and consigned it to historiography. Nonetheless, the attempt to frame the general trajectory of New Brutalism and its various international forms, constituted a turning point in Banham's vision. Other research themes would develop independently from that book, despite the shared theoretical core. In fact, Banham went so far as to identify possible new future trajectories for New Brutalism, beyond *béton brut* and towards a technological and pop world, oriented to the expression of the mechanical functioning of architecture and the definition of a new 'human environment'. It was also through the writing of *The New Brutalism: Ethic or Aesthetic?* that themes such as concrete, the environment, the habitat and finally technology became emblematic subjects for Banham, which he would discuss in subsequent publications, through historical books such as *A Concrete Atlantis* and *Architecture of the Well-tempered Environment*, or research aimed at framing contemporary phenomena such as the megastructure, pop architecture and finally high-tech.[43]

The book entered the market in a German translation in mid-September 1966 under the title *Brutalismus in der Architektur,* published by Krämer Verlag in Stuttgart, followed by an English-language edition at the beginning of December 1966, entitled *New Brutalism: Ethic or Aesthetic?* published by Architectural Press, London (see figures 39–40). Both versions consisted, as expected, of a 196-page, hardcover volume with a dust jacket featuring a photograph of one of the buildings discussed in the book set against a red background. The text, which made up two-fifths of the entire volume, was printed on grey matt paper and alternated with photographs and drawings, for a total of 303 images, printed on white glossy paper.

The diversity of the two titles is symptomatic of the variations with which the definition had spread in the international context, where it was translated from time to time as New Brutalism, Brutalismo, Brutalisme, Brutalismus. The German title of the book follows Joedicke's edited 1964 issue of *Bauen+Wohnen*. We could also affirm that the German title is expressive of a Teutonic cultural line where the focus is on architecture, offering the certainty of a Brutalism seen as a possible turning point within the discipline, through the drift away from a certain Miesian architecture against which Joedicke had always insisted. Instead, the English title raises insoluble doubts, typical of Banham and Smithson's theoretical wanderings. The addition of the two words, 'ethic' and 'aesthetic', followed by the question mark, was nevertheless decisive in bringing the question of Brutalism back into international discussions about the fate of the definition. In the end, the choice of the title reveals the different cultural aspirations of Banham and Joedicke: the former was committed to claiming an all-English origin of the phenomenon, contaminated by cultural disciplines ranging from art to music and from literature to urban planning; the latter was instead intent on demonstrating the internationalisation of the definition, rooted in a solid disciplinary framework.

---

[42] Reyner Banham, letter to Jürgen Joedicke, 5 December 1966, Krämer Verlag Archive, Stuttgart.
[43] Reyner Banham, *Megastructure: Urban Futures of the Recent Past* (London: Thames & Hudson, 1976); Reyner Banham, *A Concrete Atlantis: US Industrial Building and European Modern Architecture, 1900–1925* (Cambridge, MA: MIT Press, 1986); Reyner Banham, *The Architecture of the Well-tempered Environment* (London: The Architectural Press, 1969); see also the two volumes published posthumously: Reyner Banham, *The Visions of Ron Herron*, Architectural Monographs (London: Academy Editions, 1994); Todd Gannon, *Reyner Banham and the Paradoxes of High Tech* (Los Angeles: Getty Research Institute, 2017).

39 Cover of the German edition of Reyner Banham, *Brutalismus in der Architektur*, Krämer Verlag, Stuttgart, September 1966

40 Cover of the English edition of Reyner Banham, *New Brutalism. Ethic or Aestetic?*, Architectural Press, London, December 1966

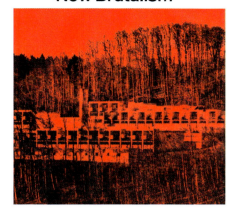

The book's promoter, Joedicke, was limited to a brief introduction presented on the dust jacket, in which he posed a series of questions summarising the issues raised by critics and architects since the definition of New Brutalism first appeared. He did not fail to notice its archetypal oscillation between movement and style. Through these questions, Joedicke presented the book's aim of investigating the vitality of Brutalism, measured against the relevance of that definition for its own founders, alluding to the Smithsons:

> Ethic or aesthetic? Was the New Brutalism a moral crusade or the reform of architecture, as its British proponents appeared to claim in the early Nineteen-Fifties, or was it simply another post-War style, or even several styles? Is it still a living movement, or has it been abandoned by its earlier practitioners?[44]

The text is articulated in a series of chapters in chronological order, following the structure indicated by Joedicke. Banham reconstructed the events starting from the origin of the definition, then illustrated its ethical principles and urban planning theories, dwelling on the artistic contaminations that had pushed New Brutalism towards an 'architecture autre', up to its affirmation as an international style, spread from America to Italy and from Switzerland to Japan. Joedicke's suggestion of including a series of chapters devoted to 'examples' was accepted by Banham, who was then able to discuss buildings he considered crucial to the debate, such as the Unité in Marseilles, the Illinois Institute of Technology, the School at Hunstanton, the Yale Art Gallery, the Maisons Jaoul, and the Flats at Ham Common. However, Banham did not follow up on his own initial intention of compiling an anthology of texts to accompany the book, but faithfully reported quotes from articles, both by Smithson and by other critics, in order to allow the various protagonists to take voice in his narrative.

For all the thematic and chronological extension, Banham was incapable of resolving the fragmentary evolution of New Brutalism in a coherent narrative. Despite the book reaffirming his authority on the subject, he reiterated an underlying disillusionment, also demonstrated in the book's brief preface: '[Joedicke] surprised me in 1963 with the proposal that the New Brutalism was a suitable subject for a serious study'.[45]

44 Joedicke, Introduction, in Banham, *The New Brutalism: Ethic or Aesthetic?*, dust cover.
45 Banham, *The New Brutalism: Ethic or Aesthetic?*, preface.

The monograph on Brutalism was tackled by Banham not so much in order to analyse the various outcomes that emerged from that definition, as to verify the validity of the Smithsons' and his intuition. If in the 1955 article Banham had maintained a detached position in order to make the definition of New Brutalism operative and internationally successful, dwelling on its theoretical and conceptual stances, in the book Banham rereads the events privileging the point of view of the 'British contribution'. Based on this parameter Banham evaluates the contributions of critics and architects who had turned New Brutalism into an international phenomenon, judging their works or comments according to whether they had respected the Smithsons' principles. Banham's book has no historical pretension and is crossed by an autobiographical and 'partisan' line, impossible for him to hide because of his first-person involvement in the genesis of the definition: 'The book has a built-in bias towards the British contribution to Brutalism: it was not a dispassionate and Olympian survey, conducted from the cool heights of an academic ivory tower'.[46] Consequently, Banham's book, instead of being purposed as a 'serious study', is closer to a narrative model, with an expositive sequence that reconstructs the events according to an apparently linear succession, and with subjects ultimately referable to a few, well-defined 'roles', identifiable in protagonists and antagonists and presented by a narrator, who was himself an actor in the events.

The whole book reveals the tension between the promising assumptions and revolutionary ambitions of Early New Brutalism and the bitter realisation of the outcomes of international Brutalism, reduced to a series of stylistic precepts. Banham never made explicit the substantial difference between the definitions of New Brutalism and Brutalism, but one can guess from the different contexts in which the two definitions were employed, although it was not a rigorous distinction: New Brutalism identified the ethical instances of the English origins, while Brutalism indicated another universally recognised international style. The book's structure reflects the coexistence of the two phenomena, New Brutalism and Brutalism, which for Banham are antagonistic: ethics versus aesthetics, theory versus practice, critics versus architects, the vision of the city versus the scale of the individual building, the truth of materials versus the virtuosity of the surface.

The book is structured on two levels of narration. The first level consists of an impassioned account of the events of the 1950s, beginning with a justification of the Smithsons' theories and an explanation of Banham's own role in the evolution of events, perhaps in response to Joedicke who had expressed scepticism about the ability of the Smithsons' to answer contemporary problems. The second level aims to pinpoint the crucial buildings in which the ethical premises of Early New Brutalism were either respected or subverted. In the first chapter, dedicated to the origin of the definition of New Brutalism, Banham traces the sequence of events that, from Asplund's invention in 1950, brought the definition to the LCC circle, and then triggered the heated debate against London's cultural elites, represented by the editors of *Architectural Review* and the 'Marxist' current of the LCC, as well as Pevsner. The book does not question New Brutalism's opposition to the nostalgic principles of the Picturesque or the sentimentalism of New Empiricism. In reconsidering the history of the term, Banham downplays the role of the Smithsons, while attributing veracity to Asplund as the author of the definition of Neo-Brutalism, later transmigrated to England and spread as New Brutalism. The change from Neo-Brutalism to New Brutalism was seen by Banham as an opportunity to clarify the difference between style and movement that he had already put forward in his 1955 article, without however specifying the ethical component that he placed at the basis of New Brutalism in his book: 'The

---

[46] Ibid., 134.

difference is not merely one of form of words: "NeoBrutalist" is a stylistic label, like Neo-Classic or Neo-Gothic, whereas "The New Brutalism" is, in the Brutalist phrase "an ethic, not an aesthetic'".[47]

The very choice of images follows the theoretical reasoning of the text. Banham does not include any photographs of the House in Soho, which was chosen by the Smithsons as a model for defining their New Brutalism, and the project only appears in a more general list of works, without being discussed further. Instead, Villa Göth, which became the object of Asplund's reflection culminating in the invention of Neo-Brutalism, is reproduced on the first page of the book. This suggests that Banham consciously wanted to discredit the Smithsons from being the authors of the definition. Moreover, the Smithsons are referred to as passive receivers of a definition already in circulation: 'The Smithsons accepted the title Brutalist'.[48] Banham picks up on Giedion and Armitage's narrative, according to which the process of appropriation of the definition by the Smithsons was enacted from a totally autobiographical perspective.[49]

For Banham, the Smithsons' contribution lay in their use of the definition as a receptacle for a series of generational concerns of an essentially theoretical nature. While in the 1955 article Banham was careful to demonstrate the operative value of New Brutalism, even identifying works that were distant from the English context, such as the Yale Art Gallery, in the book he admitted that the definition was not bound to precise buildings: 'The term was coined, in essence, before there existed any architectural movement for it to describe'. It is therefore clear that a new awareness was emerging in Banham's vision, motivated by the precise historical moment of the mid-1960s, when Brutalism had become the receptacle of a style. This supports his attempt to redeem it by restoring New Brutalism to its original impulse through the book. The absence of buildings clearly expressing the theory of New Brutalism, indicated by critics as one of the weakest points of the definition, for Banham now reveals the particular nature it had assumed in the English context: 'The New Brutalism is "an ethic, not an aesthetic". It describes a programme or an attitude to architecture'.

All of Banham's reasoning related to the early stages of New Brutalism was framed in the debates of the 1950s, particularly the Smithsons' relationship to history and their relentless drive to find 'historical justifications for its [New Brutalism] own attitude'.[50] Thus the study of Wittkower's theories on the one hand, and the renewal of the principles of the Modern Movement on the other, among whom Banham includes not only Le Corbusier, Mies, Aalto and Wright, but also Rietveld, Taut and Häring, confirm in Banham's book the intrinsic association between history and project inaugurated in England by the Smithsons. The heated debate that took place during 1961, generated by Pevsner's positions on the danger of historicism, also reiterated by Joedicke, pushed Banham to clarify the Smithsons' attitude. Their recourse to history was solely motivated by the willingness to find new values for the present, capable of emancipating architecture from ideological or stylistic dogmas: 'They were trying to see their word whole and see it true, without the interposition of diagrammatic political categories, exhausted "progressive" notions or prefabricated aesthetic preferences'.[51]

[47] Ibid., 10.
[48] Ibid., 15.
[49] 'The term "Brutalist" was doubtless applied to their [Smithson's] design ideas but it stuck to them for two reasons: firstly because they were prepared to make something serious of it; and, secondly, because Peter Smithson was known to his friends during his student days as "Brutus"'. Edward J. Armitage, 'Letter to the Editor', *Architectural Design*, vol. 27, no. 6 (June 1957): 184; Giedion had expressed this hypothesis in his response to the questionnaire on Brutalism, in Marian Z. Augustyniak and Fred T. Entwistle, *Survey of the New Brutalism*, Department of Architecture, Carnegie Institute of Technology, Pittsburgh, Pennsylvania, 1957; in the entry on 'Brutalismus', Banham also reiterated the assonance between Peter's nickname and the definition of New Brutalism, in Pehnt (ed.), *Knaurs Lexikon der modernen Architektur*.
[50] Banham, *The New Brutalism: Ethic or Aesthetic?*, 10.
[51] Ibid., 47.

Because of its nature as an 'attitude' and 'programme', the original New Brutal-ism was presented by Banham as a concept in search of an aesthetic, which found its first counterpart in the Unité: 'Behind all aspects of the New Brutalism, in Britain and elsewhere, lay one undisputed architectural fact: the concrete-work of Le Corbusier's Unité in Marseille'.[52] *Béton brut* for the Smithsons coincided with the genesis of a 'new humanism'.[53] For Banham, it acted as an 'authority' capable of concretising the still unripe concepts formulated during the first phases of New Brutalism: 'If there is one single verbal formula that has made the concept of Brutalism admissible in most of the world's western languages, it is that Le Corbusier himself described that concrete-work as "béton brut"'.[54] It was neither the heroic scale nor the typological solutions that made the Unité a building that resolved the theoretical impasse of the 1950s, but precisely the treatment of the material, capable of overcoming the 'fiction' of the 1930s and 1940s, or rather the architecture of cladding. The Smithsons' primary interest in the treatment of materials, which they extended beyond exposed concrete, derives for Banham, as he had already pointed out in 1955, from the famous phrase taken from *Vers une architecture*, where Le Corbusier had established a link between 'brutal matter' and 'moving relations'. In presenting the debates on the one hand, and Le Corbusier's model on the other, Banham set the union of ethics and aesthetics as a decisive premise for interpreting the origins of New Brutalism, which implied the revival of the heroic course of the Modern Movement, identified in the return to the cult of material, which became the 'central ambition of Brutalism'.

If the book so far appears to be the result of a linear sequence of events, the dis-cussion about the School at Hunstanton, described as a 'surprising beginning', typi-fies Banham's attitude of reinterpreting architecture according to his own cultural pro-ject. The building takes on a significance other than the demonstration of a classical composition derived from Wittkower's diagrams and is now repositioned by Banham within the debates on the role of exposed materials and the value of truth. 'The first complete building to carry the title of "New Brutalist" was not Corbusian', Banham asserts, evoking the unresolved tension between the Lecorbuserian and Miesian mod-els that still posed a seemingly insoluble dilemma. While Johnson and Pevsner had identified the impossibility of ascribing the School at Hunstanton to New Brutalism, and even Joedicke and Pehnt had clearly placed Miesian perfectionism and Brutalist tendencies in opposition to each other, Banham, on the other hand, reiterated the positions expressed on various occasions between 1954 and 1963,[55] and framed the Miesian influence in the School at Hunstanton on the conceptual level of truth and the use of materials.

Thus, in confirming the all-British model in line with his cultural project, the School at Hunstanton becomes the apex of 'precise craftsmanship', in which the assembly of welded metal elements questions above all the nature of the materials: 'Welding was as natural to this concept of steelwork as it was shuttering to concrete'. Banham does not fail to insist on the consideration of the English construction tradi-tion expressed by the School at Hunstanton, to the point of bringing back an 'intense Englishness'. In the Smithsons' synthesis of the masters' legacy, Banham underlines a fundamental update of the principles of the Modern Movement, which responds to a generational need for a new 'image': 'The fusion of the Mies image with the Corb-image was an understandable, if philosophically reprehensible, step towards the

[52] Ibid., 16.
[53] Alison and Peter Smithson, 'Some Notes on Architecture', *244: Journal of the University of Manchester Architecture and Planning Society*, vol. 1 (Spring 1954): 4.
[54] Banham, *The New Brutalism: Ethic or Aesthetic?*, 16.
[55] [Reyner Banham], 'School at Hunstanton', *Architectural Review*, vol. 116, no. 693 (September 1954): 150–62; Pehnt (ed.), *Knaurs Lexikon der modernen Architektur*.

creation of the kind of single vision of a real and convincing architecture that this generations sought'.

The ambiguity of the first phase of New Brutalism, which led to a misunderstanding both for critics and architects, is retrospectively symptomatic for Banham of the simultaneous coexistence of different concepts related to that definition, in place since 1955 and all related to the activities of the Smithsons. In the book Banham attempts to intercept different orientations within New Brutalism, expressing parallel and sometimes conflicting trajectories. In order to clarify the nature of New Brutalism, he reconsiders the various experiences and puts forward new formulations that highlight three distinct moments: a 'rappel à l'ordre' of the founding principles of the Modern Movement, where 'order' is understood as a notion that is not classical but topological, as in the example of the University of Sheffield; a 'British pragmatism' found in examples ranging from the radicalism of the School at Hunstanton, to a revisited traditionalism in the projects for the 'Patio & Pavilion' installation and for Sugden House; and finally a purely intellectual attitude against aesthetic conventions that flowed into an 'aesthetically sophisticated body of opinion', fuelled by the debates generated by the collaborations with the London avant-garde artists, which found an important outcome in the exhibition *Parallel of Life and Art* and the House of the Future. Banham's observation of the coexistence of different forms of New Brutalism, however, demonstrates the impossibility of circumscribing New Brutalism within any exhaustive definition, including its chameleon-like manifestations, which are exaggerated by avant-garde stances and nostalgic returns to traditional principles. 'Often in the history of Brutalism,' Banham states, 'the attainment of an extreme position was followed by a withdrawal to a more traditional position'.

The three moments Banham identified in the trajectory of New Brutalism already belonged to history and had already proven their design outcomes. But during the writing of the book, Banham identified a fourth definition capable of updating New Brutalism through concepts and examples rooted in the culture of the 1960s. This would demonstrate the potential of that 'architecture autre' in which he had placed his hope since 1955, and which, in overcoming the very concepts of structure and space, found its ultimate outcome in the concept of a 'total environment'.

Beyond Brutalism: 'The Total Environment'

Banham's account of the origins of New Brutalism served to demonstrate his own cultural project, far removed from the mere affirmation of the truth of materials and structure. The book demonstrates how Banham had sought to infuse New Brutalism with values that transcended architecture itself, in accordance with a truth found in the manifestation of the mechanics of design. Indeed, Banham himself confessed his attempt to shift New Brutalism towards his own cultural aspirations, admitting that since the 1955 article he had tried to apply 'some of my own pet notions on the movement'.[56]

The chapters 'Progress to a-formalism' and 'Notes on *une architecture autre*' constitute Banham's theoretical manifesto, in which he prefigures possible operative outcomes for the evolution of New Brutalism, combining topological principles and a fantastic mechanicism. By reducing the expression of architecture to a manifestation of its intrinsic mechanism, of ducts and fluids, Banham heralds the subversion of traditional architectural elements. Banham returns to the concept of *une architecture autre* in order to put into crisis and deflagrate the second principle enunciated in his 1955 triad, the one referring to the 'clear exhibition of structure': '"une architecture

[56] Banham, *The New Brutalism: Ethic or Aesthetic?*, 134.

autre" ought also to have abandoned even the idea of structure and space – or rather, it ought to abandon the dominance of the idea that the prime function of an architect was to employ structure to make spaces'.[57]

The theoretical project outlined in *The New Brutalism: Ethic or Aesthetic?* consists in taking the concepts of 'topology', 'image' and 'as found' to their extreme consequences, overcoming 'structure' and 'space' in accordance with a notion of architecture reduced to the definition of 'environments for human activities and symbols of society's cultural objectives'.[58]

Starting with the examples of the Golden Lane and Sheffield, erected as conceptual bulwarks of a generation that rejected the compromises defended by Pevsner and the elite of the *Architectural Review*, Banham reiterates the liberating potential of 'a-formalism', aimed at overcoming not only geometry, but also the very concepts of structure and space. In 1955 Banham had already specified how topology constituted the decisive presupposition for an unprecedented compositional experimentation ascribed to *architecture autre*.[59] If in the Sheffield project Banham had pieced together the clues of a new form of architecture, in the book he goes so far as to indicate in the topology the presupposition of what New Brutalism could have generated: a visionary and 'wild' urban project, 'committed to technology' and free from preconceptions of form, populated by mechanisms generated by an assembly of circulatory systems, in which the very notions of perennial and temporary are radically questioned.

A series of new and decisive examples of avowedly *architecture autre* was now ascribed to New Brutalism, to the point of completely altering the homogeneous picture that Banham had attempted to draw from the fragments of the events of the 1950s (see figure 41). Banham counts among the significant works for *une architecture autre* the geodesic domes of Buckminster Fuller, the steel pylons of Cedric Price's Fun Palace, the 'formless' Friedrick Kiesler's Endless House and Herb Greene's Normann House. Only one example of the Smithsons was included, for its alteration of the conventional elements and typology subversion, the Sudgen House. The selected examples are demonstrations of Banham's attempt to broaden the horizon of New Brutalism, to free it from the technique of *béton brut*, and finally to orient it towards a project of flexible technology, freeing architecture both from composition and from a 'rappel à l'ordre' and even from the 'as found'. These examples, which constitute a new chapter in the grand narrative on New Brutalism, testify to Banham's attention to an evolving world, close to the contemporary pop phenomena of the 1960s. In fact, the chapter on a generic definition of *une architecture autre* was not fully resolved in the book on New Brutalism and was probably included to fulfil the commission given to him by Joedicke to investigate the potential future developments of the definition.

A further manifestation of this unprecedented vision of New Brutalism was the example of the drive-in cinema. This example had puzzled Joedicke but, in Banham's reasoning, turns out to be necessary in demonstrating the dilation and inclusion of new parameters in New Brutalism. The drive-in cinema was selected as the extreme outcome of an architecture 'entirely devoid of structural elements or enclosed volume', capable of becoming a 'powerful symbol' for nomadic scenarios freed from architectural conventions, in which configurations of possible 'human social activities' are staged.[60]

---

[57] Ibid., 68.
[58] Ibid.
[59] Banham specified what he means by a-formal; informal and formal: 'It will be observed that "formal" has two antonyms in this argument: "informal" and "A-formal". The meaning to be allocated to the three words in the context of the present argument can be crudely distinguished as follows – "Formal", symmetrically composed, or ordered by some other very explicit abstract geometrical discipline; "Informal", asymmetrical and subject to some less struct visual discipline (such as Picturesque composition); "A-formal", unconcerned with geometrical or visual compositional technique of any pre-conceived type', ibid., 41.
[60] Ibid.

41 Reyner Banham, "'Art brut", "non-art" und "art autre"', *Brutalismus in der Architektur*, pp. 60–61; 68–69

From this point of view, the exhibition *Parallel of Life and Art*, indicated as the 'locus classicus' of New Brutalism, takes on new relevance. The most subversive aspects of the disruption of composition, the fantastic 'juxtaposition' and the blurring of disciplinary boundaries had remained confined to the episode of the exhibition, without ever gathering sufficient force to radically influence architecture. Attention to the truth of structure and the nature of materials had counteracted the impetuousness of the revolutionary phenomena of *Parallel of Life and Art* in architecture. From that event, only the concept of 'as found' had safeguarded a possible incursion of vital and contemporary phenomena within the design project, which the pop architecture of the 1960s was then revealing internationally. In the 1966 book, that subversive component became crucial in defining a possible outcome of New Brutalism as an alternative to the Lecorbuserian school of exposed concrete.

According to Banham, only through the examples of Buckminster Fuller and Cedric Price could an architecture 'fundamentally "other"' be achieved, in which 'the structure is simply a means towards, the space merely a by-product of, the creation of an environment'.[61] The concept of 'environment', which Banham was investigating during 1965 in articles such as 'A Home Is Not a House',[62] is to be understood as the definition of space through the control of air, light and atmospheric agents according to the activities it inhabits. 'Endless, indeterminate and a-formal' are the characteristics of an environment that for Banham represented the ultimate aim of a mechanical and adaptable architecture, which would be more precisely theorised in the article 'A Clip-on Architecture'[63] and which in the book summarised the most subversive outcome of New Brutalism. Thus transfigured, Banham's *autre* New Brutalism was no longer about the truth of matter, symbolising the 'permanence' that the Smithsons themselves had noted first in brick and then in concrete, but was freed of any composition, emancipating architecture from any monumental 'massive structure', in virtue of a renewed dynamism and flexibility.

The intuition of a 'mechanistic Brutalism', which Banham had grasped while updating Sant'Elia's paper architecture in the mid-fifties, and which was enriched by his research on the first machine age,[64] had not been followed up in the 1955 article.[65] Although Banham did not take 'mechanistic Brutalism' literally in his 1966 book, this definition summed up his hopes for a new course for New Brutalism, where the mechanics of the plan is joined to a new 'machine aesthetic'.

Banham refocused the discourse not so much on those visions theorised in the 1950s, but on the various British experiments with metallic and elastic membranes, based on principles other than structure or space. In this re-elaboration of New Brutalism towards the foundation of an alternative system based on dynamic principles, the trajectory of international Brutalism linked to the question of *béton brut* underwent a total revision. That material, as employed and established in the 1960s, was associated with another strand of the many New Brutalisms with which Banham did not identify. In fact, at the time of the apogee of exposed reinforced concrete architecture, Banham tried to outline possible and different trajectories through which New Brutalism could still survive. His hypothesis of a New Brutalism remodelled in the search for a technological and mechanical 'environment', which would eventually generate the concept of Hi-Tech, was flanked by that of a New Brutalism as a generator of 'habitat'. This orientation presupposed the dissolution of the architectural scale, and already heralded, albeit in non-explicit forms, the great theme of the megastructure, which could even be read as a further chapter of Brutalism. The overcoming of the traditional elements of architecture, by virtue of a fluid mechanism that expands to the urban scale, was the reason why Banham included a chapter in the book on urban planning principles related to New Brutalism. It should be noted that the urban scale was unexpectedly ignored by Banham in his contributions on Brutalism during the 1960s. Now, however, the ethical instances at the base of New Brutalism are expressed through principles that determine 'the end of an old urbanism'.

The reasoning conducted on the various forms of 'habitat', among which Banham included such radical proposals as the project for Sheffield, Berlin Hauptstadt and Park Hill, but also more consolidated examples such as the Harumi Apartments, Van Eyck's orphanage and the Marchiondi Institute, revealed the further possibility of renewal of the traditional architecture in the direction of a 'total environment'. The

[61] Ibid., 69.
[62] Reyner Banham, François Dallegret, 'A Home Is Not a House', *Art in America*, vol. 2, no. 1 (April 1965): 70–79.
[63] Reyner Banham, 'A Clip-on Architecture', *Design Quarterly*, vol. 63 (1965): 2–30.
[64] Reyner Banham, 'Sant'Elia', *Architectural Review*, vol. 117, no. 701 (May 1955): 84–93.
[65] Reyner Banham, *Theory and Design in the First Machine Age* (London: Architectural Press, 1960).

case of the Marchiondi Institute, also identified as a 'habitat', was emblematic in this context, because it demonstrated the vitality of the original principles of the Modern Movement. That building, which Banham had defended and celebrated as one of the most 'uncompromisingly Brutalist' examples, was erected as a bulwark of 'unsentimental' architecture, in the Italian context marked by Neo-Liberty tendencies, and constituted 'one of the major surprises of European architecture in the late Fifties'.[66] Banham, through the Marchiondi, demonstrated the possibility of a radical actualisation of the principles of rationalism through the recovery not of a 'formal aesthetic', but of a 'functional ethic', thus criticising both Pedio, who had omitted the crucial historical reference to Terragni,[67] as well as Joedicke and Pevsner who had seen in that work the affirmation of a neo-historicist tendency.[68]

In the principles of appropriation, 'cluster' and finally a 'human environment', the theme of 'habitat' demonstrated that 'an original Brutalist ethic is realised in an original version of the Brutalist aesthetic'.[69] From the mechanistic components to the 'habitat', the 'formless' and the 'environment', various concepts were included by Banham through the series of examples in New Brutalism. That definition was then radically transformed through Banham's pen, becoming the starting point for the invention of new definitions, such as those of 'megastructure', 'clip-on', 'high-tech' and 'pop', which for the time remained silent within New Brutalism. Therefore, New Brutalism, by virtue of its roots deeply linked to the principles of the Modern Movement, produced a decisive evolution in the culture of the twentieth century and, through the new components enunciated in Banham's book, was able to assume the role of a bridge between two visions: that of the pioneers and a more subversive vision that would contribute to overcoming the Modern Movement itself.

Brutalist Style

The mechanistic potential would have only a marginal continuation in the trajectory of New Brutalism, whose evolution was marked by another orientation called 'Brutalist Style'. Banham was careful to indicate a clear separation between the mechanistic and urbanistic potential faithful to the ethical demands of New Brutalism, and the style that was consolidated from the essentially Lecorbuserian model of an architecture whose expression was left to exposed concrete:

> Somewhere in the process, what the English were doing had become separated from Brutalism as the world was coming to understand it. In common international usage, the word was shedding its urbanistic and technological overtones, and becoming narrowed to a stylistic label concerned largely with the treatment of building surfaces [...] such was the prestige of Le Corbusier's béton brut that the world was becoming convinced that this heroic material was 'specifically Brutalist' [...] it was Le Corbusier who stamped his personal style upon the word.[70]

Just as Banham had indicated a precise genealogy for New Brutalism, which, starting with Asplund's invention, led to the inclusion of concepts such as 'environment' and

[66] Banham, 'Brutalismus', in Pehnt (ed.), *Knaurs Lexikon der modernen Architektur*.
[67] Renato Pedio, 'Brutalismo in funzione di libertà. Il nuovo Istituto Marchiondi a Milano', *Architettura: Cronache e Storia*, vol. 3, no. 10 (February 1959): 682–88.
[68] Pevsner, 'Modern Architecture and the Historian – or the Return of Historicism'.
[69] Banham, *The New Brutalism: Ethic or Aesthetic?*, 131.
[70] Ibid., 75.

'habitat', so too was the Brutalist Style substantiated by an alternative genealogical reconstruction. For Banham, the Brutalist Style originated in a 'Proto-Brutalism', identified in the Lecorbuserian examples of the Petite Maison du Weekend of 1935, the project for the Sainte Baume and the Maison Fueter on Lake Constance. This genealogy served to frame the model of the Maisons Jaoul as the 'spiritual source'[71] of a trajectory that included a range of works from the Flats at Ham Common by Stirling and Gowan to the Siedlung Halen complex: 'They [Maisons Jaoul] "became" Brutalism. [...] The later history of the New Brutalism has much less to do with the theoretical propositions of the Smithsons than it has to do with the progress and permutations of the style invented by Le Corbusier'. For Banham, the Maisons Jaoul embodied the inclination towards 'violence and crudity carried by the word "brutal"', which the School at Hunstanton, with its 'too thin, too elegant' expression, had failed to represent.

The Maisons Jaoul became to all intents and purposes an exemplary case for the trajectory of Brutalism narrated by Banham (see figure 42). Its first publications in magazines generated an array of architects who spoke out against their inclusion among the ranks of Brutalist examples. Architects such as Lasdun and Stirling were careful not to use this definition and even warned that the Maisons Jaoul should not be classified.[72] Although Le Corbusier had already refused the definition of New Brutalism,[73] for Banham the Maisons Jaoul 'became the common standard by which the Brutalism of other buildings could be evaluated'. Banham used the same expression as Stirling – the 'surface depth' – to definitively ascribe the Maisons Jaoul to the Brutalist style: 'Brutalism as a going style proved to be largely a matter of surfaces derived from the Jaoul'. So for Banham, even the Flats at Ham Common, the work that had become an emblematic case in England for Stirling's rejection of the definition of New Brutalism, confirmed the existence of a real 'Brutalist canon', consisting of a 'simple repertoire of banal materials, chiefly wood and fair-faced brick'.

Banham described more precisely what he recognised as a true 'Brutalist Style', by listing variants of a formal repertoire, such as the 'bird-nesting boxes', 'gargoyles' and 'exposed concrete walling', to which he also added the 'inverted L windows' used by Stirling and Gowan in the Flats at Ham Common and the 'elevated walkways' derived from the Park Hill project. Previously, such considerations were limited to an analysis of the principles of plan axiality or to freeing the composition from rigid geometries by virtue of a-formalism. Now, perhaps influenced by Joedicke's extensive disquisition on composition,[74] Banham dwelt on the devices of juxtaposition of different programmes, on the mechanism of assembly, and finally on the expression of section: 'The peculiarities of the internal section are allowed to dictate the external appearance', he stated in the case of the annexes to the Old Vic Theatre in London.

The use of traditional compositional devices, neo-Picturesque planning principles, monumental proportions, or surfaces similar to wallpaper were all symptoms of a widespread Brutalist Style. For Banham it was therefore an opportunity to take stock of the ethos of early New Brutalism and the aesthetics of international Brutalism: 'Brutalism was tamed from a violent revolutionary outburst to a fashionable vernacular'. In describing the 'commercial vernacular' drift, which also found success in England, Banham used the acclaimed examples of the control tower at Gatwick Airport, Owen Luder's office-block Eros House, Churchill College and Sussex University by Basil Spence, Peter Moro's Hille showroom, and the residential complex at St. James Place by Lasdun. Even the building that Pevsner had associated with Brutalism,

[71] Ibid., 86.
[72] Denys Lasdun, 'France, Maisons Jaoul, Paris', *Architectural Design*, vol. 26, no. 3 (March 1956): 75–77; James Frazer Stirling, 'Garches to Jaoul', *Architectural Review*, vol. 118, no. 105 (September 1955): 145–51.
[73] [n.a.], 'Cinq questions à Le Corbusier', *Zodiac*, vol. 5 (1960): 46–51.
[74] Joedicke, 'New Brutalism: Brutalismus in der Architektur'.

LXXXVI

Was ist Brutalismus in der Architektur?

Que signifie «brutalisme en architecture»?

Erstens: der deutsche Titel des englischen Originals 'The New Brutalism'

Zweitens: eine Antwort auf die Frage (siehe oben).

Drittens: ein Buch mit 68 Seiten Text. Zum Lesen (obwohl Architekten nicht gerne lesen). Und mit 144 Seiten Bildern, Grundrissen undsoweiter (obwohl wir etwas gegen Bildbande haben).

Viertens: eine Herausforderung. An die heute übliche Fassadenkosmetik. Und an die phantasielosen, glatten,

unkünstlerischen Architekturen. An die Gedankenlosigkeit (die unsere Umwelt verunstaltet).

Fünftens: und vor allem ist es ein Buch von Reyner Banham ('Revolution der Architektur'; rde). Eine gültige Darstellung des Phänomens Brutalismus (in Wort und Bild). Eine der tonangebenden Bewegungen (eine Neuformulierung des ,béton brut' Le Corbusiers).
Architekten wie (zum Beispiel) die Smithsons, das Atelier 5, Mayekawa, Ungers, Rudolph, Kahn sind „Brutalisten" Sollte Ihnen gestern der

Brutalismus noch ein Buch mit sieben Siegeln gewesen sein – morgen ist das anders. Wenn Sie heute noch Ihren Buchhändler anrufen. Wegen Banhams Buch (mit neun Kapiteln). Oder ihm schreiben.

Sechstens: erscheint das Buch in Jürgen Joedickes Reihe ,Dokumente der Modernen Architektur' Im Karl Krämer Verlag * Stuttgart·Bern. Für 76.85 Franken.

 Viel Geld für Sie. Aber ein geringer Preis für eines der wichtigsten Bücher dieses Jahrzehnts.

the LCC's Alton West complex[75] became for Banham an opportunity to ridicule the Lecorbuserian features imported into the English language: 'Anglicised, the coarse, swaggering, patchy forms of Marseilles, become stiff, formal and elegant in the "little unités" of Roehampton'. Banham's indictment of these examples was the loss of ethical instances: 'Brutalism lost some of the moral fervour that had illuminated its earlier pretensions to be an ethic'.[76]

There are several epicentres identified by Banham for the Brutalist Style that document its extension and international success. The multiform spread of New Brutalism demonstrates its complexities and aporias, yet gives credence to Banham's intuition regarding the relevance of the English debates.

One of the central nuclei of the 'Brutalist Style' is identified in the 'Swiss School', a definition used to describe the works of Schnebli, Förderer, Otto, Zwimpfer, and Atelier 5. In the 'Swiss School', Banham saw the reiteration of Lecorbuserian motives, from which his greatest 'disappointments' derive, because it demonstrated the academic declination of New Brutalism and the reduction of the complexity of the phenomenon to 'just an affair of exposed concrete'.[77] The 'Swiss School' therefore ended

---

[75] Pevsner, 'Roehampton, LCC Housing and the Picturesque Tradition'.
[76] Banham, *The New Brutalism: Ethic or Aesthetic?*, 89.
[77] Reyner Banham, letter to Jürgen Joedicke, 5 December 1966, Krämer Verlag Archive, Stuttgart.

up representing, according to Banham, the 'excesses' of the 'Brutalist Style' in its most exasperated forms, ranging from the 'mannerism' of the Haus in Rothrist and the factory in Thun, both by Atelier 5, to an 'eclectic and historical approach' by Schnebli, and an 'extremism' recognised in the school in Aesch by Förderer, Otto and Zwimpfer, guilty of reducing architecture to a game of sculptural forms.[78]

The archetypal model of the Maisons Jaoul was the work that unveiled Banham's cultural strategy and determined the birth of the 'Hard cases: the Brick Brutalists', which included a varied series of examples, from the Maihaugen Museum of Sverre Fehn and Geir Grung, to the 'puritan aesthetic and a puritan ethic' of the churches of Figini and Pollini and of Broeck and Bakema, to the erudite expressionism of Ungers' house, up to the intellectual references of Colin Wilson and Alex Cardy in Cambridge. The formal, material, and expressive variations characteristic of the works discussed presented a problem of classification. They demonstrated the limits of Brutalism as a stylistic category, totally detached from its original 'revolutionary outburst', and extended to examples that went beyond the now consolidated repertoire of exposed concrete: 'There is no agreement as to external form, detailing or spatial aesthetics. [...] What they have in common is great erudition and sophistication, worn with a flourish, about the recent history of Modern Architecture'.

Sigurd Lewerentz's Markuskyra Church was Banham's 'most enigmatic' case. Everything about the composition, from the plan to the geometry regulating the volumes, to the spatiality obtained, contradicts the canons of Brutalism as understood by Banham. Nevertheless, he identified in the 'genuine informality' of the complex, especially in the curvilinear perimeter, a 'relaxed indifference to such concepts as "rectangle"'. This indifference for the regular form suggested parallels to the principle of the cluster developed by the Smithsons. The inclusion of Lewerentz's work was functional in demonstrating the Brutalism coined by Asplund in Sweden, which could have emerged 'anyhow, without any assistance at all from Le Corbusier, Louis Kahn or the British'. Banham was in fact careful to demonstrate how Smithson's theories were able to capture 'the mood of the time', and generational concerns beyond the disparity of projects in the international manifestations of Brutalism.[79]

The oscillations and uncertainties that transpire from the text, which sees Hunstanton's reinterpretation of a never-ending Englishness, the inclusion of a fantastic mechanicism of Fuller and Price and the fascination for certain buildings such as the Marchiondi Institute, demonstrate the damnation of that definition poised between truth and aesthetics. The subsequent protagonism of exposed concrete testifies to the unresolved dialogue between New Brutalism and *béton brut*, which still persists in the contemporary debate.

In the international phenomenon of the Brutalist Style, even the habitat was progressively reduced to 'purely visual images', through the reiteration of conventional devices, embodied in the primitivistic image of 'a building like a village'. From America to Japan, there are many examples that take up the traditional elements of the city, such as the square or the street, to re-exhume a 'mythology' of the 'Mediterranean way of life', such as Rudolph's boarding school for married students at Yale, Kikutake's residential complexes, up to the new forms of Japanese democracy conceived by Tange. 'Brutalism may make tremendous bold attempts to bring the automobile phenomenon under control, but in the last resort it is in order to recreate a pedestrian city', Banham says, noting the nostalgic return of vernacular references and traditional devices, unable in substance to subvert established ways of living.

---

[78] Banham, *The New Brutalism: Ethic or Aesthetic?*, 90.
[79] Ibid., 131.

Having identified different historical phases, and in pursuit of this historiographical construction, Banham selected examples to clarify a specific phase of New Brutalism. Just as Lewerentz's church served the purpose of demonstrating that New Brutalism had an international pretension, so too was a famous Swiss complex introduced as the apex of an equally international phenomenon identified in the 'Brutalist Style': the 'habitat' of Atelier 5's Siedlung Halen in Bern. Ascribed by Banham to the phase identified as 'High-period of concrete Brutalism', the Siedlung Halen demonstrates how an ethical impulse can be revived in the 'brut' and 'heroic' aesthetics of exposed concrete.

With the hope of meeting the book's critical interpretation, Albert Winkler's photograph of the Siedlung Halen towering above the trees was selected by Joedicke for the cover of the book. In the iconographic apparatus of the book, it was therefore the work of Atelier 5 that was chosen as the example that summed up the phenomenon of Brutalism. It was on the very choice of this image that the opinions of Joedicke and Banham diverged profoundly. In the Siedlung Halen, Joedicke presumably identified a possible synthesis between ethical impulses and aesthetic factors, functional to resolving the dilemma posed by Banham in the book's subtitle. The Siedlung Halen exemplified his effort to bringing the discourse back into the certainty of built architecture. Banham, on the other hand, was radically opposed to this choice, specifying to Krämer Verlag that the image 'does not seem to typify the content of the book'.[80] Banham's misgivings show that his vision of New Brutalism diverged from the example of the Swiss school of Lecorbuserian derivation, in which he saw the end of a phenomenon that had been consumed in a triumph of styles and in the various concrete finishes, and in which the technological mechanisms of design were replaced by a repertoire of traditional devices.

The Swiss attitude of resistance to any stylistic category was expressed in the response of the members of Atelier 5 to the request for images of the Siedlung Halen by the Krämer Verlag. Like other architects, including Carlin and Stirling, Atelier 5's choice of fair-faced concrete was based on the economy of the material and the financial constraints of the construction site, in which conceptualisations linked to the debates on Brutalism were completely absent:

> As for the New Brutalism book, we cannot get involved. Hence I ask you to take our buildings off the list. In our works, we hardly ever cared about the issue of Brutalism. Even if the buildings might suggest it, the reasons are elsewhere, in limited building costs which dictate the choice of material.[81]

Following their inclusion in the historiographic construction of Brutalism, Atelier 5 clarified their position in a typewritten document entitled 'Sichtbeton', which demonstrates how exposed concrete, beyond any style, corresponded to a radicalism linked to pure construction, confirming once again the concept of rationalism that permeated the material:

> The terms beauty and clarity are related to one another. A condition for clarity in construction is visibility of construction. To judge whether a house is good or bad, you want to know how it is done. Exposed concrete is therefore not the name for a special surface treatment, but is visible concrete construction.[82]

[80] Raymond Philp, jacket for book *The New Brutalism*, letter to Nora von Mühlendahl, 25 August 1966, Krämer Verlag Archive, Stuttgart.
[81] Rolf Hesterberg, letter to Heinz Krehl, 18 December 1964, Krämer Verlag Archive, Stuttgart.
[82] Atelier 5, 'Sichtbeton', untitled typescript document, 19 November 1968, Atelier 5 archive, Bern, (1–2), 1.

Atelier 5's reasoning on monolithism, the value of the memory of the casting phases, the transformation of the surface over time and on the nature of liquid material, which can be moulded at will, converged in a vision that was always brought within the limits of an economic principle: 'The restrictions come from the economy: with as little material and formwork as simple as possible'.[83]

The Economist Building vs. Leicester University

For Banham, the phenomenon of Brutalism ended in the aporia of the dilemma posed by the book's subtitle. In attempting to provide an answer to the symbolic battle between ethics and aesthetics, Banham could not help but admit with disappointment that, by the end of the 1960s, Brutalism had been consumed with the reiteration of the Lecorbuserian model or the return of traditional devices. In spite of his heroic attempt, through the concepts of 'environment' and 'habitat', to trigger possible scenarios of development, in order not to make the ethics of New Brutalism fall into a style, in the end Banham could not but draw up a harsh appraisal of the phenomenon that he himself contributed to create:

> Brutalism, having run for ten years or more – which is [a] fair age for an '-ism' in the present century – had achieved the consummation that awaits all movements which accurately pinpoint real needs and aspirations of their period and social context. They do not achieve the dominance for which their founders hoped, but instead they 'melt into the history of their time', so that one can hardly imagine what the world could have been like before Brutalism came upon the scene.[84]

Among the various contributions that Banham attributed to New Brutalism, the only one remaining was ethics, the bulwark erected against the conservative ideology of left-wing values that Banham continued to consider retrograde: 'The face of the world does not conform to the Brutalist aesthetic, but the conscience of the world's architecture has been permanently enriched by the Brutalist ethic'.

'Memoirs of a Survivor' is the iconic title of the last chapter of the book, which constitutes Banham's farewell to the phenomenon of New Brutalism: 'As I write this "envoi", it is very clear that the biggest and most important fact about [the] British contribution is that it is over [...] the recent works of Stirling and Gowan or the Smithsons, show far less urgency of ethic or aesthetic than in the late fifties'.

One work marked, according to Banham, the symbolic end of the hopes of New Brutalism: the Smithsons' Economist Building. With its 'tender' traits it demonstrated the recovery of tradition, the incursion of theories of the Picturesque and the acceptance of an architecture for the establishment. The subversive and irreverent dimension of the origins of New Brutalism was assuaged in the perspectives for the Economist Building drawn by the theorist of Townscape, Gordon Cullen. Since the initial publication of the project for the Economist, divergent voices had been raised, with Banham on the one hand reading a possible continuity of New Brutalism in the topological organisation of the complex[85] and Pevsner on the other, distinguishing the building from the 'quirks of that trend'.[86]

[83] Ibid.
[84] Banham, *The New Brutalism: Ethic or Aesthetic?*, 133.
[85] Banham, 'Brutalismus', in Pehnt (ed.), *Knaurs Lexikon der modernen Architektur*; Reyner Banham, 'Apropos the Smithsons', *New Statesman*, 8 September 1961, 317.
[86] Nikolaus Pevsner, Brutalism, *The Penguin Dictionary of Architecture* (London: Penguin Books, 1966).

   It was only at the end of the Economist, completed in late 1964, that Banham
voiced a bitter criticism of the protagonists of New Brutalism:

>   The Smithsons' Economist building […] is a work of restudied restraint. It
>   may offer a vision of a new community structure, but it does so upon the
>   basis of an ancient Greek acropolis plan, and […] it handles the street idea
>   very tenderly indeed. Far from being an example of an 'other' architecture,
>   this is a craftmanly exercise within the great tradition.[87]

Disappointed by the retreat into tradition of a possible movement that did not man-
age to become the 'architecture autre' he had hoped for, quickly settling down into
a series of stylistic rules devoid of ethical stances, Banham admitted its failure: 'The
process of watching a movement in gestation was also a disappointment in the end.
For all its brave talk of an "ethic, not an aesthetic", Brutalism never quite broke out of
the aesthetic frame of reference'.
   The book closes with an enigmatic building, not only because of its ascription to
New Brutalism, but because Banham still saw in it an echo of the 1950s revolt that
inspired the origin of New Brutalism: Stirling and Gowan's Faculty of Engineering for
Leicester University, the only English example in which the shadow of the Lecorbuserian model had totally disappeared: '[Leicester University] comes nearer to Brutalism
in the emotional sense of a rough, tough building, and in the dramatic space-play of
its sectional organisation it carries still something of the aggressive informality of the
mood of the fifties' (see figure 43).
   The decision to close the book on New Brutalism with the work of Stirling and
Gowan must be read as a continuation of the debate with Pevsner on historicism. In
1964, Banham celebrated the work as 'a pretty extraordinary piece of contemporary
architecture'.[88] 'It combines extremism (its geometry) with reasonableness (its plan);
a strong personal vision with objectivity (about the site); aesthetic determination with
the ability to exploit happy accidents'. The use of glazing, the same patented for green-
houses and factories, demonstrates an 'unaffectedly crude' use of materials, and makes
a radical return to the principle of the 'as-found' topical, at a time when 'Brutalism has
been screwed up into the kinkiest school of elegance that architecture affords', probably referring to Smithson's Economist Building. Against the accusations of historicism
that Stirling's work might raise, and that Pevsner himself would confirm, Banham
pointed out the important legacy of the masters reinterpreted in a contemporary key
by Stirling and Gowan:

>   History and style don't bother men like these anymore; both are disen-
>   chanted with the 'white architecture of the '30s', which they regard as little
>   more than a styling gimmick. Yet, as everybody notices, the Leicester labs
>   are the first design for decades that has anything of the zip, clarity, and
>   freshness, the nonchalance, of the pioneer machine-aesthetic buildings of
>   the 1920s. It's as though they had invented modern architecture all over
>   again, and one can only wish that other architects would have the wit,
>   sophistication, sense, taste, bloody-mindedness – and in a word, character –
>   to do it, too.[89]

---

[87] Banham, *The New Brutalism: Ethic or Aesthetic?*, 134.
[88] Reyner Banham, 'The Word in Britain: Character', *Architectural Forum*, vol. 121, nos. 2–3 (August 1964): 118–
      25.
[89] Ibid., 124.

43 The Smithsons'
Economist vs. Stirling's
Leicester University,
Reyner Banham,
'Memoiren eines
Beteiligen', *Brutalismus
in der Architektur*,
pp. 190–91

Banham's 1964 commentary recalled, through the words of 'bloody-mindedness', 'nonchalance' and 'straightforwardness', the interpretation of New Brutalism that he had theorised in 1955, confirming the perseverance of the original spirit. The concurrence of the Economist Building and the Leicester University Engineering Faculty provides a direct comparison between what the ethos of New Brutalism promised and the aesthetics that resulted, between its potential and the disillusionment of what it had become.

Banham gave the definition of New Brutalism the arduous task of having represented, perhaps for the last time in the history of the Modern Movement, the ambitious relationship between ethics and aesthetics, the definition of form as a manifestation of an uncompromising attitude towards truth and honesty, and a re-actualisation of the principles of the pioneers; these principles would be radically challenged through a profound critique of New Brutalism, which would in turn open the doors to a new phase in the history of architecture: Post-Brutalism or Post-Modern.[90]

---

[90] The definition of Post-Brutalism would be used by Jencks several times to indicate the advent of what would be theorised as Post-Modern, for example in Charles Jencks, 'The Rise of Post-Modern Architecture', *Architectural Association Quarterly*, vol. 7, no. 4 (October/December 1975): 3–14.

chapter eight
the sad end
of new brutalism

Pevsner and the Anti-Pioneers

The publication of *The New Brutalism: Ethic or Aesthetic?* provoked immediate reactions, including contributions from those involved in the events and debates. The 'partisan' and autobiographical line running through Banham's book raised heated criticism about a definition that still generated stances that reaffirmed its 'provocative nature', even though it was becoming an indispensable critical tool.

Despite Banham's efforts to resolve its uncertainties, New Brutalism remained characterised by an underlying indefiniteness. The ambiguities that existed since its origins, justified by the Smithsons through the processual and evolutionary nature of New Brutalism, derived from a series of insoluble polemics, triggered by the desire to meet a generational aspiration to oppose to the architecture of the Softs. The various attempts to distance New Brutalism from accusations of nostalgia and historicism, and from the memorable image and aesthetics of *béton brut*, inevitably succumbed to a series of inconsistencies that even a skilled writer such as Banham could not resolve. All the debates on New Brutalism seem to demonstrate a lack, a void that the critics were unable to fill.

Not even Banham's book, with its accumulation of data, examples, information, and first-person accounts, managed to extrapolate a definite and 'legitimate meaning'. Even by integrating Banham's book with the comments and reviews of the leading protagonists, such as the Smithsons, one finds it impossible to arrive at a summary, or even an agreement on the basic intentions of New Brutalism and its ambivalent alterego, International Brutalism.

In the ongoing exchange between critics and architects, however potentially fruitful, one cannot help but notice how the contradictions and ambiguities of New Brutalism exceeded its very scope, to the point that its fate raised further questions. Are those contradictions intrinsic to all labels, or do they demonstrate the inability of both the Smithsons and Banham to make a 'new theory' explicit? Can New Brutalism be seen as the moment of resolution of 'Anxious Modernism' or was it merely a symptom of it?[1]

---

[1]   On the notion of 'anxious modernism', see Sarah Williams Goldhagen, Réjean Legault (eds.), *Anxious Modernism: Experimentation in Postwar Architectural Culture* (Montreal/Cambridge, MA: MIT Press, 2000).

What potential architectural trend has remained unexpressed and lies behind the theories of New Brutalism? And again, was the phenomenon of *béton brut* really a vital component or did it in fact contribute to its deflagration?

The convoluted trajectory of New Brutalism demonstrates the impossibility of translating the complexities of the profound changes of the 1950s and 1960s into a coherent synthesis. This is confirmed by the fact that New Brutalism ends up being constrained within a single interpretation which, however reductive, seems to be the only foothold that has allowed it to survive and transcend British borders: the certainty of *béton brut*.

In this sense, Pevsner's immediate reaction to the book is one that rids the debate of intellectualisation, seen as an obstacle to the search for clarifying principles. Relying on the fundamental root of the term, Pevsner articulated his arguments around what Brutalism, independently of Banham or the Smithsons, was demonstrating. Prompted by the scathing remarks directed at him by Banham, who saw him as the authority the new generation had to reject, Pevsner wrote his direct response to the book in the pages of *The Guardian*, a few days after Architectural Press released the English volume.[2]

Pevsner's vision of New Brutalism discredited not only the Smithsons, but also the entire theoretical framework that Banham had endeavoured to explain. For Pevsner, there was only one 'undisputable' certainty behind any logic of New Brutalism: the post-war work of Le Corbusier and the Townscape theories promoted by *Architectural Review*. For Pevsner, this was the only coherent trajectory, to the extent that he proposed a different genealogy of New Brutalism, one that ignored its Swedish origins, the internal debates within the LCC and even the role of the Smithsons:

> One should for the sake of definition rather start from 'brutal' than from what the term meant to Hans Asplund and Oliver Cox. [...] No: Brutalism started with Le Corbusier's Unité of 1948 and La Sainte Baume of 1948, and the Maison Jaoul of 1954. It culminated at Chandigarh. [...] Even the term Brutalism as pertinent to the 1950s and 1960s has probably more to do with béton brut as Le Corbusier boasted to use it, than with Dr. Banham's history.

'Dr. Banham takes his Brutalism seriously', joked Pevsner, who restricted Brutalism to the expression of exposed concrete. Le Corbusier was pronounced guilty of materialising a style Pevsner considered deeply disappointing: 'Brutalist architecture, then, is the architecture of béton brut, that is, of concrete exposed in large chunky masses and left rough so as to avoid all conventional beauty of surface'. The root 'brutal' allowed Pevsner to underline the violence linked to that adjective: 'Brutal is overpowering by sheer (brute) force-bashing, not stabbing. The bully is brutal, the hooligan is brutal'. To delegitimise the definition Pevsner pointed to the impossibility of ascribing the School at Hunstanton to New Brutalism in virtue of its deeply Miesian roots: 'Mies is radical but never brutal. [...] The School at Hunstanton has nothing to do with Brutalism, however the Smithsons may personally have been involved with the term'.

The origin of New Brutalism exclusively linked to the discovery of *béton brut* would persist in Pevsner's comments. When questioned by historian Marcus Whiffen about the origins of New Brutalism, Pevsner reiterated his divergence from the narrative set out in Banham's 1966 book: 'Banham's derivation of Brutalism is arrant non-sense. The term comes a) from 'beton brut' and b) from brutality'.[3] In order to

---

[2] Nikolaus Pevsner, 'Brutalism', *The Guardian*, 9 December 1966, 7.
[3] Nikolaus Pevsner, letter to Whiffen, 3 December 1969, 'Nikolaus Pevsner Miscellaneous Papers, Correspondence', Box 5, Folder Box 6, Folder 9, Correspondence 1966–1969, The Getty Research Institute, Los Angeles, USA.

understand Pevsner's view of New Brutalism, it is necessary to refer to the considerations expressed in his *Dictionary of Architecture*, published in the same year as
Banham's book, where the entry 'Brutalism' is included.[4] Pevsner differentiated two
trajectories in contemporary architecture, one anchored in the vision of the 1920s
and 1930s defined as 'international modern', and another which he associated with
tendencies towards a 'new individualism and expressionism and brutalism'. As in his
1961 lecture on historicism, Pevsner reduced Brutalism to a phenomenon of 'revival'
and a retrograde historicism deviating from the experiences of 'his' pioneers. This is
made even clearer when some of the buildings defined as Brutalist at the time, such as
those by Lasdun, Martin, Sheppard and Spence, are listed under the headings 'Greek
Revival' and 'Neo-gothic architecture'.[5] In a similar parallelism to that advanced by
Johnson and Pehnt, Pevsner indicated Brutalism's cultural root in the style of Expressionism.[6] Within the dictionary, the entry Brutalism recurs several times, whether to
indicate 'the use of salient balconies and rough concrete surfacing' of Maekawa's
Harumi Apartments, or the 'curiously dramatic and indeed aggressive' ventilation
towers of Kahn's Medical Research Building, or the machined concrete of Rudolph's
Art and Architecture Building at Yale which 'unmistakably belongs to the trend'. The
Flats at Ham Common were also a symptom of the passing 'new trend influenced by
Le Corbusier and often called Brutalism [...] They have a ruthlessness which militates
against their achieving a more than passing success'.[7]

As for the inventors of the term, the Smithsons, Pevsner devoted a dictionary
entry to them in which Brutalism was reduced to a temporary parenthesis within the
body of their work. For Pevsner, neither the 'controversial' School at Hunstanton nor
the building for the Economist in London could be ascribed to that 'quirky trend'.[8]

Banham's book can be considered a counter-history to Pevsner's *Pioneers*, after
the acclaimed example of *Theory and Design in the First Machine Age*. This is also testified by the considerations Pevsner made in a BBC broadcast with the emblematic
title 'Architecture of Our Time – The Anti-Pioneers'.[9] In taking stock of the success and
relevance of his *Pioneers*, Pevsner admitted that the ongoing revision process was initiated by Banham himself: 'Reyner Banham – my pupil, I am glad and puzzled to say
– was the first to cast doubts on it and to speak of a conspiracy of silence'.

The profound disenchantment provoked by the manifestations of contemporary
architecture, which could be summed up by the definition championed by his 'pupil'
Banham, pushed Pevsner to outline a trajectory parallel and antithetical to his Pioneers: 'What we are experiencing now is a new style completely, an anti-Pioneers style,
if my pioneers are still valid, and a style alarmingly harking back in many different,
even contradictory, ways to Art Nouveau and to Expressionism'.[10]

Pevsner's harsh criticism of Le Corbusier reveals his disagreement with Brutalism, which had become synonymous with contemporary taste. 'Brutalism has been
used to mean much, too much', he said, characterising the Anti-Pioneers, to whom
he entrusted a role diametrically opposed to his principles, and who were none other
than those architects 'in flat contradiction to the corpus of criteria to which I was committed when I wrote my Pioneers, and to which I am still committed'.

4   Nikolaus Pevsner, *The Penguin Dictionary of Architecture* (London: Penguin Books, 1966).
5   Nikolaus Pevsner, handwritten notes for the entry 'Brutalism', Nikolaus Pevsner, Miscellaneous Papers, Series II:
    Writings and Lectures, Box 12, 2003 M.34, The Getty Research Institute, Los Angeles, USA.
6   Pevsner, *The Penguin Dictionary of Architecture*, 160.
7   Ibid., 484.
8   Nikolaus Pevsner, *The Buildings of England, North and South Norfolk* (London: Penguin Books, 1962), 69; 215.
9   Pevsner's lecture was broadcast by the BBC on 3 December 1966. A summary of the broadcast can be found
    in Nikolaus Pevsner, 'The Anti-Pioneers', *Architects' Journal*, vol. 145, no. 5 (February 1967): 279–80. The full
    transcript appears in Stephen Games (ed.), *Pevsner: The Complete Broadcast Talks Architecture and Art on Radio
    and Television, 1945–1977* (Farnham: Ashgate, 2014), 474–84.
10 Pevsner, 'The Anti-Pioneers'.

The evocation of the origins of the 'Anti-Pioneers' in the wake of the phenomena of Art Nouveau and Expressionism served to deeply mark his distance from Brutalism. The examples evoked to demonstrate the axis of the 'Anti-Pioneers' included architects that were already ascribed to the origins of Brutalism, such as Gaudí and Häring with their 'rough angular forms, of rubble or of brick, and set at all kinds of nightmarish angles or its roughly drop-shaped windows and its ambiguity of what is inside and what is outside the building'. Thus, the recourse to Art Nouveau and Expressionism becomes the parameter for listing formal traits of Brutalism: 'Piers not straight but leaning or rather swaying and windows of odd shapes, [...] exaggeratedly massive concrete balcony railings and demonstrative brick cubes sticking up or out'. The return of Art Nouveau and expressionist traits was for Pevsner a problematic return, visible in three issues: 'One, self-expression of the artist-architect; two, a fervent avoidance of lightness, of anything that could be called elegant and also of anything that could be accounted for purely rationally, and three, forms of overpowering – what shall I say – yes: brutality'. Pevsner harshly criticised contemporary architecture for its tendency towards a 'randomness' in the use of architectural elements, which he attributed to architects' totally 'personal' and self-referential taste.[11]

As a final confirmation of Neo-Expressionist traits in Brutalism, Pevsner cited the Engineering Building at Leicester University by Stirling and Gowan. This choice cannot sound as a coincidence, for that building testified, for Banham, to the relevance of the fervour of early New Brutalism, entrusted to the very last pages of his book. For Pevsner, the presence of the diagonal ramps and the 'aggressive angularity' of certain 'curious prisms' find no functional justification: 'They are purely expressional and as such additional cost'. Pevsner declared himself 'irritated' by this alternative and opposing line to the pioneers and announced the brief fate to which New Brutalism would be condemned: 'Phases of so excessively high a pitch of stimulation can't last. We can't, in the long run, live our day-to-day lives in the midst of explosions'.[12]

New Brutalism's Obituary

Pevsner's criticism only fuelled the 'case' opened by Banham's book. The international debates on Brutalism prompted critics to review *The New Brutalism: Ethic or Aesthetic?* in major architectural journals as well as general culture magazines. Banham had taken care to compile a list of journals to review the book, including *Architectural Review*, *Architects' Journal*, *Architectural Design* and the *RIBA Journal*, but also more generalist periodicals such as the *New Statesman*, *New Society* and the *Observer*.[13] The reception of the book is recorded in all the major European and American magazines, and critics rapidly began commenting on the book's 'omissions' or 'incongruities', while continuing to raise doubts about the specificity of Brutalism, its origins and whether the examples collected could be filed under a single, universal definition. Through the analysis of the reviews of Banham's book, two critical strands can be outlined: one that distinguished New Brutalism as a phenomenon belonging exclusively to the Smithson's attitudes, and another as a trajectory linked to the discovery of *béton brut*. Ethics and aesthetics were thus the parameters along which international critics were divided. The main appraisal levelled at Banham's book was its partiality. Only the indications of a 'basic architecture', a definition put forward by the Smithsons in December 1953, seem to dispel the doubts of a criticism that was otherwise confused

[11] Ibid.
[12] Ibid.
[13] Reyner Banham, letter to Karl Krämer, 26 September 1966, Krämer Verlag Archive, Stuttgart.

by the various possible New Brutalisms.[14] Critics focused on the aporias of Banham's narrative, on his inability to explain the lack of coherence, the 'ruthless integrity and social intent' of a phenomenon 'à la mode'.[15] Brutalism did not seem able to defend its motto 'shock the bourgeoisie', and the collection of its varied examples turned it into the subject for a 'coffee-table book'.[16]

Robin Middleton, a friend of the Smithsons and a colleague of Banham's during his doctoral years with Pevsner, circumscribed New Brutalism to a phenomenon linked to a circle of friends, summarising the connections, events and relationships that, in his eyes, led to its origin: 'The New Brutalism was essentially a private movement – a Smithson movement. What they said and did matters, not what connotation the term Brutalism has been given in uninformed quarters'.[17] The affinities among the different buildings collected in the book on the basis of the use of a specific material, exposed concrete or bricks, only exacerbate the inconsistencies of a definition that ended up becoming synonymous with 'odder anomalies', of which Banham alone was the 'banner bearer'. The complex relationship between criticism and practice, of which the whole phenomenon of Brutalism is irrefutable proof, did not go unnoticed to Middleton: 'I propose that second period modern theory and practice is like a delta: and in architecture where streams of theory certainly exist (Smithsons, Kahn), critics hysterically try and tack all sorts of literal built statements on to it'.[18] Only in the light of individual obsessions it would be possible to understand the coherence that the critics were unable to grasp, busy as they were with outlining through Brutalism the signs of a style to come. 'Concepts' and not 'forms' are the keys around which the Smithsons' entire research should be framed, which Middleton summed up as 'fragments', 'arrangements' and 'connections'. If read along these lines, a coherent *fil rouge* emerges between references that are sometimes disparate, such as the Eames, Aalto, Wittkower or Le Corbusier, pop art and Mies. The principle of 'as found' emerges as the key to understanding the Smithsons' obsessions and their practice of 'selecting and arranging', and thus also the ultimate meaning of New Brutalism. Middleton's account anticipated some of the more recent interpretations that have emerged since the 2000s, when critics have finally had the courage to review the phenomenon of Brutalism in all its conceptual complexities, beyond the aesthetics of exposed concrete.[19]

By virtue of its 'British account', the review of Banham's book became, for other critics such as Tentori, a pretext for rereading the English events of the 1950s and for measuring the Smithsons' contribution to international culture.[20] Despite their limited output of paper architecture, the mutual support between theorists, critics and architects led to an intense debate that marked an 'extraordinarily exciting period for the evolution of ideas'. In the pages of *Zodiac*, which produced a pivotal moment for the trajectory of New Brutalism, Tentori reconstructed and documented, through an anthology of the main articles, the English events of New Brutalism.[21] Tentori's was clearly intended to be a 'restrictive' interpretation of New Brutalism, in an attempt to circumscribe Banham's 'extensive' reading of New Brutalism, which made it a

14 Silvia Kruger, 'Reyner Banham. Brutalismus in der Architektur. Ethik oder Ästhetik?', *DU: die Zeitschrift der Kultur*, vol. 27, no. 5 (May 1967): 410, 412.
15 Robin Middleton, 'The New Brutalism or a Clean, Well-lighted Place', *Architectural Design*, vol. 37, no. 1 (January 1967): 718.
16 Alison Adburgham, 'Brutalism a la mode', *Harper's Bazaar*, vol. 75, no. 5 (May 1967): 86.
17 Middleton, 'The New Brutalism or a Clean, Well-lighted Place'.
18 Robin Middleton, *Architectural Design*, vol. 35, no. 12 (December 1965).
19 See, for example, the interpretations of Dirk van den Heuvel, *Alison and Peter Smithson: A Brutalist Story, Involving the House, the City and the Everyday (Plus a Couple of Other Things)* (Delft: TU Delft, 2013); Laurent Stalder, '"New Brutalism", "Topology" and "Image": Some Remarks on the Architectural Debates in England Around 1950', *The Journal of Architecture*, vol. 13, no. 3 (2008): 263–81; Irénée Scalbert, '*Architecture as a Way of Life: The New Brutalism 1953–1956*', http://team10online.org/research/papers/delft1/scalbert.pdf.
20 Francesco Tentori, 'Phoenix Brutalism', *Zodiac*, vol. 18 (1968): 31–41.
21 Francesco Tentori, 'English Brutalism: Selection of Writings', *Zodiac*, vol. 18 (1968): 42–50.

definition that 'can accommodate almost anything'. Tentori went so far as to identifying New Brutalism exclusively with 'Banham himself or the two Smithsons'. However, he detected a subtle tension between Banham and the Smithsons: 'I don't know how willing the Smithsons are to accept the rough sharing that Banham imposes on the NB. [...] But I do know that the exchange was fruitful, in both senses, for both criticism and architectural composition'.

The expansion of New Brutalism presented by Banham through his wide range of examples, in the eyes of critics was deeply enigmatic and incoherent, and confirmed the idea of Brutalism as an 'omnivorous' definition, consumed by its own success. Banham's book represents the epitaph of a movement that was stretched to encompass a general 'catalogue of the architecture of the fifties and sixties'.[22] 'The trouble with Brutalism is that it is both too lonely and too diffuse', says Joseph Rykwert, ridiculing as 'naughty and silly' the effort to trace its history as an epic narrative of the 'battle' between a movement and a style, of which Banham was the lonely standard bearer of an incoherent doctrine based on sporadic paper projects: 'It tries to get him to believe – against the evidence of the photographic plates which accompany the text – that the work of these architects is of world-shaking significance'. For Rykwert, Banham's book demonstrated nothing more than an improper use of history, turned into a partisan narrative to conceal the absence of a coherent line, in which not even ethics could be summed up in comprehensible principles. Certainly, Pevsner's historiographical tradition was in the background to Banham's book, to the extent that Rykwert alluded to the *Pioneers* noting Banham's emphasis on describing the phases of New Brutalism: 'Dr. Reyner Banham finds it necessary to cast his narrative in an epic form modelled on those historical writings which deal with the early times of the "modern movement"'.[23]

Banham's rhetorical emphasis on the 'rebellious spirit' of English New Brutalism hurled against the decline of the Modern Movement, despite his attempts to demonstrate that 'the impact of this one regional phenomenon was world-wide', ended up as a 'timid oblique view of an episode in the life of the Smithsons'. This bitter comment is from Boyd, who had carefully followed the trajectory of New Brutalism since its origins.[24] Despite the wide range of examples demonstrating a 'diversity of visual style', Banham condemned New Brutalism to the aporia of a circle that began and ended with the Smithsons: 'One is led finally to the suspicion that the aesthetic of New Brutalism can be found in anything that was built by Alison and Peter Smithson or in anything that in Dr. Banham's opinion looks as if it might have been built by Alison and Peter Smithson'. A vague 'undefinition' runs through it, right from its very subtitle, which testifies to Banham's basic indecision about New Brutalism. For Boyd, New Brutalism's inability to fully succeed demonstrates the inapplicability of the moral principles summarised in the idea of a 'basic architecture', free of aesthetic preconceptions. That 'basic architecture' succumbs, according to Boyd, to the reality of built architecture, which must respond to the client, the context and, finally, the available materials. Banham's book thus summarises the failures of a 'paper architecture' constraint into a narrative 'of outstanding architectural talent frustrated or frozen by social conditions'. It is no longer the clash between the integrity of an ethic and the superficial drifts of an aesthetic, but the ideal of an imagined architecture set against the reality of construction. Although Banham had traced an apparently glorious history of British affairs, for Boyd, 'the book leaves behind a wistful, almost haunting sense of sadness', as he summarised in the significant title of his review, 'The Sad End

[22] Joseph Rykwert, 'Banham-Gregotti', *Domus*, no. 451 (June 1967): 2–6.
[23] Ibid.
[24] Robin Boyd, 'The Sad End of New Brutalism', *Architectural Review*, vol. 142 (1967): 9–11.

of New Brutalism', which became a veritable obituary: 'The author finally kills it [Brutalism] with his own hand on page 134 in the year 1964'.[25]

The fading trend of Brutalism, soon to be replaced by another, was foreseen by Colin Rowe. Having remained silent on the New Brutalism debate during the 1950s and 1960s, despite being called on to contribute multiple times, Rowe had not spoken publicly about New Brutalism, merely sharing his scepticism with Kahn in the letter about Banham's article.[26] In 1967, Rowe orchestrated a double review that, in the evolution of architectural history, appears prophetic. In a blurb entitled 'Waiting for Utopia', Rowe parallels Venturi's *Complexity and Contradiction in Architecture* with Banham's *The New Brutalism: Ethic or Aesthetic?*[27] The juxtaposition of Venturi and Banham was not accidental, and in the review, Rowe confessed his intentions to predict the impending clash between Brutalism and Post-Modernism:

> Connoisseurs of the ironical might extract considerable satisfaction from the simultaneous appearance of these two overtly unlike but intrinsically related offerings; the two attitudes they disclose represent the polar extremes between which architecture now oscillates.

For Rowe, New Brutalism marked the end of an era, of which Banham's book constitutes the sad 'obituary notice'. However, Rowe could not fail to profoundly criticise what was then emerging with Venturi's theory, which undermined objectivity and construction in favour of an architecture of form and symbols.[28] At this point, the debate that would soon mark the end of the trajectory of New Brutalism had already been outlined, as well as the clash that would see the promoters of 'truth' succumb to a new vision of architecture as symbol and form.

The Old Brutalism

The declared end of New Brutalism was not enough to interrupt critics' research into its origins, usually with the aim of discrediting its novelty, following a line inaugurated by Segal as early as 1954. The whole debate that followed Banham's book, which saw the reduction of this definition to the 'catalogue' of works in *béton brut* on the one hand, and solely to the Smithsons' theories on the other, witnessed the incursion of a historian who advanced a further perspective: Peter Collins. By demonstrating a genealogy that from Butterfield culminated in Perret's architecture, Collins re-read the events of Brutalism to reinforce its root in the expression of *béton brut*. All the debates that during the 1960s were extending the definition of New Brutalism to the urban scale were silenced by the primordial question of materials.

The publication of *Changing Ideals in Modern Architecture* was an opportunity for Collins to search for historical antecedents, going so far as to reread issues of Brutalism in light of a 'romantic aesthetic' that looked nostalgically at the pioneering works of Butterfield, Fergusson or Perret. In the references cited by Collins it is not difficult to discern his criticism of an architecture for an imaginary 'machine age' which Banham had derived from a technological and mechanistic expression. The manipulation of formwork for an additional 'artificial roughness' as in the

---

[25] Ibid.
[26] The letter is quoted in Braden R. Engel, 'The Badger of Muck and Brass', *AA Files*, vol. 62 (2011): 95–98
[27] Colin Rowe, 'Waiting for Utopia', *The New York Times*, 10 September 1967, 351.
[28] 'It is likewise constructable as an epitaph in advance for any such attitudes as those which Venturi propounds [...] if he feels himself obliged to condemn the Brutalists for their "esthetic" rather than "ethical" propensities, then he would feel much more disposed to condemn Venturi, who deliberately attempts to exclude "ethical" considerations and in no way tries to dissimulate his interest in form as such', ibid.

international trend of 1960s Brutalism could not be more distant for Collins from the 'technological' ideal.[29]

What Collins excluded from his argument was the New Brutalism according to the theories proposed by the Smithsons. It was instead the phenomenon of International Brutalism, crystallised in massive exposed concrete architecture, that was targeted. When Collins delved into a critique of Brutalism, he used a series of adjectives, such as 'ugliness' and 'manliness expression', which allowed him to relate it to the 'brutal design' ascribed to the works of William Butterfield, James Fergusson or William Burges, which act as deviant examples of a 'Gothic Rationalism'.[30] Butterfield, first called into question by Banham in his demonstration of the radicality and 'ruthlessness' of the School at Hunstanton,[31] and later by Summerson when demonstrating the 'Englishness' of New Brutalism,[32] was now taken up by Collins to demonstrate a 'perverted aspect of Eclecticism', where the taste for raw surfaces and the expression of structure exhumed 'sublime and picturesque' traits.

The notions of anti-art and 'ugliness', which had characterised Banham's interpretation of New Brutalism since *Parallel of Life and Art*, became for Collins, through the Butterfield and Furness's 'Ugly Style', demonstrations of a precise attitude rejecting academic canons and challenging the practice of critics who evaluated works on the basis of moral criteria such as 'good and bad'. It seems almost paradoxical that Collins traced the antecedents of Brutalism, which can be interpreted as a critical success, to a moment in history, the second half of the nineteenth century, that caused a profound break between the research of architects and the ability of critics to interpret those new trajectories.

In preparation for his review of Banham's book, significantly titled *Neo-Butterfield*, Collins carefully reviewed the main articles on New Brutalism, annotating excerpts from Smithson's and Banham's articles and reviewing the debate generated by the School at Hunstanton.[33] In the article, Collins summarised the phenomenon of New Brutalism as a 'short-lived, and hence relatively minor, architectural "movement"'.[34] Collins controversially declared New Brutalism to be a 'publicist' phenomenon, swallowed up by critics, which did not allow them to understand the reality of the works in question, as in the case of the School at Hunstanton. This building is exemplary for Collins of the mechanisms of criticism, focussing on Wittkowerian influences or the clash of the Lecorbuserian and Miesian models, in which all the polemical interpretations prevented the school from being understood beyond the debates it generated.

The arguments about surface treatment and 'crudeness' of most the examples in Banham's book led Collins to propose another decisive ancestry of Brutalism that no other critic had previously noted: Perret's concrete. In a lecture with the contentious title 'The New Brutalism of the 1920s',[35] Collins described the *béton brut* of Perret's

---

[29] Peter Collins, *Changing Ideals in Modern Architecture, 1750–1950* (London/Montreal: McGill University Press, 1965), 252.

[30] 'Today, the ideals of Gothic Rationalism assert themselves most clearly in a fondness for structural acrobatics and in a delight in rough surfaces. Just as in 1862 Fergusson demanded that the doors in dwellings should be of plain deal and that the timbers of the drawing-room ceiling should be "exposed, rudely squared, with the bolts and screws all shown", so the so-called New Brutalists today demand that concrete shall be poured into rough formwork, rather than into formwork with its surfaces in any way refined', ibid., 217.

[31] [Reyner Banham], 'School at Hunstanton', *Architectural Review*, vol. 116, no. 693 (September 1954): 150–62.

[32] John Summerson, *45–55 Ten Years of British Architecture* (London: Arts Council, 1956).

[33] Peter Collins, undated, untitled notes made in connection with the review of Banham's book, Peter Collins Collection, McGill University, Montreal, CAC 64: 016 007 Articles for Publication, box 016.

[34] Peter Collins, 'Neo-Butterfield. The New Brutalism: Ethic or Aesthetic (Reyner Banham)', *Progressive Architecture*, vol. 48, no. 3 (March 1967): 198–202.

[35] Peter Collins, 'The New Brutalism of the 1920s', typescript prepared for the Annual Meeting of the Society of Architectural Historians, 1974, Peter Collins Collection, McGill University, Montreal, CAC 64: 016 007 Articles for Publication, box 017, folder 006, 1–12. Excerpt published in *Concrete: The Vision of a New Architecture* (Montreal: McGill-Queen University Press, 2004), 315–40; 'The New Brutalism of the 1920s: The Effect of Economic Restraints at Notre Dame du Raincy', *SAH Journal*, vol. 33 (October 1974): 233–40.

church at Le Raincy: 'The crudeness of the surfaces (which has an indisputable affinity with what after World War II, was called "The New Brutalism")'. The hypothesis of Perret's influence on the phenomenon of Brutalism had already been indicated by Collins through the iconic image of the interiors of the Yale Art Gallery at the end of his monograph on Perret, *Concrete: The Vision of a New Architecture.*[36] Banham had chosen that building to announce the advent of New Brutalism to 'the new world' in 1955, through a retroactive operation to substantiate the moment of the origins of New Brutalism. Collins, on the other hand, framed the Yale Art Gallery as the final outcome of the pioneering French experiences of the mid-nineteenth century. It should be noted that Banham, in his review of Collins's book on Perret emphasised the limitations of Perret's use of concrete, which was confined to the classic beam-post system not fully explored in all its possible plastic configurations. Banham's review highlighted Collins's conservative conception of concrete architecture.[37]

Through the reciprocal reviews, a long-distance polemic emerged between Banham and Collins on the ascendancy of Brutalism and on the difference between Perret's and Le Corbusier's *béton brut*, revealing important stances on the cultural reception of that material. Collins praised Perret's choice not to retouch concrete after dismantling as an experimental and conscious intention, whereas Le Corbusier had to accept it as an a-posteriori choice, as the outcome of uncontrollable processes. Hence, he could not disagree more with Banham, who framed Le Corbusier's desire to use the technique of *béton brut* to deny an earlier view that concrete was a 'precise, machine-age material'. In Perret, Collins witnessed the synthesis of Brutalism's hesitation between ethic and aesthetic. In the Old Brutalism at Le Raincy economy and technology allied to exalt 'the most beautiful, the hardest, the most durable of those building materials which were considered, in former times, to be precious […] It was the tenacity with which he clung to such moral values as these which made "architectural theory", for him, more of an ethic than an aesthetic'. [38]

The Smithsons' Answer to Banham: Robin Hood Gardens

The undisputed protagonists of New Brutalism, the Smithsons, rushed to give their version of the facts a few days after the publication of the English edition of Banham's book. They contacted the editorial staff of *Architects' Journal*, the only weekly English architecture magazine, to write an extensive commentary entitled 'Banham's Bumper Book on Brutalism'.[39] The title immediately foreshadowed the clash between Banham and the Smithsons, present in the debates since the origin of New Brutalism.

The Smithsons recognised themselves as protagonists in the events narrated by Banham, and their commentary revealed their resentment at Banham's 'elusive' attitude, as they had already complained in response to Krämer Verlag's request for images of their projects. Although *The New Brutalism: Ethic or Aesthetic?* deploys a typical New Art History narrative, the outcome for the Smithsons was wholly unsatisfactory, starting with Banham's own method of document selection and presentation. For them, Banham's was nothing more than an 'instant history' written by a 'war correspondent' who relied on memory alone to reconstruct the events for which the protagonists were still active, 'with their wounds half healed, their minds still fresh,

[36] Peter Collins, *Concrete. The Vision of a New Architecture: A Study of Auguste Perret and His Precursors* (London: Faber and Faber, 1959). See also the introduction to the second edition of Collins's book, Réjean Legault, 'Introduction', in Peter Collins, *Concrete. The Vision of a New Architecture*, XXI–LX.
[37] Reyner Banham, 'The Perret Ascendancy', *Architectural Review*, vol. 127, no. 759 (June 1960): 373–80.
[38] Collins, 'The New Brutalism of the 1920s', 8.
[39] Alison and Peter Smithson, 'Banham's Bumper Book on Brutalism, discussed by Alison and Peter Smithson', *Architects' Journal*, vol. 144, no. 26 (December 1966): 1590–91.

and their archive in excellent order'.[40] It is evident that for the Smithsons, the book on New Brutalism could have been the occasion for a definitive historical account based on documents and interviews with the protagonists, while, in their eyes, Banham's book appeared to be a self-referential statement. The absence of a historical dimension pushed the Smithsons to consider Banham's book a biographical collection, compiled from fragmentary reconstructions and uncertain sources. Significantly, *The New Brutalism: Ethic or Aesthetic?* was referred to as 'Vasari's Lives, not a Domesday book',[41] in reference to a book that had been crucial for English historiography and had become synonymous with the authority of a definitive account based on the collection of documents.[42]

The Smithsons' commentary on Banham's book, however, constitutes a document that is only partially useful for understanding their vision of New Brutalism, whose fundamental principles, as usual in their case, were only tangentially addressed. In fact, the Smithsons merely went through Banham's text noting corrections and clarifications, through a bullet list of comments referring to specific pages of the book. Indeed, the article was admittedly written 'to be read with the book in hand', confirming their resentment at being excluded from writing on a subject they had brought to the fore.[43] The critical annotations to Banham's book thus appeared as a defence in court, drafted on the basis of a powerful impulse to clarify certain moments by resorting not only to their memory, but also to the documents in their possession. The Smithsons entered the debate on the origin of the definition, with the intention of reactivating their role as protagonists. Compared to Banham's reconstruction, through which they were discredited as mere 'users' of a definition already in circulation, their commentary decrees the invention of the definition by Alison Smithson in December 1953. 'The piece was initialled A.M.S. in typescript, but this was mistranscribed, in error or as an anti-feminist editorial gesture, as P.D.S. [...] "New Brutalism" was a spontaneous invention by A.M.S. as a word play counter-ploy to the *Architectural Review's* New Empiricism'.[44]

To confirm the Smithsons as unquestioned authors of New Brutalism, it may be recalled that at the very beginning of 1966, even before the book came out, they had returned to the subject at the urging of the editor of the Architectural Association's magazine *Arena*. On that occasion they pointed out that the absence of such a definition had already been widely discussed: 'The phrase "New Brutalism" was actually invented while we were writing this text for the Soho House. We had never heard it before'.[45]

In their commentary on Banham's book, the Smithsons recalled the article entitled 'Radiant City Lawsuit. Complaint of Brutal Realism', published in *The Times* in December 1952, preserved in their archives.[46] In confirming their invention of New Brutalism from the Unité in Marseilles, the Smithsons substantiated Banham's stance

---

[40] Ibid.

[41] This clarification is contained in another unpublished document: Alison and Peter Smithson, 'Bold Brute Bottled by the Man Banham', 1 December 1966, manuscript for an article rejected by the *New Statesman* which 'was not sure of the effect a "send-up" of the Banham style' would have, Alison and Peter Smithson Special Collection, Loeb Library, Harvard University, Cambridge, USA, folder E034.

[42] The Domesday Book is a manuscript containing the results of a large census completed in England in 1086, with the aim of quantifying the property of each owner. The valuations and estimates of the book's compilers were considered law and therefore unappealable, and the Domesday Book became synonymous with an authoritative and official text.

[43] Smithson, 'Banham's Bumper Book on Brutalism', 1590.

[44] Ibid.

[45] Alison and Peter Smithson, in Jeremy Baker, 'A Smithson File', *Arena, Architectural Association Journal*, vol. 82 (February 1966): 183.

[46] About that affair they wrote: 'The "brutal" part was taken from a French paper of a Marseilles official's attack on the Unité in construction, which described the building as "brutal"', in Smithson, 'Banham's Bumper Book on Brutalism', 1590.

that *béton brut* was the 'undisputed architectural fact' underlying New Brutalism.[47] The Smithsons ignored Asplund's role, as well as the autobiographical hypothesis linked to Peter Smithson's appellation 'Brutus' and even the internal debates within the LCC, where the definition of New Brutalism was already in use before 1953. In doing so, they contrasted Banham's complex genealogy with their unequivocal role as the leading actors from which it all originated. Where Banham discussed the origins of New Brutalism, the Smithsons pointed out: 'The people and events described on p10 were not known to this detachment'. In this exchange between 'combatants' and 'survivors', between mnemonic reconstructions and archival documents (which are in fact very rare), the Smithsons omitted to mention De Maré's letter published in *Architectural Review* certifying Asplund's invention, also kept in their archives, as well as their public admission of the Swedish origin of New Brutalism in *Byggmästaren* in 1955.[48] If one takes these coincidences into account, it is evident that the Smithsons' reconstruction was also instrumental and 'partisan', at least as much as Banham's, and promoted by other 'war correspondents'. But after all, this was precisely what New Brutalism was about.

The whole attitude underlying the article, together with the Smithsons' substantial silence on the issues of New Brutalism between 1959 and 1966, may lead one to deduce the exhaustion of New Brutalism's operative potential. Their comments, all retrospective, suggest that New Brutalism had become an accomplished phenomenon to be relegated to history, circumscribed to a precise chronological arc yet to be historicised, as they would have expected from Banham: 'Let there be no doubt, there *was* a movement, a sense of certainty about what to do, as far as we were concerned, shared at its most intense by the hard-core Team X, from 1953 to around 1963'. Through the Team X connection, the Smithsons seemed to be revealing a still unexpressed theoretical nucleus. The shift of New Brutalism towards the dimension of 'town building' had in Banham's book not significantly emerged. Thus, by matching the phenomenon of New Brutalism with the experiences of Team X and with their most intense period of theoretical reflections,[49] they consolidated the essence of that definition in 'town building'.[50] It was no longer the use of materials, nor even the revitalisation of the principles of the Modern Movement that were at the centre of the Smithsons' concerns. More than half of their response to Banham's book was in fact articulated around the genealogy of their 'street thinking', against the background of references ranging from anthropology to literature and from sociology to the history of cinema.[51] For them, the evolution of New Brutalism from materials to 'town building' demonstrated how the generational need for a new urban vision 'was in the *Zeitgeist*'.

Even their 'street-deck' principle, which Banham had interpreted as a 'subservient' attitude towards Le Corbusier and his *rue interieur*, was elected by the Smithsons as the quintessence of architecture's social dimension, to the point of defining it as the 'generator of the architectural schema'. The return to the principle of the 'street deck', present since the competition for Golden Lane, reiterated the persistence of the search for that 'new order', initially sought through the free associations of *Parallel of Life and Art*, or again through the inversion of the programme for the House in Soho, or in the topological assemblage of Sheffield. It is precisely the 'new order' intuited in

---

[47] 'Banham is marvellous on Le Corbusier', the Smithsons specify, 'and conveys the feel of his influence – especially during the building period of the Unité with great accuracy', in ibid.

[48] Alison and Peter Smithson, 'En ny engelsk skola', *Byggmästaren*, vol. 34, no. A6 (June 1955): 159–62.

[49] The collection of Team X texts, which constitutes its theoretical manifesto, was published in 1962. Alison Smithson, *Team 10 Primer. 1953–1962* (London: Standard Catalogue Co, 1962).

[50] Alison and Peter Smithson, 'Conversation on Brutalism', *Zodiac*, vol. 4 (April 1959): 73–81.

[51] The Smithsons cite novels such as Jack Common's *Kiddar's Luck*, Alan Lomax's *Mister Jelly Roll* and the works of Gwyn Thomas; documentaries and films such as *Bicycle Thieves*; and the photographs at Bethnal Green by Judith and Nigel Henderson; in Alison and Peter Smithson, 'Banham's Bumper Book on Brutalism'.

Pollock's canvases that was now related to another master of the Modern Movement: Aalto, whose absence was referred to as 'the biggest omission' in Banham's book. As early as 1955, the Smithsons had noted in the example of Aalto the evidence of a new order capable of translating the complexity of the relationship between individuals and community.[52] In the open, fluid and expressive forms of the Baker House, the Smithsons had found the essence of the New Humanism that they had been seeking since 1954, which became an alternative even to Le Corbusier's *béton brut*.[53] This very example reflected the primordial values of 'une architecture autre': 'It [Baker House] occupies the position in architecture that Pollock does in painting, and is probably the first true Brutalist building'.[54]

From Scully to Boyd and from Joedicke to Pehnt, several critics had recognised Aalto's dormitory as a precursor to the concerns expressed by the Smithsons' generation.[55] Banham's omission can only provide clues to his own vision of New Brutalism. Aalto's work appeared to Banham as being overly contaminated by a vernacular and sophisticated tone and a 'sentimental' materiality[56] to match his aspiration for a mechanistic New Brutalism. Instead, in the example of Aalto, the Smithsons identified an 'un-theoretical, non-revolutionary, un-heroic' model.[57] In this 'un-heroic' attitude they were at last able to identify the very legacy of New Brutalism, which over the course of the 1960s, from the heroic Lecorbuserian model, from an architecture and a spirit of revolt, settled down in the values of 'ordinariness' and 'common sense values'.[58]

When read through the exchanges between Banham and the Smithsons, the attempt to define and theorise New Brutalism evolved in step with contemporary concerns and revealed a trajectory in which critics and architects repeatedly chased and distanced themselves. The Smithsons' insights, which had immediately raised critical doubts because of their incoherence, had somehow benefited from the solid theoretical framework drawn up by Banham. Without Banham's intervention, the definition of New Brutalism would never have had the strength to go beyond the restricted circle of *Architectural Design*'s loyal readership and establish itself in international debates. Yet Banham, for his part, had repeatedly tried to divert the principles of New Brutalism towards his own interests, going so far in the book as to direct that *architecture autre* towards mechanistic and technological concerns, to the point that the Smithsons found it hard to identify with the definition they claim to have invented. To overcome the confusion generated by the heterogeneity of their design proposals, the Smithsons attempted to circumscribe the phenomenon of New Brutalism to the theoretical coherence of the urban and social scale, renewed through the model of the alternative rationalism of the Baker House.

[52] Alison Smithson, 'New Brutalism', 7 March 1955, Alison and Peter Smithson Special Collection, Loeb Library, Harvard University, Cambridge, USA, E009; Alison Smithson and Peter Smithson, 'The Built World: Urban Reidentification', *Architectural Design*, vol. 25, no. 6 (June 1955): 185–87.

[53] In 1954, the Smithsons declared: 'In the *béton brut* of the Unité a new human architecture has been born. Technique is seen once more as a tool: the machine as means. A new humanism has been born', in Alison and Peter Smithson, 'Some Notes on Architecture', *244: Journal of the University of Manchester Architecture and Planning Society*, vol. 1 (Spring 1954): 4.

[54] Smithson, 'Banham's Bumper Book on Brutalism', 1591.

[55] Robin Boyd, 'The Counter-Revolution in Architecture', *Harper's Magazine*, vol. 219, no. 1312 (September 1959): 40–48; Vincent Scully, *Modern Architecture* (New York: George Braziller, 1961); Wolfgang Pehnt, 'Was ist Brutalismus? Zur Architekturgeschichte des letzten Jahrfünfts', *Das Kunstwerk*, vol. 14, no. 3 (March 1960): 14–23; Jürgen Joedicke, 'New Brutalism: Brutalismus in der Architektur', *Bauen+Wohnen*, vol. 18, no. 11 (November 1964): 421–25.

[56] Reyner Banham, *Age of the Masters: A Personal View of Modern Architecture* (London: Harper & Row, 1975), 136.

[57] Peter Smithson, 'Alvar Aalto and the Ethos of the Second Generation', *ARK. Arkkitehti*, vol. 47, nos. 7–8 (July 1967): 21.

[58] Ibid.

The international trajectory of the style of Brutalism exemplified by the wide range of works presented in Banham's book, despite their Lecorbuserian common root, was for the Smithsons totally unrelated to their understanding of New Brutalism. The examples that Banham celebrated as positive manifestations of an international Brutalist style were harshly criticised by the Smithsons, who branded Lewerentz's graceful forms as 'Pre-Raphaelite', and even the Marchiondi in their eyes was 'just an old-style-ugly-building-in-a-field, to everyone except Banham'.[59] The harsh attack on Viganò or Lewerentz was probably motivated by the sharp criticism against the Economist complex, which in the book had definitively ended the trajectory of New Brutalism because it was unable to respond to Banham's own vision of *une architecture autre*.

The international outcome of Brutalism, visible in 'rough and crude' forms, contradicted what the Smithsons had specified as the essence of New Brutalism: a 'direct' construction which entailed both fidelity to the nature of materials and the – possibly urban – principle of a specific response to the specific case, as they confessed at the beginning of 1966: 'Brutalist to us meant "Direct": to others it came to be a synonym for rough, crude, oversized and using beams three times thicker than necessary. Brutalism was opposite, necessary to suit the new situation, like Kahn's work at Yale. That wasn't rough or crude or oversized'.[60] Again, Banham's insights of December 1955 were evoked by the Smithsons in their reference to the Yale Art Gallery.

The predominance in Banham's discourse of an architecture reduced to its mechanical functioning appeared in the eyes of the Smithsons to be a distortion of New Brutalism, to the point that they clearly stated: 'The people in this book are not in any way involved with technology as mystique'. The sentence contains within it the fear of technology being taken as the unquestioned bulwark of architectural, becoming an end in itself, with the consequent overshadowing of ethical and social aspects. As early as 1954, the Smithsons had stressed the importance of a certain independence of design with respect to technology.[61] In their vision of a New Brutalism as 'primarily an idea', the Smithsons limited the input of technology to being at the service of 'dynamic social ambitions and attitudes'.[62]

During the construction of the Economist, the Smithsons had also acknowledged a decisive change in their approach to technology, which concerned in particular the need to find principles for its calculated inclusion: 'Thinking about the Economist Building, we have become aware that a logical shift has taken place in our attitude towards mechanicals and services'.[63] The juxtaposition and selection of varied objects and images that the Smithsons had defined as an 'Eames Aesthetic' was here called into question for the treatment of services as well, specifying the need for a precise selection of technological or pop elements, infused with 'symbolism' by virtue of a precise and specific 'arrangement'.[64]

---

[59] Smithson, 'Banham's Bumper Book on Brutalism', 1591.

[60] Baker, 'A Smithson File', 183.

[61] In his response to a questionnaire developed by Carnegie Mellon students, Smithson specified that architecture should not be a 'byproduct of technology'. Marian Z. Augustyniak, Fred T. Entwistle, *Survey of the New Brutalism*, Department of Architecture, Carnegie Institute of Technology, Pittsburgh, Pennsylvania, 1957. See also Smithson, 'Some Notes on Architecture', 4, where they state: 'Technique is seen once more as a tool: the machine as means'.

[62] Smithson, 'Banham's Bumper Book on Brutalism', 1591.

[63] Alison and Peter Smithson, 'Concealment and Display: Meditations on Braun', *Architectural Design*, vol. 36, no. 7 (July 1966): 362–63.

[64] 'The select and arrange technique which we have used in the designing and equipping at our own houses and which we regard as a valid technique for the organisation of services and mechanicals in building when they can be known about in detail and entrained into the design process. [...] Design techniques for pop objects and appliances assume that they will be used where there are no other similar objects – the transistor radio used on a picnic on the road's edge, the Colston-type washing-up machine in the appliance-free kitchen. In these situations their symbolism can speak', in ibid.

This particular understanding of technology, which had nonetheless been a fundamental component of New Brutalism since the exposed services at the School at Hunstanton, had been supported by an important reference for the Smithsons since 1955: the automobile. In the conclusion of their commentary on Banham's book, which decreed the victory of the aesthetics of *béton brut* over the ethics of New Brutalism, the Smithsons summed up an emblematic definition, which excluded from the discourse any stylistic, formal or material reference: 'Those who still cannot see what Brutalism is about should consider this: the E type Jaguar, the Jeep, the Deux Chevaux and the DS19 are all Brutalist cars'.[65]

The models mentioned, from the Jaguar E, discussed by Peter Smithson in an article in 1965,[66] to the DS19, to which Alison Smithson would devote a book,[67] are to be linked to a complex conceptual and symbolic system ranging from mass consumer goods to industrial production and the dimension of the city based on connectivity and mobility. The reference to the automobile had become an obsession for the Smithsons over the years, symptomatic of the potential of consumer goods to transform not only lifestyles, but also the configuration of domestic and urban space, into what they had defined as 'the appliance way of life'.[68] Universalism and uniqueness come together in the example of car production, where each component is carefully designed for its specific function: 'It is a single clearly designed each part-specially-developed object'.[69] The car models become a vivid and emblematic conceptual support for the vision of an architecture that finds its raison d'être in 'completeness, uniqueness, precision of response to place, and satisfaction of need', as Peter Smithson states about the Jaguar E.[70] The reference to the car is hence crucial in reiterating the principle of a case-specific response, which appears to be the only true definition present and unchanging since the origins of New Brutalism.[71]

The Smithsons did not only draft a written response in which they summarised their visions of New Brutalism. In 1966 they started working on a project that could also be seen as another demonstration of a possible extreme outcome of New Brutalism as an intrinsic expression of 'town building': the Robin Hood Gardens residential complex. The main actors of New Brutalism thus found themselves side by side once again, on the one hand Banham, who took the opportunity to seal off his own personal account through a book, and on the other hand the Smithsons, who would make a clear statement on New Brutalism through a building in which all the discussions and themes put forward over the course of a decade would converge.

In virtue of the chronological coincidence, Robin Hood Gardens could be interpreted as a revenge on Banham's book by the Smithsons, ousted from the phenomenon of international Brutalism. But it was also through Robin Hood Gardens that the Smithsons finally succeeded in giving a concrete and coherent configuration to New

[65] Smithson, 'Banham's Bumper Book on Brutalism', 1591.
[66] Peter Smithson, 'The Rocket: A Statement on the Present State of Architecture, Giving a Certain Rationality to Our Instinctive Judgements on It', *Architectural Design* (1965): 322–23.
[67] Alison Smithson, *AS in DS: An Eye on the Road* (Delft: Delft University Press, 1983). In Alison Smithson's novel, *A Portrait of the Female Mind as a Young Girl* (1966), the Cadillac is mentioned several times.
[68] See the chapter 'Vehicles of Desire', in M. Christine Boyer, *Not Quite Architecture: Writing Around Alison and Peter Smithson* (Cambridge, MA: MIT Press, 2017), 195–228.
[69] Smithson, 'The Rocket: A Statement on the Present State of Architecture'.
[70] 'For example, the "E-type" Jaguar appears to be modelled in some universal material – certainly the actual materials and the machinery are not overtly displayed. Such buildings which have been carried to an equivalent level of the logic of their own development, for example 900 Lake Shore Drive (on the outside), Union Carbide (on the Inside), are "designed" to a point of refinement entirely missed by a popular taste which assumes them to be routine catalogue stuff, when they are in fact unique and one-off', in ibid.
[71] 'Today we are in a period where in many cases there is no longer an economic argument in favour of using mass-produced building components – we can machine-produce exactly what we want even for small runs – and we may soon be in a period when there will no longer be a social argument. [...] As far as architecture is concerned this new situation will knock the lynch-pin out of the "only acceptable components are the mass-produced components" argument', in ibid.

Brutalism, after theoretical hesitations had led to a series of incongruences. Robin Hood Gardens is the Smithsons' constructed testament to New Brutalism, compensating for the incongruity of their writings and in which the enigma of the Miesian model of the School at Hunstanton, the Lecorbuserian interpretations of Golden Lane, the pop drifts of House of the Future or the picturesque compromises of the Economist were resolved in the coherence of a 'brutalist' project from every point of view, even if no longer 'new'. It is difficult not to grasp in the forms of Robin Hood Gardens – and their similarity to the 1950s Golden Lane – the same nostalgic vein that aroused Smithsons's criticism of the Marchiondi Institute.

Nonetheless, the theories of New Brutalism are made explicit in Robin Hood Gardens through the principles of 'town building', through an organism that participates in the urban form through principles of identity, relationship and mobility: the two slabs are traversed by the movement of circulation, flexing to interweave these connections and to define a 'space in between' as the fulcrum of the project. The two buildings also bear the consequences of the Smithsons' research on the re-actualisation of the Unité in Marseille which had obsessed them since the competition for Golden Lane, against the background of the debates within the LCC and the principles for reconstruction.

The concern for social issues, fomented also by the *Architectural Review* and by the criticism that in England had invested the Unité, found its configuration and application also in virtue of the 'un-heroic' example of Aalto's Baker House, which acted as the previous model of a building deformed by the manifestation of circulation. Aalto's example, which emerged strongly in the commentary on Banham's book, was thus decisive in its understanding and demonstration of the possibility of *une architecture autre* capable of translating the example of Pollock's Action Painting into a series of slabs that shape a new topography, through a composition that goes beyond that of traditional rationalism. In the integration of the analysis of the urban fabric, in the definition of a new landscape and finally in the organism that flexes and expands through new connections, the Smithsons assumed an 'un-revolutionary, un-heroic' posture, giving meaning to the adjective 'new' in the definition of New Brutalism, understood as an overcoming of the Lecorbuserian matrix. By updating the Unité model in the perspective of the 'town building' based on a principle of unity and relationship, even the materiality of concrete undergoes an important alteration. In the early stages of the project, the Smithsons envisaged a building made entirely of *béton brut*. However, in December 1966, on the suggestion of Arup's engineers, they opted for a mixed system involving prefabricated elements for the residential parts and a cast structure for the communal areas. The vitalism that the Smithsons had infused into their vision of materials was revived through the terminology used to describe the various parts of building, referred to as 'head, neck, joints and tail'.[72]

Robin Hood Gardens is not only a re-actualisation of the Lecorbuserian model, but also of the Miesian aesthetic, which since the School at Hunstanton had been relegated to an enigmatic ancestor of New Brutalism. The series of regular, non-load-bearing mullions that punctuate the façades, installed as an acoustic device, and made using plastic-coated formwork, demonstrate the Smithsons' obsession with polished, perfect concrete, not the 'brutal realism' employed in Marseilles. Peter Smithson was personally responsible for checking the quality of the concrete and the homogeneous finish, requiring the contractor to carry out several tests, which ended up delaying the

[72] 'These terms have been adopted as the plan of the block resembles a jointed worm', in, Frank Allum, 'Job No. 1903 – Robin Hood Lane, Tower Hamlets, London, E14', *Arup Newsletter Supplement*, no. 33 (May 1969), quoted in Alejandra Albuerne, 'Robin Hood Gardens: Reinforced Concrete Design and Construction of a Museum Artefact in Reinforced Concrete', in James W. P. Campbell (ed.), *Iron, Steel and Buildings. Studies in the History of Construction. Proceedings of the Seventh Conference of the Construction History Society*, Cambridge, 2020, (612–624), 613. Over the complex history of Robin Hood Gardens see Nicholas Thoburn, *Brutalism as Found. Housing, Form, and Crisis and Robin Hood Gardens*, (London: Goldsmiths Press, 2022).

completion of the work. The mullions, which seem to have been designed on the basis of the perfection of the metal profiles in Mies's works, are far from the 'brut' aesthetics of the international Brutalism and were an 'extremely complicated' part of the project, as Arup engineer Frank Allum recalled. Robin Hood Gardens is therefore an only apparently ordinary building. Instead, it contains within it the Smithsons' pressing concern for the perfection and uniqueness that they had included in the definition of New Brutalism through the parallel with cars.

Thus, if one reads in the example of Robin Hood Gardens the apex and closure of the phenomenon of New Brutalism, the conflict between the Miesian and Lecorbuserian models was resolved in a coherent and reciprocal contamination, in which converged all the complexities that the Smithsons tried to suggest through the laborious elaboration of the definition of New Brutalism, ranging from the role of technology, the vision of materials, the technical perfection of the modes of manufacture identified in the reference to cars, and the 'town building'. All the debates about the meaning of New Brutalism, and ultimately Banham's stance expressed in the book, can therefore be seen as an incentive for the Smithsons to approach the building in a critical and 'uncompromised' manner and, consequently, to consciously demonstrate the principles of New Brutalism.

The Smithsons would continue to reiterate their distance from the style of international Brutalism and also identify Banham as an accomplice in a widespread distortion of their definition, which for the Smithsons continued to be something else entirely: 'New Brutalism had not much to do with the Brutalism that popularly became lumped into the style outlined in Reyner Banham's The New Brutalism'.[73]

This is why they felt the urge to return to the genealogy of New Brutalism even in their 1973 collection of writings entitled *Without Rhetoric*. Le Corbusier would remain a fixed point in the Smithsons' narrative of the origins of that definition, testifying to an 'attitude' that persisted throughout the 1970s:

> The coining of the name New Brutalism – the English only think in terms of words – made possible the recognition in England of those ideas we had developed in our first working years. The nearest thing to what we were looking for was then being built in Marseille by Le Corbusier.[74]

By adding the prefix 'new', the Smithsons confessed not only to having wanted to mock the labels in vogue at the beginning of the 1950s, but also to having sought a re-actualisation of the master's intentions, as they perhaps ultimately succeeded through Robin Hood Gardens:

> Coined on sight of a newspaper paragraph heading which called (by poor translation of Beton Brut?) the Marseille Unité 'Brutalism in Architecture' – that was for us 'New', both because we came after Le Corbusier, and in response to the going literary style of the Architectural Review which – at the start of the 'fifties – was running articles on the New Monumentality, the New Empiricism, the New Sentimentality, and so on.[75]

*

---

[73] Alison and Peter Smithson, *Without Rhetoric: An Architectural Aesthetic 1955–1972* (Cambridge, MA: MIT Press, 1973), 6.

[74] Ibid., 4.

[75] Alison and Peter Smithson, 'The 'Fifties / The Response to the Impact of American Advertising', in *Without Rhetoric: An Architectural Aesthetic 1955–1972*, 2, footnote 2; also confirmed in Peter Smithson and Hans-Ulrich Obrist, *Smithson Time: A Dialogue* (Cologne: Verlag der Buchhandlung Walther König, 2005), 17.

Towards the end of the 1960s and coinciding with the exhaustion of ethical aspirations into aesthetic choices, the passing of Brutalism into style can be said to have been definitively accomplished – not the last feat in its long history. The cultural and theoretical vision that had pushed architects to investigate anew the nature of materials, in the direction of the truth of the structure and towards urban principles linked to a new order, was then bent into a series of expedients of surface finishing, modelling of volumes and recognizable compositional traits.

The decline of the ethical stances ascribed to New Brutalism can be determined through the swirling publication of historical retrospectives that revealed the proliferation of new tendencies, to the point of surpassing the very style of Brutalism. Following Banham's essay, critics and historians focused on drawing up retrospective accounts of post-war architecture and publishing critical essays, illustrated histories or guides to styles that presented a drastic alteration to the interpretation of the Brutalist phenomenon and contributed to the documentation of new buildings and models, confirming the multiple possible understandings of the definition of Brutalism and the spread of a popular taste for exposed concrete buildings.

From this point of view, the considerations expressed on Brutalism on the threshold of the 1970s focused on stylistic analyses based mainly on the external appearance of buildings. Even the act of classification itself was linked to a principle of identification that had become popular.[76] Such critical operations engendered a canonical vision of Brutalism, variously unfolding according to precise stylistic characteristics, in which the image of the building reigns supreme.

The ironic fate of the 'quality' that Banham himself had placed at the head of the principles of Brutalism, the 'memorability as an image', can only be seen in architecture reduced to an image. Critical revisions of the trajectory of Brutalism have, however, gone so far as to modify the parameters of interpretation according to a vast range of regional variants and technical solutions, setting in motion the process of canonising Brutalism. In order to grasp the extremes of the definition of Brutalism that still remain in architectural culture today, it is important to point out that the process of canonisation and simplification of that definition was part of concatenation of critical operations that followed Banham's book.

---

[76] 'The classification of modern architecture presented here started from external appearance of the building and was concerned with the nature of the relationship between appearance and spatial content. Any classification, however, is simply a means of identification, nothing more. Proof of its rightness comes from use', in Jürgen Joedicke, *Architecture Since 1945: Sources and Directions* (London: Pall Mall Press, 1969), 28.

Bibliography:
Primary Sources

[n.a.], 'Editorial. Programme', *Architectural Review*, vol. 93, no. 556, April 1943, p. 85.

[n.a.], 'Rebuilding Britain', *Architectural Review*, vol. 93, no. 556, April 1943, pp. 87–112.

[n.a.], 'A Plea for Texture', *Architectural Review*, vol. 95, no. 566, February 1944, p. 30.

[n.a.], 'A Village Planned to Be Picturesque', *Architectural Review*, vol. 95, no. 566, February 1944, pp. 39–43.

[n.a.], 'Price on Picturesque Planning', *Architectural Review*, vol. 95, no. 566, February 1944, pp. 47–50.

[n.a.], 'Cavalcanti House', *Architectural Review*, vol. 95, no. 569, May 1944, p. 130.

[n.a.], 'The New Humanism', *Architects' Journal*, vol. 100, no. 2600, 23 November 1944, pp. 375–76.

[n.a.], 'Metals and Minerals Research Building, Illinois Institute of Technology', *Architects' Journal*, vol. 103, no. 2658, 3 January 1946, pp. 7–15.

[n.a.], 'How Building and Planning are Organised in the URSS', *Architects' Journal*, vol. 104, no. 2688, 1 August 1946, pp. 79–86.

[n.a.], 'Lesson from Germany', *Architects' Journal*, vol. 104, no. 2689, 8 August 1946, pp. 93–95.

[n.a.], 'Astragal: Notes & Topics: In Search of a Word', *Architects' Journal*, vol. 104, no. 2966, 17 October 1946, pp. 274–75.

[n.a.], 'Le Corbusier in U.S.', *Architectural Forum*, vol. 84, no. 2, December 1946, p. 23.

[n.a.], 'Un immeuble d'habitation collectif type I.N.A.I. à Marseille', *L'Architecture d'Aujourd'hui*, vol. 17, no. 9, December 1946, pp. 4–6.

[n.a.], 'Reconstruction in the USSR', *Architectural Review*, vol. 101, May 1947, pp. 177–84.

[n.a.], 'A Dormitory that Explores New Ideas of Student Life: M.I.T. Senior House, Alvar Aalto, Architect, Perry, Shaw and Hepburn, Associated', *Architectural Record*, vol. 102, December 1947, pp. 97–99.

[n.a.], 'Concrete. Construction: Surface Treatments and Finishes', *Architectural Design*, vol. 17, no. 12, December 1947, pp. 328–29.

[n.a.], 'TVA Dam, Fontana, Tennessee', *Progressive Architecture*, vol. 28, December 1947, pp. 46–48.

[n.a.], 'A Letter from the U.S.S.R.', *Architectural Review*, vol. 103, no. 615, March 1948, pp. 75–76.

[n.a.], 'The Dutch Melting-Pot', *Architectural Review*, vol. 104, no. 616, April 1948.

[n.a.], 'High Gothic', *Architects' Journal*, vol. 108, no. 2787, July 1948, p. 29.

[n.a.], 'Standardisation of Building. Editor's Notes', *Architects' Journal*, vol. 108, no. 2790, July 1948, p. 85.

[n.a.], 'The Gothic Roots of the Highly Developed Craft', *Architects' Journal*, vol. 108, no. 2790, July 1948, p. 79.

[n.a.], 'Marginalia. Architectural Symposium', *Architectural Review*, vol. 104, no. 620, August 1948, pp. 97–98.

[n.a.], 'In Search of a New Monumentality', *Architectural Review*, vol. 104, no. 621, September 1948, pp. 117–28.

[n.a.], '2eme numéro hors-série consacré aux arts plastiques', *L'Architecture d'Aujourd'hui*, 1949 (monograph issue).

[n.a.], 'Le Corbusier and the Minister', *Building*, vol. 24, March 1949, p. 75.

[n.a.], 'LCC Housing: The Need for a Critical Assessment', *Architects' Journal*, vol. 109, no. 2823, March 1949, pp. 251–54.

[n.a.], 'Monumentality through Magnitude', *Architectural Review*, vol. 105, no. 628, April 1949, p. 201.

[n.a.], 'College Dormitory, *Architectural Forum*, vol. 91, no. 2, August 1949, pp. 61–67.

[n.a.], 'Inside the Pub', *Architectural Review*, vol. 106, no. 634, October 1949, pp. 209–22.

[n.a.], 'Unité d'Habitation, Marseille', *Architectural Design*, vol. 19, December 1949, pp. 295–96; 308–09.

[n.a.], 'Recommended Change of Responsibility', *Architects' Journal*, vol. 110, no. 2864, December 1949, p. 725.

[n.a.], 'Senior Dormitory Massachusetts Institute of Technology', *Arkitekten. Finland*, no. 4, 1950, pp. 53–64.

[n.a.], 'The Functional Tradition', *Architectural Review*, vol. 107, no. 637, January 1950, pp. 3–65.

[n.a.], 'First Winning Design in Competition for Secondary School at Hunstanton', *Architects' Journal*, vol. 111, no. 2883, 11 May 1950, pp. 576–77.

[n.a.], 'Competition: Secondary Modern School, Hunstanton', *The Builder*, 12 May 1950, pp. 642–43.

[n.a.], 'Competition: Winning Design by Alison and Peter Smithson', *The Architect and Building News*, 12 May 1950, pp. 486–88.

[n.a.], 'Progress at Marseille', *Architectural Design*, vol. 20, no. 2, February 1951, p. 51.

[n.a.], 'The Next Fifty Years', *Architectural Forum*, vol. 96, no. 6, June 1951, pp. 152–70.

[n.a.], 'South Bank Exhibition', *Architectural Review*, vol. 110, no. 656, August 1951, pp. 73–142.

[n.a.], 'Golden Lane Competition: A Selection of the Unsuccessful Entries', *Architects' Journal*, vol. 115, no. 2977, March 1952, pp. 358–62.

[n.a.], 'Marseille Building Experiment: Symbol of L.C.C. Dispute', *The Manchester Guardian*, 9 April 1952.

[n.a.], 'Villa I Uppsala', *Byggmästaren*, vol. A/12, December 1952, pp. 256–58.

[n.a.], 'Radiant City Lawsuit: Complaint of Brutal Realism', *The Times*, 4 December 1952.

[n.a.], 'On the Responsibility of the Architect', *Perspecta*, vol. 2, 1953, pp. 45–55.

[n.a.], 'Corb Triumphant', *Architects' Journal*, vol. 117, no. 3018, 1 January 1953, pp. 103–05.

[n.a.], 'Le Corbusier Vindicated', *Architectural Review*, vol. 113, no. 674, February 1953, p. 132.

[n.a.], 'Welded Steel Fabrication Used at Hunstanton Secondary Modern School', *The National Builder*, April 1953, pp. 280–81.

[n.a.], 'Warehouse, Birmingham', *Architectural Design*, vol. 23, no. 5, May 1953, pp. 125–28.

[n.a.], 'Ica Exhibition', *Architectural Design*, vol. 23, no. 9, September 1953, pp. 266–67.

[n.a.], 'Secondary School at Hunstanton', *Architects' Journal*, vol. 118, no. 3054, 10 September 1953, pp. 323–28.

[n.a.], 'Men of the Year. Alison and Peter Smithson', *Architects' Journal*, vol. 119, no. 3073, 21 January 1954, pp. 68–73.

[n.a.], 'Unité d'habitation Le Corbusier à Marseille', *L'Architecture d'Aujourd'hui*, no. 4, February 1954, pp. 12–21.

[n.a.], 'For Architects Only', *Architectural Forum*, vol. 100, no. 3, March 1954, p. 174.

[n.a.], 'L'école secondaire à Hunstanton', *L'Architecture d'Aujourd'hui*, vol. 53, March 1954, pp. 64–67.

[n.a.], 'The New Brutalism, Future', *Architectural Review*, vol. 115, no. 688, April 1954, pp. 274–75.

[n.a.], 'The New Formalism', *Architectural Design*, vol. 24, no. 4, April 1954, p. 94.

[n.a.], 'Astragal. Disreputable Elements', *Architects' Journal*, vol. 119, no. 3094, 17 June 1954, p. 723.

[n.a.], 'England - Hunstanton Secondary Modern School, Norfolk', *Architects' Year Book*, vol. 6, 1955, pp. 193–200.

[n.a.], 'The Evolution of the Craftsman?', *Perspecta*, vol. 3, 1955, pp. 64–75.

[n.a.], 'Three Approaches to Architecture', *Architectural Forum*, vol. 102, no. 5, May 1955, pp. 142–45.

[n.a.], 'Jaoul Completed', *Architectural Review*, vol. 119, no. 709, February 1956, p. 12.

[n.a.], 'Le Corbusier e la poetica di un'architettura brutale', *Architettura: Cronache e Storia*, vol. 26, supplement no. 3, March 1956, pp. 75–77.

[n.a.], 'New Brutalism. Defined at Last', *Architects' Journal*, vol. 123, no. 3189, 12 April 1956, p. 339.

[n.a.], 'Luigi Figini e Gino Pollini', *Domus*, vol. 318, May 1956, pp. 11–12.

[n.a.], 'Le Corbusier a terra', *Architettura: Cronache e Storia*, vol. 1, no. 8, June 1956, p. 111.

[n.a.], 'This is Tomorrow', *Architectural Design*, vol. 26, no. 10, October 1956, p. 334.

[n.a.], 'Exhibitions', *Architectural Review*, vol. 120, no. 718, November 1956, pp. 332–33.

[n.a.], 'Thoughts in Progress; The New Brutalism', *Architectural Design*, vol. 27, no. 4, April 1957, pp. 111–13.

[n.a.], 'Thoughts in Progress, Aesthetic Control', *Architectural Design*, vol. 27, no. 6, June 1957, pp. 182–83.

[n.a.], 'Letter from Paris. Unesco Building Under Construction', *Architectural Design*, June 1957, p. 216.

[n.a.], 'Ancora contro Ronchamp', *Architettura: Cronache e Storia*, vol. 3, no. 21, July 1957, p. 216.

[n.a.], 'Thoughts in Progress, The Pavillon Suisse as a Seminal Building', *Architectural Design*, vol. 27, no. 7, July 1957, pp. 223–24.

[n.a.], 'Thoughts in Progress, Detail', *Architectural Design*, vol. 27, no. 9, September 1957, pp. 300–01.

[n.a.], 'Thoughts in Progress, Summing Up II-The Missing Term in the Equation-The Gap Between Inspiration and Technology and the Method of Bridging it', *Architectural Design*, vol. 27, no. 11, November 1957, pp. 395–96.

[n.a.], 'Thoughts in Progress, Summing Up III. The "Objects Found" Philosophy', *Architectural Design*, vol. 27, no. 12, December 1957, pp. 435–36.

[n.a.], 'Un modo di invecchiare', *Architettura: Cronache e Storia*, vol. 3, no. 26, December 1957, pp. 540–41.

[n.a.], 'Hauptstadt: Berlin', *Architect and Building News*, vol. 214, 1958, pp. 7–10.

[n.a.], 'Le béton brut de décoffrage et son application', *Construction Moderne*, vol. 74, 1958, pp. 91–114.

[n.a.], 'Protective in Italy', *Architectural Forum*, vol. 108, no. 2, February 1958, p. 178.

[n.a.], 'Organico Giapponese?', *Architettura: Cronache e Storia*, vol. 4, no. 32, May 1958, pp. 110–11.

[n.a.], 'Metamorphosis of Rubbish: Mr. Paolozzi Explains His Process', *The Times*, 2 May 1958, p. 7.

[n.a.], 'Architectural Coxcombry or the Desire for Ornament', *Perspecta*, vol. 5, 1959, pp. 4–15.

[n.a.], 'Astragal. Brutalism for the Backward', *Architects' Journal*, vol. 129, no. 3338, 19 February 1959, pp. 287–88.

[n.a.], 'Milanese Boys' Town', *Architectural Forum*, vol. 110, no. 3, March 1959, pp. 223–25.

[n.a.], 'Vittoriano Viganò', *Zodiac*, vol. 4, April 1959, pp. 174–79.

[n.a.], 'Death of CIAM', *Architectural Design*, vol. 29, October 1959, p. A/5.

[n.a.], 'The Monotonous Curtain Wall', *Architectural Forum*, vol. 111, no. 4, October 1959, pp. 142–50.

[n.a.], 'Sekundarschule in Hunstanton', *Bauen+Wohnen*,

vol. 12, no. 11, November 1959, pp. 373–77.

[n.a.], 'Neoliberty, The Debate', *Architectural Review*, vol. 126, no. 754, December 1959, pp. 341–44.

[n.a.], 'Cinq questions à Le Corbusier', *Zodiac*, vol. 5, 1960, pp. 46–51.

[n.a.], 'Architecture After 1960', *Architectural Review*, vol. 127, no. 755, January 1960, p. 9.

[n.a.], 'Glaus Si, e Kenzo Tange?', *Architettura: Cronache e Storia*, vol. 5, no. 52, February 1960, p. 652.

[n.a.], 'Annessi al teatro "The Old Vic" a Londra', *Architettura: Cronache e Storia*, vol. 5, April 1960, pp. 832–33.

[n.a.], 'Epigonen', *Architectural Review*, vol. 127, no. 758, April 1960, p. 224.

[n.a.], 'No. 5 Building (Nihon University Block by Miyagawa)', *Architectural Review*, vol. 127, no. 758, April 1960, p. 224.

[n.a.], 'Brutalismo nella monumentalità', *Architettura: Cronache e Storia*, vol. 5, no. 51, May 1960, p. 115.

[n.a.], 'L'istituto Marchiondi di Milano', *Vitrum*, vol. 120, July 1960, pp. 21–27.

[n.a.], 'Fortress of Faith', *Architectural Forum*, vol. 113, October 1960, pp. 130–35.

[n.a.], 'Eight Annual Design Awards', *Progressive Architecture*, vol. 42, no. 1, January 1961, pp. 96–199.

[n.a.], 'Enrico Castiglioni', *Architectural Review*, vol. 129, no. 767, January 1961, pp. 2–3.

[n.a.], 'Il complesso di casa', *Architettura: Cronache e Storia*, vol. 6, no. 63, January 1961, p. 625.

[n.a.], 'Kurashiki: Town Hall by Kenzo Tange', *Architectural Review*, vol. 129, no. 767, January 1961, pp. 3–5.

[n.a.], 'Beyond Brutalism', *Architectural Review*, vol. 129, no. 768, February 1961, p. 135.

[n.a.], 'Church in Sheffield', *Architectural Review*, vol. 129, no. 768, February 1961, pp. 116–17.

[n.a.], 'Biblioteca per l'università di Yale', *Domus*, vol. 376, March 1961, pp. 1–4.

[n.a.], 'Vittoriano Viganò, Baggio, Milan, Italy', *Architectural Design*, vol. 31, no. 3, March 1961, pp. 304–07.

[n.a.], 'Non è di legno', *Architettura: Cronache e Storia*, vol. 6, no. 66, April 1961, p. 830.

[n.a.], 'Psychiatric Institute in Milan', *Architectural Review*, vol. 129, no. 78, May 1961, pp. 304–07.

[n.a.], 'British Use of Materials', *Architectural Review*, vol. 130, no. 773, July 1961, p. 66.

[n.a.], 'Casabella Strikes Back', *Architectural Review*, vol. 130, no. 773, July 1961, p. 148.

[n.a.], 'Mies smussato: il nuovo Economist', *Architettura: Cronache e Storia*, vol. 7, no. 74, December 1961, p. 542.

[n.a.], 'Notes in Passing', *Arts and Architecture*, vol. 78, no. 12, December 1961, p. 9.

[n.a.], 'History Repeats: A Discussion of Two Papers by Professor Pevsner and Dr. Reyner Banham', *Architectural Association Journal*, vol. 77, 1962, pp. 158–69.

[n.a.], 'Contrastes', *L'Architecture d'Aujourd'hui*, vol. 32, no. 100, February 1962, p. XIL.

[n.a.], 'What Architecture of Technology?', *Architectural Review*, vol. 113, no. 780, March 1962, pp. 97–99.

[n.a.], 'Labyrinthian Environs', *Progressive Architecture*, vol. 43, no. 5, May 1962, pp. 181–87.

[n.a.], 'Caos 1962', *Architettura: Cronache e Storia*, vol. 8, no. 61, July 1962, pp. 181–81.

[n.a.], 'La Tourette Comes to Boston: Boston City Hall', *Architects' Journal*, vol. 136, 4 July 1962, pp. 2; 11.

[n.a.], 'New Masterpiece in Concrete', *Architectural Forum*, vol. 117, no. 3, September 1962, pp. 78–96.

[n.a.], 'Villa di Erskine a Lindigö', *Architettura: Cronache e Storia*, vol. 8, no. 86, December 1962, pp. 538–39.

[n.a.], 'Boston City Hall', *Casabella-Continuità*, no. 271, January 1963, pp. 17–27.

[n.a], 'Le Corbusier at Harvard: A Disaster, or a Bold Step Forward?', *Architectural Forum*, vol. 119, no. 4, April 1963, pp. 104–07.

[n.a.], 'The New Boston City Hall', *Progressive Architecture*, vol. 44, April 1963, pp. 132–53.

[n.a.], '*Arts and Architecture* Opens at Yale', *Architectural Forum*, vol. 119, December 1963, no. 6, p. 7.

[n.a.], 'Gerhard Kallmann Shows the New Boston City Hall', *Architectural Association Journal*, vol. 79, 1964, pp. 313–16.

[n.a.], 'Il parlamento di Chandigarh', *Architettura: Cronache e Storia*, vol. 100, no. 9, February 1964, pp. 755–57.

[n.a.], 'Smooth and Brutal', *Architectural Review*, vol. 804, February 1964, p. 85.

[n.a.], 'A Great Plaza for Boston's Government Center', *Architectural Record*, vol. 135, March 1964, pp. 190–200.

[n.a.], 'Faculté d'art et architecture de l'université de Yale', *L'Architecture d'Aujourd'hui*, vol. 113, no. 114, April 1964, pp. 182–87.

[n.a.], 'Ornament? Ohne Ornament', *Domus*, vol. 432, November 1965, p. 56.

[n.a.], 'Concrete Poetry', *Architectural Review*, vol. 139, no. 830, April 1966, pp. 308–09.

[n.a.], 'Concrete: Where Do We Go from Here?', *Progressive Architecture*, vol. 61, October 1966, pp. 172–238.

[n.a.], 'Pre-Corb', *Architectural Review*, vol. 140, no. 836, October 1966, pp. 291–96.

[n.a.], 'Instant History: The New Brutalism', *Architects' Journal*, vol. 144, no. 26, 28 December 1966, p. 1580.

[n.a.], 'Brutalismus: Rauh und Rissig', *Der Spiegel*, 12 November 1967, pp. 188–93.

[n.a.], 'What it Took to Bring about the Best Public Building of our Time', *Contract Interiors*, vol. 128, no. 9, 1969, pp. 115–33.

[n.a.], 'After the Boston City Hall', *Architectural Forum*, vol. 130, no. 1, January 1969, pp. 54–57.

[n.a.], 'Boston's City Hall', *Architectural Forum*, vol. 130, no. 1, January 1969, pp. 38–53.

[n.a.], 'The New Boston City Hall', *Architectural Record*, vol. 145, no. 2, February 1969, pp. 133–44.

[n.a.], 'Arson Suspected in Fire at Yale', *The New Haven Register*, 15 June 1969, p. 1.

[n.a.], 'Boston's Open Center', *Architectural Forum*, vol. 132, no. 5, 1970, pp. 24–31.

[n.a.], 'Brutalismo-cromatismo: quattro interventi nel Trentino di Leo Salvotti', *Architettura: Cronache e Storia*, vol. 25, 1979, pp. 88–97.

Aalto Alvar, 'The Humanizing of Architecture', *Architectural Forum*, vol. 73, December 1940, pp. 505–06.

Aalto Alvar, 'L'oeuf de poisson et le saumon', *Werk*, vol. 36, February 1949, pp. 43–44.

Ackerman James, 'A Theory of Style', *Journal of Aesthetics and Art Criticism*, vol. 20, 1962, pp. 227–37.

Adburgham Alison, 'Brutalism à la mode', *Harper's Bazaar*, vol. 75, no. 5, May 1967, p. 86.

Aikman Alexander, 'The Hunstanton School', *Architectural Design*, vol. 25, no. 3, March 1955, p. 96.

Ain Gregory, 'Form Follows Faction', *Architectural Record*, vol. 137, May 1965, pp. 108–09.

Alfieri Bruno, 'João Vilanova Artigas: ricerca brutalista', *Zodiac*, vol. 7, 1960, pp. 96–107.

Alfieri Bruno, 'English Brutalism – Selected Writings', *Zodiac*, vol. 13, 1968, pp. 30–41.

Alloway Lawrence, *Collages and Objects*, exhibition catalogue, Institute of Contemporary Art, London, 1953.

Alloway Lawrence, 'Art News from London', *Art News*, vol. 53, no. 6, October 1954, p. 54.

Alloway Lawrence, 'Re: Vision', *Art News*, vol. 6, January 1955, p. 5.

Alloway Lawrence, 'Eduardo Paolozzi', *Architectural Design*, vol. 26, no. 4, April 1956, p. 135.

Alloway Lawrence, 'Dada in Our Times', *Architectural Design*, vol. 27, no. 7, July 1957, pp. 249–50.

Alloway Lawrence, 'The Arts and the Mass Media', *Architectural Design*, vol. 28, no. 2, February 1958, pp. 84–85.

Alloway Lawrence, *The Development of British Pop*, Thames & Hudson, London, 1966.

Alloway Lawrence, Banham Reyner, Lewis David, McHale John, Crosby Theo, *This Is Tomorrow*, exhibition catalogue, Whitechapel Gallery, London, 1956.

Anderson Lawrence, 'The Architect in the Next Fifty Years', *Journal of Architectural Education*, vol. 14, 1959, no. 1, pp. 3–9.

Argan Giulio Carlo, 'A Debate on the Moral Grounds of Architecture', *Casabella-Continuità*, vol. 209, February 1954, pp. 5–7.

Armitage Edward John, 'Letter to the Editor', *Architectural Design*, vol. 27, no. 6, June 1957, p. 184.

Arnheim Rudolph, 'From Function to Expression', *Journal of Aesthetics and Art Criticism*, no. 1, Autumn 1964, pp. 29–41.

Arup Ove, 'Structural Honesty', *Architects' Journal*, vol. 119, no. 3087, 29 April 1954, pp. 514–15.

Augustyniak Marian, Entwistle Fred, *Survey of the New Brutalism*, Bachelor thesis, Department of Architecture, Carnegie Institute of Technology, Pittsburgh, Pennsylvania, May 1958.

Backström Sven, 'A Swede Looks at Sweden', *Architectural Review*, vol. 94, no. 561, September 1943, p. 80.

Backström Sven, Kidder Smith Everard George, Holford William, 'Swedish Peace in War', *Architectural Review*, vol. 94, no. 561, September 1943, p. 59.

Baker Jeremy, 'A Smithson File', Arena, *Architectural Association Journal*, vol. 82, February 1966 (monographic issue).

Baljeu Joost, *Attempt at a Theory of Synthesist Plastic Expression*, Alec Tiranti, London, 1963.

Banham Reyner, 'Painting and Sculpture of Le Corbusier', *Architectural Review*, vol. 113, no. 678, June 1953, pp. 401–04.

Banham Reyner, 'Parallel of Life and Art', *Architectural Review*, vol. 114, no. 682, October 1953, pp. 259–60.

Banham Reyner, 'Pelican World History of Art', *Architectural Review*, vol. 114, no. 683, November 1953, pp. 285–88.

Banham Reyner, 'Object Lesson', *Architectural Review*, vol. 115, no. 690, June 1954, pp. 403–06.

Banham Reyner, 'Astragal at the Bartlett', *Architects' Journal*, vol. 120, no. 3097, July 1954, p. 6.

Banham Reyner, 'Mendelsohn', *Architectural Review*, vol. 116, no. 692, August 1954, pp. 84–93.

[Banham Reyner], 'School at Hunstanton', *Architectural Review*, vol. 116, no. 693, September 1954, pp. 152–62.

Banham Reyner, 'Façade', *Architectural Review*, vol. 116, no. 695, November 1954, pp. 302–08.

Banham Reyner, 'Vision in Motion', *Art*, vol. 5, January 1955, p. 4.

Banham Reyner, 'The Machine Aesthetic', *Architectural Review*, vol. 117, no. 700, April 1955, pp. 225–28.

Banham Reyner, 'Sant'Elia', *Architectural Review*, vol. 117, no. 701, May 1955, pp. 84–93.

Banham Reyner, 'A Rejoinder', *Design*, vol. 19, July 1955, pp. 24–25.

Banham Reyner, 'Man, Machine and Motion', *Architectural Review*, vol. 119, no. 703, July 1955, pp. 51–54.

Banham Reyner, 'Space for Decoration', *Design*, vol. 79, July 1955, pp. 24–25.

Banham Reyner, 'Vehicles of Desire', *Art*, vol. 1, September 1955, p. 3.

Banham Reyner, 'Where Man Meets Machine', *The Listener*, vol. 54, September 1955, pp. 332–33.

Banham Reyner, 'Art in British Advertising', *Art News & Review*, vol. 7, no. 22, November 1955, p. 3.

Banham Reyner, 'Industrial Design and Popular Art', *Civiltà delle Macchine*, vol. 3, no. 6, November 1955, pp. 81–86.

Banham Reyner, 'The New Brutalism', *Architectural Review*, vol. 118, no. 708, December 1955, pp. 354–61.

Banham Reyner, 'New Look in Cruiserwights', *Ark*, vol. 16, Summer 1956, pp. 44–47.

Banham Reyner, 'Ateliers d'artistes', *Architectural Review*, vol. 120, no. 715, August 1956, pp. 75–83.

Banham Reyner, 'Not Quite Painting or Sculpture Either', *Architects' Journal*, vol. 124, no. 3207, 16 August 1956, pp. 217–29.

Banham Reyner, 'This is Tomorrow', *Architectural Review*, vol. 120, no. 716, September 1956, pp. 186–87.

Banham Reyner, 'Hair-Cut, You!', *Architects' Journal*, vol. 124, no. 3214, 4 October 1956, pp. 469, 471.

Banham Reyner, 'Egg-Head Exposed?', *Architects' Journal*, vol. 124, no. 3216, 18 October 1956, p. 546.

Banham Reyner, 'Alloway and After. Not Quite Architecture', *Architects' Journal*, vol. 126, no. 3278, 26 December 1957, p. 941.

Banham Reyner, *The Theory of Modern Architecture 1907–1927*, PhD Thesis, University of London, Courtauld Institute of Art, 1958.

Banham Reyner, 'Top Pop Boffin', *Architects' Journal*, vol. 127, no. 3286, 20 February 1958, pp. 269, 271.

Banham Reyner, 'Space, Fiction and Architecture', *Architects' Journal*, vol. 127, no. 3294, 17 April 1958, pp. 557–59.

Banham Reyner, 'Plucky Jims', *New Statesman*, vol. 49, 19 July 1958, pp. 83–84.

Banham Reyner, 'Machine Aesthetes', *New Statesman*, vol. 52, 16 August 1958, pp. 192–93.

Banham Reyner, 'Corb Goes to Liverpool', *New Statesman*, 20 December 1958, pp. 882–83.

Banham Reyner, 'Neoliberty. The Italian Retreat from Modern Architecture', *Architectural Review*, vol. 125, no. 747, March 1959, pp. 231–35.

Banham Reyner, 'Home of Taste', *New Statesman*, 11 October 1959, pp. 488–89.

Banham Reyner, *Theory and Design in the First Machine Age*, Architectural Press, London, 1960.

Banham Reyner, 'Stocktaking', *Architectural Review*, vol. 127, no. 756, February 1960, pp. 93–100.

Banham Reyner, 'A Throw-Away Aesthetic', *Industrial Design*, March 1960 [1955], pp. 61–65.

Banham Reyner, 'History Under Revision', *Architectural Review*, vol. 127, no. 759, May 1960, pp. 325–32.

Banham Reyner, 'The Perret Ascendancy', *Architectural Review*, vol. 127, no. 759, June 1960, pp. 373–80.

Banham Reyner, 'Futurism for Keeps', *Arts*, vol. 35, December 1960, pp. 33–39.

Banham Reyner, 'The History of the Immediate Future', *RIBA Journal*, vol. 68, 1961, pp. 252–57.

Banham Reyner, 'Ego-Image Adjuster', *New Statesman*, vol. 61, 6 January 1961, p. 482.

Banham Reyner, 'Black and White Magazine Show', *New Statesman*, 2 June 1961, p. 889.

Banham Reyner, 'Apropos the Smithsons', *New Statesman*, 8 September 1961, p. 317.

Banham Reyner, 'The World of the Brutalists. Opinion & intention in British Architecture, 1951–60', *Texas Quarterly*, vol. 4, no. 3, October 1961, pp. 129–38.

Banham Reyner, 'Park Hill Housing', *Architectural Review*, vol. 130, no. 778, December 1961, pp. 402–40.

Banham Reyner, 'Views and Reviews: Book Reviews - Aesthetic or Technic?', *Architectural Review*, vol. 130, no. 778, December 1961, p. 375.

Banham Reyner, *Guide to Modern Architecture*, Architectural Press, London, 1962.

Banham Reyner, 'Who is This Pop?', *Motif*, vol. 10, March 1962, pp. 3–13.

Banham Reyner, 'The Buttery-Hatch Aesthetic', *Architectural Review*, vol. 113, April 1962, pp. 203–06.

Banham Reyner, 'England His England', *New Statesman*, 28 September 1962, p. 427.

Banham Reyner, 'Brutalismus', in Pehnt Wolfgang (ed.), *Lexikon Der Moderne Architektur*, Berl Knaur, Köln, 1963, pp. 557–59.

Banham Reyner, 'At Aspen. On the American Image Abroad', *Design*, no. 177, September 1963, p. 58.

Banham Reyner, 'Convenient Benches and Handy Hooks: Functional Considerations in the Criticism of the Art and Architecture', in Whiffen Marcus (ed.) *The History, Theory and Criticism of the Art of Architecture*, Papers from the 1964 AIA-ACSA Seminar, MIT Press, Cambridge, 1964, pp. 91–105.

Banham Reyner, 'New Brutalism', in Pehnt Wolfgang (ed.), *Encyclopedia of Modern Architecture*, Harry N. Abrams, New York, 1964, pp. 557–59.

Banham Reyner, 'The Atavism of the Short-Distance Mini- Cyclist', *Living Arts*, vol. 3, 1964, p. 89.

Banham Reyner, 'The Word in Britain: Character', *Architectural Forum*, vol. 121, no. 2–3, August-September 1964, pp. 118–25.

Banham Reyner, 'A Clip-On Architecture', *Design Quarterly*, vol. 63, 1965, pp. 2–30.

Banham Reyner, 'Economist Building', *New Statesman and Nation*, 20 January 1965, pp. 113–20.

Banham Reyner, Dallegret François, 'A Home is Not a House', *Art in America*, vol. 2, no. 1, April 1965, pp. 70–79.

Banham Reyner, 'Motherwell & Others', *Architectural Review*, vol. 140, no. 833, July 1965, pp. 59–62.

Banham Reyner, 'Im dienst der Öffentlichkeit', *Form*, vol. 32, December 1965, p. 15.

Banham Reyner, *The New Brutalism: Ethic or Aesthetic?*, Architectural Press, London, 1966.

Banham Reyner, *Brutalismus in der Architektur*, Krämer Verlag, Stuttgart, 1966.

Banham Reyner, 'The Last Formgiver', *Architectural Review*, vol. 139, no. 834, August 1966, pp. 97–98.

Banham Reyner, 'All that Glitters is not Stainless', *Architectural Design*, vol. 37, no. 8, August 1967, pp. 351–52.

Banham Reyner, 'Revenge of the Picturesque: English Architectural Polemics, 1945–65', in Summerson John, *Concerning Architecture: Essays on Architectural Writers and Writing Presented to Nikolaus Pevsner*, Allen Lane, London, 1968, pp. 265–73.

Barnett Jonathan, 'Philip Johnson Interview', *Architectural Record*, vol. 128, no. 16, December 1960, p. 238.

Barr Alfred Hamilton et al., 'What is Happening to Modern Architecture?: A Symposium at the Museum of Modern Art', *Museum of Modern Art. Bulletin*, vol. 15, no. 3, 1948, pp. 4–21.

Belluschi Pietro, 'The Spirit of the New Architecture', *Architectural Record*, vol. 114, October 1953, pp. 143–49.

Beresford Peter, 'School at Hunstanton', *Architectural Review*, vol. 116, no. 695, November 1954, p. 282.

Berkeley Ellen Perry, 'More Than You May Want To Know About The Boston City Hall',

Architecture Plus, vol. 1, no. 1, 1973, pp. 72–77.

Bill Max, *Robert Maillart*, Verlag Für Architektur, Erlenbach- Zürich, 1949.

Bill Max, 'The Beginning of a New Epoch in Architecture', *Architectural Design*, vol. 25, no. 11, November 1955, pp. 335–38.

Blake Peter, 'Modern Architecture: Its Many Faces', *Architectural Forum*, vol. 108, no. 3, March 1958, pp. 76–81.

Blake Peter, 'Form Follows Function–or Does It?', *Architectural Forum*, vol. 108, no. 4, April 1958, pp. 99–103.

Blake Peter, 'The Difficult Art of Simplicity', *Architectural Forum*, vol. 108, no. 5, May 1958, pp. 126–31.

Blake Peter, *The Master Builders*, Knopf, New York, 1960.

Blake Peter, 'Are you Illiterate About Modern Architecture?', *Vogue*, no. 404, September 1961, pp. 180–82.

Blake Peter, 'The Secret Scrapbook of an Architectural Scavenger', *Architectural Forum*, vol. 121, no. 2, August 1964, pp. 81–114.

Bloc André, 'Le Corbusier. Artistes chez eux', *L'Architecture d'Aujourd'hui*, vol. 20, 1949, pp. 52–55.

Boesiger Willy (ed.), *Le Corbusier. Œuvre Complète 1938–1946*, vol. 4, Éditions Girsberger, Zurich, 1946.

Boesiger Willy (ed.), *Le Corbusier. Œuvre Complète 1938–1946*, vol. 4, 2nd ed., Éditions Girsberger, Zurich, 1950.

Boesiger Willy (ed.), *Le Corbusier. Œuvre Complète 1946–1952*, vol. 5, Éditions Girsberger, Zurich, 1953.

Boesiger Willy (ed.), *Le Corbusier. Œuvre Complète 1952–1957*, vol. 6, Éditions Girsberger, Zurich, 1957.

Bonelli Renato, 'Estetica contemporanea e critica dell'architettura', *Zodiac*, vol. 4, April 1959, pp. 22–29.

Bordier Roger, 'La synthèse des arts. L'art est un service sociale', *Art d'Aujourd'hui*, vol. 5, no. 4–5, May 1954, pp.13–31.

Bourne Russell, 'Yale's Paul Rudolph', *Architectural Forum*, vol. 108, no. 4, April 1958, pp. 128–29.

Boyd Andrew, 'A Review of the Symposium - The Kind of Architecture We Want in Britain', *Keystone. Journal of the AASTA* [Associations of Architects, Surveyors and Technical Assistants], May 1949, p. 96.

Boyd Andrew, Penn Colin, (eds.), *Homes for the People. How Modern Building Technique Can Provide High Standard Dwellings Quickly. How They Could Be Planned and Built; What They Could Look Like And How We Can Get Them*, Paul Elek Publishers, London, 1946.

Boyd Robin, 'A New Eclecticism?', *Architectural Review*, vol. 110, no. 657, September 1951, pp. 151–54.

Boyd Robin, 'The Functional Neurosis', *Architectural Review*, vol. 119, no. 710, February 1956, pp. 84–88.

Boyd Robin, 'Engineering of Excitement', *Architectural Review*, vol. 124, no. 742, November 1958, pp. 295–308.

Boyd Robin, 'Has Success Spoiled Modern Architecture?', *Architectural Forum*, vol. 111, no. 1, July 1959, pp. 98–103.

Boyd Robin, 'The Counter-Revolution in Architecture', *Harper's Magazine*, vol. 219, no. 1312, September 1959, pp. 40–48.

Boyd Robin, *The Australian Ugliness*, F. W. Cheshire, Melbourne, 1960.

Boyd Robin, *Kenzo Tange*, George Braziller, New York, 1962.

Boyd Robin, *The Puzzle of Architecture*, Melbourne University Press, Carlton, 1965.

Boyd Robin, 'The Sad End of New Brutalism', *Architectural Review*, vol. 142, no. 812, July 1967, pp. 9–11.

Boyd Robin, *New Directions in Japanese Architecture*, George Braziller, New York, 1968.

Brett Lionel, 'The Space Machine: An Evaluation of the Recent Work of Le Corbusier', *Architectural Review*, vol. 102, no. 604, June 1947, pp. 147–52.

Brett Lionel, 'Architecture. Paris and London', *The London Magazine*, June 1963, pp. 66–68.

Bucher Francois, 'A Failure of Architectural Purism', *Perspecta*, vol. 6, 1960, pp. 5–8.

Bullivan Dargan, 'Hunstanton Secondary Modern School', *Architectural Design*, vol. 23, no. 9, September 1953, pp. 238–97.

Bullrich Francisco, *New Directions in Latin American Architecture*, George Braziller, New York, 1969.

Burchard John Ely, 'The Dilemma of Architecture', *Architectural Record*, vol. 117, May 1957, pp. 193–98.

Burchard John Ely, 'Pilgrimage: Ronchamp, Raincy, Vézelay', *Architectural Record*, vol. 123, no. 3, March 1958, pp. 171–78.

Burchard John Ely, 'Architecture in a Restless Age', *Architectural Record*, vol. 125, May 1959, pp. 174–77.

Burchard John Ely, 'A Parable Via Milano and Roma', *Architectural Record*, vol. 128, no. 1, July 1960, pp. 123–30.

Bush-Brown Albert, 'Notes Toward a Basis for Criticism', *Architectural Record*, vol. 121, October 1959, pp. 185–89.

Butterly Daniel R., *The Architecture of Vision:*

Or the Theory of Composition in Plane-Surface Design, Beechhurst, New York, 1947.

Caquot Albert, 'Le béton dans la reconstruction de la France', *L'Architecture d'Aujourd'hui*, vol. 17, no. 5, December 1946, pp. 37–43.

Carey O., 'Unité d'Habitation', *Architects' Year Book*, vol. 4, 1949, pp. 130–36.

Carlin Earl, 'P/A Design Award. Central Fire Station', *Progressive Architecture*, vol. 42, no. 7, July 1961, pp. 132–35.

Carter Edward, 'Soviet Architecture To-Day', *Architectural Review*, vol. 92, no. 5, November 1942, pp. 107–14.

Casson Hugh, 'Art by Accident', *Architectural Review*, vol. 96, no. 573, September 1944, pp. 63–70.

Castellano Luca Luigi, 'Noi insistiamo! Il Brutalismo. Realismo panico del costruire', *Linea Sud*, vol. 0, 1963, p. 6.

Collins Peter, *Concrete: The Vision of a New Architecture. A Study of Auguste Perret and his Precursors*, Faber & Faber, London, 1959.

Collins Peter, 'Aspects of Ornament', *Architectural Review*, vol. 129, no. 772, June 1961, pp. 373–78.

Collins Peter, 'Whither Paul Rudolph?', *Progressive Architecture*, vol. 42, August 1961, pp. 130–33.

Collins Peter, 'Action Architecture', *The Guardian*, 13 September 1962, n.p.

Collins Peter, 'Critique', *Progressive Architecture*, vol. 154, no. 4, April 1963, pp. 146–47.

Collins Peter, 'Review: Modern Architecture. The Architecture of Democracy by Vincent Scully, Jr.', *Journal of the Society of Architectural Historians*, vol. 22, no. 2, May 1963, p. 108.

Collins Peter, 'Sincerity', *Architectural Review*, vol. 135, no. 805, March 1964, pp. 165–68.

Collins Peter, *Changing Ideals in Modern Architecture, 1750–1950*, McGill University Press, London/Montreal, 1965.

Collins Peter, 'Neo-Butterfield. The New Brutalism: Ethic or Aesthetic (Reyner Banham)', *Progressive Architecture*, vol. 48, no. 3, March 1967, pp. 198–202.

Collins Peter, 'The New Brutalism of the 1920. The Effect of Economic Restraints at Notre Dame du Raincy', *Society of Architectural Historian Journal*, vol. 33, October 1974, pp. 233–40.

Colquhoun Alan, 'Twentieth Century Picturesque', *Architectural Review*, vol. 116, no. 691, July 1954, p. 2.

Coombe June S., 'The New Brutalism: Suitable for St. Trinians', *Architects' Journal*, vol. 120, no. 3113, October 1954, p. 516.

Cowburn Bill, Pearson Michael, 'Art in Architecture', *244: Journal of the University of Manchester Architecture and Planning Society*, vol. 2, Winter 1954, p. 20.

Cowburn N. A., 'School at Hunstanton', *Architectural Review*, vol. 116, no. 695, November 1954, p. 282.

Cowburn W. G., 'New Brutalism', *Architectural Design*, vol. 06, no. 27, June 1957, p. 184.

Creighton Thomas Hawk, 'P.S.', *Progressive Architecture*, vol. 38, no. 1, January 1957, p. 216.

Creighton Thomas Hawk, 'The Intellectual Fringe', *Progressive Architecture*, vol. 38, no. 6, June 1957, p. 366.

Creighton Thomas Hawk, 'The New Sensualism', *Progressive Architecture*, vol. 40, no. 9, September 1959, pp. 141–54.

Creighton Thomas Hawk, 'The New Sensualism II', *Progressive Architecture*, vol. 40, no. 10, October 1959, pp. 180–87.

Creighton Thomas Hawk, 'The Sixties. A P/A Symposium on the State of Architecture. Part III', *Progressive Architecture*, vol. 42, no. 5, May 1961, pp. 136–41.

Creighton Thomas Hawk, *American Architecture*, Robert B. Luce, Washington, 1964.

Crosby Theo, 'Parallel of Life and Art', *Architectural Design*, vol. 23, no. 10, October 1953, pp. 297–98.

Crosby Theo, 'The New Brutalism', *Architectural Design*, vol. 25, no. 1, January 1955, p. 1.

Crosby Theo, 'The Search for the Image', *Architectural Design*, vol. 25, no. 3, March 1955, p. 103.

Crosby Theo, 'This is Tomorrow', *Architectural Design*, vol. 26, no. 9, September 1956, pp. 302–04.

Crosby Theo, 'Detail, 3', *Architectural Design*, vol. 28, no. 3, March 1958, pp. 123–23.

Crosby Theo, 'Towards a New Rationality', *Architectural Design*, vol. 37, no. 7, July 1967, p. 302.

Cullen Gordon, 'Hazards. On the Art of Introducing Obstacles into the Urban Landscape without Inhibiting the Eye', *Architectural Review*, vol. 103, no. 625, March 1948, pp. 99–105.

Cullen Gordon, 'The Economist Building, St. James', *Architectural Review*, vol. 137, no. 816, February 1965, pp. 114–24.

Curcic Slobodan, 'Review of the New Brutalism. Ethic or Aesthetic', *Journal of Aesthetic Education*, vol. 3, no. 2, 1969, pp. 171–73.

Dardi Costantino, *Il gioco sapiente: tendenze della nuova*

architettura, vol. 2, Marsilio Editori, Padua, 1971.

Davies Richard, 'Letter. The New Brutalism', *Architectural Review*, vol. 116, no. 691, July 1954, p. 2.

De Maré Eric, 'The Antecedents and Origins of Sweden's Last Style', *Architectural Review*, vol. 103, no. 623, January 1948, pp. 8–22.

De Maré Eric, 'Eric De Maré Pays a Return Visit to Sweden', *Architects' Journal*, vol. 121, no. 3125, January 1955, pp. 101–10.

De Maré Eric, 'Et Tu, Brute?', *Architectural Review*, vol. 120, no. 715, August 1956, p. 72.

De Maré Eric, 'Brazil's Architecture', *The Manchester Guardian*, 22 January 1957, p. 4.

Dearstyne Howard, 'Letters', *Journal of the Society of Architectural Historians*, vol. 24, no. 3, October 1965, pp. 254–57.

Deasy C. M., 'Letter. The New Brutalism', *Architectural Forum*, vol. 103, no. 2, August 1955, p. 72.

Derek A., De Abbott, G., 'The New Brutalism', *Architects' Journal*, vol. 120, no. 3108, 23 September 1954, p. 366.

Derpool James Grote Van, 'Review: Early Victorian Architecture in Britain by Henry-Russell Hitchcock', *Journal of the Society of Architectural Historians*, vol. 15, no. 2, May 1956, pp. 30– 31.

Dixon John, 'Corbu's Center Rises at Harvard', *Progressive Architecture*, vol. 43, no. 12, December 1962, p. 43.

Dorfles Gillo, 'L'istituto Marchiondi Spagliardi a Milano', *Edilizia Moderna*, vol. 67, August 1959, pp. 35–46.

Dorfles Gillo, 'Cosa è cambiato a Londra?', *Domus*, vol. 368, July 1960, pp. 1–2.

Dorfles Gillo, 'Edizioni per architetti', *Domus*, vol. 379, June 1961, p. 32.

Dorfles Gillo, 'Gestaltungsprobleme der Gegenwart', *Das Werk*, vol. 51, no. 3, March 1964, pp. 102–05.

Drew Jane, Fry Maxwell, Smithson Alison and Peter, 'Conversation on Brutalism', *Zodiac*, vol. 4, April 1959, pp. 73–81.

Drew Philip, *Third Generation: The Changing Meaning of Architecture*, Pall Mall Press, London, 1972.

Dubuffet Jean, *Prospectus aux amateurs de tout genre*, Gallimard, Paris, 1946.

Dubuffet Jean, *L'art brut préféré aux arts culturels*, Compagnie de l'Art Brut, Paris, 1949.

Dubuffet Jean, *Publications de la Compagnie de l'Art Brut*, Compagnie de l'Art Brut, Paris, 1964.

Dubuffet Jean, *Prospectus et tous écrits suivants*, Gallimard, Paris, 1967.

Eames Charles, cover, *Architectural Review*, vol. 106, no. 635, November 1949.

Eastwick-Field J., 'Out of the Form', *Architectural Review*, vol. 125, no. 749, June 1959, pp. 386–97.

Edman Bengt, Holm Lennart, 'Tegelspråk', *Tegel*, vol. 40, no. 2, 1950, pp. 46–50.

Fein Albert, 'Review: American Architecture and Urbanism by Vincent Scully', *Journal of the Society of Architectural Historians*, vol. 31, no. 1, March 1972, pp. 71–73.

Feuerstein Günther, *New Directions in German Architecture*, George Braziller, New York, 1968.

Fisker Kay, 'The History of Danish Domestic Architecture', *Architectural Review*, vol. 104, no. 623, November 1948, pp. 219–26.

Fitch James Marston, 'Wellesley's Alternative to "Collegiate Gothic" – Criticism', *Architectural Forum*, vol. 111, no. 1, July 1959, pp. 93–95.

Fitch James Marston, 'The Shifting Base of Contemporary Criticism', *Progressive Architecture*, vol. 37, April 1956, pp. 143, 192, 194, 197, 202, 208, 210, 212, 218, 222.

Fitch James Marston, 'A Building of Rugged Fundaments', *Architectural Forum*, vol. 113, July 1960, pp. 82–87.

Fitch James Marston, 'City Hall, Boston', *Architectural Review*, vol. 147, June 1970, pp. 398– 411.

Five Architects, 'What the Smithsons Think', *Architects' Journal*, vol. 119, no. 3078, 25 February 1954, p. 240.

Frampton Kenneth, 'The Economist and the Hauptstadt', *Architectural Design*, vol. 137, no. 2, February 1965, pp. 61–62.

Fry Maxwell, *Fine Building*, Faber & Faber, London, 1944.

Fry Maxwell, 'Future of Architecture', *Architects' Year Book*, vol. 1, no. 1, 1945, pp. 7–10.

Gardner-Medwin Robert, 'A Flight from Functionalism', *American Institute of Architects Journal*, vol. 31, May 1959, pp. 21–28.

Giedion Sigfried, 'Mars & ICA', *Architects' Journal*, vol. 108, no. 2796, 9 September 1948, pp. 251–52.

Giedion Sigfried, 'Alvar Aalto', *Architectural Review*, vol. 107, no. 638, February 1950, pp. 77–84.

Giedion Sigfried, *A Decade of Contemporary Architecture*, Editions Girsberger, Zurich, 1954.

Giedion Sigfried, 'The State of Contemporary Architecture', *Architectural Record*, vol. 115, January 1954, pp. 132–37.

Giedion Sigfried, *Space, Time and Architecture*, 2a Edition, Harvard University Press, Cambridge Massachusetts, 1962.

Giedion Sigfried, 'Architecture in the 1960s: Hopes and Fear', *Zodiac*, no. 11, 1963, pp. 24–35.

Gloag John, *The English Tradition of Design*, Penguin Books, London, 1946.

Goff Bruce, 'A Young Architect's Protest for Architecture', *Perspecta*, vol. 13/14, 1971, pp. 330–57.

Goodhart-Rendel H. S., 'Rogue Architects of the Victorian Era', *RIBA Journal*, vol. 47, no. 4, April 1949, pp. 251–59.

Gordon Cullen, 'Premeditated Concrete', *Architects' Journal*, vol. 119, no. 3073, January 1954, pp. 99–104.

Gowan James, 'Notes on American Architecture', *Perspecta*, vol. 7, 1961, pp. 77–82.

Gregotti Vittorio, *New Directions in Italian Architecture*, George Braziller, New York, 1968.

Gropius Walter, 'Eight Steps Toward a Solid Architecture', *Architectural Forum*, vol. 100, no. 2, February 1954, pp. 156–57.

Guégen Pierre, 'Art Brut', *L'Architecture d'Aujourd'hui*, vol. 20, 1949, pp. 48–51.

Guggenheimer Richard, *Sight and Insight: A Prediction of New Perceptions in Art*,

Harper & Brothers, London, 1945.

Gutheim Frederick A., 'Tennessee Valley Authority: A New Phase in Architecture', *Magazine of Art*, vol. 33, no. 9, September 1940, pp. 520–21.

Habasque Guy, 'L'œil de l'architecte vous présente les constructeurs italiens et certaines de leurs réalisations les plus remarquables', *L'Œil*, vol. 61, January 1960, pp. 68–77; 101.

Hambly Maya, 'En Ny Engelsk Skola', *Byggmästaren*, vol. 34, no. A6, June 1955, pp. 159–62.

Haskell Douglas, 'The New Image of Architecture', *Architectural Forum*, vol. 107, no. 4, October 1957, pp. 111–13.

Haskell Douglas, 'Ornaments Rides Again', *Architectural Forum*, vol. 108, no. 4, April 1958, pp. 99–103.

Haskell Douglas, 'Big Change on the Campus', *Architectural Forum*, vol. 118, no. 3, March 1963, pp. 76–82.

Haskell Douglas, 'Muscles, Mirrors and Wire', *Architectural Forum*, vol. 120, no. 1, January 1964, p. 118.

Haskell Douglas, '75 Years of Change-Mostly Unpredicted', *Architectural Forum*, vol. 121, no. 2–3, August 1964, pp. 73–80.

Hastings Hubert De Cronin, 'The Court Style', *Architectural*

Review, vol. 105, no. 625, January 1949, pp. 3–10.

Herbert Gilbert, 'Notes in Passing', *Arts & Architecture*, vol. 78, no. 12, December 1961, p. 9.

Hersey G. L., Hill John T, 'Replication Replicated, or Notes on American Bastardy', *Perspecta*, vol. 9/10, 1965, pp. 211–48.

Heyer Paul, *Architects on Architecture: New Directions in America*, Allen Lane, New York, 1966.

Hiroshi Sasaki, 'Alison and Peter Smithson: the New Brutalism of Tomorrow', *Kokusai Kenchiku*, vol. 27, 1960, pp. 35–38.

Hitchcock Henry Russell, 'The International Style, Twenty Years After', *Architectural Record*, vol. 110, no. 2, August 1951, pp. 89–97.

Hitchcock Henry Russell, *Architecture: Nineteenth and Twentieth Centuries*, Penguin Books, Harmondsworth A.O, 1958.

Hitchcock Henry Russell, 'Food for Changing Sensibility', *Perspecta*, vol. 6, 1960, pp. 2–4.

Hitchcock Henry Russell, 'Notes of a Traveller: Wright and Kahn', *Zodiac*, vol. 6, 1960, pp. 15–21.

Hitchcock Henry Russell, 'The Rise to World Prominence of American Architecture', *Zodiac*, vol. 8, 1961, pp. 1–5.

Hitchcock Henry Russell, 'English

Architecture in the Early 1960s', *Zodiac*, vol. 12, 1963, pp. 18–47.

Hitchcock Henry-Russell, 'The Decade 1929–1939', *Journal of the Society of Architectural Historians*, vol. 24, no. 1, 1965, pp. 1–5.

Hitchcock Henry-Russell, 'Modern Architecture - A Memoir', *Journal of the Society of Architectural Historians*, vol. 27, no. 4, December 1968, pp. 227–33.

Hitchcock Henry Russell, Drexler Arthur (eds.), *Built in USA: Post-War Architecture*, Simon & Schuster, New York, 1952.

Hitchcock Henry Russell, Johnson Philip, 'The Buildings we See', in O'Connor Flannery (ed.), *New World Writing*, New American Library, New York, 1952, pp. 109–30.

Hitchcock Henry-Russell, Kidder Smith George Everard, 'Aalto Versus Aalto: The Other Finland', *Perspecta*, vol. 9/10, 1965, pp. 131–66.

Holm Lennart, 'Ideologioch Form', *Byggmästaren*, vol. 27, no. 15, 1948, pp. 264–72.

Holmes Burton H., 'Exposed Concrete Today', *Progressive Architecture*, vol. 45, no. 10, October 1960, pp. 150–57.

Hopkinson Tom, 'Editorial', *Manchester Guardian*, 22 September 1953, p. 1.

Huber Benedikt, 'Epigonen', *Das Werk*, vol. 46, no. 12, April 1959, pp. 419–22.

Hudnut Joseph, 'A New Eloquence for Architecture', *Architectural Record*, vol. 119, January 1956, pp. 139–46.

Hulten Bertil, *Building Modern Sweden*, Penguin, London, 1951.

Hurst Sam, Burchard John Ely, 'In Search of Theory', *Arts and Architecture*, vol. 81, no. 6, June 1963, p. 17.

Huxley Julian, 'TVA. An Achievement of Democratic Planning', *Architectural Review*, vol. 93, no. 558, June 1943, pp. 138–66.

Huxtable Ada Louis, 'Concrete technology in the U.S.A.', *Progressive Architecture*, vol. 113, no. 1, October 1960, pp. 144–65.

Jackson Eric W., *Achievement: A Short History of the LCC*, Longmans, London, 1965.

Jacobs Theo, 'Letter. The New Brutalism', *Architectural Design*, vol. 25, no. 3, March 1955, p. 96.

Jacobus John, 'Modern Architecture', in Seton Lloyd, Copplestone Trewin (eds.), *World Architecture: An Illustrated History*, Paul Hamlyn, London, 1963, pp. 297–341.

Jacobus John, *Twentieth-Century Architecture; The Middle Years, 1940–65*, Thames & Hudson, London, 1966.

Jellicoe G. A., 'A Philosophy of Landscape I', *Architects' Year Book*, vol. 1, 1945, pp. 39–42.

Jellicoe G. A., 'A Philosophy of Landscape II', *Architects' Year Book*, vol. 2, 1947, pp. 36–40.

Joedicke Jürgen, *Geschichte der Modernen Architektur: Synthese aus Form, Funktion und Konstruktion*, Hatje, Stuttgart, 1958.

Joedicke Jürgen, 'Häring at Gargkau', *Architectural Review*, vol. 127, no. 759, May 1960, pp. 313–18.

Joedicke Jürgen, *A History of Modern Architecture*, Architectural Press, London, 1961.

Joedicke Jürgen, *Architektur und Städtebau das Werk van den Broek und Bakema*, Karl Krämer, Stuttgart, 1963.

Joedicke Jürgen, 'New Brutalism: Brutalismus in der Architektur', *Bauen+Wohnen*, vol. 18, no. 11, November 1964, pp. 421–25.

Joedicke Jürgen, *Für eine lebendige Baukunst. Notizen und Kommentare*, Krämer Verlag, Stuttgart, 1965.

Joedicke Jürgen, *Hugo Häring: Schriften, Entwürfe, Bauten*, Krämer Verlag, Stuttgart, 1965.

Joedicke Jürgen, 'Britische Architektur: von Kontinent Aus Gesehen', *Bauen+Wohnen*, vol. 21, no. 12, December 1967, pp. 447–49.

Joedicke Jürgen, *Architecture Since 1945: Sources and Directions*, Pall Mall Press, London, 1969.

Joedicke Jürgen, *Moderne Architektur: Strömungen und Tendenzen*, Karl Krämer, Stuttgart, 1969.

Johnson Philip, 'School at Hunstanton. Comment by Philip Johnson as an American Follower of Mies van Der Rohe', *Architectural Review*, vol. 116, no. 693, September 1954, pp. 148–49.

Johnson Philip, 'Where Are We At?', *Architectural Review*, vol. 127, no. 763, September 1960, pp. 173–75.

Johnson Philip, 'Retreat from the International Style to the Present Scene', *Philip Johnson Writings*, Oxford University Press, New York, 1979.

Jones Cranston, *Architecture Today and Tomorrow*, McGraw-Hill, New York, 1961.

Jordan Robert Furneaux, 'Societies and Institutions', *Architects' Journal*, vol. 109, no. 2825, 31 March 1949, p. 303.

Jordan Robert Furneaux, 'Lubetkin', *Architectural Review*, vol. 118, no. 703, July 1955, pp. 36–44.

Jordan Robert Furneaux, 'LCC: New Standards in Official Architecture', *Architectural Review*, vol. 120, no. 718, November 1956, pp. 303–24.

Jordan Robert Furneaux, 'Bilancio dell'architettura inglese', *Casabella*, no. 250, April 1961, pp. 3–12.

Jordan Robert Furneaux, 'Piazza St. James', *The Observer*, 16 July 1961, p. 28.

Jordy William Henry, 'Humanism in Contemporary Architecture: Tough- and Tender-Minded', *Journal of Architectural Education*, vol. 15, no. 2, 1960, pp. 3–10.

Jordy William Henry, 'The Formal Image: USA', *Architectural Review*, vol. 127, no. 757, March 1960, pp. 156–65.

Jordy William Henry, 'The International Style in the 1930s', *Journal of the Society of Architectural Historians*, vol. 24, no. 1, 1965, pp. 10–14.

Kahn Louis, 'Toward a Plan for Midtown Philadelphia', *Perspecta*, vol. 2, 1953, pp. 10–27.

Kahn Louis, 'Order and Form', *Perspecta*, vol. 3, 1955, pp. 47–63.

Kahn Louis, 'Louis Kahn. Interview', *Perspecta*, vol. 7, 1961, pp. 9–28.

Kahn Louis, 'Kahn sull'architettura', *Architettura: Cronache e Storia*, vol. 10, November 1964, pp. 480–81.

Kallmann Gerhard Michael, 'The New Uncertainty', *Architectural Review*, vol. 100, no. 583, March 1946, pp. 95–98.

Kallmann Gerhard Michael, 'Towards a New Environment. The Way through Technology: America's

Unreleased Potential', *Architectural Review*, vol. 108, no. 648, December 1950, pp. 407–14.

Kallmann Gerhard Michael, 'Modern Tower in Old Milan', *Architectural Forum*, vol. 108, February 1958, pp. 108–11.

Kallmann Gerhard Michael, 'Vital Impulses', *Journal of Architectural Education*, vol. 14, no. 2, Autumn 1959, pp. 38–41.

Kallmann Gerhard Michael, 'The 'Action' Architecture of a New Generation', *Architectural Forum*, vol. 111, no. 4, October 1959, pp. 132–37.

Kallmann Gerhard Michael, 'New Perspectives for the Second Machine Age', *Four Great Makers of Modern Architecture*, Columbia University. School of Architecture, New York, 1961, pp. 279–85.

Kallmann Gerhard Michael, 'La "Action Architecture" di una generazione nuova', *Casabella-Continuità*, no. 269, November 1962, pp. 29–49.

Kennedy Robert Woods, 'After the International Style–Then What?', *Architectural Forum*, vol. 99, no. 3, September 1953, pp. 130–33; 186–90.

Kerr Robert, 'Notes on Architectural Style', *Architectural Review*, vol. 110, no. 657, September 1951, p. 205.

Kidder Smith George Everard, *Sweden Builds: Its Modern Architecture and Land Policy Background, Development and Contribution*, A. Bonnier, New York, 1950.

Kidder Smith George Everard, *The New Architecture of Europe. An Illustrated Guidebook and Appraisal*, World Publishing, New York, 1961.

Koeper Frederick H., 'The Discussions: at the Summit', *Journal of Architectural Education*, vol. 14, no. 2, 1959, pp. 5–9.

König Giovanni Walter, 'La seconda crisi, oggi', *Architettura:*

Cronache e Storia*, vol. 7, no. 73, January 1962, pp. 628–29.

Kornwolf James D., 'High Victorian Gothic; Or the Dilemma of Style in Modern Architecture', *Journal of the Society of Architectural Historians*, vol. 34, no. 1, March 1975, pp. 37–47.

Kultermann Udo, *Baukunst der Gegenwart: Dokumente des neuen Bauens in der Welt*, Wasmuth, Tübingen, 1958.

Kultermann Udo, 'Une Architecture Autre. Ein neugeknüpfter Faden der architektonischen Entwiklung', *Baukunst und Werkform*, vol. 11, no. 8, August 1958, pp. 425–41.

Kultermann Udo, *Dynamische Architektur*, Lucas Cranach, Munich, 1959.

Kultermann Udo, *Neues Bauen in Japan*, Wasmuth, Tübingen, 1960.

Kultermann Udo, *Neue Plastik, Neue Architektur*, Kupferberg, Mainz, 1963.

Kultermann Udo, *Neues Bauen in Afrika*, Wasmuth, Tübingen, 1963.

Kultermann Udo, *Neues Bauen in Der Welt*, Wasmuth, Tübingen, 1965.

Kultermann Udo, *Leben und Kunst: Zur Funktion der Intermedia*, E. Wasmuth, Tübingen, 1970.

Kultermann Udo, *Radikaler Realismus*, Wasmuth, Tübingen, 1972.

Kultermann Udo, *Neue Formen des Bildes*, Wasmuth, Tübingen, 1975.

Lancaster Osbert, 'The Relevance of the Past', *Architectural Review*, vol. 105, no. 628, April 1949, pp. 159–60.

Landau Royston, *New Directions in British Architecture*, Studio Vista, London, 1968.

Langer Susanne K., *Feeling and Form: A Theory of Art*, Scribner, New York, 1953.

Lannoy Richard, 'Two Buildings in India. Mill Ownes' Association Building, Ahmedabad', *Architectural Design*, vol. 26, January 1956, pp. 18–20.

Lannoy Richard, 'India. House at Ahmedabad', *Architectural Design*, vol. 26, March 1956, pp. 93–95.

Lasdun Denys, 'France, Maison Jaoul, Paris', *Architectural Design*, vol. 26, no. 3, March 1956, pp. 75–77.

Lasserre F., 'Letter. New Brutalism', *Architectural Review*, vol. 123, no. 733, January 1958, p. 88.

Le Corbusier, 'Marseille. Projet pour un immeuble d'état', *Techniques et Architecture*, vol. 6, July 1945, no. 7–8, pp. 346–48.

Le Corbusier, 'Unité d'Habitation à Marseille de Le Corbusier', *L'Homme et l'Architecture*, no. 11–14, 1947.

Le Corbusier, *Le Modulor*, Éditions de L'Architecture d'Aujourd'hui, Boulogne, 1948.

Le Corbusier, *Towards a New Architecture*, Architectural Press, London, 1948.

Le Corbusier, 'Unité', *L'Architecture d'Aujourd'hui*, April 1948, numéro hors série, n.p.

Le Corbusier, *New World of Space*, Reynal & Hitchcock, New York, 1948.

Le Corbusier, 'L'unità urbana verticale di Marsiglia', *Domus*, vol. 235, no. 3, April 1949, pp. 1–4.

Le Corbusier, *Œuvre Complète 1938–1946*, Éditions Girsberger, Zurich, 1950.

Le Corbusier, 'L'Unité d'Habitation de Marseille', *Le Point*, vol. 38, November 1950.

Le Corbusier, *Œuvre Complète 1946–1952*, vol. 5, Éditions Girsberger, Zürich, 1953.

Le Corbusier, *The Marseilles Block*, Harvill Press, London, 1953.

Le Corbusier, *Le Modulor 2*, Editions de L'Architecture d'Aujourd'hui, Boulogne, 1955.

Le Ricolais Robert, Scully Vincent, 'Louis I. Kahn', *L'Architecture d'Aujourd'hui*, no. 173, 1974, pp. 5–6.

Ling Arthur G., 'Architecture in the URSS', *RIBA Journal*, vol. 48, June 1941, pp. 155–58.

Ling Arthur G., *Planning and Building in the USSR*, Bantam Books, London, 1943.

Lippard Lucy R., *Pop Art*, Praeger, New York, 1966.

London County Council Division, 'Le Corbusier's Unité d'Habitation', *Architectural Review*, vol. 109, no. 653, May 1951, pp. 292–300.

Lyons Ellis Israel, 'Annex to the Old Vic', *Architectural Review*, vol. 124, no. 743, December 1958, pp. 361–64.

Macfarlane Stephen, 'Unité d'Habitation', *Plan: Architectural Students Association Journal*, vol. 4, 1949, pp. 23–27.

Malcolmson Reginald F., 'A Curriculum of Ideas', *Journal of Architectural Education*, vol. 14, no. 2, 1959, pp. 41–43.

Marshall D. G., 'Letter. Hunstanton: is it "introspective"?', *Architects' Journal*, vol. 120, no. 3112, October 1954, p. 486.

Maxwell Fry Edward, 'The Architect and his Time', *Architects' Year Book*, vol. 3, no. 3, 1949, pp. 9–12.

Maxwell Fry Edward, 'Twenty-Five Years of Modern Architecture in England', *Architectural Design*, vol. 25, no. 11, November 1955, pp. 338–41.

Maxwell Fry Edward et al., 'Ornamented Modern & Brutalism', *Zodiac*, vol. 4, April 1959, pp. 68–81.

McCullough David G., 'Architectural Spellbinder', *Architectural Forum*, vol. 111, no. 3, September 1959, pp. 136–37; 191; 202.

McQuade Walter, 'Architect Louis Kahn and His Strong-Boned Structures', *Architectural Forum*, vol. 107, no. 4, October 1957, pp. 134–43.

McQuade Walter, 'Toughness – Before Gentility Wins in Boston', *Architectural Forum*, vol. 117, August 1962, pp. 96–99.

McQuade Walter, 'Rudolph's Roman Road', *Architectural Forum*, vol. 118, no. 2, February 1963, pp. 100–09.

McQuade Walter, 'A Building that is an Event', *Architectural Forum*, vol. 120, no. 2, February 1964, pp. 62–89.

Mellor T., 'Letter. New Brutalism', *Architectural Review*, vol. 115, no. 690, June 1954, p. 364.

Melville Robert, 'Exhibitions', *Architectural Review*, vol. 119, no. 703, July 1955, p. 50.

Middleton Robin, 'Editorial', *Architectural Design*, vol. 35, no. 12, December 1965, p. 1.

Middleton Robin, 'The New Brutalism or a Clean, Well-Lighted Place', *Architectural Design*, vol. 37, no. 1, January 1967, p. 718.

Middleton Robin, 'Disintegration', *Architectural Design*, vol. 37, no. 5, May 1967, p. 203.

Miller Richard, 'Disenchantment and Criticism: The State of Modern Architecture', *Journal of Architectural Education*, vol. 14, no. 1, Spring 1959, pp. 9–12.

Mills Edward David, *The New Architecture in Great Britain, 1946–1953*, Standard Catalogue, London, 1953.

Mitchell Neal B., 'The Proposal', *Journal of Architectural Education*, vol. 14, no. 2, 1959, pp. 43–45.

Mitchell Neal B., 'A Proposal for a Sequence of Structure Courses', *Journal of Architectural Education*, vol. 15, no. 4, 1961, pp. 29–32.

Moffett Noel William, 'Le Corbusier's Unité d'Habitation at Marseille: A Critical Analysis', *Architectural Design*, vol. 21, January 1951, pp. 1, 3–7.

Moholy-Nagy László, *Vision in Motion*, P. Theobald, Chicago, 1947.

Moholy-Nagy Sibyl, 'The Future of the Past', *Perspecta*, vol. 7, 1961, pp. 65–76.

Moholy-Nagy Sibyl, 'The Measure: A Critical Appraisal of the Building and its Place in Contemporary Architecture', *Architectural Forum*, vol. 120, no. 2, February 1964, pp. 76–89.

Moholy-Nagy Sibyl, 'Review: Changing Ideals in Modern Architecture 1750-1950 by Peter Collins', *Journal of the Society of Architectural Historians*, vol. 26, no. 4, December 1967, pp. 316–18.

Moholy-Nagy Sibyl, 'Review of Architecture since 1945, Sources and Directions, Juergen Joedicke', *Journal of the Society of Architectural Historians*, vol. 29, no. 4, 1970, pp. 360–60.

Monotti Carlo, 'Chiesa della Madonna dei poveri', *Architettura: Cronache e Storia*, vol. 3, no. 25, November 1957, pp. 452–57.

Mumford Lewis, 'Monumentalism, Symbolism and Style', *Architectural Review*, vol. 105, no. 628, April 1949, pp. 173–80.

Musgrave Clifford, 'A New Edition of Pevsner's "European Architecture"', *The Burlington Magazine*, vol. 103, no. 704, 1961, pp. 469–70.

Nehls Werner, 'New Brutalism: Beginn einer neuen Epoche', *Baumeister*, vol. 64, January 1967, pp. 75–85.

Newman Oscar, *Ciam '59 in Otterlo: Arbeitsgruppe für die Gestaltung Soziologischer und Visueller Zusammenhänge*, vol. 1, Girsberger, Zurich, 1961.

Norton Paul F., 'World's Fairs in the 1930s', *Journal of the Society of Architectural Historians*, vol. 24, no. 1, 1965, pp. 27–30.

Olivier Marc, 'L'architecture japonaise après 1945', *L'Architecture d'Aujourd'hui*, vol. 34, no. 113/114, April-May 1964, pp. 182–87.

Osborn Frederic James, 'Concerning Le Corbusier. Part I', *Town & Country Planning*, vol. 20, no. 99, July 1952, pp. 311–16.

Osborn Frederic James, 'Concerning Le Corbusier. Part II', *Town & Country Planning*, vol. 20, no. 100, August 1952, pp. 359–63.

Paulhan Jean, *Guide d'un petit voyage en Suisse*, Gallimard, Paris, 1947.

Pedio Renato, 'Brutalismo in funzione di libertà. Il nuovo Istituto Marchiondi a Milano', *Architettura: Cronache e Storia*, vol. 3, no. 10, February 1959, pp. 682–88.

Pedio Renato, 'Costume inglese in due opere di Lyons, Israel & Ellis', *Architettura: Cronache e Storia*, vol. 77, March 1962, pp. 750–57.

Pedio Renato, 'Brutalista in Sicilia', *Architettura: Cronache e Storia*, vol. 24, no. 3, 1978, pp. 156–63.

Pehnt Wolfgang, 'Was ist Brutalismus? Zur Architekturgeschichte des letzten Jahrfünfts', *Das Kunstwerk*, vol. 14, no. 3, March 1960, pp. 14–23.

Pehnt Wolfgang (ed.), *Knaurs Lexikon der modernen Architektur*, Hatje, Munich, 1963.

Pehnt Wolfgang, *German Architecture*, New York-Washington, 1970.

Pevsner Nikolaus, *Pioneers of the Modern Movement: From William Morris to Walter Gropius*, Faber & Faber, London, 1936.

Pevsner Nikolaus, *An Enquiry into Industrial Art in England*, Cambridge University Press, Cambridge, 1937.

Pevsner Nikolaus, *Academies of Art, Past and Present*, Cambridge University Press, Cambridge, 1940.

Pevsner Nikolaus, *An Outline of European Architecture*, Penguin, London, 1942.

Pevsner Nikolaus, 'A Short Pugin Florilegium', *Architectural Review*, vol. 94, no. 560, August 1943, pp. 31–34.

Pevsner Nikolaus, 'The Genesis of the Picturesque', *Architectural Review*, vol. 96, November 1944, pp. 139–46.

Pevsner Nikolaus, 'Books. The New Humanism', *Architectural Review*, vol. 98, no. 584, August 1945, pp. 59–60.

Pevsner Nikolaus, 'The Architecture of Mannerism', in Grigson Geoffrey (ed.), *The Mint*, Routledge, London, 1946, pp. 120–32.

Pevsner Nikolaus, 'The Function of Craft in an industrial Age', *Art for Everyone Art and the State*, BBC Radio, 16-18-19 June 1946, London.

Pevsner Nikolaus, 'Apollo or Baboon', *Architectural Review*, vol. 104, no. 624, December 1948, pp. 271–79.

Pevsner Nikolaus, 'Canons of Criticism', *Architectural Review*, vol. 109, no. 649, January 1951, pp. 3–6.

Pevsner Nikolaus, *The Englishness of English Art*, Frederick A. Prager, New York, 1955.

Pevsner Nikolaus, 'Time and Le Corbusier', *Architectural Review*, vol. 125, no. 746, March 1959, pp. 159–65.

Pevsner Nikolaus, 'Roehampton, LCC Housing and the Picturesque Tradition', *Architectural Review*, vol. 125, no. 750, July 1959, pp. 21–35.

Pevsner Nikolaus, 'Modern Architecture and the Historian - or the Return of Historicism', *RIBA Journal*, no. 68, April 1961, pp. 230–40.

Pevsner Nikolaus, *The Penguin Dictionary of Architecture*, Penguin Books, London, 1966.

Pevsner Nikolaus, 'Brutalism', *The Guardian*, 9 December 1966, p. 7.

Pevsner Nikolaus, 'The Anti-Pioneers', *Architects' Journal*, vol. 145, no. 5, 1 February 1967, pp. 279–80.

Pevsner Nikolaus, *Studies in Art, Architecture, and Design*, Thames & Hudson, London, 1968.

Pidgeon Monica, 'Editorial', *Architectural Design*, vol. 21, no. 1, January 1951, p. 1.

Pierrefeu François De, *The Home of Man*, Architectural Press, London, 1948.

Piper John, 'Colour and Textures', *Architectural Review*, vol. 95, no. 566, February 1944, pp. 51–52.

Piper John, 'Pleasing Decay', *Architectural Review*, vol. 102, September 1947, pp. 85–94.

Ponti Gio, 'Forma', *Domus*, vol. 250, September 1950, pp. 4–5.

Ponti Gio, 'Giovinezza d'oggi o splendida età di Le Corbusier?', *Domus*, vol. 320, July 1956, pp. 1–4.

Ponti Gio, 'Si fa con i pensieri', *Domus*, vol. 379, June 1961, pp. 1–34.

Ponti Gio, 'Per una abbazia benedettina nel Minnesota', *Domus*, vol. 391, June 1962, pp. 1–6.

Ponti Gio, 'A Westport, Connecticut, sulla riva del Mare', *Domus*, vol. 397, December 1962, pp. 15–18.

Ponti Gio, 'Immagini dei due 'colleges' di Saarinen a Yale, con le sculture di Nivola', *Domus*, vol. 399, February 1963, pp. 17–26.

Pope Huge, 'Letter on New Brutalism', *Architectural Review*, vol. 115, no. 690, June 1954, p. 364.

Portoghesi Paolo, 'Dal Neorealismo al Neoliberty', *Comunità*, vol. 12, no. 65, December 1958, pp. 69–79.

Portoghesi Paolo, *Dizionario enciclopedico di architettura e urbanistica*, Istituto Editoriale Romano, Roma, 1968.

Poulsen C., 'Brutalism fra Hunstanton til the Economist', *Arkitekten*, vol. 64, 1967, pp. 542–47.

Raafat Aly Ahmed, *Reinforced Concrete in Architecture*, Reinhold Publishing Corporation, New York, 1958.

Ragon Michel, 'Was wird aus der amerikanischen Architektur? = Où va l'architecture americaine?, *Bauen+Wohnen*, vol. 19, no. 1, January 1965, pp. 37–44.

Randell Barbara, Pidgeon Monica, 'About Ourselves. Editorial', *Architectural Design*, vol. 16, no. 12, December 1946, p. 132.

Reilly Paul, 'British Architects' Response to the Problems of Modern Living', *The Manchester Guardian*, 2 April 1956, p. 5.

Ricci Leonardo, 'Nascita di un villaggio per una nuova comunità, Sicilia', *Domus*, vol. 409, December 1963, pp. 7–13.

Richards James Maude, *An Introduction to Modern Architecture*, Penguin Books, Harmondsworth, 1940.

Richards James Maude, *The Castles on the Ground: The Anatomy of Suburbia*, Architectural Press, London, 1946.

Richards James Maude, 'The Second Half Century', *Architectural Review*, vol. 101, no. 601, January 1947, pp. 21–36.

[Richards James Maude], 'The New Empiricism: Sweden's Last Style', *Architectural Review*, vol. 102, no. 606, June 1947, pp. 199–204.

Richards James Maude, 'The Bay Region Domestic', *Architectural Review*, vol. 104, no. 631, October 1948, p. 164.

Richards James Maude, 'The Wrong Turning', *Architectural Review*, vol. 105, no. 627, March 1949, pp. 107–12.

Richards James Maude, 'The Next Step', *Architectural Review*, vol. 107, no. 639, March 1950, pp. 165–68.

Richards James Maude, 'Le Corbusier's Œuvre Complète. Shorter Notice', *Architectural Review*, vol. 110, no. 657, September 1951, p. 204.

Richards James Maude, 'Preview', *Architectural Review*, vol. 115, no. 685, January 1954, pp. 7–13.

Richards James Maude, 'Buildings of the Year', *Architects' Journal*, vol. 121, no. 3125, 20 January 1955, pp. 85–100.

Richards James Maude, *The Functional Tradition in Early Industrial Buildings*, Architectural Press, London, 1958.

Richards James Maude, 'The Functional Tradition in Early industrial Building', *Motif*, no. 2, 1959, pp. 77–78.

Robertson Howard P., *Architecture Arising*, Faber & Faber, London, 1944.

Rogers Ernesto Nathan, 'Appunti sull'Inghilterra e l'Italia', *Casabella-Continuità*, vol. 250, April 1961, pp. 1–2.

Rosenberg Harold, 'The American Action Painters', *Art News*, vol. 51, no. 8, December 1952, pp. 22–50.

Rosenberg Harold, 'The Premises of Action Painting', *Encounter*, vol. 20, no. 5, May 1963, p. 47.

Rossi Aldo, 'Arredamento e Architettura', in Canella Guido, Gregotti Vittorio (ed.), *Nuovi disegni per il mobile italiano*, catalogue curated by Osservatorio delle arti industriali, March 1960.

Rossi Aldo, 'Il convento de la Tourette di Le Corbusier', *Casabella-Continuità*, vol. 246, December 1960, p. 4.

Rossi Aldo, 'L'esperienza inglese e i nuovi problemi urbanistici', *Casabella-Continuità*, vol. 250, April 1961, pp. 13–14.

Roth Alfred, 'Architectural Education', *Architects' Year Book*, vol. 2, 1947, pp. 115–20.

Rowe Colin, 'The Mathematics of the Ideal Villa: Palladio and Le Corbusier Compared', *Architectural Review*, vol. 101, no. 602, February 1947, pp. 101–04.

Rowe Colin, 'Mannerism and Modern Architecture', *Architectural Review*, vol. 107, no. 641, May 1950, pp. 289–300.

Rowe Colin, 'Dominican Monastery of La Tourette, Eveux-sur-Arbresle, Lyons', *Architectural Review*, vol. 129, no. 772, June 1961, pp. 401–10.

Rowe Colin, 'Waiting for Utopia', *The New York Times*, Book review section, 10 September 1967, p. 351.

Royston Landau, *New Directions in British Architecture*, Studio Vista, London, 1968.

Rudolph Paul, 'The Changing Philosophy of Architecture', *Architectural Forum*, vol. 101, no. 1, July 1954, pp. 120–21.

Rudolph Paul, 'Regionalism in Architecture', *Perspecta*, vol. 4, 1957, pp. 12–19.

Rudolph Paul, 'Creative Use of Architectural Materials', *Progressive Architecture*, vol. 40, April 1959, pp. 92–94.

Rudolph Paul, *The Architecture of Paul Rudolph*, Thames and Hudson, London, 1970.

Rykwert Joseph, 'Review of a Review', *Zodiac*, vol. 4, April 1959, pp. 13–14.

Rykwert Joseph, 'Banham-Gregotti', *Domus*, no. 451, June 1967, pp. 2–6.

Saarinen Eero, 'The Six Broad Currents of Modern Architecture', *Architectural Forum*, vol. 99, no. 1, July 1953, pp. 110–15.

Saarinen Eliel, *Search for Form; A Fundamental Approach to Art*, Reinhold Pub. Corp, New York, 1948.

Sachs Lisbeth, 'Studentenheim des Massachusetts Institute Technology, Cambridge (USA)', *Werk*, vol. 37, April 1950, pp. 97–102.

Sainsbury Geoffrey, *The Marseille Block*, The Harvill Press, London, 1954.

Samonà Giuseppe, 'La lettura della cappella a Ronchamp', *Architettura: Cronache e Storia*, vol. 8, June 1956, p. 111.

Samonà Joseph [Giuseppe], 'Man, Matter and Space', *Architects' Year Book*, vol. 5, 1953, pp. 110–22.

Santini Pier Carlo, 'The Focus is on the Young Architects', *Zodiac*, vol. 4, April 1959, pp. 174–79.

Saxl Fritz, 'Visual Education', *The Listener*, 23 September 1943, p. 356.

Schinneller James A., 'Art Programs for all Secondary School Students', *Art Education*, vol. 17, no. 3, 1964, pp. 11–14.

Schmertz M., 'The New Boston City Hall', *Architectural Record*, vol. 145, February 1969, pp. 144–50.

Schmertz Mildred, 'Movement Systems as Generators of Built Form', *Architectural Record*, vol. 158, no. 7, November 1975, pp. 105–16.

Scott Brown Denise, 'Team 10, *Perspecta* 10, and the Present State of Architectural Theory', *Journal of the American Institute of Planners*, vol. 33, no. 1, January 1967, pp. 42–50.

Scott Brown Denise, 'On Pop Art, Permissiveness, and Planning', *Journal of the American Institute of Planners*, vol. 35, no. 3, May 1969, pp. 184–86.

Scott Kenneth, 'Letter', *Architectural Review*, vol. 115, no. 688, April 1954, p. 274.

Scott Keith, 'Letters: Egg-Heads Exposed?', *Architects' Journal*, vol. 124, no. 3216, 18 October 1956, p. 546.

Scully Vincent, 'Archetype and Order in Recent American Architecture', *Art in America*, vol. 42, December 1954, pp. 251–61.

Scully Vincent, 'Wright vs. the International Style', *Art News*, vol. 53, March 1954, pp. 32–35, 64–66.

Scully Vincent, 'Order and Form', *Perspecta*, vol. 3, 1955, pp. 64–75.

Scully Vincent, 'Art Gallery and Design Center, Yale University, New Haven', *Museum: A Quarterly Review*, vol. 9, no. 2, 1956, pp. 110–13.

Scully Vincent, 'Modern Architecture: Toward a Redefinition of Style', *Perspecta*, vol. 4, 1957, pp. 4–11.

Scully Vincent, 'Louis Sullivan's Architectural Ornament: A Brief Note Concerning Humanist Design in the Age of Force', *Perspecta*, vol. 5, 1959, pp. 73–80.

Scully Vincent, 'The Precisionist Strain in American Architecture', *Art in America*, vol. 48, no. 3, 1960, pp. 46–53.

Scully Vincent, *Modern Architecture*, George Braziller, New York, 1961.

Scully Vincent, *Louis I. Kahn*, George Braziller, New York, 1962.

Scully Vincent, 'Wright, International Style and Kahn', *Arts*, vol. 36, March 1962, pp. 67–71, 77.

Scully Vincent, 'Art and Architecture Building, Yale University', *Architectural Review*, vol. 135, no. 805, May 1964, pp. 324–32.

Scully Vincent, 'Light, Form and Power; New Work of Louis Kahn', *Architectural Forum*, vol. 121, August/September 1964, pp. 162–70.

Scully Vincent, 'A Search for Principle Between Two Wars', *RIBA Journal*, June 1969, pp. 240–47.

Scully Vincent, *American Architecture and Urbanism*, Praeger, New York, 1969.

Segal Walter, 'The New Brutalism', *Architectural Design*, vol. 24, no. 2, February 1954, p. 7 (ad).

Serenyi Peter, 'Le Corbusier's Changing Attitude Toward Form', *Journal of the Society of Architectural Historians*, vol. 24, 1965, no. 1, pp. 15–23.

Sert José Luis, 'Complicated and Delicate, Opinions on the Yale Art Gallery', *Progressive Architecture*, vol. 35, no. 4, May 1954, pp. 15–16, 22, 24.

Sert José Luis, 'Le Corbusier, What Became of Ciam?', *Architectural Review*, vol. 129, March 1961, p. 154.

Shahn B., 'Realism Reconsidered', *Perspecta*, vol. 4, 1957, pp. 28–35.

Sharp Dennis, *Modern Architecture and Expressionism*, George Braziller, New York, 1966.

Sharpe Richard, 'Gobbledigook', *Architectural Review*, vol. 119, no. 712, May 1956, p. 222.

Shear Knox John, 'Architecture for the Complete Man', *Architectural Record*, pp. 201–02.

Shepheard Peter, 'Inaugural Address by President', *Architects' Journal*, vol. 120, no. 3114, November 1954, pp. 567, 569–70.

Smith Donald, 'Towards a Theory', *Architectural Review*, vol. 137, no. 816, February 1965, pp. 101–04.

P.D.S. [Smithson Alison], 'House in Soho', *Architectural Design*, vol. 23, no. 12, December 1953, p. 342.

Smithson Alison, 'But Today We Collect Ads', *Ark*, vol. 18, November 1956, pp. 49–50.

Smithson Alison, 'Couvent de la Tourette, Eveux-sur-Arbresle, Nr. Lyon, France', *Architectural Design*, vol. 28, November 1958, p. 462.

Smithson Alison, 'Caravan-Embryo Appliance House', *Architectural Design*, vol. 29, no. 9, September 1959, p. 348.

Smithson Alison, 'A Photograph and Some Auto-Biographical Notes, *Bauen+Wohnen*, vol. 12, no. 9, October 1959, p. 348.

Smithson Alison, 'The Function of Architecture on Cultures-in-Change', *Architectural Design*, vol. 30, April 1960, pp. 32–38.

Smithson Alison, 'Not Quite Architecture: War Reporter Looks Back', *Architects' Journal*, vol. 5, January 1961, pp. 1–3.

Smithson Alison, 'La generazione del '47', *Casabella*, vol. 250, April 1961, pp. 27–28.

Smithson Alison, *Team 10 Primer*, Standard Catalogue Co, London, 1962.

(Signed) Surprised [Alison Smithson], 'Not Quite Architecture: Toward an Instant Architecture', *Architects' Journal*, vol. 136, no. 16, October 1962, pp. 897; 899.

Camini p. W. [Alison Smithson], 'What Happened to the Lovely Crispy Pollocks?', *Architectural Design*, vol. 35, March 1965.

Chippendale I. [Alison Smithson], 'The L.C.C. Was Our Uncle', *Architectural Design*, vol. 35, no. 9, September 1965, p. 428.

Smithson Alison and Peter, 'Correspondence. Architectural

Principles in the Age of Humanism', *RIBA Journal*, vol. 59, no. 4, February 1952, p. 140.

Smithson Alison and Peter, 'Statement', in *Parallel of Life and Art*, exhibition catalogue, ICA, London, 1953.

Smithson Alison and Peter, 'An Urban Project: Golden Lane Housing', *Architects' Year Book*, vol. 5, 1953, pp. 48–55.

Smithson Alison and Peter, 'Some Notes on Architecture', *244: Journal of the University of Manchester Architecture and Planning Society*, vol. 1, Spring 1954, p. 4.

Smithson Alison and Peter, 'Secondary School at Hunstanton', *Architects' Journal*, vol. 120, no. 3107, September 1954, pp. 341–52.

Smithson Alison and Peter, 'The Built World: Urban Reidentification', *Architectural Design*, vol. 25, no. 6, June 1955, pp. 185–87.

Smithson Alison and Peter, 'Alternative to the Garden City Idea', *Architectural Design*, vol. 26, no. 7, July 1956.

Smithson Alison and Peter, 'Cluster Patterns: Images from Scrap Book', *Architect and Building News*, July 1956.

Smithson Alison and Peter, 'Aesthetic of Change', *Architects' Year Book*, no. 8, 1957, pp. 14–22.

Smithson Alison and Peter, 'The New Brutalism: Alison and Peter Smithson Answer the Criticism on the Opposite Page', *Architectural Design*, vol. 27, no. 4, April 1957, p. 113.

Smithson Alison and Peter, 'Cluster City: A New Shape for the Community', *Architectural Review*, vol. 122, no. 730, November 1957, pp. 333–36.

Smithson Alison and Peter, 'Mobility Road Systems', *Architectural Design*, vol. 28, no. 10, October 1958, pp. 385–88.

Smithson Alison and Peter, 'Implications of Appliances: A Symposium', *Design 119*, November 1958.

Smithson Alison and Peter, 'On Teaching', *Architectural Prospect*, Autumn 1959.

Smithson Alison and Peter, *Uppercase*, no. 3, Whitefriars, London, 1960.

Smithson Alison and Peter, 'Architecture and Art', Le *Carré Bleu*, no. 2, May 1960.

Smithson Alison and Peter, 'Louis Kahn', *Architects' Year Book*, vol. 9, August 1960.

Smithson Alison and Peter, 'Education for Town Building', *Byggkunst*, 8 November 1960.

Smithson Alison and Peter, 'Fix', *Architectural Review*, vol. 128, no. 766, December 1960, pp. 437–39.

Smithson Alison and Peter, 'Architect's Own House, Tisbury, Wiltshire', *Architectural Review*, vol. 133, no. 791, February 1963, pp. 135–36.

Smithson Alison and Peter, 'Celebratory Gears: Flags', *Architectural Design*, vol. 31, no. 2, February 1966.

Smithson Alison and Peter, 'Concealment and Display: Meditations on Braun', *Architectural Design*, vol. 36, no. 7, July 1966, pp. 362–63.

Smithson Alison and Peter, 'Banham's Bumper Book on Brutalism, Discussed by Alison and Peter Smithson', *Architects' Journal*, vol. 144, no. 26, December 1966, pp. 1590–91.

Smithson Alison and Peter, *Ordinariness and Light*, MIT Press, Cambridge, Massachusetts, 1970.

Smithson Peter, 'Architect's Own House in Rotterdam', *Architectural Design*, vol. 24, no. 8, August 1954, pp. 227–30.

Smithson Peter, 'Modern Architecture in Holland', *Architectural Design*, vol. 101, no. 3, August 1954, pp. 68–70.

Smithson Peter, 'Lesson of Le Havre: Perret', *Architectural Design*, vol. 101, no. 4, September 1954.

Smithson Peter, 'Maison Jaoul: Tile by Le Corbusier', *Architectural Design*, vol. 25, no. 12, December 1955, pp. 302–11.

Smithson Peter, 'Futurism: Comment on Banham's Talk', *RIBA Journal*, February 1957.

Smithson Peter, 'Discussion', *Architectural Design*, vol. 27, no. 6, June 1957, p. 185.

Smithson Peter, 'House at Watford Herts, *Architectural Review*, vol. 122, no. 728, September 1957, pp. 194–97.

Smithson Peter, 'Letter to America', *Architectural Design*, vol. 28, no. 3, March 1958, pp. 93–102.

Smithson Peter, 'Footnote on the Seagram Building', *Architectural Review*, vol. 124, no. 743, December 1958, pp. 374–82.

Smithson Peter, 'Ludwig Mies van der Rohe', *Architectural Association Journal*, October 1959, p.n.n.

Smithson Peter, 'Le Corbusier: Contribution to a Symposium', *Architectural Association Journal*, May 1959, pp. 254–62.

Smithson Peter, 'N.Q.A. Not with a Bang but with a Flicker: End of Machine Aesthetics', *Architects' Journal*, vol. 131, 28 May 1959.

Smithson Peter, 'On Louis Kahn', *Architects' Year Book*, vol. 9, 1960, pp. 27–28.

Smithson Peter, 'The Idea of Architecture in the '50s', *Architects' Journal*, vol. 21, 21 January 1960, pp. 121–26.

Smithson Peter, 'The Revolution in Architectural Thinking since 1950', *Husmellon*, vol. 1, May 1960.

Smithson Peter, 'Class of '47', *Casabella-Continuità*, vol. 251, May 1961.

Smithson Peter, 'My Own Debt to Mies Van Der Rohe', *Bauen+Wohnen*, vol. 20, no. 5, May 1965, p. 206.

Smithson Peter, 'The Rocket: A Statement on the Present State of Architecture, Giving a Certain Rationality to Our instinctive Judgements on it', *Architectural Design*, vol. 35, no. 7, July 1965, pp. 322–23.

Smithson Peter, 'Without Rhetoric', *Architectural Design*, vol. 37, no. 1, January 1967, pp. 38–39.

Smithson Peter, 'Alvar Aalto and the Ethos of the Second Generation', *Ark. Arkkitehti*, vol. 47, no. 7–8, July 1967, p. 21.

Sottsass Ettore Jr., 'Le Corbusier e il Mediterraneo', *Domus*, vol. 291, February 1954, p. 44.

Spade Rupert, *Paul Rudolph*, Thames & Hudson, London, 1968.

Spring Bernard P., Canty Donald, 'Concrete, The Material That Can Do Almost Anything', *Architectural Forum*, vol. 117, no. 3, March 1962, pp. 78–96.

Stearn Gerald Emanuel, *McLuhan, Hot & Cool*, Dial Press, New York, 1967.

Stern Robert Arthur Morton, 'Relevance of the Decade', *Journal of the Society of Architectural Historians*, vol. 24, no. 1, 1965, pp. 6–10.

Stern Robert Arthur Morton, *New Directions in American Architecture*, George Braziller, New York, 1969.

Stern Robert Arthur Morton, 'Yale 1950-1965', *Oppositions*, vol. 4, 1974, pp. 35–62.

Stirling James Frazer, 'From Garches to Jaoul', *Architectural Review*, vol. 118, no. 705, September 1955, pp. 145–51.

Stirling James Frazer, 'Ronchamp, Le Corbusier's Chapel and the Crisis of Rationalism', *Architectural Review*, vol. 119, no. 711, March 1956, pp. 155–61.

Stirling James Frazer, 'Regionalism and Modern Architecture', *Architects' Year Book*, vol. 8, 1957, pp. 62–68.

Stirling James Frazer, 'Young Architects. A Personal View of the Present Situation', *Architectural Design*, vol. 28, no. 6, June 1958, pp. 232–40.

Stirling James Frazer, 'Plucky Jim's New Brutalism', *New Statesman*, vol. 50, July 1958, p. 116.

Stirling James Frazer, 'Flats at Ham Common', *Architectural Review*, vol. 124no. 741, October 1958, pp. 223–26.

Stirling James Frazer, 'Flats at Langham House, Ham Common, Richmond', *Architectural Design*, vol. 28, no. 11, November 1958, pp. 123–24.

Stirling James Frazer and Gowan James, 'Afterthoughts on the Flats at Ham Common', *Architecture and Building*, May 1959, pp. 167–69.

Summerson John, 'The London Suburban Villa', *Architectural Review*, vol. 104, no. 620, August 1948, pp. 63–72.

Summerson John, 'William Butterfield, or the Glory of Ugliness', *Heavenly Mansions: and Other Essays on Architecture*, The Cresset Press, London, 1949, pp. 159–76.

Summerson John, *Heavenly Mansions and Other Essays on Architecture*, The Cresset Press, London, 1949.

Summerson John, *Architecture in Britain 1530 to 1830*, Penguin Books, London, 1953.

Summerson John, *45–55 Ten Years of British Architecture*, Arts Council of Great Britain, London, 1956.

Summerson John, 'The Case for a Theory of "Modern" Architecture', *RIBA Journal*, vol. 64, June 1957, pp. 307–10.

Summerson John, 'Nikolaus Pevsner 1967 Gold Medallist',

RIBA Journal, vol. 74, August 1967, p. 316.

Summerson John, *Concerning Architecture: Essays on Architectural Writers and Writing Presented to Nikolaus Pevsner*, Allen Lane, London, 1968.

Sylvester Anthony David Bernard, 'Architecture in Modern Painting', *Architectural Review*, vol. 109, no. 650, February 1951, pp. 81–90.

Sylvester Anthony David Bernard, 'Round the London Art Galleries, *The Listener*, September 1953, p. 512.

Tafuri Manfredo, *L'architettura moderna in Giappone*, Cappelli Editore, Bologna, 1964.

Tafuri Manfredo, *Teorie e Storia dell'architettura*, Editori Laterza, Roma-Bari, 1968.

Tanner Ogden, 'Architecture in Transition', *Architectural Forum*, vol. 121, August 1964, no. 2–3, pp. 71–163.

Taylor Nicholas, 'Honest to Brut', *New Statesman*, 10 March 1967, pp. 334–35.

Tentori Francesco, 'English Brutalism: Selection of Writings', *Zodiac*, vol. 18, 1968, pp. 42–50.

Tentori Francesco, 'Phoenix Brutalism', *Zodiac*, vol. 18, 1968, pp. 31–41.

The Editors, 'Exterior Furnishing or Sharawaggi: The Art of Making Urban Landscape', *Architectural Review*, vol. 95, no. 565, January 1944, pp. 3–11.

Theron Danil, 'The New Brutalists', *Theoria: A Journal of Social and Political Theory*, vol. 24, June 1965, pp. 49–52.

Thiel Philip, 'City Hall at Kurashiki, Japan', *Architectural Review*, vol. 131, February 1962, pp. 107–14.

Thomas M. H., 'Yale Art Gallery', *Architectural Design*, vol. 25, no. 1, January 1955, pp. 20–21.

Tunnard Christopher, 'The Conscious Stone', *Perspecta*, vol. 3, 1955, pp. 22–78.

Tunnard Christopher et al., 'Man Made America: A Special Number of the Architectural Review for December 1950', *Architectural Review*, vol. 108, no. 648, December 1950.

Turner Robert, 'Where Are We Going', *Architects' Journal*, vol. 108, no. 2799, September 1948, pp. 307–08.

Van Eckhardt Wolf, 'The Age of Anti-Architecture', *Saturday Review*, 23 February 1965, pp. 19–21; 62.

Van Goethem Jan, 'Casa dei ragazzi ad Amsterdam', *Architettura: Cronache e Storia*, vol. 7, no. 72, October 1961, pp. 386–402.

Van Trump James D., 'Henry Hornbostel: the New Brutalism', *Charette*, vol. 46, no. 5, 1966, pp. 8–11.

Vassiliadis E. D., 'Hunstanton', *Architectural Review*, vol. 117, no. 698, February 1955, p. 82.

Veronesi Giulia, 'Alvar Aalto', *Emporium*, vol. 115, 1952, pp. 98–104.

Veronesi Giulia, 'New Look on the Hills Near Florence', *Zodiac*, vol. 4, April 1959, pp. 10–11.

Veronesi Giulia, 'Yamasaki and Stone', *Zodiac*, vol. 8, 1961, pp. 128–139.

Veronesi Giulia, 'Paul Rudolph', *Zodiac*, vol. 8, 1961, pp. 149–54.

Veronesi Giulia, 'Les gares du ciel: Orly', *Zodiac*, vol. 9, 1962, pp. 182–87.

Veronesi Giulia, *Profili: disegni - architetti - strutture - esposizioni*, vol. 3, Vallecchi, Firenze, 1969.

Viganò Vittoriano, 'L'istituto Marchiondi a Milano-Baggio. L'internato per ragazzi difficili', *Comunità*, vol. 12, no. 57, February 1958, pp. 64–69.

Viganò Vittoriano, 'An Interview with Vittoriano Viganò', *Casabella*, vol. 339, no. 340, August 1969, pp. 46–51.

Voelcker John, 'Correspondence. Architectural Principles in the Age of Humanism', *RIBA Journal*, vol. 59, no. 4, February 1952, pp. 140–41.

Voelcker John, 'Hunstanton Provides a Sense of Location', *Architects' Journal*, vol. 120, no. 3111, October 1954, p. 456.

Voelcker John, 'New Brutalism', *Architectural Design*, vol. 06, no. 27, June 1957, p. 184.

Weeks John, 'Formalism Avoided', *Architects' Journal*, vol. 118, no. 3059, October 1953, p. 499.

West Gerald, 'Astragal at the Bartlett', *Architects' Journal*, vol. 120, no. 396, July 1954, p. 3.

West Thomas Wilson, *A History of Architecture in Italy*, Hodder & Stoughton, London, 1968.

Whiffen Marcus, *American Architecture Since 1780: A Guide to the Styles*, MIT Press, Cambridge, Massachusetts, 1969.

Wilson Colin St John, 'The Vertical City', *The Observer*, 17 February 1952, p. 8.

Wilson Colin St John, 'Open Letter to an American Student', *Architectural Design*, vol. 35, no. 3, March 1965, pp. 6–7.

Wittkower Rudolf, 'Federico Zuccari and John Wood of Bath', *Journal of the Warburg and Courtauld Institutes*, vol. 6, 1943, pp. 220–22.

Wittkower Rudolf, 'Principles of Palladio's Architecture', *Journal of the Warburg and Courtauld Institutes*, vol. 7, 1944, pp. 102–22.

Wittkower Rudolf, *Architectural Principles in the Age of Humanism*, Warburg Institute, London, 1949.

Zegel Sylvain, 'A Vertical Community: Le Corbusier's Project at Marseille', *The Manchester Guardian*, 2 February 1949, p. 75.

Zevi Bruno, *Verso un'architettura organica: saggio sullo sviluppo del pensiero architettonico negli ultimi cinquant'anni*, Giulio Einaudi Editore, Torino, 1945.

Zevi Bruno, *Frank Lloyd Wright*, Il Balcone, Milan, 1947.

Zevi Bruno, *Erik Gunnar Asplund*, Il Balcone, Milan, 1948.

Zevi Bruno, 'Dormitorio degli studenti del Massachusetts Institute of Technology a Cambridge', *Metron*, vol. 35–36, 1949, pp. 14–22.

Zevi Bruno, 'Riconoscimento dell'architettura Post-

Razionalista', *Comunità*, vol. 5, September 1949, pp. 28–29.

Zevi Bruno, *Realtà dell'architettura Organica*, L'airone, Rome, 1950.

Zevi Bruno, *Storia dell'architettura moderna*, Einaudi, Torino, 1950.

Zevi Bruno, *Storia dell'architettura moderna*, Ed. 3, Einaudi, Torino, 1955.

Zevi Bruno, 'I ragazzi non scappano', *L'Espresso*, 2 March 1958, p. 16.

Zevi Bruno, 'Brutalismo in funzione di libertà: il nuovo Istituto Marchiondi a Milano', *Architettura: Cronache e Storia*, vol. 40, no. 2, February 1959, pp. 683–90.

Zevi Bruno, 'La registrazione veritiera di Le Corbusier', *Architettura: Cronache e Storia*, vol. 7, no. 68, June 1961, pp. 74–75.

Zevi Bruno, 'Architettura e Pop- Art', *Architettura: Cronache e Storia*, vol. 10, no. 111, January 1965, pp. 574–75.

Zevi Bruno, 'La misura umana del tramonto lecorbusieriano', *Architettura: Cronache e Storia*, vol. 11, no. 117, July 1965, pp. 142–43.

Zevi Bruno, 'Nikolaus Pevsner denuncia gli Anti-Pioneers', *Architettura: Cronache e Storia*, vol. 138, April 1967, pp. 772–73.

Bibliography:
Secondary Sources

Acayaba Marlene, 'Brutalismo caboclo e as residências paulistas', *Projeto*, vol. 73, March 1985, pp. 46–48.

Acayaba Marlene, 'Vilanova Artigas, amado mestre', *Projeto*, vol. 76, December 1985, pp. 50–54.

Acayaba Marlene, 'Reflexões sobre o brutalismo caboclo', *Projeto*, vol. 78, April 1986, pp. 68–70.

Ackerman James Sloss, 'Rudolf Wittkower's Influence on the History of Architecture', *Source: Notes in the History of Art*, vol. 8/9, no. 4/1, July 1989, pp. 87–90.

Aitchison Matthew, *Visual Planning and the Picturesque*, Getty Publications, Los Angeles, 2010.

Albuerne Alejandra, 'Robin Hood Gardens: Reinforced Concrete Design and Construction of a Museum Artefact in Reinforced Concrete', in James W. P. Campbell et. al. (eds.), *Iron, Steel and Buildings. Studies in the History of Construction. Proceedings of the Seventh Conference of the Construction History Society*, Cambridge, 2020, pp. 612–24.

Allen Stan, 'Banham's Material Ecologies', *Journal of Architectural Education*, vol. 71, no. 2, July 2017, pp. 262–63.

Alloway Lawrence (ed.), *Modern Dreams: The Rise and Fall and Rise of Pop*, MIT Press, Cambridge, 1988.

Artigas Rosa, 'Sobre Brutalismo, mitos e bares', *AU. Arquitetura e Urbanismo*, vol. 7, no. 9, December 2000, pp. 61–63.

Artigas Vilanova João Batista, *Caminhos da arquitetura*, Cosac Naify, São Paulo, 1981.

Artigas Vilanova João Batista, 'Em branco e preto', *AU. Arquitetura e Urbanismo*, vol. 17, April 1988, p. 78.

Artigas Vilanova João Batista, 'Fragmentos de um discurso complexo', *Projeto*, vol. 109, April 1988, pp. 91–94.

Artigas Vilanova João Batista, 'As posições dos anos 50', *Projeto*, vol. 109, April 1988, pp. 95–102.

Artigas Vilanova João Batista, *A função social do arquiteto*, Nobel, São Paulo, 1989.

Artigas Vilanova João Batista, *Vilanova Artigas*, Editorial Blau, Lisboa, 1997.

Atelier van Lieshout, Navid Nuur, Pieter Vermeersch, Franz Erhard Walther, Christoph Weber, *Three Positions. Six Directions: The Brutalist Ideal*, exhibition, König Gallery, Berlin, 21 January – 12 February 2017.

Aynsley Jeremy (ed.), *The Banham Lectures: Essays on Designing the Future*, Design History Society, Oxford, 2009.

Bacon Mardges, *Le Corbusier in America. Travels in the Land of the Timid*, MIT Press, Cambridge, 2001.

Bacon Mardges, 'Le Corbusier and Postwar America: The TVA and Béton Brut', *Journal of the Society of Architectural Historians*, vol. 74, no. 1, March 2015, pp. 13–40.

Banham Mary (ed.), *A Critic Writes: Essays by Reyner Banham*, University of California Press, Berkeley, 1990.

Banham Mary, Interview by Corinne Julius, National Life Story Collection: Architects' Lives, British Library Sound Archive, Oral History, C467/67, 2001.

Banham Reyner, *The Architecture of the Well-Tempered Environment*, Architectural Press, London, 1969.

Banham Reyner, *Age of the Masters: A Personal View of Modern Architecture*, Architectural Press, London, 1975.

Banham Reyner, *Critique Architecturale*, Institut de l'Environnement, Paris, 1975.

Banham Reyner, *Megastructure: Urban Futures of the Recent Past*, Thames and Hudson, London, 1976.

Banham Reyner, 'Arts in Society: The Valley of the Dams', *New Society*, vol. 41, July 1977, pp. 138–39.

Banham Reyner, *Fathers of Pop*, Arts Council of Great Britain, Concord Video & Film Council, UK, 1979.

Banham Reyner, *A Concrete Atlantis: U.S. Industrial Building and European Modern Architecture, 1900-1925*, MIT Press, Cambridge, 1986.

Banham Reyner, *The Visions of Ron Herron*, Academy Editions, London, 1994.

Baudoui Rémi (ed.), *Le Corbusier. Correspondance lettres à la famille 1926-1946*, Infolio Éditions, Paris/Lausanne, 2013.

Beanland Christopher (ed.), *Concrete Concept: Brutalist Buildings Around the World*, Frances Lincoln, London, 2016.

Becker Margret, *Der Raum des Öffentlichen. Die Escola Paulista und der Brutalismus in Brasilien*, Reimer Verlag, Berlin, 2012.

Bédarida Marc (ed.), *Le Corbusier: Aventures photographiques*, Editions De La Villette, Paris, 2014.

Bedford Joseph, 'Stirling's Rational Facade: Self-Division within the Reading of Garches and Jaoul', *ARQ: Architectural Research Quarterly*, vol. 14, no. 2, June 2010, pp. 153–64.

Bell Clive, *Art*, Stokes, New York, 1914.

Benelli Francesco, 'Rudolf Wittkower Versus Le Corbusier: A Matter of Proportion', *Architectural Histories*, vol. 3, no. 1, May 2015, pp. 1–11.

Benevolo Leonardo, *L'ultimo capitolo dell'architettura moderna*, Laterza, Roma-Bari, 1985.

Benevolo Leonardo, *L'architettura nell'Italia contemporanea*, Laterza, Rome, 1998.

Bergdoll Barry, Massey Jonathan, *Marcel Breuer: Building Global Institutions*, Lars Müller Publishers, Zurich, 2018.

Bernardi Donatella (ed.), *Art & Crisis*, Zürcher Hochschule Der Künste Jrp|Ringier, Zurich, 2018.

Bilò Federico, 'Salto triplo: gli Smithson dal Pittoresco al "Conglomerate Ordering" attraverso il Neobrutalismo', *Parametro*, vol. 36, no. 264–265, 2006, pp. 114–22.

Bloomfield Julia, 'A Bibliography of Alison and Peter Smithson', *Oppositions*, vol. 2, January 1974, pp. 104–23.

Boissonnas Edith, *La vie est libre: correspondance et critiques, 1945–1980*, Éditions Zoe, Carouge-Genève, 2014.

Bonifazio Patrizia, *Tra guerra e pace: società, cultura e architettura nel secondo dopoguerra*, Franco Angeli, Milan, 1998.

Bortoluci José H., 'Brutalism and the People: Architectural Articulations of National Developmentalism in Mid-Twentieth-Century São Paulo', *Comparative Studies in Society and History*, vol. 62, no. 2, April 2020, pp. 296–326.

Boyer Christine, 'An Encounter with History: The Postwar Debate between the English Journals of *Architectural Review* and *Architectural Design* (1945–1960)', in *Team 10 - Between Modernity and the Everyday*, conference at TU Delft, the Netherlands, 5–6 June 2003.

Boyer Mary Christine, *Not Quite Architecture: Writing around Alison and Peter Smithson*, MIT Press, Cambridge, 2017.

Bradley John Lewis, *Ruskin: The Critical Heritage*, London, 1984.

Bradnock Lucy, *Lawrence Alloway: Critic and Curator*, Getty Research Institute, Los Angeles, 2015.

Braun Ana María, *Betonbau & architektonische Identität in Argentinien und Brasilien von 1900 bis 1970*, Akademischer Verlag, Munich, 2008.

Bruand Yves, *L'architecture contemporaine au Brésil*, Lille, Cahiers Des Amériques Latines, Thèse d'état, Atelier de reproduction des thèses de Lille III, no. 1971PA040016, 1968.

Brun Jean Baptiste, *Dubuffet et le paradigme primitiviste, 1944– 1951*, Université Paris Ouest Nanterre, Paris, 2013.

Bruno J. Hubert (ed.), *Louis I. Kahn. Le Yale Center for British Art*, Editions Parenthèses, Marseille, 1992.

Buchanan Peter, 'Corb Born 1887: Master of a Misunderstood Modernism', *Architectural Review*, vol. 181, no. 1079, January 1987, pp. 18–83.

Buckley Craig, 'Clipping: The Promiscuous Attachments of Reyner Banham', in *Graphic Assembly. Montage, Media and Experimental Architecture in the 1960s*, University of Minnesota Press, Minneapolis, 2019, pp. 33–72.

Bullock Nicholas, 'La politica del London County Council 1945-1951', *Rassegna di Architettura e Urbanistica*, vol. 54, no. 2, June 1993, pp. 50–57.

Bullock Nicholas, *Building the Post-War World: Modern Architecture and Reconstruction in Britain*, Routledge, London, 2002.

Busse Anette, 'Was ist Brutalismus?' in *Baumeister*, vol. 111, no. 2, February 2014, pp. 82–85.

Busse Annette, 'Was ist Brutalismus? Teil II', *Baumeister*, vol. 111, no. 3, March 2014, pp. 86–89.

Busse Anette, 'Was ist Brutalismus? Teil III', *Baumeister*, vol. 111, no. 4, April 2014, pp. 90–94.

Calder Barnabas, 'A Terrible Battle with Architecture: Denys Lasdun in the 1950s, Part. 2', *ARQ: Architectural Research Quarterly*, vol. 12, no. 1, March 2008, pp. 59–68.

Calder Barnabas, *Raw Concrete: The Beauty of Brutalism*, Cornerstone, London, 2016.

Calvocoressi Peter, *The British Experience, 1945–75*, Penguin Books Ltd, London, 1978.

Carolin Peter, 'Sense, Sensibility and Tower Blocks: The Swedish Influence on Post- War Housing in Britain', in Harwood Elain, Powers Alan (eds.), *Housing the Twentieth Century, Twentieth Century Society*, London, 2008, pp. 98–112.

Casini Giovanni, 'Richard Hamilton at the Slade School of Fine Art (1948–51) and his "Abstract" Paintings of the Early 1950s', *Burlington Magazine*, vol. 1350, September 2015, pp. 623–30.

Castle Helen, *Modernism and Modernization in Architecture*, Wiley, Chichester, 1999.

Chadwick Peter, *Archi Brut*, Phaidon Press, Paris, 2016.

Chadwick Peter, *This Brutal World*, Phaidon Press, London, 2017.

Champigneulle Bernard, *Histoire de l'architecture*, Somogy, Paris, 1972.

Chasin Noah, *Ethics and Aesthetics: New Brutalism, Team 10 and Architectural Change in the 1950s*, City University of New York, New York, 2002.

Cheetham Mark, *Britain: The 'Englishness' of English Art Theory Since the Eighteenth Century*, Ashgate, Farnham, 2012.

Cheney Sheldon, *The Story of Modern Art*, The Viking Press, New York, 1941.

Cinqualbre Olivier, Migayrou Frédéric (ed.), *Le Corbusier – Mesure de l'homme*, Centre Pompidou, Paris, 2015.

Clement Alexander, *Brutalism: Post-War British Architecture*, Crowood Press, London, 2011.

Cole G. D. H. (ed.), *William Morris*, Nonesuch Press, London, 1934.

Colegio oficial de arquitectos de cataluña y baleares, *Le Corbusier et le livre: les livres de Le Corbusier dans leurs éditions originelles*, Actar, Barcelona, 2005.

Collins Bradford, *Pop Art: The Independent Group to Neo Pop, 1952–90*, Phaidon Press, London, 2012.

Collins Peter, *Architectural Judgement*, McGill University Press, Montreal, 1971.

Collins Peter, 'The New Brutalism of the 1920s', *Concrete: The Vision of a New Architecture*, McGill-Queen University Press, Montreal, 2004, 2nd edition, pp. 315–40.

Colomina Beatriz, 'Koppels = Couplings', *OASE: Tijdschrift Voor Architectuur = OASE: Architectural Journal*, no. 51, 1999, pp. 20–33.

Colomina Beatriz, 'Unbreathed Air 1956', *Grey Room*, vol. 15, Spring 2004, pp. 28–59.

Colomina Beatriz, Smithson Peter, 'Friends of the Future: A Conversation with Peter Smithson', *October*, vol. 94, Spring 2000, pp. 3–30.

Colquhoun Alan, *Essays in Architectural Criticism: Modern Architecture and Historical Change*, MIT Press, Cambridge, Massachusetts, 1981.

Contier Felipe, Anelli Renato, 'João Vilanova Artigas and the Meanings of Concrete in Brazil', *The Journal of Architecture*, vol. 20, no. 3, June 2015, pp. 445–73.

Cook John Wesley, Scully Vincent, Klotz Heinrich (eds.), *Conversations with Architects: Philip Johnson, Kevin Roche, Paul Rudolph, Bertrand Goldberg, Morris Lapidus, Louis Kahn, Charles Moore, Robert Venture & Denise Scott Brown*, Lund Humphries, London, 1973.

Cornu Marcel, 'L'affaire du Brutalisme', *Architecture Mouvement Continuité*, vol. 21, no. 4, April 1971, pp. 15–42.

Costa Da Valerie, *Jean Dubuffet: Works, Writings and Interviews*, Poligrafa, Barcelona, 2007.

Costanzo Denise, 'Text, Lies and Architecture: Colin Rowe, Robert Venturi and Mannerism', *The Journal of Architecture*, vol. 18, no. 4, 2013, pp. 455–73.

Costelloe Timothy, *The British Aesthetic Tradition: From Shaftesbury to Wittgenstein*, College of William and Mary, New York, 2013.

Crinson Mark (ed.), *James Stirling: Early Unpublished Writings on Architecture*, Routledge, London, 2010.

Crinson Mark, Kite Stephen, Zimmerman Claire (eds.), *Neo-Avant-Garde and Postmodern: Postwar Architecture in Britain and Beyond*, YC British Art, London, 2010.

Crinson Mark, Williams Richard, 'From Image to Environment-Reyner Banham's Architecture',

The Architecture of Art History. A Historiography, Bloomsbury Visual Art, London, 2019, pp. 75–93.

Critchley Matthew, 'Continuity or Crisis? Aldo Rossi Versus Reyner Banham', *OASE: Tijdschrift Voor Architectuur = OASE: Architectural Journal*, vol. 97, 2016, pp. 71–90.

Curtis William, *Modern Architecture Since 1900*, Phaidon Press, Oxford, 1982

D'arcy Michael, Nilges Mathias, *The Contemporaneity of Modernism: Literature, Media, Culture*, vol. 61, Routledge, New York, 2016.

Dardi Costantino, *Il gioco sapiente*, Marsilio Editori, Padua, 1971.

Darling Elizabeth, *Re-Forming Britain: Narratives of Modernity Before Reconstruction*, Routledge, New York, 2007.

David Bruce Brownlee, De Long David Gilson, *Louis I. Kahn: in the Realm of Architecture*, Rizzoli, New York, 1991.

Davies Colin, *A New History of Modern Architecture: Art Nouveau, The Beaux-Arts, Expressionism, Modernism, Constructivism, Art Deco, Classicism, Brutalism, Postmodernism, Neo-Rationalism, High Tech, Deconstructivism*, Digital Futures, Laurence King Publishing Ltd, London, 2017.

Day Kirsten, Raisbeck Peter, 'The Last Laugh and its Afterlife: Emerging Narratives in 1970s Melbourne Architecture', *Fabrications*, vol. 31, no. 3, 2021, pp. 336–56.

Day Nicholas Merhyr, *The Role of the Architect in Post-War Housing: A Case Study of the Housing Work of the London County Council 1939–1956*, PhD thesis, University of Warwick, Warwick, 1988.

De Alba Roberto, *Paul Rudolph – The Late Work*, Princeton Architectural Press, New York, 2003.

De Franclieu Françoise (ed.), *Le Corbusier: Carnets*, Herscher & Dessain et Tolra, Paris, 1981.

De Smet Catherine, *Le Corbusier, Architect of Books*, Lars Müller Publishers, Baden, 2005.

De Smet Catherine, *Vers une architecture du livre. Le Corbusier: édition et mise en pages, 1912–1965*, Lars Müller Publishers, Baden, 2007.

Deyong Sarah, 'An Architectural Theory of Relations: Sigfried Giedion and Team X', *Journal of the Society of Architectural Historian*, vol. 73, no. 2, June 2014, pp. 226–47.

Dijkema Pieter, *Innen und Aussen: die Frage nach der Integration der Künste und der Weg der Architektur*, Van Saane, Hilversum, 1960.

Dorfles Gillo, *L'architettura Moderna*, Garzanti, Milan, 1972.

Dorfles Gillo, *Architetture ambigue: dal Neobarocco al Postmoderno*, Dedalo, Bari, 1984.

Dreher Florian, 'Fundstücke des Alltäglichen. New Brutalism as Found', *Archithese*, vol. 6, June 2010, pp. 72–77.

Eisenmann Peter, 'From Golden Lane to Robin Hood Gardens. or if you Follow the Yellow Brick Road, it May Not Lead to Golders Green', *Oppositions*, vol. 1, September 1973, pp. 27–56.

Elser Oliver, Kurz Philip, Cachola Schmal Peter, *SOS Brutalism: A Global Survey*, exhibition, DAM, Deutsches Architekturmuseum, Frankfurt am Main, Germany, 9 November 2017 – 2 April 2018.

Elser Oliver, Kurz Philip, Cachola Schmal Peter (eds.), *SOS Brutalism: A Global Survey*, vol. 1, Park Books, Zurich, 2017.

Elser Oliver, Kurz Philip, Cachola Schmal Peter (eds.), *SOS Brutalism: A Global Survey. Contributions to the International Symposium in Berlin 2012*, vol. 2, Park Books, Zurich, 2017.

Emili Anna Rita, *Brutalismo Paulista: l'architettura brasiliana tra teoria e progetto*, Manifestolibri, Castel San Pietro Romano, 2020.

Engel Braden, 'The Badger of Muck and Brass', *AA Files*, vol. 62, 2011, pp. 95–98.

Eriksson Agneta, Ronnefalk Weronica, *Bengt Edman: Samlade Verk = Complete Works*, Eriksson & Ronnefalk, Stockholm, 1998.

Erten Erdem, *Shaping 'The Second Half Century': The Architectural Review, 1947–1971*, PhD thesis, Massachusetts Institute of Technology, Cambridge, 2004.

Erten Erdem, *Alternative Visions of Post-War Reconstruction: Creating the Modern Townscape*, Routledge, London, 2015.

Fair Alistair, '"Brutalism Among the Ladies": Modern Architecture at Somerville College, Oxford, 1947–67', *Architectural History*, vol. 57, 2014, pp. 357–92.

Fausch Deborah, *The Context of Meaning is Everyday Life: Venturi and Scott Brown's Theories of Architecture and Urbanism*, Princeton University, Proquest Dissertations Publishing, 1999.

Fausch Deborah, 'She Said, He Said: Denise Scott Brown and Kenneth Frampton on Popular Taste', *Footprint*, vol. 5, no. 1, August 2014, pp. 77–90.

Ferraz Marcelo (ed.), *Vilanova Artigas, Instituto Lina Bo e P. M. Bardi*, São Paulo, 1997.

Flanders Architecture Institute, *The General Representation of the Government of Flanders in the United Kingdom, Brutalism on a Human Scale. Post-war Architecture by Léon Stynen (1899–1990)*, exhibition, London Festival of Architecture, Silver Building, 6 June 2019 – 30 June 2019.

Forty Adrian, 'Le Corbusier's British Reputation', Benton Tim (ed.) *Le Corbusier, Architect of the Century*, Hayward Gallery, London, 1987, pp. 35–41.

Forty Adrian, 'Reyner Banham, "One Partially Americanized European"', Campbell Louise (ed.), *Twentieth- Century Architecture and its Histories*, Society of Architectural Historians of Great Britain, London, 2000, pp. 195–205.

Forty Adrian, *Concrete and Culture. A Material History*, Reaktion Books, London, 2012.

Foster Hal, *The Anti-Aesthetic: Essays on Postmodern Culture*, Bay Press, Port Townsend, Washington, 1983.

Foster Hal, 'Savage Minds (A Note on Brutalist Bricolage)', *October*, vol. 136, 2011, pp. 182–91.

Frampton Kenneth, *Modern Architecture: A Critical History*, Thames & Hudson, London, 1980.

Frampton Kenneth, Prospects for a Critical Regionalism, *Perspecta*, vol. 20, 1983, pp. 147–62.

Frampton Kenneth, *Le Corbusier*, Thames and Hudson, London, 1997.

Frampton Kenneth, 'Notes sur la réception critique de Le Corbusier en Grande- Bretagne, 1946-1972', *Cahiers de la recherche architecturale et urbaine*, vol. 24, no. 25, 2009, pp. 21–40.

Frampton Kenneth, 'Homage à Monica Pidgeon: An AD Memoir', *AA Files*, vol. 60, 2010, pp. 22–25.

Frampton Kenneth, 'Nigel Henderson: I.C.A. Gallery', *October*, vol. 136, 2011, pp. 48–50.

Franc Helen M. (ed.), *Philip Johnson. Writings*, Oxford University Press, New York, 1979.

Francone Marcello, *A come Architettura: Vittoriano Viganò*, Electa, Milan, 1992.

Franklin Geraint, Howell, Killick, Partridge & Amis, *Historic England*, Swindon, 2017.

Franzke Andreas, *Dubuffet*, Harry N. Abrams, Cologne, 1990.

Gallis Johan (ed.), *Brutalismus in Österreich 1960-1980: eine Architekturtopografie der Spätmoderne in 9 Perspektiven*, Böhlau Verlag, Vienna, 2022.

Games Stephen, Pevsner Nikolaus, *Pevsner: The Complete Broadcast Talks Architecture and Art on Radio and Television, 1945–1977*, Ashgate, Farnham, 2014.

Gannon Todd, *Reyner Banham and the Paradoxes of High Tech*, Getty Research Institute, Los Angeles, 2017.

Gargiani Roberto, *Louis I. Kahn: Exposed Concrete and Hollow Stones, 1949–1959*, EPFL Press, Lausanne, 2014.

Gargiani Roberto, *A New Era of American Architectural Concrete. From Wright to SOM. 1940 – 1980*, vol. 1-2-3, EPFL Press, Lausanne, 2020.

Gargiani Roberto, *Razionalismo emozionale per l'identità democratica nazionale 1945-1966*, Eretici italiani dell'architettura Razionalista, vol. 2, Skira, Milan, 2021.

Gargiani Roberto, Bologna Alberto, *The Rhetoric of Pier Luigi Nervi: Concrete and Ferrocement Forms*, EPFL Press, Lausanne, 2016.

Gargiani Roberto, Rosellini Anna, *Le Corbusier: Béton Brut and Ineffable Space 1940-1965, Surface Materials and Psychophysiology of Vision*, EPFL Press, Lausanne, 2011.

Gargiani Roberto, Rosellini Anna, 'La découverte du béton brut avec malfaçons: chronique du chantier de l'Unité d'Habitation à Marseille', Sbriglio Jacques (ed.),

Le Corbusier et la question du Brutalisme, Parenthèses, Paris, 2013, pp. 152–79.

Garnham Trevor, *Architecture Re- Assembled: The Use (and Abuse) of History*, Routledge, Abingdon, 2013.

Garric Jean-Philippe (ed.), *Le livre et l'architecte: actes du colloque organisé par l'Institut National d'Histoire de l'Art et l'École Nationale Supérieure d'Architecture de Paris- Belleville, Paris, 31 Janvier – 2 Février 2008*, Editions Mardaga, Wavre, 2011.

Gatley Julia, King Stuart, *Brutalism Resurgent*, Routledge, London, 2016.

Ghirardo Diane, 'What Did Banham See?', *Journal of Architectural Education*, vol. 71, no. 2, July 2017, p. 266.

Giedion Sigfried, *Space, Time and Architecture; The Growth of a New Tradition*, Harvard University Press, Cambridge, 1941.

Girieud Corine, *La Revue Art d'Aujourd'hui (1949–1954): une vision sociale de l'art*, PhD thesis, Paris IV Sorbonne, 2011.

Girouard Mark, *Big Jim: The Life and Work of James Stirling*, Pimlico, London, 2000.

Goad Philip, 'Bringing it all Home: Robin Boyd and Australia's Embrace of Brutalism, 1955–71', *Fabrications*, vol. 25, no. 2, June 2015, pp. 176–213.

Goldhagen Sarah Williams, Legault Réjean (eds.), *Anxious Modernisms: Experimentation in Postwar Architectural Culture*, Canadian Centre for Architecture, Montreal, 2000.

Goldhagen Sarah Williams, *Louis Kahn's Situated Modernism*, Yale University Press, New Haven, 2001.

Graf Franz, Tedeschi Letizia (eds.), *L'istituto Marchiondi Spagliardi di Vittoriano Viganò*, Mendrisio Academy Press, Mendrisio, 2009.

Grandorge David, 'Lessons in More: Alison and Peter Smithson at Hunstanton', *Architecture Today*, no. 137, 2003, pp. 30–32; 34.

Green Nigel, Wilson Robin, *Rewiring Brutalism. Architectural Futures Through Musique Concrète*, exhibition, Life Rewired Hub, Barbican Center, London, 28 August – 1 September 2019.

Grindrod John, *How to Love Brutalism*, Pavilion Books, London, 2018.

Groaz Silvia, 'La genèse du livre The New Brutalism. Ethic or Aesthetic? À travers les échanges épistolaires de Banham et Joedicke', *Matiéres*, no. 14, 2018, pp. 90–101.

Groaz Silvia, 'Le béton apparent dans la culture suisse. Mythe de la perfection et de l'economie de matériau', *Tracés*, no. 3503, November 2020, pp. 14–19.

Groaz Silvia, 'The New Brutalism: Ethic Vs. Marxism? Ideological Collisions in Post- War English Architecture', *HPA. Histories of Postwar Architecture*, no. 7, 2021, pp. 104–23.

Groaz Silvia, 'La semplicità democratica del calcestruzzo', *Archi. Rivista di architettura, ingegneria e urbanistica*, vol. 5, August 2021, L'eredità di Robert Maillart, pp. 13–17.

Groaz Silvia, 'The Swiss Principle of Béton Brut: "Betonkonstruktion". A Debate Between Theory and Practice, 1940s–1960s', in Aprea Salvatore, Navone Nicola, Stalder Laurent (ed.), *Concrete in Switzerland. Histories from the Recent Past*, EPFL Press, 2021, pp. 105–14.

Groaz Silvia. 'Robin Hood Gardens. La barre non-héroïque du town building anglais', *Matières*, no. 17, 2022, pp. 20-25.

Grossmann Vanessa, 'João Batista Vilanova Artigas, Le Corbusier and Imperialism (1951)', *Pidgin*, vol. 10, 2011, pp. 138–51.

Guillery Peter, *British Architecture and the Vernacular*, Routledge, London, 2011.

Gutheim Frederick A., 'Tennessee Valley Authority: A New Phase in Architecture', *Magazine of Art*, vol. 33, no. 9, September 1940, pp. 520–21.

Hamilton Richard, *Collected Words: 1953-1982*, Thames & Hudson, London, 1982.

Harries Susie, *Nikolaus Pevsner: The Life*, Pimlico, London, 2011.

Harris Jennifer, *William Morris Revisited: Questioning the Legacy*, Crafts Council, London, 1996.

Hartoonian Gevork, *Time, History and Architecture: Essays on Critical Historiography*, Routledge, Taylor & Francis Group, London, New York, 2018.

Harwood Elain, 'Butterfield & Brutalism', *AA Files*, no. 27, 1994, pp. 39–46.

Harwood Elain, *Space, Hope and Brutalism: English Architecture, 1945-1975*, Yale University Press, New Haven, 2015.

Hell Julia, *Ruins of Modernity*, Duke University Press Books, Durham, 2010.

Henley Simon, *Redefining Brutalism*, RIBA Publishing, Newcastle Upon Tyne, 2017.

Herschdorfer Nathalie, (ed.) *Construire l'image: Le Corbusier et la photographie*, Éditions Textuel, Paris, 2012.

Hewison Robert, *In Anger: British Culture in the Cold War, 1945-60*, Oxford University Press, Oxford, 1981.

Hibbard Howard, 'Obituary for Rudolf Wittkower', *Burlington Magazine*, vol. 114, March 1972, p. 175.

Higgott Andrew, *Mediating Modernism: Architectural Cultures in Britain*, Routledge, London, 2006.

Higgott Andrew, 'Eric De Maré in Search of the Functional Tradition', *AA Files*, no. 70, 2015, pp. 144–51.

Highmore Ben (ed.), 'Rough Poetry: Patio and Pavilion Revisited', *Oxford Art Journal*, vol. 29, no. 2, 2006, pp. 1–22.

Highmore Ben, 'Walls Without Museums: Anonymous History, Collective Authorship and the Document', *Visual Culture in Britain*, vol. 8, no. 2, 2007, pp. 1–20.

Highmore Ben, 'Image-Breaking, God-Making: Paolozzi's Brutalism', *October*, vol. 136, 2011, pp. 87–104.

Highmore Ben, *The Art of Brutalism: Rescuing Hope from Catastrophe in 1950s Britain*, Yale University Press, New Haven, 2017.

Hight Christopher, *Architectural Principles in the Age of Cybernetics*, Routledge, New York, 2008.

Hillman Roman, 'Ist "béton brut" brutal?', *Kritische Berichte*, vol. 32, no. 1, 2004, pp. 88–91.

Hobhouse Niall (ed.), *Architecture is not Made with the Brain: The Labour of Alison and Peter Smithson*, Architectural Association Publications, London, 2005.

Hopkins Owen (ed.), *Lost Futures: The Disappearing Architecture of Post-War Britain*, Royal Academy of Arts, London, 2017.

Isla Fernández Maria José, 'Peter Smithson [interview]', *Arquitectura*, vol. 310, 1997, pp. 93–94.

Jacquet Nicolas Bruno, *Londres, capitale du Post- Modernisme?: Transformations des modèles et des pratiques de l'architecture dans la culture britannique à la fin du XXe Siècle*, PhD thesis, École Polytechnique Fédérale de Lausanne, Lausanne, 2016.

Jencks Charles, 'Pop-Non Pop', *AAQ: Architectural Association Quarterly*, vol. 1, no. 1, April 1969, pp. 48–64.

Jencks Charles, *Meaning in Architecture*, Barrie & Rockliff, The Cresset Press, London, 1969.

Jencks Charles, 'Does American Architecture Really Exist?', *AAQ: Architectural Association Quarterly*, vol. 2, no. 2, 1970, pp. 62–65.

Jencks Charles, *Architecture 2000: Predictions and Methods*, Praeger, New York, 1971.

Jencks Charles, *Modern Movements in Architecture*, Penguin, Harmondsworth, 1973.

Jencks Charles, *Le Corbusier and the Tragic View of Architecture*, Allen Lane, London, 1973.

Jencks Charles, 'The Rise of Post Modern Architecture', *AAQ: Architectural Association Quarterly*, vol. 7, no. 4, October 1975, pp. 15–21.

Jencks Charles, *The Language of Post-Modern Architecture*, Academy Editions, London, 1977.

Jencks Charles, *Bizarre Architecture*, Academy Editions, London, 1979.

Jenger Jean (ed.), *Le Corbusier: choix de lettres*, Birkhauser Verlag, Basel, 2002.

Jenkins David, *Unité d'Habitation*, Marseilles: Le Corbusier, Phaidon Press, London, 1993.

Johnson Philip, *Mies van der Rohe*, Museum of Modern Art, New York, 1947.

Johnston Pamela, Smithson Alison and Peter (eds.), *Architecture Is Not Made with the Brain: The Labour of Alison and Peter Smithson*, Architectural Association, London, 2005.

Jolivette Catherine, *British Art in the Nuclear Age*, Ashgate, Farnham, 2014.

Kamita João Masao, 'Affinità elettive: Affonso Eduardo Reidy e il Brutalismo Paulista', *Rassegna di Architettura e Urbanistica*, vol. 48, no. 142/143, January 2014, pp. 31–41.

Katinsky Júlio Roberto, 'Arquitetura Paulista. Uma perigosa montagem ideológica', *AU, Arquitetura e Urbanismo*, vol. 17, April 1988, pp. 66–71.

Kei Yat Shun Juliana, 'New Brutalism Again', *Architecture and Culture*, vol. 7, no. 2, 2019, pp. 271–90.

Kei Yat Shun Juliana, 'New Brutalism and the Myth of Japan', *HPA. Histories of Postwar Architecture*, vol. 2, no. 4, 2020, pp. 242–55.

Kenley Stefania, *Du fictif au réel: dix essais sur le pop art anglais et le Nouveau Brutalisme en architecture*, Les Presses du Réel, Dijon, 2016.

Kennedy John Fitzgerald, 'The Vigor We Need', *Sports Illustrated*, vol. 17, no. 3, July 1962, pp. 12–15.

Kent Cheryl, 'Softening Brutalism: is Anything Lost?', *Architectural Record*, vol. 184, no. 8, August 1996, pp. 21–22.

Kitch Carolyn, 'Models for Understanding Magazines', Abrahamson David (ed.), *The American Magazine: Research Perspectives and Prospects*, Iowa State University Press, Ames, 1995, pp. 9–21.

Kite Stephen, 'Softs and Hards: Colin St John Wilson and the Contested Vision of 1950s London', in Crinson Mark, Zimmerman Claire (eds.), *Neo-Avant-Garde and Postmodern: Postwar Architecture in Britain and Beyond*, YC British Art, London, 2010, pp. 55–78.

Kitnick Alex, 'New Brutalism', *October*, vol. 136, Summer Summer 2011, pp. 3–62.

Kitnick Alex, 'The Brutalism of Life and Art', *October*, vol. 136, 2011, pp. 63–86.

Klotz Heinrich, Cook John Wesley, *Architektur im Widerspruch: Bauen in den USA von Mies van der Rohe bis Andy Warhol*, Verlag für Architektur Artemis, Zurich, 1981.

Krause Linda, 'The New Brutalism: Frampton Reconsidered', *Circa*, vol. 53, October 1990, pp. 20–31.

Krucker Bruno, *Komplexe Gewöhnlichkeit - Der Upper Lawn Pavillon von Alison und Peter Smithson*, gta Verlag, Zurich, 2002.

Kulić Vladimir, 'Yugoslavia: Brutalism and Sophistication', *ARQ: Architectural Research Quarterly*, vol. 23, no. 4, December 2019, pp. 381–83.

Langevin Jared, 'Reyner Banham: In Search of an Imageable, Invisible Architecture', *Architectural Theory Review*, vol. 16, no. 1, April 2011, pp. 2–21.

Le Corbusier. *Vers une architecture*, Editions G. Crès et Cie, Paris, 1923.

Le Corbusier, interview by Georges Charensol and Robert Mallet, edited by Frémeaux et Associés, recording from Archives de l'Institut National de l'Audiovisuel, Vincenne, FA5173, 2007.

Lefaivre Liane, 'Peter Smithson After the Rebellion', *Architecture: the AIA Journal*, vol. 89, no. 1, January 2000, pp. 51–53; 146.

Legault Réjean, 'Material and Modernity', *Rassegna di Architettura e Urbanistica*, vol. 14, no. 49/1, March 1992, pp. 58–65.

Legault Réjean, 'Introduction', in Peter Collins, *Concrete: The Vision of a New Architecture*, McGill-Queen University Press, Montreal, 2004, pp. XXI– LX.

Legault Réjean, 'I.M. Pei's East Building and the Postwar Culture of Materials', in Alofsin Anthony (ed.), *A Modernist Museum in Perspective. The East Building, National Gallery of Art*, Yale University Press, New Haven/ London, 2005, pp. 81–105.

Legault Réjean, de Jonge Wessel, Lagae Johan, 'Ambivalent positions on modern heritage:

a dialogue between and Réjean Legault and Wessel de Jonge', *OASE: Tijdschrift Voor Architectuur = OASE: Architectural Journal*, no. 69, 2006, pp. 46–58.

Legault Réjean, 'The Idea of Brutalism in Canadian Architecture', in Liscombe Windsor Rhodri (ed.), *Architecture and the Canadian Fabric*, UBC Press, Vancouver, 2011, pp. 313–40.

Legault Réjean, 'The Architecture of Paul Rudolph', *Journal of Architectural Education*, vol. 70, no. 1, February 2016, pp. 177–78.

Legault Réjean, 'The Trajectories of Brutalism. England, Germany and Beyond', in Elser Oliver, Kurz Philip, Cachola Schmal Peter (eds.), *SOS Brutalism: A Global Survey*, Park Books, Zurich, 2017, pp. 21–25.

Lampariello Beatrice, *Aldo Rossi e le forme del razionalismo esaltato. Dai progetti scolastici alla 'città analoga', 1950-1973*, Quodlibet, Macerata, 2017.

Lending Mari, *Plaster Monuments: Architecture and the Power of Reproduction*, Princeton University Press, Princeton, 2017.

Levine Neil (ed.), *Scully Modern Architecture and other Essays*, Princeton University Press, New York, 2002.

Lichtenstein Claude, Schregenberger Thomas (ed.), *As Found: The Discovery of the Ordinary*, Lars Müller Publishers; Zurich Museum, 2001.

Lima Sergio, 'Alguns dados sobre a construção interessada de uma ausência: a do surrealismo no Brasil', *Organon*, vol. 22, 1994, pp. 183–206.

Lima Zeuler Rocha Mello De Almeida, *Lina Bo Bardi*, Yale University Press, New Haven, 2013.

Liscombe Rhodri Windsor, *Architecture and the Canadian*

Fabric, University of British Columbia Press, Vancouver, 2011.

Lotery Kevin, *The Long Front of Culture: The Independent Group and Exhibition Design*, MIT Press, Cambridge, Massachusetts, 2020.

Lucan Jacques, *Composition, non- composition: architecture et théories XIXᵉ-XXᵉ siècles*, Presses Polytechniques et Universitaires Romandes, Lausanne, 2009.

Luis E. Carranza. (ed.), *Modern Architecture in Latin America: Art, Technology, and Utopia*, University of Texas Press, Austin, 2014.

Macarthur John, 'The Nomenclature of Style: Brutalism, Minimalism, Art History and Visual Style in Architecture Journals', *Architectural Theory Review*, vol. 10, no. 2, 2005, pp. 100–08.

Macarthur John, *The Picturesque: Architecture, Disgust and Other Irregularities*, Routledge, London, 2007.

Macarthur John, 'The Revenge of the Picturesque', *Journal of Architecture*, vol. 17, no. 5, 2012, pp. 643–53.

Maniacque Caroline, *Le Corbusier et les Maisons Jaoul projet et fabrique*, Picard, Paris, 2005.

Maniacque Caroline, 'Back to Basics: Maisons Jaoul and the Art of the mal foutou', *Journal of Architectural Education*, vol. 63, no. 1, October 2009, pp. 31–40.

Martin Jean-Hubert, *Dubuffet & l'Art Brut*, Collection de L'Art Brut, Milan/Lausanne, 2005.

Massey Anne, *The Independent Group: Modernism and Mass Culture in Britain, 1945–1959*, Manchester University Press, Manchester, 1995.

Massey Anne, 'The Independent Group: Towards a Redefinition', *The Burlington Magazine*, vol. 129, no. 1009, April 1987, pp. 232–42.

Massey Anne, Muir Gregor, *Institute of Contemporary Art: 1946-1968*, Roma Publications, Amsterdam, 2014.

Maxwell Robert, 'Reyner Banham: The Plenitude of Present', *Architectural Design*, vol. 51, no. 6/7, June 1981, pp. 52–57.

Maxwell Robert, *Buildings and Projects: James Stirling, Michael Wilford and Associates*, Thames & Hudson, London, 1984.

Maxwell Robert, 'Truth Without Rhetoric: The New Softly Smiling Face of Our Discipline', *AA Files*, vol. 28, 1994, pp. 3–11.

May Kyle (ed.), 'Brutalism', *Clog*, February 2013 (monograph issue).

McLeod Mary, 'Architecture or Revolution: Taylorism, Technocracy, and Social Change', *Art Journal*, vol. 43, no. 2, 1983, pp. 132–47.

McLeod Mary, Ockman Joan, *Architecture, Criticism, Ideology*, Princeton Architectural Press, Princeton, New Jersey, 1985.

McLeod Mary, 'Architecture and Politics in the Reagan Era: from Postmodernism to Deconstructivism', *Assemblage*, no. 8, February 1989, pp. 23–59.

McLeod Mary, *Urbanism and Utopia: Le Corbusier from Regional Syndicalism to Vichy*, Princeton University Press, Princeton, 1985.

McLeod Mary, 'First interlude: on the Nuances of Historical Emancipation', *The Journal of Architecture*, vol. 7, no. 3, January 2002, pp. 245–47.

Mellor Leo, *Reading the Ruins: Modernism, Bombsites and British Culture*, Cambridge University Press, Cambridge, 2011.

Mendelson Edward, 'Forum: Promising Directions in American Architecture', *Precis*, vol. 4, 1983, pp. 6–17.

Menin Sarah, Kite Stephen, *An Architecture of Invitation*, Ashgate Publishing Limited, London, 2005.

Middleton Robin, 'Working for Monica', *AA Files*, vol. 60, 2010, pp. 22; 26–27.

Miele Chris, *From William Morris: Building Conservation and the Arts and Crafts Cult of Authenticity, 1877–1939*, Studies in British Art, vol. 14, Paul Mellon, London, 2005.

Miller Tyrus, 'Modernism Under Review: Reyner Banham's Theory and Design in the First Machine Age (1960)', *Modernist Cultures*, vol. 12, no. 3, November 2017, pp. 331–44.

Million Henry, 'Rudolph Wittkower, Architectural Principles in the Age of Humanism: Its Influence on the Development and Interpretation of Modern Architecture', *Journal of the Society of Architectural Historians*, vol. 31, May 1972, pp. 83–91.

Molinari Luca, 'The Italian Way to New Brutalism. The Experience of Vittoriano Viganò', Elser Oliver, Kurz Philip, Cachola Schmal Peter (eds.), *SOS Brutalism: A Global Survey. Contributions to the International Symposium in Berlin 2012*, vol. 2, Zurich, 2017, pp. 85–94.

Monk Tony (ed.), *The Art and Architecture of Paul Rudolph*, Wiley-Academy, Chichester, 1999.

Montaner Joseph Maria, *Dopo il Movimento Moderno*, ITA Edizione/Laterza, Roma/Bari, 1996.

Monteyne David, 'Boston City Hall and a History of Reception', *Journal of Architectural Education*, vol. 65, no. 1, October 2011, pp. 45–62.

Montpied Bruno, 'Quelques notes sur les origines de l'Art Brut', *S.U.R.R.*, vol. 3, no. 53–56, July 1999, pp. 69–71.

Montpied Bruno, 'D'où vient l'Art Brut? Esquisses pour une généalogie de l'Art Brut', *LIGEIA, Devenir de l'art brut*, no. 53, July-December 2004, pp. 155–64.

Mumford Eric, *The CIAM Discourse on Urbanism 1928-1960*, MIT Press, Cambridge, Massachusetts, 2000.

Murray Andrew, 'Brutal Beginnings: The New Brutalism and Western Australia in the 1950s', *The Journal of Architecture*, vol. 26, no. 8, 2021, pp. 1219–40.

Murray Irena (ed.), *Le Corbusier and Britain: An Anthology*, Oxon, Abingdon, 2009.

Neumann Eva-Marie, 'Architectural Proportion in Britain 1945–957', *Architectural History*, vol. 39, 1996, pp. 197–221.

Niebrzydowski Wojciech, 'The Impact of Avant-Garde Art on Brutalist Architecture', *Buildings*, vol. 11, no. 7, June 2021, pp. 1–31.

Nolan Rachel, 'Arts, Crafts and Brutalism', *Architecture Australia*, vol. 101, no. 6, November 2012, pp. 110–11.

O'Sullivan Kevin, *Concrete Expressions: Brutalism and the Government Buildings Precinct*, University of South Australia Architecture Museum, Adelaide, 2013.

Ockman Joan, 'The Road Not Taken: Alexander Dorner's Way Beyond Art', Somol Robert (ed.), *Autonomy and Ideology: Positioning an Avant-Garde in America*, Monacelli Press, New York, 1997, pp. 82–120.

Ockman Joan, 'New Empiricism and New Humanism', *Design Book Review*, no. 41/42, Winter/ Spring 2000, pp. 18–21.

Ockman Joan, 'Modernism in the U.S. After World War II', *Special Issue of Docomomo*, vol. 31, 2004, p.n.n.

Ockman Joan, 'How America Learned to Stop Worrying

and Love Brutalism', in Casciato Maristella (ed.), *Modern Architecture: The Rise of a Heritage*, Mardaga, Wavre, 2012, pp. 37–42.

Ockman Joan, 'The School of Brutalism: from Great Britain to Boston (And Beyond)', Pasnik Marc, Kubo Michael, Grimley Chris (eds.), *Heroic, Concrete Architecture and the New Boston*, The Monacelli Press, New York, 2015, pp. 30–47.

Ockman Joan, 'The American School of Brutalism. Transformations of a Concrete Idea', in Elser Oliver, Kurz, Philip, Cachola Schmal Peter (eds.), *SOS Brutalism: A Global Survey. Contributions to the International Symposium in Berlin 2012*, vol. 2, Zurich, 2017, pp. 105–16.

Ockman Joan, 'How America Learned to Stop Worrying and Love Brutalism', *OASE: Tijdschrift Voor Architectuur = OASE: Architectural Journal*, no. 108, March 2021, pp. 37–44.

Oliveira De Olívia, 'Lina Bo Bardi: Obra construída=Built Work', Gustavo Gili, Barcelona, *2G: Revista internacional de Arquitectura*, 2002.

Olmo Carlo (ed.), *Dizionario dell'architettura del XX Secolo*, Istituto dell'enciclopedia italiana, Rome, 2003.

Onians John, 'Wilde, Pevsner, Gombrich: la "Kunstgeschichte" en Grande-Bretagne', *Perspective. Actualité en histoire de l'art*, vol. 2, 2007, pp. 194–206.

Orwell George, *The Lion and the Unicorn: Socialism and the English Genius*, Secker & Warburg, London, 1941.

Panzeri Miriam. *Architettura Moderna e progetto umanistico storia, formazione, comunità 1945–1965*, Jaca Book, Milano, 2013.

Parkins Wendy, *William Morris and the Art of Everyday Life*, Cambridge Scholars Publishing, Newcastle Upon Tyne, 2010.

Parnell Steve. *Architectural Design, 1954–1972*, PhD thesis, University of Sheffield School of Architecture, Sheffield, 2011.

Parnell Steve. 'Architecture Magazines: Playgrounds and Battlegrounds', in Long Kieran, Bose Shumi (ed.), *Common Ground: A Critical Reader*, Marsilio, Venezia: Marsilio, 2012, pp. 305–08.

Parnell Steve. 'Brute Forces', *Architectural Review*, vol. 231, no. 1384, June 2012, pp. 18–19.

Parnell Steve, Sawyer Marc, 'In Search of Architectural Magazines', *ARQ: Architectural Research Quarterly*, vol. 25, no. 1, March 2021, pp. 43–54.

Partridge John, 'Roehampton Housing', in Harwood Elain et al. (eds.), *Housing the Twentieth Century*, Twentieth Century Society, London, 2008, pp. 114–20.

Pasnik Marc, Kubo Michael, Grimley Chris (eds.), *Heroic, Concrete Architecture and the New Boston*, The Monacelli Press, New York, 2015.

Paulhan Jean, 'Guide d'un petit voyage en suisse au mois de juillet 1945', *Œuvres Complètes*, Gallimard, Paris, vol.1, 2006, pp. 321–49.

Payne Alina, 'Rudolf Wittkower and Architectural Principles in the Age of Modernism', *Journal of the Society of Architectural Historians*, vol. 53, no. 3, September 1994, pp. 322–42.

Pedreira Lívia Alvarez, 'Arquitetura, política e paixão, a obra de um humanista', *AU. Arquitetura e Urbanismo*, vol. 1, January 1985, pp. 23–34.

Pehnt Wolfgang, *Das Ende der Zuversicht. Architektur in diesem Jahrhundert. Ideen-Bauten-Dokumente*, Siedler Verlag, Berlin, 1983.

Peiry Lucienne (ed.), *L'Art Brut*, Flammarion, Paris, 1997.

Penner Barbara, 'The Man Who Wrote Too Well', *Places Journal*,

September 2015, p.n.

Pevsner Nikolaus, *An Enquiry into Industrial Art in England*, Cambridge University Press, Cambridge, 1937.

Pevsner Nikolaus, *Academies of Art, Past and Present*, Cambridge University Press, Cambridge, 1940.

Phillips Andrea et al., *Fifty Years of the Future: A Chronicle of the Institute of Contemporary Arts*, Institute of Contemporary Art, London, 1998.

Phipps Simon, *Brutal London*, September Publishing, London, 2016.

Phipps Simon, *Finding Brutalism: Eine Fotografische Bestandsaufnahme Britischer Nachkriegsarchitektur*, Park Books, Zurich, 2017.

Pidgeon Monica, interview by Charlotte Benton, National Life Story Collection: Architects' Lives, British Library Sound Archive, Oral History, F7494 Side A, 29 April 1999.

Piva Antonio (ed.), *Vittoriano Viganò*, Gangemi, Rome, 2008.

Portoghesi Paolo, *Album degli anni cinquanta*, Laterza, Roma-Bari, 1977.

Potts Alex, 'Realism, Brutalism, Pop', *Art History*, vol. 35, 2012, pp. 288–313.

Potts Alex, *Experiments in Modern Realism: World Making, Politics and the Everyday in Postwar European and American Art*, Yale University Press, New Haven, 2013.

Powers Alan, *Britain*, Reaktion Books, London, 2007.

Powers Alan (ed.), *Robin Hood Gardens Re-Visions*, Twentieth Century Society, London, 2010.

Puntoni Álvaro, *Vilanova Artigas: Arquitetos Brasileiros = Brazilian Architects*, Blau, Instituto Lina Bo Bardi/Fundação Vilanova Artigas, São Paulo, 1997.

Pütz Udo, 'Die Weiterführung der Moderne durch den Brutalismus', *Deutsches Architektenblatt*, vol. 22, no. 4, April 1990, pp. 551–54.

Ragon Michel, *Histoire mondiale de l'architecture et de l'urbanisme modernes*, vol. 2, Casterman, Tournai, 1971.

Rattray Charles, 'What is it About the Smithsons?', in Davies Paul, Schmiedeknecht Torsten (eds.), *An Architect's Guide to Fame: A Collection of Essays on Why They Got Famous and you Didn't*, London, Architectural Press, 2005, pp. 3–16.

Read Herbert, *Art Now; An Introduction to the Theory of Modern Painting and Sculpture*, Harcourt, Brace & Company, New York, 1937.

Ribstein Susannah, *The Pursuit of the Unfamiliar: A Short History of American Brutalism*, School of the Art Institute of Chicago, Chicago, 2013.

Risselada Max, 'Tussenruimte = the Space Between', *OASE: Tijdschrift Voor Architectuur = OASE: Architectural Journal*, no. 51, June 1999, pp. 46–53.

Risselada Max (ed.), *Alison and Peter Smithson: A Critical Anthology*, Ediciones Poligrafa, Barcelona, 2011.

Robbins David, *The Independent Group: Postwar Britain and the Aesthetics of Plenty*, MIT Press, Cambridge, 1990.

Rohan Timothy, 'Rendering the Surface: Paul Rudolph's Art & Architecture Building at Yale', *Grey Room*, vol. 1, Autumn 2000, pp. 84–107.

Rohan Timothy, 'Challenging the Curtain Wall: Paul Rudolph's Blue Cross and Blue Shield Building', *Journal of the Society of Architectural Historians*, vol. 66, no. 1, March 2007, pp. 84–109.

Rohan Timothy, *The Architecture of Paul Rudolph*, Yale University Press, New Haven, 2014.

Rosellini Anna, 'Oltre il "béton brut": Le Corbusier e la "Nouvelle Stéréotomie"', in Bardati Flaminia, Rosellini Anna (eds.), *Arte e Architettura. Le cornici della storia*, Bruno Mondadori, Milan, 2007, pp. 231–58.

Rosellini Anna, *Le Corbusier e la superficie, dal rivestimento d'intonaco al béton brut*, Aracne, Rome, 2013.

Rosellini Anna, *Louis I. Kahn, Towards the Zero Degree of Concrete 1960–1974*, EPFL Press, Lausanne, 2014.

Rosellini Anna, 'Unité d'Habitation in Marseille - Experimental Artistic Device', in Baumeister Ruth (ed.), *What Moves Us?: Le Corbusier and Asger Jorn in Art and Architecture*, Scheidegger & Spiess, Zurich, 2015, pp. 38–45.

Rosso Michela, 'John N. Summerson and Tales of Modern Architecture', *The Journal of Architecture*, vol. 5, no. 1, 2000, pp. 65–89.

Rowe Colin, *James Stirling: Buildings and Projects. James Stirling, Michael Wilford and Associates*, Architectural Press, London, 1984.

Rowe Colin, *As I Was Saying: Recollections and Miscellaneous Essays*, MIT Press, Cambridge, Massachusetts, 1996.

Rykwert Joseph, *Louis Kahn*, Harry N. Abrams, New York, 2001.

Sanderson Warren, *International Handbook of Contemporary Developments in Architecture*, Westport-London, 1981.

Sanvitto Maria Luiza, *Brutalismo, uma análise compositiva de residências paulistanas entre 1957 e 1971*, Propar/Ufrgs, Porto Alegre, 1997.

Sarno Francesca, 'O lugar do pensamento: la concretezza poetica della FAU di Artigas', *Rassegna di Architettura e Urbanistica*, vol. 48, no. 142/143, January 2014, pp. 97–107.

Sbriglio Jacques (ed.), *Le Corbusier. L'Unité d'Habitation de Marseille*, Parenthèses, Marseille, 1992.

Sbriglio Jacques, *LC au J1. Le Corbusier et la question du Brutalisme*, exhibition, Gare Maritime J1, Marseille, 11 October–22 December 2013.

Sbriglio Jacques (ed.), *Le Corbusier et la question du Brutalisme: LC au J1*, Parenthèses, Marseille, 2013.

Scalbert Irénée, *Architecture as a Way of Life: The New Brutalism 1953–1956*, http://www. team10online.org/research/ papers/delft1/scalbert.pdf, n.n.p., s.d.

Scalbert Irénée, 'Architecture Is Not Made with the Brain: The Smithsons & the Economist Building Plaza', *AA Files*, vol. 30, 1995, pp. 17–25.

Scalbert Irénée, 'Siedlung Halen: Between Standards and Individuality', *ARQ: Architectural Research Quarterly*, vol. 2, Autumn 1996, pp. 14–24.

Scalbert Irénée, 'The Value of Plenty', *ARQ: Architectural Research Quarterly*, vol. 7, Spring 1997, pp. 18–25.

Scalbert Irénée, 'The Value of Objectivity', *OASE: Tijdschrift Voor Architectuur = OASE: Architectural Journal*, vol. 49/50, 1998, pp. 12–23.

Scalbert Irénée, 'Towards a Formless Architecture: The House of the Future by A+P Smithson', *Archis*, September 1999, pp. 34–47.

Scalbert Irénée, 'Parallel of Life and Art', *Daidalos*, vol. 75, May 2000, pp. 52–65.

Scalvini Maria Luisa, *L'immagine storiografica dell'architettura Contemporanea da Platz a Giedion*, Officina Edizioni, Rome 1984.

Schnoor Christoph, 'Colin Rowe: Space as Well-Composed Illusion', *Journal of Art Historiography*, vol. 5, December 2011, pp. 1–22.

Schregenberger Thomas, '"As Found": Ein aktuelle Blick auf den Brutalismus', *Archithese*, vol. 27, no. 2, February 1997, pp. 42–45.

Schweikher Robert Paul, *Oral History of Robert Paul Schweikher*, interview by Blum Betty, Chicago Architects Oral History Project, 1984.

Scimemi Maddalena, 'Peter e Alison Smithson: scuola secondaria, Hunstanton, 1949–54', *Casabella*, vol. 71, no. 750–51, January 2007, pp. 28–41.

Scott Brown Denise, 'A Worm's Eye View of Recent Architectural History', *Architectural Record*, vol. 172, no. 2, February 1984, pp. 69–81.

Scott Brown Denise, Venturi Robert, Izenour Steven, *Learning from Las Vegas*, MIT Press, Cambridge, 1972.

Scott Brown Denise, Venturi Robert, 'Interview with Denise Scott Brown and Robert Venturi: Is and Ought', *Perspecta*, vol. 41, January 2008, pp. 36–41.

Scott Geoffrey, *The Architecture of Humanism: A Study in the History of Taste*, Houghton Mifflin Company, Boston/ New York, 1914.

Scrivano Paolo, *Storia di un'idea di architettura moderna. Henry-Russell Hitchcock e l'International Style*, Franco Angeli, Milan, 2001.

Scrivano Paolo, *Building Transatlantic Italy: Architectural Dialogues with Postwar America*, Ashgate, Farnham – Burlington, 2013; new edition: Routledge, London – New York, 2016.

Scrivano Paolo, Jannière Hélène (eds.), 'Committed, Politicized, or Operative: Figures of Engagement in Criticism from 1945 to Today', *HPA Histories of Postwar Architecture*, vol. 4, no. 7 (monograph issue), 2020.

Segawa Hugo, 'Artigas o mestre desconocido', *Projeto*, vol. 72, 1985, pp. 42–44.

Segawa Hugo, 'Duas entrevistas inédits de Vilanova Artigas', *Projeto*, vol. 109, 1988, pp. 92–102.

Segawa Hugo, *Architecture in Brasil, 1990-1990*, Springer, São Paulo, 1998.

Sharp Denis, *Twentieth Century Classics*, Phaidon Press, London, 1999.

Sirman Brian M., *Concrete Changes: Architecture, Politics, and the Design of Boston City Hall*, Bright Leaf, Amherst, 2018.

Smith Otto Saumarez, 'Graeme Shankland: A Sixties Architect-Planner and the Political Culture of the British Left', *Architectural History*, vol. 57, 2014, pp. 393–422.

Smith Terri C., *Aggregate: Art and Architecture. A Brutalist Remix*, exhibition, Westport Arts Center, 25 September – 22 November 2009.

Smithson Alison and Peter, *Without Rhetoric: An Architectural Aesthetic 1955– 1972*, MIT Press, Cambridge, 1974.

Smithson Alison and Peter, 'The Space in Between', *Oppositions*, vol. 4, October 1974, pp. 75–78.

Smithson Alison and Peter, 'Ohne Rhetorik/Sans Rhétorique', *Werk-Archithese*, vol. 64, no. 1, January 1977, pp. 11–28.

Smithson Alison and Peter, *The Shift Alison + Peter Smithson*, vol. 7, Academy Editions, (Architectural Monographs), London, 1982.

Smithson Alison, *The Emergence of Team 10 Out of C.I.A.M.: Documents*, Architectural Association, London, 1982.

Smithson Alison, *AS in DS: An Eye on the Road*, Delft University Press, Delft, 1983.

Smithson Alison and Peter, *Italian Thoughts*, International Laboratory of Architecture and Urban Design, s.l., 1993.

Smithson Alison and Peter, *Changing the Art of Inhabitation: Mies' Pieces, Eames' Dreams*, Artemis, London/ Zurich 1994.

Smithson Alison and Peter, *The Charged Void: Architecture*, Monacelli Press, New York, 2002.

Smithson Alison and Peter, *The Charged Void: Urbanism*, Monacelli Press, New York, 2002.

Smithson Alison and Peter, 'Patio and Pavilion Reconstructed', *AA Files*, 2002, pp. 37–45.

Smithson Peter, Interview by Brodie Louise, National Life Story Collection: Architects' Lives, British Library Sound Archive, Oral History, F5951 Side A, September 4, 1997.

Smithson Peter, 'Reflections on Hunstanton', *ARQ: Architectural Research Quarterly*, vol. 2, Summer 1997, pp. 32–43.

Smithson Peter, Obrist Hans Ulrich, *Smithson Time: Peter Smithson & Hans Ulrich Obrist: A Dialogue*, Walther König Auflage, Cologne, 2004.

Smithson Peter, *Peter Smithson: Conversations with Students, a Space for Our Generation*, Princeton Architectural Press, New York, 2005.

Spencer Catherine, 'The Independent Group's "Anthropology of Ourselves"', *Art History*, vol. 35, no. 2, 2012, pp. 314–35.

Stalder Laurent, '"New Brutalism", "Topology" and "Image": Some Remarks on the Architectural Debates in England Around 1950', *Journal of Architecture*, vol. 13, no. 3, 2008, pp. 263–81.

Stalder Laurent, 'Cluster Buildings', in Hassler Uta (ed.), *Bauten Der Boomjahre*, infolio, Zurich, 2010, pp. 44–55.

Stalder Laurent, 'AS in DS. Alison und Peter Smithson und ihre Publikation AS in DS: an Eye on the Road', *Scholion*, vol. 6, 2010, pp. 171–83.

Stalder Laurent, 'Circuits, Conduits, et cetera. Quelques notes sur le caractère normatif des infrastructures dans l'architecture de l'après- guerre', *Matières*, vol. 12, 2015, pp. 23–31.

Stalder Laurent, Denton Jill, 'Air, Light, and Air-Conditioning', *Grey Room*, no. 40, July 2010, pp. 84–99.

Stalder Laurent, Gleich Moritz, Denton Jill, 'Stirling's Arrows', *AA Files*, vol. 72, 2016, pp. 57–67.

Štanský Peter, *Redesigning the World: William Morris, the 1880s, and the Arts and Crafts*, Princeton University Press, New York, 1985.

Steiner Hadas, 'Brutalism Exposed: Photography and the Zoom Wave', *Journal of Architectural Education*, vol. 59, February 2006, pp. 15–27.

Steiner Hadas, 'Life at the Threshold', *October*, vol. 136, 2011, pp. 133–55.

Stierli Martino, Kulić Vladimir, *Toward a Concrete Utopia. Architecture in Yugoslavia, 1948–1980*, exhibition, MoMA New York, 15 July 2018–13 January 2019.

Stocchi Attilio (ed.), *Vittoriano Viganò: etica brutalista*, Testo & Immagine, Torino, 1999.

Stoller Ezra, *The Yale Art + Architecture Building, Building Blocks*, Princeton Architectural Press, New York, 1999.

Sunwoo Irene, 'Whose Design? MoMA and Pevsner's Pioneers', *Getty Research Journal*, no. 2, 2010, pp. 69–82.

Tafuri Manfredo, Dal Co Francesco, *Storia dell'architettura contemporanea*, Electa, Milan, 1979.

Tafuri Manfredo, *Storia dell'architettura Italiana 1944-85*, Einaudi, Torino, 1982.

Tafuri Manfredo, *Ricerca del rinascimento: principi, città, architetti*, vol. 760, Einaudi, Torino, 1992.

Taniguchi Maria, *Horror in the Modernist Block*, exhibition, Ikon Gallery, Birmingham, 25 November 2022-19 February 2023.

Tedeschi Letizia, 'Il contributo italiano al brutalismo: la ricezione critica dell'Istituto Marchiondi Spagliardi di Vittoriano Viganò. 1958– 1968', in Reichlin Bruno, Tedeschi Letizia (eds.), *L'Istituto Marchiondi Spagliardi di Vittoriano Viganò*, Mendrisio Academy Press, Mendrisio, 2009, pp. 29–59.

Terrill Simon, Assemble Collective, *The Brutalist Playground, exhibition*, The US Architecture Gallery, RIBA, London, UK, 10 June – 16 August 2015.

Thévoz Michel, *L'art brut*, Albert Skira, Geneva, 1975.

Thévoz Michel, *Dubuffet*, Albert Skira, Geneva, 1986.

Thoburn Nicholas, 'Concrete and Council Housing: The Class Architecture of Brutalism "As Found" at Robin Hood Gardens', *City*, vol. 22, no. 5–6, 2018, pp. 612–32.

Thoburn Nicholas, *Brutalism as Found. Housing, Form, and Crisis and Robin Hood Gardens*, Goldsmiths Press, London, 2022.

Tigerman Stanley, 'Mies Van Der Rohe: A Moral Modernist Model', *Perspecta*, vol. 22, 1986, pp. 112–35.

Timothy M. Rohan, *Reassessing Rudolph*, Yale School of Architecture, New Haven Connecticut, 2017.

Valcarce María Teresa, 'El nuevo brutalismo: una aproximación y una bibliografía', *Cuaderno de notas*, vol. 7, 1999, pp. 131–44.

Van Acker Wouter (ed.) *Architecture and Ugliness: Anti-Aesthetics and the Ugly in Postmodern Architecture*, Bloomsbury Publishing, London, 2020.

Van Den Heuvel Dirk, *Alison and Peter Smithson: A Brutalist Story, Involving the House, The City and the*

Everyday (Plus a Couple of Other Things), PhD thesis, Tu Delft, Delft, 2013.

Van Den Heuvel Dirk, 'Between Brutalists: The Banham Hypothesis and the Smithson Way of Life', *Journal of Architecture*, vol. 20, no. 2, 2015, pp. 293–308.

Van Den Heuvel Dirk, Risselada Max, *Alison and Peter Smithson: From the House of the Future to a House of Today*, 010 Publishers, Rotterdam, 2004.

Van Uffelen Chris, *Massive, Expressive, Sculptural: Brutalism Now and Then*, Braun, Salenstein, 2018.

Vidler Anthony, 'Toward a Theory of the Architectural Prog', *October*, vol. 106, 2003, pp. 59–64.

Vidler Anthony, *Histories of the Immediate Present: Inventing Architectural Modernism 1930-1975*, PhD Thesis, TU Delft, Delft, 2005.

Vidler Anthony, *James Frazer Stirling: Notes from the Archive*, Yale Center for British Art/Yale University Press, New Haven, 2010.

Vidler Anthony, 'Another Brick in the Wall', *October*, vol. 136, 2011, pp. 105–32.

Vidler Anthony, 'Learning to Love Brutalism', *International Working-Party for Documentation and Conservation of Buildings, Sites and Neighbourhoods of the Modern Movement*, no. 47, 2012, pp. 4–9.

Vidler Anthony, 'Brutalism, Ethic or Aesthetic?', *Clog*, 2013, pp. 132–33.

Vidler Anthony, 'Troubles in Theory V: The Brutalist Moment(s)', *Architectural Review*, vol. 235, no. 1404, 2014, pp. 96–101.

Vidotto Marco, Spanna Annalaura, Mazzini Augusto, *A+P Smithson: pensieri, progetti e frammenti fino al 1990*, Sagep, Genoa, 1991.

Vidotto Marco, *Alison + Peter Smithson, Obras y proyectos = Works and Projects*, Gustavo Gili, Barcelona, 1997.

Vieira Filho Carlos Alberto, 'Vilanova Artigas e a Arquitetura Paulista', *Projeto*, vol. 66, August 1984, pp. 97–101.

Viganò Vittoriano, *A Come Architettura, exhibition catalogue*, Electa, Milano, 1992.

Von Moos Stanislaus, Bachmann Jul, *New Directions in Swiss Architecture*, George Braziller, New York, 1969.

Von Moos Stanislaus, *Le Corbusier. L'architecte et son mythe*, Horizons de France, Paris, 1971.

Von Moos Stanislaus, 'Space, Time and Turbulence', in Baltzer Nanni (ed.), *Art History on the Move*, Diaphanes Verlag, Zurich, 2010, pp. 217–31.

Von Moos Stanislaus, *Le Corbusier: Une Synthèse*, Parenthèses, Marseille, 2013.

Von Moos Stanislaus, '"L'Europe après la pluie" ou, le Brutalisme face à l'histoire', in Sbriglio Jacques (ed.), *Le Corbusier et la question du Brutalisme*, Parentheses, Marseille, 2013, pp. 64–87.

Walker John, *Cultural Offensive: America's Impact on British Art Since 1945*, Pluto Press, London, 1998.

Wallis Brian (ed.), *Modern Dreams, The Rise and Fall and Rise of Pop*, MIT Press, Cambridge, 1988.

Walmsley Dominique, 'Leicester Engineering Building: Its Post- Modern Role', *Journal of Architectural Education*, vol. 42, no. 1, 1988, pp. 10–17.

Walsh Victoria, *Nigel Henderson: Parallel of Life and Art*, Thames & Hudson, London, 2001.

Ward Stephen V., 'Soviet Communism and the British Planning Movement: Rational Learning or Utopian Imagining?', *Planning Perspectives*, vol. 27, no. 4, October 2012, pp. 499–524.

Watkin David, *Morality and Architecture: The Development of a Theme in Architectural History and Theory from the Gothic Revival to the Modern Movement*, Clarendon Press, Oxford, 1977.

Watkin David, *The Rise of Architectural History*, The Architectural Press, London, 1980.

Webb Sidney, *Soviet Communism: A New Civilisation?*, Longmans, Green and Co., New York, 1935.

Webster Helena, *Modernism Without Rhetoric: Essays on the Work of Alison and Peter Smithson*, John Wiley & Sons, London, 1997.

Wells Matthew J., 'The Practice of History: The Smithsons, Colin St John Wilson, and the Writing of Architectural History', *Journal of Art Historiography*, vol. 14, June 2016, p. 9.

Whiteley Nigel, 'Banham and 'Otherness': Reyner Banham (1922–1988) and His Quest for an Architecture Autre', *Architectural History*, vol. 33, 1990, pp. 188–221.

Whiteley Nigel, *Reyner Banham: Historian of the Immediate Future*, MIT Press, Cambridge, Massachusetts, 2002.

Williams Richard J., *Reyner Banham Revisited*, Reaktion Books, London, 2021.

Wilson Colin St John, 'Sigurd Lewerentz and the Dilemma of the Classical', *Perspecta*, vol. 24, 1988, pp. 51–77.

Wiryomartono Bagoes, 'Reyner Banham and Modern Design Culture', *Frontiers of Architectural Research*, vol. 1, no. 3, 2012, pp. 272–79.

Wisnik Guilherme, 'Architettura paulista ieri e oggi', *Rassegna di Architettura e Urbanistica*, vol. 48, no. 142/143, January 2014, pp. 42–49.

Wright Caroline Sophie, *The New Brutalism: Reyner Banham's Definition and its Application to 1950's Sculpture*, PhD Thesis, Cortauld Institute of Art, 1998.

Zaknic Ivan, 'Review of "In the Footsteps of Le Corbusier"', *Journal of Architectural Education*, vol. 46, no. 2, 1992, pp. 108–11.

Zein Verde Ruth, *Brutalist Connections. A Refreshed Approach to Debates & Buildings*, Altamira Editorial, São Paulo, 2014.

Zevi Bruno, *Storia dell'architettura moderna*, Einaudi, Torino, 1975.

Zimmerman Claire, 'From Legible Form to Memorable Image: Architectural Knowledge from Rudolph Wittkower to Reyner Banham', *Candide*, vol. 5, no. 2, February 2012, pp. 93–110.